# ESSAYS IN MODERN EUROPEAN

# HISTORIOGRAPHY

CLASSIC EUROPEAN HISTORIANS

A SERIES EDITED BY LEONARD KRIEGER

# ESSAYS IN MODERN EUROPEAN HISTORIOGRAPHY

Edited and with an Introduction
by S. William Halperin

THE UNIVERSITY OF CHICAGO PRESS
CHICAGO & LONDON

ISBN: 0–226–31445–6 (clothbound); 0–226–31446–4 (paperbound)
Library of Congress Catalog Card Number: 79–116920

THE UNIVERSITY OF CHICAGO PRESS, Chicago 60637
THE UNIVERSITY OF CHICAGO PRESS, Ltd., London

# Contents

# Series Editor's Preface

It has been said about literary fashions that the social realism "welcomed enthusiastically in Paris . . . in 1890 . . . would get to Chicago and New York in the 1930s,"[1] and much the same may be said about history. Social realism in modern history is compounded of economic and social history, and since the 1930's these fields have developed steadily in this country to their present position of preeminence as the appropriate dimensions of a truly democratic history. Perhaps the most immediately relevant, then, among the following essays on European historians who wrote or were trained around the turn to the twentieth century will be those on the progenitors of economic and social history in the modern mode. In Germany, it is true, their protagonists have until very recently been regarded either as pariahs of the historical profession or as practitioners of a neighboring discipline, such as economics or sociology, in its historical dimension. But in France social and economic history has formed the main thread of twentieth-century historiography. In Europe as a whole, social and economic history grew into an autonomous form of the historical discipline, laying its claim, from the start, to be the only valid form of the discipline, in the context and with the support of a general idea about history which comes out of late nineteenth-century European culture. As Professor Halperin's illuminating

1. Mary M. Colum, *From These Roots: Ideas That Have Made Modern Literature* (New York, 1944), pp. 312–13.

introduction shows, the concomitant of early social and economic history was the idea that the application of science to history required historians to make what was the impersonal, multiple, collective, and massive in human affairs the proper objects of their concern. To identify the intellectual and ideological components of this early scaffolding and to determine which of them have dropped away and which covertly absorbed into the current focus upon the masses of the inarticulate and the unheralded in history is certainly essential to an awareness of the assumptions behind contemporary historiography.

The volume affords a second historiographic lesson as well: traditional forms of history persisted alongside the innovations and even to some degree interacted with them. This lesson follows from Professor Halperin's skillful classification of the historians here considered. That the eighty years of historical writing covered by this collection—roughly from 1880 to 1960—should include a goodly representation of the early professional historians who established history as an independent and specialized discipline essentially on the basis of *political* history in the largest sense—that is, including constitutions, war, and diplomacy as well as intrigues and policy—should come as no surprise in view of the prominent role which the critical study of political sources and the critical analysis of political events has played in establishing the academic historical standards which have dominated the profession in our century. But what may be surprising—and valuable—is the discovery, in these essays, of grounds for the longevity of such traditional forms of history which go beyond the inherited conservatism of the academic guild. We are reminded first that political historians have continuously advanced their own claims to be *the* authentic applicators of science to history, by dint of their empirical approach to their materials and their inductive fidelity to the specificity of their results. The persistence of political history can also be explained by the sophistication of political history and political biography in Renouvin and Gooch, by its combination with religious, social, and economic factors in Mathiez and with intellectual history in Gooch, and by the juncture of traditional legal history with large-scale cultural history in Altamira. These adaptations indicate a resiliency in historiographic traditions which is worth remembering in these days when they are being subjected to strenuous challenge.

*Essays in Modern European Historiography* registers a departure from the usual format of Classic European Historians, since the classic historians are here rather the subjects than the authors of the reprints (a condition, certainly, which may be amended by the passage of time). But because the series is aimed as much at the clarification of European historiography as at the republication of European history, the inclusion of these essays is well within the spirit of the series. It is hoped that the essays will assist in our understanding of the historical approaches which characterize our own century, when the population explosion of historians has rendered them more susceptible to organization by representative groups than to the isolation of outstanding individuals.

LEONARD KRIEGER

# Editor's Introduction

THE sixteen scholars dealt with in this volume represent or reflect certain tendencies that have manifested themselves in modern European historiography in the course of the past hundred years. Needless to say, the writings of each of them bear the stamp of the author's individuality. But despite their obvious differences, these historians can be divided into groups on the basis of certain similarities of approach and emphasis or according to the necessarily overlapping yet distinguishable categories of subject matter—political, diplomatic, intellectual, economic, social, cultural, and so forth—on which they chose to dwell. With the single exception of military history, each of the subject-matter categories discussed in this introduction is represented by two or more of the historians considered here.

During the long time span covered by the careers of these men, European modernists of talent and distinction have of course produced an immense variety of works. Amid this diversity, the biographical approach stands out as one of the most recurrent. C. V. Wedgwood's balanced statement, made apropos of the life and career of a specific individual, Richelieu, may be said to typify the way in which all but the most extreme partisans of the biographical approach tend to view their respective heroes:

> The part played by the Great Man in history is usually overestimated; on the other hand the modern fashion of allowing no influence to the individual at all, and ascribing all historical de-

velopments to social or economic forces seems equally mistaken. If forces beyond individual control—the spiritual force of a great religious revival, the economic and social forces, driving France towards national consciousness and expansion—played an important part in the creation of the French monarchy, it is difficult to imagine quite how these forces would have found expression under other guidance than that of Cardinal Richelieu. It is the measure of his greatness that it should be so difficult to imagine the growth of the French monarchy, or the development of Europe in the seventeenth century, without him.[1]

Of the historians considered here, no fewer than half have at one time or another employed the biographical approach. In so doing, they have subscribed, at least implicitly, to the view that the individual, as distinguished from the complex of circumambient forces and conditions, is almost always a key to an understanding of the past, at times even the single most powerful factor among the many that have shaped the course of human history. Thus Rafael Altamira on Philip II;[2] Hans Delbrück on Gneisenau; G. P. Gooch on Frederick the Great, Maria Theresa, Catherine the Great, and Louis XV as well as on the pre-1914 diplomats; Gabriel Hanotaux on Richelieu, Poincaré, and Joan of Arc (the latter two viewed by the author, whose sense of balance deserted him here, as the agents of Providence); Ernest Lavisse on Frederick the Great; Sir Richard Lodge on Richelieu; Erich Marcks on Gaspard de Coligny, William I, and Bismarck; Francesco Ruffini on Cavour and Manzoni—all bear witness to the tendency of scholars of different backgrounds and preconceptions to underscore the historical role played by individuals. In these biographical studies, the authors have almost without exception followed the well-established practice of depicting the times as well as the persons and fortunes of their central figures.

Antipodal to the implications of the biographical approach is the conception of history held by those who regard collectivities

1. *Richelieu and the French Monarchy*, rev. ed. (New York: Crowell-Collier, 1962), pp. 9–10.

2. In his *Ensayo sobre Felipe II, hombre de estado, su psicología general y su individualidad humana* (Mexico City, 1950), a study that came out several years after the publication of the volume in which the essay by John E. Fagg, one of our contributors, originally appeared.

and classes, conditions and circumstances, as the main motive force, the strongest propulsive agent, of the historical process. Four of the scholars surveyed in this volume—Karl Lamprecht, Henri Sée, Albert Mathiez, and Georges Lefebvre—adhered quite explicitly to such a view and directed most of their researches accordingly. Lamprecht, seeking the "laws" of history through investigations of the collective psyche in successive periods, was influenced by positivism, scientism, and the psychological studies of Wilhelm Wundt as well as by a revulsion against the alleged inadequacies of the individualistic tendencies that continued to dominate the historical scholarship of his time. For him, the history of individuals and even of heroic figures was infinitely less significant than that of the masses of mankind. The many, he insisted, "domineered over the genius." Sée, although rejecting any materialistic interpretation of history, nevertheless viewed individuals as incapable of prevailing against "the force of things." Both Mathiez and Lefebvre, although by no means wholly at one in their interpretation of the French Revolution, were obviously influenced by Marxism and its concept of the class struggle. Of course, they did not neglect the actions of individuals, but almost invariably subordinated them to the role of impersonal factors. According to Mathiez, a highly complex phenomenon like the French Revolution was in essence the product of circumstances. Lefebvre for his part went out of his way to stress mass behavior in his reconstruction of the great cataclysm that erupted in 1789. His predilection for the study of groups was so strong that he carefully avoided writing even a single biography. Delving deeply and systematically into the psyche of the crowd, he enriched the literature on the French Revolution with a pioneering study entitled *La grande peur de 1789*. Unlike Lamprecht, however, Lefebvre betrayed surprisingly little interest in the ground-breaking work of contemporaneous psychologists and made virtually no attempt to apply their findings to the study of history. The position of these four men on the relative importance of the individual and the group, of the human will and the ensemble of circumstances, typifies the approach of many other European modernists of the first rank. Nevertheless, the individualist emphasis continues to be abundantly represented in the Continent's great outpouring of historical literature.

This antinomy finds something of a parallel in the prolonged controversy between the defenders and critics of political history. Interest in the role of individuals leads quite naturally to a partiality for political history, just as preoccupation with the life of the masses, with the multidimensional impact of circumstances and the varied manifestations of the collective psyche, leads to a preference for socioeconomic or cultural history.

Throughout the second half of the nineteenth century and the first part of the twentieth, the vogue of political history continued despite the growing number of able and influential researchers who showed by their work that they rejected the notion that the actions and vicissitudes of states and governments should be the historian's principal concern. The preeminence of political history until the era of World War I, and the very strong pull it has continued to exert thereafter, reflect a widespread, steadfastly held belief about the nature and dynamics of the historical process. According to this view, the root phenomenon, triggering and shaping all the others, is the struggle for and exercise of political power. Therefore, the proper task of the historian is to probe political history.

This is precisely what several of the historians considered here have done. Two of them, Hanotaux and Alphonse Aulard, paid little or no attention in their principal works to nonpolitical developments despite their oft-reiterated affirmation of interest in an approach that would comprehend history's multifarious data. The others—Lavisse, Marcks, and Charles Seignobos—are more representative of the so-called political school insofar as they did not content themselves with mere lip service to a broader view of their subject matter. Lavisse's masterly account of the reign of Louis XIV deals amply with the cultural, religious, commercial and industrial aspects of French national life during that period. In Marcks' classic *Der Aufstieg des Reiches,* social and cultural movements (but not economic forces) are thoroughly treated as integral parts of German history in the nineteenth century rather than as addenda belatedly tacked on. The still unsurpassed volumes contributed by Seignobos to Lavisse's cooperative *Histoire de France contemporaine, 1789–1919* contain substantial sections on socioeconomic and intellectual developments.

Although most political historians showed an increasing awareness of the interdependence and interaction of history's many aspects, they nonetheless focused the bulk of their attention on states and governments and on the men who headed or directed them. Against this emphasis a reaction set in. The scholars who challenged the dominant school not only charged that political history ignored or underestimated nine-tenths of the human past (to use Frederick Harrison's well-known computation); they also maintained that the dynamics of the historical process must be sought far more outside than within the political domain. Boasting such disparate predecessors as Voltaire, Buckle, and Burckhardt, some of the dissenters contended that the historian could do justice to the past and penetrate its innermost core only by sifting all the significant aspects of human civilization.

Prominent among the paladins of cultural history are two of the scholars discussed in this volume, Lamprecht and Altamira. Lamprecht, in keeping with his stress on the collective psyche, his use of the genetic method, his interest in causation, and his quest for "laws," attempted to apply his own version of positivist and scientific principles to the data of history which he culled, according to his many vociferous critics among Germany's professional historians, in a one-sided, haphazard, and careless manner. Lamprecht proceeded on the assumption that the manifold expressions of culture in each of a series of epochs are parts of a single whole which the historian must seek to fix and illuminate. Altamira, on the other hand, is far more typical of the history-of-civilization school insofar as he did not try to extrapolate "laws" or impose upon his variegated data an artificial, all-subsuming unity. Nevertheless, he was not content merely to compile and juxtapose. Discoursing on one occasion about the merits of his *Historia de España y de la Civilización Española,* he noted that it represented something more than a collection of the fruits of modern monographic research on Spanish history. Its distinctive contribution, he pointed out, was to provide an integral and organic picture of the life of the Spanish people based on a systematic classification and ordering of the facts.

Another prime feature of modern European historiography, and largely identical with the anti-individualist trend, is the steadily accelerating gravitation toward economic and social history. Spurred either by an independent interest in the rapidly evolving social sciences or by a revulsion against the preponderance of political history, the economic and social historians forged ahead during the several decades that preceded the outbreak of World War I, creating all the while a considerable intellectual stir. They made giant strides after 1918, ultimately becoming a dominant group among the Continent's modernists. No other trend in recent European historiography stands out more sharply or possesses greater significance.

A few of the scholars dealt with here—Gustav von Schmoller, Sée, Mathiez, and Lefebvre—figure prominently in this trend. Schmoller, a man of endless energy and inventiveness whose interests were so wide-ranging that they embraced all of the social sciences, exerted enormous influence during the emergence of the historical school of national economics in Germany, a period that coincided with the most productive phase of his own professional career. Undeterred by the fact that most professional German historians had hitherto been reluctant to deal with economic and social history, he helped to establish a tradition in this area. His *Zur Geschichte der deutschen Kleingewerbe im 19. Jahrhundert,* a collection of essays published in 1870, made a deep impression on aspiring students of economic history in Germany and abroad and affected to a considerable extent the direction of their researches for the better part of a generation. The task of placing the mercantilist policies of the seventeenth and eighteenth centuries in a historical setting was successfully performed by Schmoller in another fundamental contribution; and the influence which this work exerted on others was aided by the fact that in it he developed an evolutionary conception of economic growth.

An economist turned historian, Schmoller was far less successful when he attempted to make historical generalization virtually a substitute for economic theory. He conceived of economic history not as an end in itself but as a means of testing economic theories, as a proving ground for the principles of economics. In this Schmoller was influenced by Wilhelm Roscher, an economic historian who was among the first to employ the historical method in economics. Although Schmoller's efforts to replace economic theory with historical research proved abortive and in some respects prejudicial to the subsequent development of both the economic and historical disciplines in Germany, he did succeed in making economics more historical, just as he succeeded in making history more economic. The close connection between economic phenomena on the one hand and the life of the state and society on the other was underscored with tremendous emphasis in most of his writings. He was equally consistent in pressing his conclusion that economic processes and institutions play a determinative role in the social and cultural domains. He was thus among the first to encourage a tendency in modern European historiography that has been gaining momentum ever since the latter part of the nineteenth century and that seems currently to be nearing its apogee.

Sée too was something of a pioneer in his own country. Prior to his time, French scholars had paid insufficient attention to economic and social history. Sée set an example that elicited emulation and thereby contributed to the growing importance of this genre in twentieth-century French historiography. Trained under such rigorous methodologists as Fustel de Coulanges, Monod, Luchaire, Lavisse, and Seignobos, Sée stands out for his critical as well as for his exhaustive utilization of source materials in the domain of economic history. Striving systematically to synthesize the results of his researches and to place them in a broad historical setting, he underscored the constant interplay between economic phenomena and the milieu in which they evolve. Collective entities and institutions drew the bulk of his attention because he regarded knowledge of the social order, of its concerns, values, and procedures, as the proper culmination of historical research. In this context he referred to history as the "science of human societies." Hoping to contribute thereto, he chose economic and social history, and to a lesser extent the history of ideas, as the surest roads to his goal. He deprecated political and military history along with the biographical approach because, in his opinion, the complex of economic necessities plays a preponderant role in the evolution of societies. At the same time he repudiated explanations that focus on a single factor or on a single category of factors while excluding all others. This was at the bottom of his rejection of the Marxist interpretation of history, a position to which he steadfastly adhered despite his lifelong fidelity to the socialist ideal.

Mathiez, whose tirelessness as an investigator was matched by his desire to see the so-called lessons of the past find meaningful application to the problems of the present, moved away from the political approach of his teacher, Aulard, and went on to blaze new trails in the very same area where Aulard had already made his mark. The economic and social history of the French Revolution, treated as the clue to what was happening in the political domain during the successive phases of the great upheaval, was clearly Mathiez' forte. Influenced by the studies of Jean Jaurès as well as by the ideas of Karl Marx, Mathiez examined the struggles within and between classes and ascribed a decisive role to the impact of material circumstances upon the ensemble of French society. In any retrospective review of the researches done on the French Revolution by so many different hands, Mathiez stands out as an extraordinarily fertile figure. His influence was tremendous, and for an entire generation he dominated the historiography of the revolution.

Lefebvre's development resembles Mathiez' in that he too was influenced quite early by Marxist thought. Like Mathiez, Lefebvre regarded changing material conditions and the concomitant class conflicts as the prime source of the French Revolution. In his view, modern capitalism was far more effective than intellectual ferment in undermining the old regime. Author of a voluminous chef-d'oeuvre on agrarian conditions in France before and during the rush of events set off in 1789, a virtuoso in the art of combining several techniques, including the statistical, to master a veritable mountain of perplexing data, he was instrumental in accelerating a fruitful trend in the historiography of the French Revolution: the dissection of class structure. Although the work of Lefebvre parallels Mathiez' researches in some important aspects, it is more original and penetrating. Lefebvre's uncannily perceptive analyses of both milieu and social structure, his lifelike recreations of the relations between classes and between subdivisions of the same class, together with his marvelous portrayal of the collective mentality of a huge, heterogeneous segment of French society galvanized into revolutionary action by a unique combination of factors, assure him a preeminent place in recent historical scholarship. The radiation and prestige of his studies are inseparable from the cresting vogue of socioeconomic history in present-day France.

In the history of ideas, long one of the main areas of scholarly interest on both sides of the Atlantic and a magnet for some of the best brains in the historical profession, only two of our historians, Gooch and Sée, have made systematic contributions. These, although erudite and lucid, are cast in a conventional mold. Neither Gooch nor Sée was primarily concerned with the history of ideas; their writings in this field lack the fullness and depth one encounters in the works of Europe's foremost intellectual historians. Nevertheless, their accomplishments are far from inconsiderable, and the respect that their studies on the history of political thought still command is indicative of how representative they are of the painstaking work that has been and continues to be done by many Europeans in this immensely active domain.

In the zealously tilled, traditionally prestigious field of diplomatic history, which is well represented by three of the men considered here—Lodge, Gooch, and above all Pierre Renouvin—the customary emphasis on the relations of states and governments and on the role of individual statesmen and diplomats has continued to be dominant. The contributions of Lodge and Gooch and the early writings of Renouvin belong to the substantial number of first-class works of this genre that European scholars have turned out over the past several decades. But of late there has been a marked trend toward greater breadth and depth in the treatment of diplomatic history. Renouvin's concern, in his more recent writings, with underlying forces and impersonal factors, as well as with the not inconsiderable number of remarkable individuals who indubitably influenced and at times determined the course of diplomatic history, his insistence on the need to reconstruct the relations of peoples as well as the relations of states and governments, may be regarded as symptomatic of this trend. In *Introduction à l'histoire des relations internationales*,[3] a work authored jointly with J.-B. Duroselle and which one knowledgeable admirer has described as a "learned and systematic contribution to the historical sociology of international relations," Renouvin elucidates the kind of approach to diplomatic history that seeks out the various factors and influences at work and that he himself had to some extent applied in his masterly four-volume coverage of the period from 1815 to 1945.

The treatment of military history has likewise tended to become broader. Almost exclusive concentration on armaments, battles, tactics, and strategy has progressively given way to increasing concern with relevant institutional developments in the political and socioeconomic domains. To be sure, the work of one of our historians, Delbrück, bears witness to the continuing hold of the traditional approach; it therefore represents a tendency that has retained a significant place in the annals of modern European historiography. At the same time, however, the contributions of Delbrück to the history of the art of war have helped to point the way toward the current trend which emphasizes the interaction and interplay of nonmilitary and military factors. Delbrück's success in fitting military developments into the larger picture of politico-diplomatic history is the aspect of his work that has proved especially influential.

It nevertheless remains true that for those military historians who continue to concentrate mainly on strategy and tactics, Delbrück's massive *Geschichte der Kriegskunst im Rahmen der politischen Geschichte* still provides guidelines of fundamental value. A close student of Clausewitz, Delbrück correctly notes that just as there are two kinds of war—unlimited and limited—so there must be two kinds of strategy. One is designed to annihilate the

3. Paris: Librairie Armand Colin, 1964.

enemy; the other aims at exhausting him. The decisive battle is the prime goal in the first, whose most celebrated practitioners of course include Napoleon. In the second kind of strategy, which was pursued by many leaders, notably Wallenstein, Gustavus Adolphus, and Frederick the Great in the modern period, such expedients as economic offensives, along with engagements on the battlefield, clearly count as means toward the end in view. Delbrück's analysis produced a lively and fruitful discussion among historians, particularly those concerned with the modern makers of strategy. It continues to figure in the historiography of war despite the soundness of some of the criticisms that have been leveled at it.

A striking feature of recent historical scholarship in France is the revival of interest in religious history. Among the historians surveyed here, Francesco Ruffini, apostle as well as chronicler of religious toleration, stands out as an early and important contributor to the revival. Not without influence are the relevant writings of Aulard and especially Mathiez. Both men produced trenchant studies on some of the religious aspects of the history of the French Revolution. Insofar as the general approach of Ruffini, Aulard, and Mathiez is politico-ecclesiastical in character, it reflects in large measure the spirit of their own times; yet their work continues to interest writers in this field despite the current shift toward a one-sided emphasis on the sociological aspects of religious history.

Considerably more significant as an indicator of the direction in which a large number of European researchers are currently moving is the amount of attention being lavished on local or regional history. Several of our historians—notably Schmoller, Lamprecht, Aulard, Altamira, Sée, and Lefebvre—lent impetus to this trend and also revealed the rich potentialities of such investigations by giving a limited geographical frame to some of their researches. Schmoller's role as pacemaker and model deserves special notice here. His *Das strassburger Tücher- und Weberzunft* (1879) spurred a wave of monographic research on the history of guilds and related local bodies in other German cities. For Schmoller and those of his contemporaries who followed his lead, inquiries into local history were not only rewarding in themselves; they were also designed to provide a foundation for the writing of national history. It is in such a dual perspective that most present-day explorers of municipal, provincial, and regional archives in western and central Europe likewise view their work.

Our sixteen historians are of course but a tiny part of the great stream of modern European historiography. However, because they typify to a greater or lesser degree so much of it, they may be looked upon as approximating in their totality a cross section of the branch of learning to which they, as historians and modernists, belong. For this reason, the essays in the following pages should prove instructive.[4]

S. WILLIAM HALPERIN

4. All of these essays have been previously published. The essays on Altamira, Aulard, Delbrück, Hanotaux, Lamprecht, Lavisse, Lodge, Marcks, Mathiez, Ruffini, Schmoller, Sée, and Seignobos first appeared in *Some Historians of Modern Europe*, edited by Bernadotte E. Schmitt (Chicago: University of Chicago Press, 1942). The essays on Gooch, Lefebvre, and Renouvin have been reproduced from *Some Twentieth Century Historians: Essays on Eminent Europeans*, edited with an introduction by S. William Halperin (Chicago: University of Chicago Press, 1961). Four of our sixteen historians—Altamira, Gooch, Hanotaux, and Seignobos—were still living when the essays on them were written.

Anyone who wishes to do additional reading might consult the following works: Herman Ausubel, J. B. Brebner, and E. M. Hunt, eds., *Some Modern Historians of Britain* (New York, 1951); Harry E. Barnes, *A History of Historical Writing*, 2d rev. ed. (New York, 1963); Georg von Below, *Die deutsche Geschichtsschreibung von den Befreiungskriegen bis zu unsern Tagen* (Munich and Berlin, 1924); Benedetto Croce, *Storia della storiografia italiana nel secolo decimonono*, 2 vols., 4th ed. (Bari, 1964); Matthew A. Fitzsimons, Alfred G. Pundt, and Charles E. Nowell, eds., *The Development of Historiography* (Harrisburg, Pa., 1954); Eduard Fueter, *Geschichte der neueren Historiographie* (Munich, 1925); G. P. Gooch, *History and Historians in the Nineteenth Century*, rev. ed. (London, 1952); John R. Hale, ed., *The Evolution of British Historiography from Bacon to Namier* (Cleveland, 1964); Louis Halphen, *L'Histoire en France depuis cent ans* (Paris, 1914); John Higham, Leonard Krieger, and Felix Gilbert, *History* (Englewood Cliffs, N.J., 1965); *Histoire et historiens depuis cinquante ans*, 2 vols. (Paris, 1927); Walter Z. Laqueur and George L. Mosse, eds., *The New History* (New York, 1967); Boyd C. Shafer et al., *Historical Study in the West* (New York, 1968); Heinrich Ritter Von Srbik, *Geist und Geschichte vom deutschen Humanismus bis zur Gegenwart*, 2 vols. (Munich, 1950, 1951); James Westfall Thompson and Bernard J. Holm, *The History of Historical Writing*, 2 vols. (New York, 1942).

# ESSAYS IN MODERN EUROPEAN

## HISTORIOGRAPHY

# I

## Rafael Altamira (1866–1951)

John E. Fagg

Men of learning in Spain have frequently been conscious of an obligation to their less erudite compatriots. They have sought to diffuse knowledge both of the outside world and of Spanish past grandeur in the hope of stimulating a national revival. One of the most public spirited of these missionary-intellectuals is Rafael Altamira y Crevea, whose outstanding contribution has been a monumental history of Spanish civilization. He believed that humanity usually behaved in line with its conception of experience, in accordance with its historical memory, and that, therefore, it should at least know the facts about its past. An investigator who observed the highest standards of research, he was eager to simplify and to popularize the results of his inquiries. To him the historian's duty was first to arrive at the truth and then to communicate it to the lay reader.[1]

Born in Alicante on February 10, 1866, of undistinguished parentage, Altamira was well known in Spanish intellectual circles

1. His chief writings in the field of history are: *Historia de la propiedad comunal* (Madrid, 1890), *La enseñanza de la historia* (Madrid, 1895), *Historia de España y de la civilización española* (4 vols.; Barcelona, 1900–1911; rev. ed., 1913–14), *Cuestiones de historia del derecho y de legislación comparada* (Madrid, 1914), and chapters on Spain in the *Cambridge medieval history* and the *Cambridge modern history*. Many of his essays and lectures are included in *De historia y arte* (Madrid, 1898), *Psicología del pueblo español* (Madrid, 1902), *Temas de historia de España* (Madrid, 1929), and *Cuestiones modernas de historia* (Madrid, 1935).

by the time he was twenty-one. As a student at the University of Valencia he was singled out by the remarkable mental powers, the personality, and the industry that were to characterize him through life. His activities ranged from political agitation as a republican and anticlerical to publishing novels, literary criticisms, and articles on historical subjects and pedagogical questions.[2] In common with most Spanish men-of-letters, he was fated to study law, and in 1886 he went to Madrid to complete his studies under the direction of Spain's leading professors. Readily accepted into a group of prominent scholars and public men, including such figures as Azcárate, Giner de los Ríos, and Salmerón, the gifted young Valencian was soon one of their peers.

Altamira's career took the shape it was to hold in the atmosphere of the last decade of the nineteenth century. Spain was dormant in most respects; but her intelligentsia were alive to the currents of thought that were altering world-outlook, and, above and beyond the sphere of politics, they sought to divert them into the peninsula. From his youth, Rafael Altamira labored enthusiastically in the self-imposed task of popularizing the historical, literary, and sociological trends with which he was in touch. With unswerving confidence he preached that Spain could rise again as a great civilization if her citizens accepted the proper instruction. It was not unnatural that a man of his temperament and wide interests should embrace the "new history" or that there should be many aspects of his career other than historian. In his chief life-mission, however, that of promoting national regeneration, he was primarily concerned as a student of the past.

Until he won a chair in 1897 at the University of Oviedo by means of the Spanish custom of competition, Altamira was scarcely a professional historian. He delivered public lectures on historical subjects, published a few articles on legal history, and regularly contributed bibliographical essays to the *Revue historique* and the *Jahresberichte der Geschichtswissenschaft*. But, as secretary of the national pedagogical museum, most of his

2. *Diccionario enciclopédico hispano-americano de literatura, ciencias, y artes* ( 28 vols.; Barcelona, 1887–99 ), XXIV, 125.

4

efforts were devoted to educational reform. He also founded and edited the *Revista crítica de historia y literatura españolas, portuguesas, y hispano-americanas,* a unique little journal which proved a boon to Spanish scholars during its brief career. Altamira's appetite for work was not satisfied until he had published several novels, countless literary criticisms, and fugitive articles in the republican press. With abundant enthusiasm for all branches of his activity—literature, education, history, and law—he won some distinction in each.

His excursions into literature, which for a time furnished part of his livelihood, did not bring Altamira renown. None of his novels even approached success on the book market, although one was deemed to show promise.[3] In 1907 he finally abandoned literature for concentration on his historical and other interests, but he continued to regard it somewhat nostalgically as blessed relief from the unlovely features of human conduct contemplated by the historian.[4] His literary criticisms were numerous and, for the most part, meritorious. His reviews were said to be distinguished for their reflection and justice;[5] his guiding principle was that the critic should "have a heart."[6] But neither was his reputation in this field outstanding nor has it endured. Through his literary interests, however, he came to associate with other Spanish writers and scholars, such as Leopoldo Alas, Menéndez y Pelayo, Unamuno, Pérez Galdós, and Menéndez Pidal. If his literary efforts affected his historical writing in later years, its influence was probably salutary, for his style of composition, hopelessly awkward in his first attempts, improved markedly as he continued writing. And it is likely that the attentive study he devoted to national and European literature further equipped him as a historian of culture.

Acutely conscious of the influence exercised by historical knowledge or misinformation on the thoughts and actions of na-

3. *Revue hispanique,* I (1894), 214.
4. *Arte y realidad* (Barcelona, 1921), p. 10.
5. Prologue of Leopoldo Alas in *Mi primera campaña* (Madrid, 1893), p. x.
6. *De historia y arte,* p. 252.

tions, Altamira believed that history should inform the individual of his true juncture with the evolution of world-civilization. He appeared to consider the pedagogical function of a historian as inseparable from his capacity as an investigator of the past. His early maturity in questions of education was revealed in a book he circulated privately in 1891 and published four years later, *La enseñanza de la historia*. The reception of this work abroad was favorable,[7] and in Spain it became the principal guide in matters of historical methodology and pedagogy. He urged, among other things, that students be taught history from their beginning school years, on the grounds that it would awaken the critical spirit, imbue a respect for truth, provide a sense of perspective, and form habits of reaching conclusions through factual knowledge.[8] Although its power of example might be weak, Altamira insisted that history maintained the traditional spirit of a people and inspired sentiments and ideals of vast importance in the present.[9] It would condition the approach of the public to contemporary problems with a consciousness of the peculiarities of the nation's development.

The methods of teaching proposed in *La enseñanza de la historia* recalled in many respects the ancient conception that history was a mode of inquiry. Altamira would have each youth work with documents, make excursions to sites of famous events of the past, and study monuments, inscriptions, and relics.[10] As he considered every phase of the past within the proper scope of history, he would encourage students to undertake personal investigations of the sources in any field, provided they learned to think in terms of evolutionary development. Aware of the continuity of civilization and trained in the best techniques of historical method, they should become capable citizens. Veritably, Altamira considered every man his own historian.

In comparison with the educational policies in other countries, which he analyzed with characteristic thoroughness, Altamira

7. *RH*, XLVIII (1891), 450, and *AHR*, I (1896), 316–18.
8. *La enseñanza de la historia*, p. 11.
9. *Ibid.*, pp. 370–71.
10. *Ibid.*, pp. 413–16.

described conditions in Spain as "detestable."[11] The universities suffered from politics and bureaucracy, and the lower schools from dry rot. The state of the archives and libraries was discouraging to scholarly enterprises. In the case of history-teaching, students were fed mischievous legends long discarded by specialists and were compelled to memorize passages of rhetorical beauty. Textbooks embalmed absurd myths which misinformed Spaniards and antagonized foreigners. Furthermore, Altamira complained, there was in existence no creditable book on the history of Spanish civilization. He called for such a work—a lucid, accurate survey primarily for students and the general public but also acceptable to scholars. And, he stipulated, only a Spaniard who was saturated with the spirit of the past was adequately qualified for the task.[12] One may well conjecture that he had himself in mind.

To remedy those shortcomings in Spanish education Altamira worked indefatigably during much of his lifetime. From his university days on he published articles and books on pedagogy, expounded his liberal ideas in lectures, and participated in international congresses.[13] As secretary of the pedagogical museum from 1889 until 1897, he was active in educational reform work and in the campaign to overcome the blight of illiteracy. When he went to Oviedo as a professor of history he instituted the seminar method and carried out other favorite ideas that brought student and teacher into co-operative research. More spectacular was his foundation of the university extension, by means of which the assumed blessings of enlightenment were carried to the unlettered workmen of Asturias and Santander. When he held the post of director-general of primary teaching from 1911 to 1913, Altamira energetically pushed his program for revitalizing the system of public education. Academic duties, he preached, were national duties.[14] As for the history book of Spanish civilization, whose

11. *Ibid.*, p. 457.
12. *Ibid.*, pp. 350–51.
13. *Enciclopedia universal ilustrada europeo-americana* (Apéndice, 10 vols.; Barcelona, 1930–33), I, 418–20.
14. *Psicología del pueblo español*, p. 196.

absence he had lamented, that, too, was to be provided by the active professor at Oviedo.

Altamira attained full stature as a historian-patriot of national importance after the disastrous events of 1898. In that year the catastrophic defeat suffered by Spain at the hands of the United States spoke with crashing eloquence of the decadence and isolation of the peninsular kingdom. Many of the intellectuals were jolted into patriotic introspection, and out of the prevailing despondency they undertook to bring about a national renaissance. This so-called "generation" of 1898 proposed to borrow selectively from other civilizations, to look into the Spanish past for instruction, and, by means of stimulating artistic activity, to rejuvenate the genius of Spain. Much of the literature they produced was devoted to a searching analysis of the spirit of the people and the potentialities of the national character. The humiliating defeat of 1898 had wrenched Altamira's soul,[15] and he joined this movement, which to some extent he had anticipated—his role to be that of a historian who resurrected the achievements of the past in order to counteract discouragement as to the future.

His chief production in the ensuing patriotic campaign was a collection of essays mistitled *Psicología del pueblo español,* the purpose of which was to discover whether or not Spain still possessed a "right to life."[16] As befitted a "scientific" historian, Altamira concentrated much less on a psychological appraisal of the people than on the effect of historical evolution. Analyzing the Hispanophobe writings of the past, he was astonished at the strength of the legends that blackened the Spanish name with acts of cruelty and bigotry. More than ever he was convinced that both native and foreign historians had perpetuated fables that imbued in Spaniards grotesque notions of the factors in the past which had brought them to their present state. The decadence of Spain he considered the result not of temperamental weakness but of misguided economic activities.[17] In addition, unfortunate distractions at critical moments had ruinously dispersed

15. *Ibid.,* p. 11.
16. *Ibid.,* p. 13.
17. *Ibid.,* p. 127.

national energy and had thus accelerated the decline.[18] Certainly there was nothing deficient in Spanish cultural and intellectual contributions, although the driving force that had once dominated Europe and subdued a new world had almost dried up. The burden of the message of *Psicología del pueblo español* was that a survey of the past indicated that Spain's national character was wholesome, that she was still capable of greatness.

While he often labeled himself a patriot, Altamira was no egotistical nationalist, disdainful of other lands and aggressively proud of his own. On the contrary, he was a pacifist who believed that each people should be free to cultivate its own distinctive note in the concert of civilization. He once translated Fichte's *Reden an die deutsche Nation* in the hope that the German philosopher's appeal would stir the Spanish as it had the Prussians a century before, but he was careful to reject the militaristic-imperialistic implications of the work.[19] Misoneism and flamboyant patriotism were repugnant to him. His "patriotic campaign," a strand of varied interests manifest throughout his career, consisted only of the harmless desire to arouse the Spanish to the value of foreign ideas and to inspire them with their truly remarkable accomplishments in the past.

Altamira's historical writing was rarely disfigured by undue attributions to Spain, and he was not a genuine nationalistic historian. If he presumed to edify his countrymen with an abstract of their civilized existence, it was not to flatter them. Nor did he expect to discover ironclad principles of conduct in the past. Rather, he hoped to correct misconceptions in the national self-consciousness and to lay the foundation of the future on the basis of earlier achievements. The Spanish people were geared to a psychology of failure after the 1898 debacle, and the hopeful historian believed most firmly that the work of regeneration could not proceed until credit had been restored to their history.[20] To be sure, he had once complained that no scholarly book for this purpose was available, but at last he was ready to fill the need.

18. *Ibid.*, p. 129.
19. *Ibid.*, p. 11.
20. *Ibid.*, p. 139.

Altamira's preparations for a history of Spanish civilization gathered momentum during the depth of the malaise following the events of 1898. His original impulse was admittedly didactic, but soon fascination with the work was alone enough to impel him to continue.[21] The task was indeed formidable, however compelling his inspiration, for it was difficult enough in any case to clear the way in cultural and social history. In Spain, however, the chaotic state of archives and libraries made the obstacles all the more forbidding. Vital monographs on certain important phases of history were lacking, thus necessitating a large amount of investigation on his part. Hallowed national legends cluttered his path, to mislead him if they were accepted and to haunt him if he passed them over. Apparently he did without the aid of research assistants and collaborators. And the work was carried on during years when duties as a professor, publicist, and man-of-letters diverted the full force of his energy.

His qualifications for the undertaking were likewise imposing. He was familiar with the latest aids in methodology employed by foreign historians, and he had read widely in history in addition to his various bits of research. His breadth of information and his vast capacity for assimilating data were refined by a solid wisdom. That Altamira was not exclusively a professional historian was probably advantageous, for he brought to the task the perspective and originality of a man of extensive interests. Thus he was enabled to treat widely varied aspects of history intelligently, if not with equal authority.

The first volume of Altamira's *Historia de España y de la civilización española* was published in 1900. A distinctive work, it traced the evolution of Spain from primitive times through the middle ages. The reception of this volume on the part of specialists in history was enthusiastic, and he was urged to continue the work.[22] Yet in the preface he had disclaimed any pretensions that it was erudite or exhaustive; he modestly presented it as a manual for use in secondary schools and for the general public.

21. *Manuel de historia de España* (Madrid, 1934), preface, p. 18.
22. *RH*, LXXXVII (1904), 156–58, and *Revista crítica de historia y literatura*, V (1900), 382–85.

The second volume, completing the period of Ferdinand and Isabella, appeared in 1902. The third and longest, published in 1906, was originally intended to bring the work to a close, but it only finished up the reign of the House of Austria. Other activities and fatigue because of the colossal labor involved delayed the final volume until 1911.[23] With it the narrative terminated at the year 1808.

Altamira declined to treat recent history in this set because the sources were too overwhelming,[24] certainly not because he hesitated to touch contemporary subjects. Since he could not be prevailed upon to carry this particular study down to the present, it was eventually done by another historian.[25] In the course of three decades it was corrected, revised, and sent through two more editions. Condensations of it were published in several languages, the English version becoming available in 1918 with Professor Charles E. Chapman's *A history of Spain,* based on Altamira's four volumes. The *Historia de España* was the most famous production of Spanish historical scholarship abroad at the time; more than twenty years passed before it came to be superseded in part by the more elaborate work of Antonio Ballesteros.[26] In Spain its renown was such that an editor could justly refer to it as a national enterprise.[27]

The organic concept of Spanish civilization and the hierarchy of organization indicated Altamira's most uniform mastery of the field. The work was nearly mathematically proportioned; and the aims of simplicity, factual presentation, and cautions interpretation were evident throughout. Significantly enough, the first sentence announced that Spain was located on a peninsula in the extreme southwest of Europe. In such an elementary and clear

23. Reviews by Desdevises du Dezert, in *RH,* CIX (1912), 158–63, and in *Revue hispanique,* VI (1900), 522–25, and IX (1902), 528–32.

24. *Historia de España y de la civilización española,* III, 741–42 (advertencia).

25. Pío Zabala y Lera, *Historia de España y de la civilización española,* Vol. V (Barcelona, 1930).

26. *Historia de España y de su influencia en la historia universal* (8 vols.; Barcelona, 1918–34).

27. Statement by Zabala.

fashion the history of Spain until the chosen termination point of 1808 was subjected to close scrutiny. Political and diplomatic events were treated dutifully at the beginning of each period, but without the details usually lavished on them by the earlier historians. Then the little essays on the manifold topics ensued. Usually they were generalizations of monographs, although in many cases Altamira had extracted new and instructive facts in his own investigations. Such varied phases of civilization as law, society, institutions, military establishments, women, education, subject peoples, ecclesiastical affairs, commerce, art, industry, philosophy, architecture, scholarship, and many others were illuminated with skill. By no means were they discussed as incidental to the course of civilization; instead they were given ample sections of each volume.

Although most of the work was purely descriptive, the author ventured to set forth guiding interpretations. They were not obtrusive, however, for Altamira endeavored to achieve his effect by piling facts upon facts until the general lines were, or should be, obvious. The details he amassed tended to indicate his position on the Romanization of Spain, the role of the Visigoths, the importance of the municipalities, the expulsion of the Jews, and the activities of the Catholic Inquisition—all controversial issues among historians at that time. A prominence unorthodox in a Spanish history was given to the achievements of the Moors and Arabs. The chapters on the middle ages threw light into many a dim corner, while ancient myths were ignored or relegated disdainfully to their proper niche. In handling the history of the church, Altamira was objective and frank; he was prudent enough to document the shortcomings he described. He broke tradition in granting considerable space to economic matters, but he did not often interpret the past according to the materialistic view. Other innovations in the work were the adequate consideration devoted to the colonial empire and the refreshingly indulgent treatment of French influence in eighteenth-century Spain. Himself a man of enthusiasm, Altamira could narrate the exploits of others with sympathy. He had a gift for portraying the opinions and actions of individuals, no matter how unpopular as historical characters, in their setting, with the result that their attitudes were shown as comprehensible or even inevitable.

From flaws his set was by no means exempt. This grandiose synthesis of hundreds of aspects of Spanish history was naturally subject to errors of detail and inference. Painstaking though he was, Altamira was far from being an expert in all the ages he studied. His discussion of the Moorish period in particular was later deemed deficient.[28] He treated political and military history sketchily, if not contemptuously. On the other hand, the descriptions of the various topics in each period in every region of the Spanish possessions were at times repetitious and encyclopedic. He reached no happy solution of the problems involved in listing the illustrious men of science and literature, and some sections were only catalogues of names. And perhaps too often he speculated on might-have-beens at critical junctures in the past.

Altamira's circle of admirers widened as each volume of his *Historia de España* appeared. His work won the warm approval of his countrymen, although certain ecclesiastics and aristocrats found parts of it displeasing. His conscience as a historian could be amply satisfied, for modern methods of style, organization, and criticism had been observed. The various themes of Spanish history had been correlated with one another and treated as evolutionary forces, in accordance with the dictum he had once laid down in *La enseñanza de la historia*. Furthermore, his liberal political and religous prejudices were rarely offensive to objective students; neither diatribes nor eulogies had a place in his work. In spite of his much advertised patriotism, the sober pages seldom smacked of nationalistic distortion of the truth. The educator in Altamira could well regard the set as a success, for it was filled with cross-references and other teaching aids for the benefit of students. He could hardly be disappointed if his volumes had surpassed their mere pedagogical aim and had become a famous work of history. And yet the *Historia de España* surprisingly approached failure in one respect. In presenting a "scientific" book of history, replete with details, Altamira was too confident that it

28. *AHR*, XXIV (1919), 720–21.

would suggest its own conclusions, and he neglected to write large in order to emphasize the broad lines of development. Its effect in guiding the Spanish nation in the tradition of its past was diminished by the author's evident apprehension that he should appear to be shouting.

Another of Rafael Altamira's chief interests in life has been the Pan-Hispanic movement for the furtherance of greater intimacy between Spain and her estranged daughters in the western hemisphere. His association with it dates back to 1895, and in subsequent years he had been active as a historian and publicist in its promotion. The animosity borne by the Spanish-speaking nations of the new world toward the mother-country was, he was early convinced, in large part the product of fancied historical grievances.[29] Even in the peninsula it was fashionable for liberals to vilify the work of Spain in colonization. Irritated at this persistence of the "black legend," he attempted to set the record as straight as possible in the *Historia de España*. This work was, as he once noted with pride,[30] one of the first books of national history to consider the colonial empire as an integral part of Spanish civilization, and Altamira was among the earliest of the leftist writers to vindicate the imperial achievements of his country. Although his sections devoted to the new world in the *Historia de España* were compendious, they served to inter many a poisonous legend of Spanish misgovernment and cruelty.

His researches in Hispanic-American history were otherwise not significant. But he dedicated much effort to making source material available for the use of other scholars. He compiled a bibliography of colonial history[31] and published a large collection of constitutions and texts of legislation.[32] Always desirous of raising standards, he cautioned historians against the indiscriminate use of the old chronicles as source material of equal value,[33] and

29. *La huella de España en América* (Madrid, 1924), p. 14.
30. *Escritos patrióticos* (Madrid, 1929), p. 75.
31. *Bibliographie d'histoire coloniale (1900–30): Espagne* (Paris, 1932).
32. *Constituciones vigentes . . . y colección de textos para el estudio de la historia de las instituciones de América* (5 vols.; Madrid, 1926).
33. *La huella de España en América*, p. 57.

14

late in life he accepted the responsibility of directing the edition of documents and monographs for the history of Spanish America.

Convinced, as he was, that Spain's colonial record had been great and creditable, Altamira made known the possibilities of the harvest and recruited scholars to gather it. In an address to the American Historical Association, for example, he dwelt upon the superficial nature of historical studies of the field and called attention to the rich and almost undisturbed archives of the Indies at Seville.[34] While he held the chair of professor of the civil and political institutions of America at the University of Madrid he directed his students in ambitious research projects in Hispanic-American history. It seems likely, however, that some of Altamira's disciples carried a surplus of patriotism into their work, for too often recent Spanish scholars have mistaken the letter of legislation in behalf of the colonies for its fulfilment. When foreign historians published books on Spanish imperial history they received a cordial salute from the "restorer" of the history of Spain. Not only did their findings contribute to the fund of historical information, but his beloved *patria* usually emerged with a cleaner reputation.

Regarding Latin America as a proving-ground where the Spanish people were demonstrating their vitality anew,[35] Altamira was full of projects to stimulate the intellectual communion of Spaniards on both sides of the Atlantic. He was long a publicist for the Pan-Hispanic movement, and in 1908 he was entrusted with an important good-will mission to learned groups in the western hemisphere. His receptions as he lectured in Argentina, Uruguay, Chile, Peru, Mexico, and Cuba were flattering,[36] and his tour was considered a spectacular success for Pan-Hispanism. In the first years of his propagandist career he restricted the aims of the movement to a spiritual reconquest of the former empire. But encouraging results in that direction later led him to sponsor diverse political and economic arrangements to solidify the Span-

34. *AHR*, XV (1910), 476.
35. *La huella de España en América*, p. 44.
36. *Mi viaje a América* (Madrid, 1911).

ish-speaking world.[37] While this work was not out of harmony with his ideal of a historian who was at the same time an active patriot, his ardor was somewhat unrestrained, and his writings were unworthy of his scholarly gifts.

Altamira's erudite production in legal history was far more substantial than his Hispanic-American studies, and his works brought him great prestige as a jurist. More often than not his professorial duties were concerned with the history of law and institutions. He was elected president of international juridical societies, he served as arbitrator for the government in labor disputes, and he won awards for his research. The crowning honor came in 1920, when he was commissioned, along with other distinguished jurists, by the Council of the League of Nations to draw up a plan for the Permanent Court of International Justice. Having publicized the Allied cause in Spain during the war of 1914–18,[38] he was now moderately optimistic about the potentialities of world-peace machinery.[39] For some years after 1922 he was a judge on the Permanent Court of International Justice at The Hague.

His doctoral dissertation, *La historia de la propiedad comunal*, marked Altamira as a member of the illustrious liberal school of Spanish jurists. His research was thorough, his enunciation of legal ideas bold. From the first he hoped to demolish illusions that institutions were not mutable,[40] and he skilfully, though hurriedly, traced the evolution of common property through the centuries. While teaching at the University of Oviedo, he published various bits of research in articles and a preliminary study of the history of law.[41] An attractive monograph on the life and customs in his natal region of Alicante won a prize from the

37. His other chief books of this nature are *Cuestiones hispano-americanos* (Madrid, 1900), *España en América* (Valencia, 1908), *España y el programa americanista* (Madrid, 1917), *La política de España en América* (Valencia, 1921), and *Ultimos escritos americanistas* (Madrid, 1929).

38. *La guerra actual y la opinión española* (Barcelona, 1915).

39. *La sociedad de las naciones y el proyecto del tribunal permanente de justicia internacional* (Madrid, 1920).

40. P. 36.

41. *Historia de derecho español: cuestiones preliminares* (Madrid, 1903).

## John E. Fagg

Academy of Political and Moral Sciences.[42] A work published under the title of *Cuestiones de historia del derecho y de legislación comparada,* containing summaries of his own lecture courses and a survey of Spanish law, was warmly approved by foreign scholars.[43] In the *Historia de España* the recurring themes of jurisprudence in the different periods of Spanish history were discussed with a fulness that bordered on emphasis. Altamira's treatment of legal history was distinctive at the time for his conception of law as a vital expression of national life springing from social requirements.

Long a steadfast upholder of scientific methodology in historical research, Altamira struggled to improve Spanish standards through his own teachings and writings. His smaller historical works attested to his own observance of refined critical methods. He even went to the extreme of conducting lengthy battles for authority among sources in the very pages of his early studies. The *Historia de España* was primarily a work of generalization, and footnote citations to sources were not employed. But documents were inserted in the text when the author seemed to anticipate that verification of his points would be required. Customs and institutions were considered along with documents as relics of historical significance. At the end of the last volume was a bibliography which, in spite of its brevity and the modest value he placed on it,[44] was for years a leading guide to the materials of the history of Spain. His other bibliographical articles and collections were valuable to students, but he was not able to fill his early aspiration for an exhaustive study of the sources of Spanish history.[45]

Possibly as a result of his reaction against the rhetorical and philosophical sallies of the older historians, Altamira's literary style was factual and subdued. His first works were made disagreeable by involved sentences, some of them more than two

42. *Derecho consuetudinario y economía popular de la provincia de Alicante* (Madrid, 1905).

43. *RH,* CXVIII (1915), 375–76, and *AHR,* XX (1914), 185–86.

44. *Historia de España,* IV, 457.

45. Preface of R. Altamira to B. Alonso Sánchez, *Fuentes de la historia española* (Madrid, 1919).

17

RAFAEL ALTAMIRA

hundred words long. But his skill increased with practice, and by the time he composed the *Historia de España* his style was lucid and his arrangement logical. He did not often attain eloquence, but neither was his effectiveness vitiated by a self-conscious striving for effect. Unadorned and straightforward, his literary technique also was governed by standards of common sense and good taste.

Altamira declared in his first book that historical research had its own finality independent of application in the present,[46] but in many of his works he admitted a preoccupation with contemporary affairs. He never weakened in his stand that solutions of modern questions could assuredly be suggested by a scientific scrutiny of experience;[47] historical studies were an erudite pastime if they did not serve to guide humanity in the light of its past development. For a consciousness of history was imbedded in the minds of men. They often turned to it for precedents and records of experience, which affected, if they did not actually direct, social and national opinion. Thus it was essential, Altamira urged in his inaugural address to the Real Academia de la Historia, to narrow the chasm between the information of the specialists and the impressions of the public.[48]

The position of the historian in his own age was therefore one of great influence, for his publications helped to shape the course of events in the present and in the future. Altamira was convinced that behind the research of the historian, whether he always realized it or not, lay the yearning to discover the best means of improving humanity.[49] These he was more likely to strike if he worked the mine of all-embracing history of civilization. Once he had fitted the minuscule fragments of the past into a comprehensible picture, he should present it in simple form so that even the uncultured could participate in the maintenance of the traditional spirit. As exemplified by his lifelong activities and his nearly

46. *Historia de la propiedad comunal*, p. 36.
47. *De historia y arte*, p. 165.
48. *Cuestiones modernas de historia*, p. 163.
49. "The theory of civilization," *Rice Institute pamphlet* (Houston, Texas, 1915), III, 282.

18

sixty volumes of writing, Altamira's own career was in keeping with that conception. Not only did he preach to his colleagues that the historian was a man of great moral and political responsibility,[50] but he himself took quite seriously his role as a guide to his fellow-men in everyday affairs.

In speaking upon one occasion of the philosophy of history,[51] Altamira posited questions as to whether there was an end toward which humanity was moving blindly, perhaps directed by something transcendental to itself. He complained that most historians had dodged the true problems of philosophy, but he did not attempt to formulate a system of speculation to define and predict the course of mankind. That there was an eternal striving toward liberty, sincerity, and justice he did once affirm,[52] and in the substratum of his history of Spanish civilization this vein can be detected. But he hesitated to inquire whether these longings tended to triumph in conflicts with opposing forces for fear, he said, that the answer would be in the negative.[53] Progress in its highest form he considered the awakening of humanity to the idealistic qualities behind its actions, and the experience of history demonstrated that such progress had been made—but only in certain features.[54] For the element of evil was still undominated and defiant in such moral aberrations as envy, anger, cupidity, ambition, and the craving for luxury. In spite of a "clamor for the ethical basis to life, a demand for the reign of justice in the sphere of jurisprudence, of the good in the sphere of morality,"[55] he doubted that men could purge themselves of those natural impulses.

As Altamira entered old age his impressive range of activities hardly diminished. He labored at revising his prolific writings and publishing them in a set of *obras completas*. He continued to

50. *AHR*, XXI (1915), 10.
51. "The problem of the philosophy of history," *Rice Institute pamphlet*, III, 256–78.
52. "Philippe II d'Espagne," *Hommes d'état* (3 vols.; Paris, 1937), II, 513.
53. *La huella de España en América*, p. 207.
54. "The theory of civilization," *loc. cit.*, p. 307.
55. *Ibid.*, p. 311.

direct students in historical research and to publicize his various causes. An eminent historian of world-wide reputation, he was invited to give courses at such European universities as Cambridge, Oxford, London, Brussels, the Sorbonne, the Collège de France, and in Spanish intellectual centers, where he was always a prized guest. Having addressed learned audiences both in the United States and in Latin America, he was well known in the New World as an inspiring and brilliant orator. His very appearance and personality were in keeping with the distinguished position he held in scholarly circles. Tall, erect, slender, and handsome, he typified Spanish dignity. He was respected for his character and for his unswerving idealism; and, with it all, he was unassuming, kindly, and beloved of his friends.

In a lecture delivered in the United States in 1912 the historian of Spanish civilization expressed pessimism concerning the future of human civilization in general. His contemplation of the past had stirred him with the victory of man over nature and the consequent betterment of certain social and material aspects of life. But, he mused, might not all these advances be "doomed to immolation before a sudden metamorphosis of human thought and opinion"—illogical, perhaps, but not unprecedented?[56] Between the enormous disproportion in achievements in the material order and those of the ethical there lay spirit-chilling perils. And, he added, "who can escape the bitter confusion that moral development is still exiguous, that customs are not improving all around, and that the higher ethical doctrines remain untranslated into action in the practical life of the majority?"[57]

Rafael Altamira witnessed events in his later years that may have justified in his mind those forebodings. In common with men great and humble the world over, he saw the aspirations he cherished for humanity frustrated. If the spread of public education and the popular diffusion of history had results, they could scarcely have been those he had anticipated. His ideal Spain appeared on the stage in 1931, but it perished in agony soon after making its bow. The Pan-Hispanic movement of which he had

56. *Ibid.*, pp. 297–98.
57. *Ibid.*, pp. 299–300.

been a guiding spirit altered its temper and aggressively increased its aims. Having labored in international peace arrangements and proclaimed the conciliation of peoples, he saw his efforts mocked as the world again plunged down the cascades to war.

Futile as Altamira's design for his contemporary world may have proved, his work as a historian has a lasting value. His books were profoundly influential in clarifying the national traditions of Spain, and his career was a boon to Spanish scholarship. Even with the corrosion that the passing of time and new findings wreak on the authority of the facts and interpretations he set forth, his books form a general structure of knowledge that is hardly weakened. History he wrote, taught, and even preached. Not often in recent times has its value been affirmed with more spirited consistency than it has by Rafael Altamira.

# II

## *Alphonse Aulard (1849–1928)*

JAMES L. GODFREY

TODAY the world is in a revolutionary movement which threatens to leave its imprint upon action and thought in just as indelible a manner as did the French Revolution of a century and a half ago. From one point of view the present revolution may be considered the true counterrevolution to that which brought the eighteenth century to a close, for in many respects the values and ideas created and fostered then have just now been challenged by new social and political conceptions. This fact in itself should direct the attention of the student back to that most formative period of western European culture when the men of those countries and that time entered upon a heritage that now seems on the point of exhaustion. Those who do turn their attentions back will soon be conscious of the fact that they have incurred a debt to Alphonse Aulard, who, more than anyone else, has been responsible for the excellent work in writing and in documentation that has characterized the historical treatment of the French Revolution over the last fifty years.

Scholars of the French Revolution in this country would have little difficulty in agreeing that the major portion of their deference should go to Aulard and Albert Mathiez; these two men seem to dominate the historical work on the period just as Danton and Robespierre seemed for a time to dominate the period itself. The analogy may be even more fully drawn, for it is well known that Aulard considered himself the champion of Danton, while

Mathiez portrayed the virtues of the incorruptible Robespierre. This favoritism gives a clear insight into the personal feelings of the two authors as they consider the Revolutionary period. It seems apparent that Aulard would have been content had the Revolution abated before the apogee of internal violence was reached under Robespierre, if the gains that had been made could have been solidified under Danton's capacity for compromise; while Mathiez, without the advent of Robespierre and his connotations of economic and social change, would have considered the entire movement as incomplete—the beginning of a syllogism that refused to continue itself beyond the minor premise. The basis for a lively feud[1] becomes obvious, and even yet it is difficult not to take sides, for the Revolutionary movement is eloquent in its appeal to partisanship. It is possible, however, without entering this controversy, to judge Aulard on the basis of his historical influence, his methodology, his success as a teacher, his devotion to scholarship, his products of research, and the great impetus which he gave to the study of history of the Revolution. Most of these qualities and contributions Aulard shares with few peers; their common residence in one personality explains why Aulard is usually considered as "the grand old man" of French Revolutionary history.

Of Aulard's early life but little has been ascertained.[2] He was born on July 19, 1849, at Monthron in Charente. His father was an inspector of secondary education. Economically, the family was probably of the lower middle class but with a more preten-

1. See the anecdote recounted in the introduction to Herman Wendel, *Danton* (New Haven, 1935). Aulard's explanation of why he championed Danton is an interesting one. He saw in Danton the spirit of the embattled Revolution, the incarnation of the national defense against all of its foes. This picture of Danton had been understood before by such men as Villaume, Despois, Bougeart, and Sorel, but harm had been done by the fact that Auguste Comte and his disciples had distorted the character of Danton by presenting an untrue Danton—free of error but lacking on the positive side. Aulard thus felt it his mission to rescue Danton from the dialectic of the positivists. An account of this can be found in "Auguste Comte et la Révolution française," in *La Révolution française*, XXIV (1893), 5–9.

2. For a biographical skeleton of Aulard's life and activities see "Notice biographique," *La Révolution française*, LXXXI (1928), 293 ff. Also *Grande encyclopédie*, IV (Paris, *s.d.*), 671.

tious claim to an intellectual rating. It is known that young Alphonse studied at the College of Sainte-Barbe and at the Lycée Louis-le-Grand in Paris. At the age of eighteen he entered the École Normale Supérieure, where his studies were interrupted by his voluntary enlistment (though legally exempt) for service in the Franco-German War. The following year, 1871, he became an *agrégé des lettres.* He spent the period following graduation in the south of France, serving successively as professor of humanities at the lycées of Nîmes and Nice. In 1877 he received the degree of *docteur ès lettres*, submitting for his thesis one paper in Latin on Asinius Pollion, under the title of *De Caii Asinii Pollionis vita et scriptis*, and one in French on Leopardi, the Italian poet. It is interesting to note that Aulard's formal training was in literature, where he showed promise, rather than in history, where he achieved fame. Between 1878 and 1884 he served as professor of French literature at Aix, Montpellier, Dijon, and Poitiers. After this extensive apprenticeship in the provinces, he returned to Paris in 1884 as professor of rhetoric at the Lycée Janson-de-Sailly. The following year the municipality of Paris endowed at the University of Paris a chair of the history of the French Revolution, which Aulard accepted and filled with distinction until his retirement in 1922.

That a person prepared in literature should be appointed to an important chair in history must have been a matter of chagrin in historical circles. The election, however, was justified not only by future hopes but by past performances. Aulard had devoted a great portion of his time spent in the provinces to research in the history of the Revolutionary period. In 1822 he began to publish a series entitled *L'éloquence parlementaire pendant la Révolution française.*[3] The work, by later standards, was modest enough, but it was favorably received at the time as embodying a pleasing and impartial presentation of the legislative aspects of selected figures in the Revolutionary assemblies.[4] In a later (1905) and extended edition of the book Aulard admits that he approached his first

3. Vol. I, *Les orateurs de l'Assemblée Constituante* (Paris, 1882); Vols. II, III, *Les orateurs de la Legislative et de la Convention* (Paris, 1885–86).
4. Ch. Bemont, "Bulletin historique," *RH*, XXX (1886), 395.

study from a literary point of view and that many errors were incorporated in the text; but the work had virtue, for it was undertaken at a time when there existed but "few examples of the application of the historical method to the Revolutionary period." In 1884 Aulard began his contributions to journals, publishing with some success under the name of "Santhonax" in Clemenceau's journal *Justice*.[5] And so it was not a man entirely unknown and unvouched for who in 1885 honored the municipality of Paris by his acceptance of its generosity.

Why did Aulard turn from his first chosen field to devote his talents to historical research, and why in the Revolutionary period? Georges Lefebvre suggests that a solution might be found in the fact that Aulard belonged to a generation which from 1870 to 1875 had struggled to form a parliamentary and secular democracy in France.[6] The study of the Revolutionary period might be calculated to constitute the most effective historical background for such an attempt; it was the period of French history which best exhibited, shorn of its popular excesses, the political society which a depressed and humiliated France sought to recapture. The study of such a period during the years following the Franco-German War would certainly have the psychological compensation of contemplating more glorious days. In addition, the study of parliamentary figures from the standpoint of their speeches might, with some courtesy, be considered as a legitimate interest for a teacher of French literature. Then, again, it may be that the journalistic tendencies of Aulard—those who regarded him from the opposite side of the historical fence were very vocal in

5. A. Mathiez, "M. Aulard, historien et professeur," *Le Révolution française*, LV (1908), 59. Also *Grande encyclopédie*, IV, 671. In *La Révolution française*, XII (1887), 670–72, will be found an interesting list of ninety-five articles under the title "Lundis révolutionnaires" published from Dec. 29, 1884, through Dec. 27, 1886, in *Justice*. These articles include, among other subjects, some treatment of the following men: Taine, Danton, Marat, Dubois-Crancé, Quinet, Dufour, Jullien de Paris, Couthon, Robespierre, Vergniaud, Billaud-Varennes, Legendre, Hérault de Sechelles, Bazire, Desmoulin, Saint-Just, Barère, Ducos, Royer-Fonfrède, Guadet, Isnard, Lanjuinais, Fauchet, Fauriel, Moreau, Carrier, Lindet, and Babeuf.

6. G. Lefebvre, "L'œuvre historique d'Albert Mathiez," *Annales historiques de la Révolution française*, IX (1932), 194.

their opinion that Aulard was essentially a journalist—led him to an examination of the Constituent Assembly, sensing that he would find there political sentiments which could be useful in consolidating the Third Republic.

There is another item in this conversion which must be mentioned. Aulard was, in the better sense of the word, a nationalist. He possessed too much intellectual integrity, he had too sane a perspective on the fluctuations of both private and national life, to feel personally humiliated by his country's defeat of 1870–71. Yet he was conscious that as a result of the ill fortunes of war French culture experienced a sickening sag, that the public mind lost tone and resilience. France needed to be revived—and one of the first therapeutic aids to revival was teaching.[7] Add to that belief in the efficacy of teaching, Aulard's personal attitude toward history, and one can estimate the strong intellectual and emotional tug which must have drawn Aulard from the formal study of literature to the more utilitarian (politically) study of history. Léon Cahen, a contemporary professional colleague, classifies Aulard as the spiritual son of Michelet, Quinet, and the men of '48, for whom history was the highest form of human culture, the foundation of political science, and the basis of progress.[8] Surely here was an opportunity that a man of Aulard's convictions and predilections could scarcely have refused: the occasion, a psychopathic depression of the national ego; the therapeutic method, teaching; and the therapeutic dose, history. In any case, it is not so strange that Aulard turned to the study of French Revolutionary history as it was that Revolutionary history waited for his turning.

Since Aulard placed such a premium upon the ministration of teaching, it should be of interest, now that he was in Paris and on his way to becoming the center of a historical constellation, to observe his methods and something of his successes as a teacher. As occupant of the new chair created by the Paris municipality,

7. L. Cahen, "Alphonse Aulard," *Revue universelle*, I (1929), 304.
8. *Ibid.*, p. 303.

Aulard delivered his first lecture on March 12, 1886.[9] From that time until his retirement in 1922 he was actively engaged in imparting to others the attitudes and methods which, watered by his own genius, had been made to bear rich fruit for himself.[10] This does not mean that Aulard was concerned with indoctrination. Such an imputation would have been received by him with a sense of aggrievement; he was too aware of the changing evaluations of scholarship, of the evolution of all sciences, and of the ephemeral character of facts and ideas—"the definitive of today is the provisional of tomorrow"[11]—to seek to set the intellectual bonds too tightly. The object of teaching, according to his conviction, was "to purify the passions through the action of the intelligence." His ideal was that of Dante, "une lumière intellectuelle pleine d'amour."[12] The result and comfort of work should be the joy of understanding—an understanding which comprehended not only the texts but—perhaps more important and certainly more difficult—the men themselves. Such a general attitude has enough of "sweetness and light" to be appealing; enough of intellectual integrity and toughness—when one considers the character of the man—to be a formidable and compelling intellectual discipline.

We are told by Pierre Flottes, a professional colleague, in the issue of *La Révolution française* devoted to the memory of Aulard, that Aulard discounted the role of memory. For him the "good life," intellectually, resided not in the retention of details but in

9. "Leçon d'ouverture du cours d'histoire de la Révolution française à la faculté des lettres de Paris," *Études et leçons sur la Révolution française*, I (Paris, 1901), 3–39.

10. The most interesting information—though of an impersonal nature—concerning Aulard as a teacher is contained in a report prepared by himself and published under the title, "L'enseignement de l'histoire de la Révolution française à la Sorbonne (1886–1911)," in *La Révolution française*, LXI (1911), 442–55. This article lists the subjects considered in the public course each year from 1886 through 1911 and reveals the rich variety of Aulard's work. Some of his outstanding students and their publications are given along with the publications of the author and many interesting items concerning his professional relationships with students.

11. A. Mathiez, *loc. cit.*, p. 58.

12. E. Herriot, *La Révolution française*, LXXXI (1928), 306–7.

the power of analysis, in the possession of "l'esprit de finesse."
He never reproached a student for not knowing a thing. "If he
does not know it, it is perhaps because he has a bad memory!
It may be that he has not had time to learn it! There are so
many things to learn."[13] This intellectual compassion, this generosity of attitude, represented a deliberate choice on the part of
Aulard. To him it was of great value to catch what he considered
to be the essence of things; he would have been derelict in his
duty—in his mission—had he not allowed his students the same
latitude.

The fact that Aulard emphasized the quality of analysis rather
than that of tenacious memory must not be interpreted to mean
that he possessed no rigorous standards or that he was lax in his
methodology. Camille Bloch, the general secretary of the Société
de l'Histoire de la Révolution, who delivered modest reminiscences at the funeral of Aulard, has recalled that Aulard at the
beginning of an academic year habitually passed to his classes
the following observations:

> Always use the sources; say nothing that one does not know
> from the originals; write nothing without producing the appro-
> priate references; avoid assertions without proof; work from the
> texts; distinguish between the important and interesting facts and
> those that are insignificant and without interest; emphasize the
> former and neglect the latter; estimate the value of a historical
> fact in terms of its degree of influence upon the evolution of the
> individual, group, or society that is being studied; present the

13. P. Flottes, "Aulard professeur," *La Révolution française*, LXXXI
(1928), 341. This immensity of what there was to know may have left
Aulard with the opinion that too much time was frequently spent on learning that which it was not necessary to know. At least he carried on a running fight against the requirement that the minor thesis submitted for the
*doctorat* be in Latin when the work done is in modern and contemporary
history. This point was brought up in the notices that Aulard wrote on the
examinations of Philippe Sagnac ("Le doctorat de M. Sagnac," *La Révolution
française*, XXXVI [1899], p. 7) and Paul Gautier ("Le doctorat de M. Paul
Gautier," *ibid.*, XLIV [1903], 174–75). Evidently, Aulard felt that his
criticisms had possessed some weight, for the same article stated that the
University Council would take up the question at its session in June, 1903.
He pointed out that the *petite thèse* is now written in French ("Le doctorat
de M. Arnaud," *ibid.*, XLVIII [1905], 49). To have helped in this reform is
to have spread one's benefactions to an undoubtedly eager group of students.

facts in an impartial and objective manner; in publishing that which is new [*inédit*] the pertinent facts should not be buried beneath that which is insignificant and of the character of rubbish [*fatras*]; and, finally, let the research be long and the results short.[14]

It would not, I think, be irreverent to refer to these admonitions as "M. Aulard's decalogue for historical study."

These would be virtues enough for a teacher, but to them must be added certain qualities which, while not professional in character, serve to adorn the professor. Albert Mathiez, the most brilliant student to know Aulard as a teacher, has recorded that he was cordial with his students, that he used his Sundays to receive and counsel those who studied under him.[15] Easily approachable, he appears as a democrat by birth and instinct as well as by reason. Those who knew him appreciated this quality, and one friend remembered him for these few words spoken when he gave a small sum of money to a needy student: "It is an occasion when a small sum of money can save a man."[16] From his mind, his spirit, and his pocket he gave to those who came seeking him.

So far, most of the evidence for Aulard's ability as a teacher has been of the inferential variety; for those who must have the pragmatic test of accomplished results, the evidence is no less convincing. Mathiez assures us that Aulard had a very productive influence on his students and cites in affirmation a short list of works, the inspiration for which came from Aulard. They comprise: *L'Isle de France sous Decaen,* by Henri Prentout; *Fouché,* by Louis Madelin; *Jeanbon Saint-André,* by Léon Lévy-Schneider; and *Phillippeaux* and *Histoire de le théophilanthropie,*

14. These advisory remarks are a very free translation of Bloch's arrangement of them. See C. Bloch, "Notre Deuil," *La Révolution française,* LXXXI (1928), 291–92.

15. *Loc. cit.,* p. 53. Professor M. B. Garrett, of the University of North Carolina, was kind enough to share with the writer his impressions of Aulard gained from a Sunday afternoon call. He confirms the opinion that Aulard had an abundance of sympathy and patience. A picture of Aulard (*La Révolution française,* LXXXI [1928] facing p. 289) reveals that he had a delightfully French appearance.

16. Flottes, *loc. cit.,* p. 341.

by Paul Mautouchet.[17] In addition, Professor Louis Gottschalk, recently described by an academic rival of Oxford as the leading exponent of the Mathiez school in America, considers Mathiez himself as one of the most persuasive arguments for the thesis that Aulard was a great teacher.[18] In the perverse world of education it is considered—and correctly so—something of a triumph to have been the teacher of the man who later does more than anyone else to question the definitive quality of your work and to threaten you in the role of the leading authority. On this particular score the evidence is fairly complete and consistent—Aulard was a great teacher.

Aulard, however, was no academic orchid seeking his sustenance from the air. He paid for his success in the good hard coin of devoted and consistent work. From the time in southern France when as a teacher of French literature Aulard first began to consider seriously the historical sources of the French Revolution, he was never for long free from the fascination which the documents of the Revolutionary period held for him. Always he seems to have worked with a triple purpose: to understand the documents; to use them faithfully in his accounts of the Revolution; and to make them, as far as possible, available for the students who were to follow him. In the first lecture delivered from his new post, Aulard reviewed the work that had been done in Revolutionary history and lamented the sad lack of scientific documentation. His spirits were sustained, however, by the knowledge that with some regrettable exceptions the documents remained and could be made to yield their true evidence to an unimpassioned investigator.[19] Ample room there was for this, for he estimated that not over a fourth or a third of the documents pertaining to the period had ever been catalogued. And so he set for himself the task not only of portraying the Revolution but of making available its remnants as his chief witnesses, speaking their testimony to any who might inquire of them.

From the man to his writings is but a natural step, for Aulard

17. Mathiez, *loc. cit.*, p. 53.
18. L. Gottschalk, "Professor Aulard," *JMH*, 1 (1929), 86.
19. "Leçon d'ouverture," *Études et leçons*, I, 18–28.

faithfully reflected in his writings the qualities and ideas which characterized him as a teacher. The only thing surprising is the fact that a man who gave so much time to his teaching should have produced, as writer and editor, the vast quantity of careful work that now bears his name. It must have been that in a fortunate mental synthesis he combined the two so that they aided, rather than hindered, each other, for the catalogue of the Bibliothèque Nationale lists under his name some sixty volumes. Even when the appropriate discount is made for the works that were merely edited, almost thirty volumes remain. This is even more imposing when one considers the rigor of his method and the historical worth of his contribution. And as this long and fruitful life expressed itself in scholarly work, it is only fair to say that Aulard maintained with remarkable consistency his personal attitude toward the Revolution—there seems to have been some subtlety of association that enabled them to draw the best from each other.

Indeed, it may be said that the Revolution occupied for Aulard something of the place that social cynics usually attribute to a satisfactory wife of several years' standing. He took "her" seriously; he considered himself "her" official defender; and for "her" contributions to his intellectual and emotional happiness he repaid "her" by a lifelong devotion. To him the French Revolution represented the most important era in the history of France,[20] for he saw it not as a period but as a continuous process which had its origins before 1789 and which was still moving toward fulfilment. According to Mathiez, he held the view that the Revolution was not made but was in a process of making itself.[21] The period of Revolution proper he described as a mirror held before France in which she could discern her true lineaments. "Without the Revolution, one would have never known that our nation could be all at once so lusty [*forte*] and so sensitive [*sensible*], so gay and so dead, so loving and so irritable, so generous and so dreadful."[22] He aptly summed it up when he con-

20. *Ibid.*, p. 6.
21. *Loc. cit.*, p. 60.
22. *Études et leçons*, I, 6.

cluded that for France to know the Revolution was for her to know herself.

Having established for himself the position of the Revolution, Aulard warned that the historian approaching the subject should do so with clean hands. Partisanship should be avoided; judgments *en bloc* should yield themselves to a more selective method. This is rigorous enough, but, as is so often the case with Aulard, it is subject to a softening touch: "He who does not sympathize with the Revolution sees only the surface. In order to understand it, it is necessary to love it."[23] Such an attitude, such an affection toward any subject, would bring its own rewards in the shape of fervor and emotional zeal in the actual process of the work; and, truly, sympathy is almost a necessary condition to a fair understanding. Yet it is questionable if such an attachment would yield appreciable dividends in the way of impartiality and objectivity. It is said that whom the Lord loveth, he chasteneth. But could Aulard do the same? Or did he feel for certain aspects of his subject emotional predilections that predisposed him in his judgments? And Aulard realized fully that judgment was a legitimate province of the historian.[24] This is not an indictment of Aulard; if anything, it is an indictment of the fallacy of a complete objectivity, and a preparation for an exposition of how Aulard's personality—his emotional affinities—influenced, to a degree beyond that encompassed by the term "purely scientific," his reactions to the study of Revolutionary history.

For the purpose of explaining more fully Aulard's attitude toward the Revolution, we may do violence to chronology and select not his first published works but his *Histoire politique de la Révolution française*.[25] This work, published in 1901, gives such a complete picture of the historian of the Revolution that it is necessary to consider his lesser works of authorship only *en passant* in order to care for a few specialized views. Of all the works which

23. *Ibid.*, p. 16.
24. *Ibid.*, p. 12.
25. Paris, 1901. The copy most frequently found in American libraries is a translation with notes made by Bernard Miall from the third French edition: *The French Revolution, a political history, 1789–1804* (New York, 1910).

Aulard could call his own in the sense that they took their being from the impact of facts upon his mind, this was his favorite one— and even here, in justice to Aulard's appreciation of the transitory nature that works of scholarship carry about them, it should be said that he pledged his claim to lasting recognition not upon this book but upon a work which he edited and which will be mentioned later.

It is doubtful if many historical contributions have been made in which the contributor was in more complete control of the technical apparatus of his craft than was Aulard in offering his political history to the world of scholars and to the public.[26] Twenty years of research in the sources made their valuable contribution to the narrative,[27] while invaluable experience as a teacher, author, and editor was utilized to adorn the tale. Within the chronological limitations of the period between 1789 and 1804 Aulard proposed to depict the political history of the Revolution "au point de vue des origines et du développement de la démocratie et de la république." It seemed clear to him that "la conséquence logique du principe de l'égalité, c'est la démocratie. La conséquence logique du principe de la souveraineté nationale, c'est la république."[28] In such a limitation Aulard recognized the hazard that critics would accuse him of painting but a partial picture: of leaving out items and influences that had a legitimate—some would say, paramount—claim to consideration; of neglecting to present the information that would show, alongside the political, the socioeconomic manifestations of the movement. This could not be avoided: history is very demanding, and life is short; there must be a limitation to the material in

26. James Harvey Robinson, after pointing out the difficulties of a partisan and emotional nature which beset the period, commends Aulard's fairness and judgment and adds the glowing tribute that "there is no reason to suppose that anyone in the world knows more than he about the sources" (*Political science quarterly*, XXVI [1911], 133–41). It is unfortunate, however, that Aulard's principal work should have reached the English and American reader through such a bad translation. Robinson complains in the critical article just quoted of the bad translation by Miall—a judgment partly concurred in by H. E. Bourne in *AHR*, XVI (1910–11), 386.

27. *Histoire politique*, p. x.

28. *Ibid.*, p. iii.

the sources that can be thoroughly covered in a lifetime. In this regard Aulard wrote:

> Si on n'est pleinement satisfait ni de ma méthode ni de mon plan, j'espère qu'on aura du moins, quant à ma documentation, une sécurité, qui vient de la nature de mon sujet. Je veux dire qu'on n'aura pas à craindre qu'il m'ait été matériellement impossible de connaître toutes les sources essentielles. Il n'en est pas de même pour d'autres sujets. L'histoire économique et sociale de la Révolution, par exemple, est dispersée en tant de sources qu'il est actuellement impossible, dans le cours d'une vie d'homme, de les aborder toutes ou même d'en aborder les principales.[29]

There is little doubt, however, that Aulard in selecting the political field for his efforts was at the same time doing that which was most congenial with his intellectual interests and tastes.

Having once set his goal, Aulard proceeded with some persuasiveness. The acquisition of a democratic republic, which characterized, according to Aulard, the French government from 1792 to 1795, was not a march of events in which logic played a large part. To the author, events unfolded themselves, ideas germinated and grew, from the mutual interaction of men and circumstances—an interaction which on its political side exhibited "ni unité de plan, ni continuité de méthode, ni suite logique dans les divers remaniements de l'édifice politique."[30] From this welter of interacting forces came the "ups and downs" of the graph of historical events, as now this, now that, combination of men and circumstances dominated the scene. An excellent illustration of the manner in which Aulard viewed these manifestations was his belief that the establishment of the democratic republic was the true revelation of the Revolutionary movement; yet in 1789, when the movement was already well under way, he failed to discern anywhere in France the semblance of a republican party. The men were there who were perfectly capable of such a government, but circumstance had not as yet claimed them for its own. Not until the king sought the eastern border in the flight to Varennes did circumstances and men combine for the

29. *Ibid.*, p. ix.
30. *Ibid.*, p. vii.

formation of a truly republican party. Probably, in the short run, Aulard would not have subscribed to any historical doctrine which contemplated an orderly and logical marshaling and ful-filling of historical events. The possibilities of combination were too infinite. It is also possible, however, that as one lengthened the period under consideration Aulard would have admitted an in-creasing possibility not for the elimination of, but for the reduc-tion of the operation of chance. His contention that the Revolu-tionary process continued through the France of his day may be taken to indicate that, in the long run, certain patterns and com-binations tend to predominate. While this is far from affording the historian a foundation from which he can view without trepi-dation the symmetrical unfolding of sequences, it, at least, gives some assurance for the patient and long-lived that there is in his-tory, the magnetic effect of a trend which eventually will make itself felt and establish a compulsive force about which the events of history will cluster.

To Aulard must go considerable credit for predicating his treatment of the Revolution upon fairly sound consideration of the external relationships of France during the period. The in-vasions were largely responsible for Revolutionary government and the Terror, though there is a possibility that Aulard attributed too much significance to the military troubles in his explanation of this period of the Revolution. If the character of man is an active factor, along with circumstances, in the determination of events, then it is all too probable that events cannot be explained in terms of one alone. To the provinces also goes a liberal portion of Aulard's attention. We must credit Aulard with his view of the Revolution as not born of a doctrine but imposed as a fact,[31] and the contribution that came from his distribution of emphasis be-tween Paris and the provinces as centers of the Revolutionary movement.[32]

This political history is the chief opus of its author. The faults

31. *Revue historique*, LXXVII (1901), 368.
32. A good statement of this point of view is found in a speech given by Aulard on June 9, 1900 (just before the publication of the *Histoire poli-tique*) at the general meeting of the Congrès des Sociétés Savantes. This

that characterize it will also characterize him. Great though Aulard is when considered as a whole, he is not flawless in detail. While Aulard prided himself upon his methodology and his assiduous cultivation of the documents, it is reasonably doubtful whether his method of selection was that best calculated to give a true picture. The citations in the political history—in fact, in most of Aulard's works—are overwhelmingly from the official reports. While no one would begrudge the historian the comfort and assurance that such sources give, it must be pointed out that official sources, especially during a revolutionary period, are to be regarded with some suspicion. They are too apt to deal with propaganda, too inclined to place either the best or the worst construction on important facts; such documents, before being admitted into the text of history, should be most carefully evaluated. This matter of excessive reliance on official documents has made Aulard fair game for more than one critic; H. Chobaut,[33] writing in a rival journal and under a rival flag, cites it as one of the dangers that must be guarded against when reading Aulard, while Augustin Cochin, in defense of Taine, administers to Aulard a critical drubbing equaled only by that previously administered by Aulard to Taine.[34] The result of this method has been to make of Aulard's work more of a façade than what a great work of history, in the modern sense, should be.

---

speech was subsequently printed as "L'histoire provinciale de la France contemporaine," *La Révolution française*, XXXVIII (1900), 481–99. The relationship is clearly set forth: "On est d'accord à comprendre que, dans l'histoire comme dans la réalité, Paris et la province sont inséparables, qu'on ne connaît vraiment la France que quand on la considère en ces deux éléments, qui se pénètrent et se mêlent sans cesse, et que, puisqu'on connaît assez bien l'histoire de Paris, il est temps d'étudier l'histoire de la province d'une manière complète et méthodique" (*ibid.*, p. 484).

33. H. Chobaut, "L'œuvre d'Aulard et l'histoire de la Révolution française," *Annales historiques de la Révolution française*, VI (1929), 2–3.

34. A. Cochin, *La crise de l'histoire révolutionnaire* (Paris, 1909), pp. 21 ff. This attack upon Taine as a historian is so well known through Aulard's *Taine, historien de la Révolution française* (2d ed.; Paris, 1908), that one is apt to get the impression that Aulard has a critical viciousness that operated against the work of anyone whom he did not consider a professional historian. As a pleasant contrast to this one might read the words of praise that Aulard has for Jean Jaurès in "M. Jaurès historien de la Révolution." *La Révolution française*, XLIII (1902), 289–99.

Another indictment has been offered in the charge that Aulard paid too much attention to ideas and not enough to personalities. That a work of history should show concern for the intellectual attributes of the subject it treats is in itself a matter for congratulations, but there is the danger that one will forget that the basis for intellectual manifestations is in the personalities of the men who make ideas and in the personality of the age that influences the men. This must be considered, and considered seriously, if the resultant treatment is to be more than an abstraction of an abstraction. Aulard has too little concerned himself with the intricacies and irrationalities of personality.

Perhaps as a result of the previous lack, it is true that Aulard has not enough occupied himself with the diverse social groups that comprise the whole of society. Just as there was too great emphasis placed upon official documents, it is possible to say that the author placed too great an emphasis upon what might be termed an "official group." This prevented an adequate appreciation of all the forces that combined in forming the specific movement that Aulard describes so well.

These faults are not minor ones; they would have crushed a smaller man. But, fortunately, faults may be considered as relative to virtues: the latter increase, the former decrease. Even the most sadistic critic must admit that, despite the maladies that beset the historical person of Aulard, he will live. His work had sufficient vitality to conquer for itself one of the strongest of the entrenched positions, and it would seem that that which it conquered it can hold against all, save possibly the historical revulsions which time may bring.

Although the *Histoire politique* must obviously overshadow the other historical works of Aulard, he would not be entirely without credit if he depended upon them alone. His minor works often strike a rich vein of Revolutionary history and bring from the genius of Aulard a very welcome illumination of dark corners. One of his earlier attempts was *Le culte de la raison et le culte de l'Être suprême,*[35] a monograph which, though short, is indispens-

35. Paris, 1892.

able in any serious study of Revolutionary religious aberrations.[36] About a decade later, undoubtedly stirred by the nature and spirit of the clerical question in France,[37] Aulard added another volume on the subject of religious history during the Revolutionary period with the publication of *La Révolution française et les congrégations*.[38] This additional venture was not well advised, for his treatment of the religious question was not lacking in superficiality, especially in the view that the French people were not deeply attached to the Catholic church. It is quite possible that Aulard, through his personal sympathies that were undoubtedly stirred by the controversy about him, allowed himself certain liberties more in keeping with his occasional role as a polemnist than with that of a historian. In 1905 a new and revised edition of his work on Revolutionary oratory was issued, and in 1911 he made a contribution to the history of the Napoleonic period with *Napoleon 1er et la monopole universitaire*.[39] It was undoubtedly with great pleasure that Aulard came to the conclusion that the educational policy of Napoleon, instead of bolstering his personal position and his government, actually contributed to the downfall of both. With the publication of *La Révolution française et le régime féodal*[40] Aulard entered still another field. He had always been conscious of the fact that his work in the history of the Revolution lacked those elements of economic history which younger writers were using to such good effect. This work may be considered a belated effort to repair this deficiency. Although Aulard assumed no special competence in economic history, he was always interested in it and played an important part on the committee charged with the collection and publication of materials relating to the economic history of the Revolutionary period. In

36. This work received the following description from a German critic: "Der Werth des Buches liegt nicht in dieser künstlichen, ganz willkürlichen Hypothese, sondern in der Erzählung des Thatsächlichen, in der Sammlung zahlreicher historische Notizen über jenen kurzlebigen revolutionären Kultus in Paris und in denProvinzen" ( *HZ*, LXIX [1892], 562).

37. F. M. Fling, "Some recent works on the French Revolution," *AHR*, X ( 1904–5), 889.

38. Paris, 1903.

39. Paris, 1911.

40. Paris, 1919.

addition to these formidable publications, all during this period Aulard was collecting the articles that he contributed to periodicals, especially his own *La Révolution française,* and issuing them as volumes in a series entitled *Études et leçons sur la Révolution française.*[41] Beyond this one finds him making contributions to the following journals: *Justice, Matin, Journal, Dépêche de Toulouse, Populaire* (Nantes), *l'Heure, Nouvelles Littéraires, l'Œuvre, Progrès civique, Quotidien, l'Ère nouvelle,* and *Lumière.*[42] Under the pressure of such an accomplishment the quality of the work done represents a tribute to Aulard's rich endowment in industry and in genius.

One of the great interests of Aulard's professional career was to make the documents of the Revolutionary period available to students. This was not merely a sideline to Aulard's work: it was of equal rank with his teaching and writing. Indeed, there is reason to suppose that Aulard considered it, in the final analysis, the most important aspect of his work. He is said to have considered his work in editing the documents of the Committee of Public Safety[43]—*Recueil des actes du Comité de Salut Public, avec la correspondance officielle des représentants en mission*—as the most likely to prevent his contributions to history from perishing.[44]

Such a belief reflected sound judgment on the part of Aulard. The work (comprising twenty-six large volumes) is of the highest importance; it constitutes an indispensable collection of documents for the study of the Revolution. The Committee of Public Safety was the most important governmental body during the period of Revolutionary government; its decrees and reports, along with the reports sent to it by the deputies on mission, are matters of permanent concern. Most of these documents are chronologically arranged and reprinted in full, though some, of less importance, are only summarized. An attempt on the part of

41. 9 vols.; Paris, 1901–24.
42. "Notice biographique," *La Révolution française,* LXXXI (1928), 294.
43. 26 vols.; Paris, 1889–1923. Despite its great length, this marvelous collection was never fully completed.
44. Bloch, *loc. cit.,* p. 312.

Chobaut to treat this work as a hodgepodge in which the material and the immaterial are jumbled together, shows not only a critical viciousness but an embarrassing lack of judgment.[45] There must be at least fifty thousand documents in the collection either given in full or summarized; that some should be more important than others is patent. The importance of any one document, however, depends as much on the subject which the researcher is studying as it does upon the intrinsic worth of the document itself. The collection is a monument to skill and industry; its completeness must be considered as a vindication rather than as an indictment of Aulard's scholarship.

As companion pieces Aulard has offered *La société des Jacobins: recueil des documents pour l'histoire du club des Jacobins de Paris*,[46] and three shorter collections dealing with the municipal history of the city of Paris under the titles: *Paris pendant la réaction thermidorienne et sous le Directoire, Paris sous le Consulat,* and *Paris sous le premier Empire.*[47] While less extensive than the series of volumes on the Committee of Public Safety, they all represent work that needed to be done. The documents on the Jacobin Club are especially important in view of the fact that the club for the greater part of its existence occupied a semiofficial position in the political structure. It will be noticed that practically all of this documentary material appeared before Aulard wrote his political history and offered tangible proof of intense industry during the twenty years which he claimed to have spent in the archives.

Another great historical service of Aulard's was his editorship of *La Révolution française,* a professional journal devoted to the publication of work done in the Revolutionary period. This journal had been founded in 1881 by Dide and Charavay; Aulard assumed the editorship in 1887 and exerted such an influence upon its character that the personalities of the journal and its

45. Chobaut, *loc. cit.,* p. 2.
46. 6 vols.; Paris, 1889–97. This collection was made under the auspices of the municipal council of Paris and is compiled from numerous sources, many of them newspapers.
47. 5 vols., Paris, 1898–1902; 4 vols., Paris, 1903–9; Paris, 1912.

editor tended to blend. The maintenance, in full vigor, of such a journal, offering, as it did, a publisher for meritorious work, was a steady incentive for students of the period. It is interesting to note that the first differences between Aulard and Mathiez appeared over the interpretation which should have been made in an article submitted by Mathiez to the journal.[48] Also in connection with his editorial duties, Aulard prepared much private literature for publication, the list including such works as: *Mémoires secrets de Fournier l'Americain,*[49]*Notes historiques . . .* of Delbrel,[50] and the *Mémoires de Chaumette sur la révolution du 10 août 1792.*[51] With the completion of this appreciation of Aulard as an editor, there remains but one other phase of his activities for our consideration.

Aulard was also something of a public man. At all times he seems to have given freely of himself to academic and social movements in which he believed. His activities on academic committees were considerable and of high order. During the course of his life he served in the following capacities: in the ministry of public instruction Aulard was president of the section on modern history; at the ministry of foreign affairs he was a member of the committee on diplomatic archives and the committee for the publication of the diplomatic documents on the origin of the war of 1914;[52] he was a member of the committee for publication of the history of the city of Paris; and he served with considerable interest and assistance on the committee for the collection and publication of documents relating to the economic history of the

48. *Annales historique de la Révolution française,* IX (Paris, 1932), p. 219. This is in a letter from Mathiez to Gottschalk dated Paris, Nov. 23, 1930.
49. Paris, 1890.
50. Paris, 1893.
51. Paris, 1893.
52. Aulard interestingly enough contributed to various periodicals a number of articles on the subject of the war of 1914. These were collected and issued under the title: *La guerre actuelle commentée par l'histoire; vues et impressions au jour le jour (1914–1916)* (Paris, 1916). There was also a later volume entitled: *1914–1918; histoire politique de la grande guerre, publiée sous la direction de A. Aulard . . . avec la collaboration de E. Bouvier . . . et A. Ganem* (Paris, 1924).

French Revolution. In the professional historical societies outside that of his own field he held a membership in the Société d'Histoire Moderne, the Société d'Histoire de la Guerre Mondiale, and the Société d'Histoire de la Révolution de 1848.

In the sociopolitical groups Aulard identified himself with several that attracted his sympathies. He was at one time vice-president of the Ligue Française des Droits de l'Homme et du Citoyen and a member of the council of the Fédération Internationale des Ligues des Droits de l'Homme. He served as both president and vice-president of the Mission Laïque Française. His interest in peace and his prestige secured for him the presidency of the Association Française pour la Société des Nations, and in 1927 he presided over an international union of national associations.[53] His death, in the fall of the following year, closed a career that had been given without stint to his colleagues, his people, and the world.

A final paragraph which catches and holds for display the man who was Alphonse Aulard is very difficult. He was a person who lived with some intensity; such people are not easy to impale with rigid formulas. It is difficult also to determine whether or not Aulard should be considered a truly great historian. As a thinker he would have profited from a little more brilliance; as a writer a trifle more of grace and suavity of style would have been an appreciable benefit; as a craftsman a more latitudinarian use of the sources would have contributed to his finality. What patience, interest, and skill, combined with a deep feeling for the historical, can do, Aulard did. Great or not, he continues to dwarf the many who have followed him, though they have added height by standing upon his shoulders. Great or not, the day is long hence when serious works on the French Revolution will not bear citations from the works written and edited by Aulard. Until such a time comes let those who use him do him honor.

53. Most of this material is from "Notice biographique," *La Révolution française,* LXXXI (1928), 293 ff. The complete list includes membership in a few groups not mentioned in this essay.

# III

## *Hans Delbrück (1848–1929)*

Richard H. Bauer

During the third quarter of the nineteenth century German historiography was largely dominated by an influential group of political historians. Led by such eminent historians as Dahlmann, Droysen, Sybel, and Treitschke, whose patriotic and nationalistic sentiments had been profoundly stirred by the contemporary political developments of Europe, they vigorously advocated the unification of Germany under the leadership of Prussia. Hence they were sometimes called the *kleindeutsch* historians. Moreover, they favored the establishment of a constitutional monarchy resting on a national foundation. In general, they considered themselves as belonging to the school of historians founded by Leopold von Ranke. Some of them, as a matter of fact, had received their historical training from him. All accepted both his methodology and his interpretation of history. They agreed with him that history should confine itself primarily to political matters; that it should emphasize the role of the state as the supreme cultural and political achievement of mankind; and finally, that it should particularly stress the relations of the states to one another and the effect of these relations on their internal policies. Unlike Ranke, who insisted upon treating all states on a basis of equality and without partiality, they gave preference and special consideration to their own state. In other words, his approach to history was largely universal; theirs was definitely nationalistic.

Basically, however, they differed from him in degree rather than in substance.[1]

As one of the last important representatives of the political historians, the name of Hans Delbrück should be mentioned. Long after their influence had declined, he continued to emphasize political history and to defend it against all attacks. His interesting career and noteworthy achievements deserve careful examination.

Hans Delbrück was born of a distinguished family of Prussian officials on November 11, 1848, in Bergen on the island of Rügen. Among his ancestors were noted jurists, theologians, and university professors.[2] One of his great-uncles, Johann Friedrich Gottlob Delbrück (1768–1830), had served as tutor to two Prussian kings, Frederick William IV and William I. During the nineteenth century several of his relatives achieved distinction as Prussian statesmen. His father, Berthold Delbrück, was a judge of the district court in Bergen and was later promoted to the court of appeals in Greifswald. His mother was a highly gifted woman, the daughter of Dr. Leopold von Henning, who had been a professor of philosophy at the University of Berlin and an enthusiastic disciple of Hegel. Undoubtedly, young Delbrück's devotion to Hegel can be traced to his maternal grandfather.

He received his preparatory training at the *Gymnasium* in Greifswald. Protestant in its outlook and dominated intellectually by the local university, this institution gave him an excellent humanistic education. It was here that he met Max Lenz,[3] with whom he established a lifelong friendship. He continued his higher education at the universities of Heidelberg, Greifswald, and Bonn. Deeply interested in history, he attended the lectures

1. Georg von Below, *Die deutsche Geschichtsschreibung von den Befreiungskriegen bis zu unsern Tagen* (Munich and Berlin, 1924), pp. 38–63.
2. A few of his more important relatives were: Rudolf von Delbrück (1817–1903), Prussian minister of state and later president of the imperial chancellery under Bismarck; Clemens von Delbrück (1856–1921), Prussian minister of commerce and later secretary of the interior of the German Empire; Berthold Delbrück (1842–1922), a noted philologist; Max Delbrück (1850–1919), a brother, who distinguished himself as a chemist.
3. A distinguished German historian (1850–1932), known especially for his writings on Bismarck and other historical essays.

of such prominent historians as Noorden, Schäfer, and Sybel, from whom he gained an insight into Ranke's methodology and approach to history. They also imbued him with their political ideals and objectives. According to his own testimony, he was particularly grateful to Noorden, an intimate friend of the family, for advice and guidance.[4]

In the meantime his career as a university student was briefly interrupted by two events. Keenly interested in the political developments of Germany, he gave enthusiastic support to Bismarck's plan for the unification of Germany under the leadership of Prussia. He was profoundly stirred by patriotic sentiments and eagerly awaited the opportunity to serve Prussia. When he realized that war with France was inevitable, he enlisted in the army and as a lieutenant of the reserves took part in the battle of Gravelotte and the siege of Metz. Moreover, for a short period he tutored Crown Prince Gustav of Sweden.

Like most doctoral candidates of this period, he published his dissertation, *Über die Glaubwürdigkeit Lamberts von Hersfeld,* on a medieval topic. Since this thesis contained the main characteristics of his later writings, it proved to be a most revealing contribution. After carefully examining and evaluating the writings of Lambert von Hersfeld, a German monk and chronicler of the eleventh century, whose *Annales* and other works heretofore had been generally accepted by reputable historians, Delbrück concluded that numerous passages were totally unreliable. With remarkable insight and clarity of expression, he proved that Lambert von Hersfeld was an untrustworthy source of information. In doing so he did not hesitate to challange the conclusions of Giesebrecht, who was considered an authority on medieval German history. In short, the dissertation reflected his independent spirit, his sharp critical faculties, his ability to present historical material in clear and logical fashion, and his fearlessness in challenging accepted beliefs and traditions. Nothing gave him more satisfaction than the opportunity to destroy historical legends.

4. See autobiographical sketch in *Die Glaubwürdigkeit Lamberts von Hersfeld* (Bonn, 1873), p. 78.

In 1874 Delbrück was appointed tutor of Prince Waldemar, one of the younger sons of Crown Prince Frederick. He held this position for five years until the premature death of Prince Waldemar in 1879. As tutor he often accompanied the royal family to various parts of Europe, thereby increasing his geographic knowledge and understanding of other countries. He became intimately acquainted with the crown prince and crown princess, for both of whom he had the deepest respect and admiration. Not only was he frequently consulted by them in matters pertaining to the education of Prince Waldemar, but he was given many opportunities to discuss problems of general interest with them. In all his relations with the royal family he never acted the part of a courtier or flatterer but always remained true to his nature. He never hesitated to express his sincere and honest convictions.

His experiences as tutor were extremely profitable. In the first place, they enabled him to gain a better insight into the contemporary political scene. It was his firm belief that every historian should concern himself with current affairs and should never lose sight of the present. In meeting various higher officials of the government he made many valuable political observations. Moreover, his contacts with the crown princess, a gifted and intelligent daughter of Queen Victoria of England, stimulated his interest in English history. As a result he wrote several essays dealing with the development of English political parties and the nature of the English monarchy.[5] Finally, it was during this period that he decided to make military history his particular field of specialization.

It is rather difficult to explain the circumstances which finally led him to concentrate on military history—all the more so because he himself could give no satisfactory explanation. Perhaps his experiences during the Franco-German War, or perhaps his associations with army leaders at court, were partly responsible for his growing interest in military matters. According to his own version, he gradually discovered that such topics as the organiza-

5. Consult *Deutsches biographisches Jahrbuch* (Stuttgart and Berlin, 1917–20).

tion of the army and its relations to the state had a peculiar fascination for him.[6] He became deeply interested in analyzing the campaigns and strategy of famous military leaders. While attending military exercises in Wittenberg in the spring of 1874, a copy of Rüstow's *History of Infantry* fell into his hands. This book influenced him profoundly and stimulated him to do further research. Most important in strengthening his decision to write military history was the request he received in 1877 from Countess Hedwig Brühl to complete the unfinished biography of her illustrious grandfather, Neidhardt von Gneisenau, a work that had been begun by Georg Heinrich Pertz, the noted historian. In accepting this request he realized that a comprehensive understanding of the campaigns of the War of Liberation was essential for evaluating the work of Gneisenau. He therefore made a thorough study of Clausewitz, whose complete works had been presented to him by the crown prince, and consulted leading military experts, including such authorities as Field-Marshal Count Blumenthal, General von Gottberg, General von Winterfeld, and others.

With his appointment in 1881 as Privatdozent to the University of Berlin, he finally realized his ambition to become a professor of history. He began his long and distinguished career at that institution by offering a series of lectures on "The war of 1866." These were shortly followed by others on "The war of 1870," "The general history of the art of war from the Persian wars to the present," and "The main battles of Frederick the Great and Napoleon." As a teacher he was unusually successful. From the very beginning he attracted many students to his classes and as his popularity increased, the largest auditorium of the university was assigned to him.[7] His genial personality, combined with an ability to organize and present his material in a clear and stimulating manner, largely explained his success. He knew how to make past historical scenes live in the minds of his students.

6. *Geschichte der Kriegskunst im Rahmen der politischen Geschichte* (Berlin, 1900), I, vii.
7. Roy S. MacElwee in his introduction to Delbrück's *Government and the will of the people* (New York, 1923), p. vii. See n. 25 below.

With rare humor and irony he explained many historical legends.

Unfortunately, his promotion at Berlin was very slow. His independent attitude in military and political matters antagonized influential army and state officials. His new viewpoints on the strategy of Frederick the Great and Napoleon gave rise to a bitter controversy that lasted over a decade. Some of his opponents in the army tried to silence him by demanding that the university drop all courses in military history. Unsuccessful in this attempt, they managed to place obstacles in the way of his promotion. That explains why he had to wait until 1897, shortly after Treitschke's retirement from the faculty, for his promotion to the rank of Professor. In that same year he was asked by Dr. Friedrich Althoff, the Prussian minister of education, to offer a course in world-history. The magnitude of the assignment did not frighten him. As a matter of fact, he believed that the offering of such a course was not only justified but imperative, especially in view of the glaring lack of general historical knowledge displayed by the average student of history. Using his knowledge of military history as a framework, he soon prepared a long series of lectures on world-history. From 1896 to 1920 his course on world-history, offered in cycles of four semesters each, proved to be one of the most popular courses in history at the University of Berlin.

Unlike the typical German professor, he did not believe in removing himself from the realities of life by secluding himself behind the cloistered walls of a university. Following in the footsteps of Treitschke and Sybel, he remained in close touch with all political developments.[8] As a member of the Prussian legislature from 1882 to 1885 and as a member of the Reichstag from 1884 to 1890, he gained valuable political experience. In fact, he considered this experience as an indispensable preparation for his professional work as a historian. He was no parliamentarian of the stature of Richter, Bebel, or Windthorst. He preferred to play the role of observer to that of active participant. Nominally belonging to the Free Conservative Party, which had given loyal support to the policies and program of Bismarck, he was really no

8. Eugen Schiffer, "Delbrück als Politiker," *Preussische Jahrbücher,* CCXVIII (1929), 290 f.

"party man" at all. He was too independent to give blind obedience to any party program or leadership. Party discipline irked him. He liked to think of himself as standing above all parties and classes. Hence, he judged all measures independently on their own merits, no matter what party had proposed them. At times he even supported measures sponsored by left-wing parties. When the crown princess once asked him to state his political affiliations and beliefs, he smilingly replied: "I am a conservative social democrat."[9]

Delbrück, to be sure, was a conservative. But his conservatism was not class-conscious like that of the Prussian military nobility, which sought to achieve an aristocratic self-administration by opposing the omnipotence of the bureaucracy.[10] On the contrary, his conservatism was rooted in the traditions of the bureaucracy, with which administrative group his family had been identified for generations. He accepted the monarchy as a reasonable institution and favored the administration of government by a group of educated officials. He did not object to the privileged economic position of the landed aristocracy, since he felt that its welfare was essential to the morale and strength of the Prussian corps of army officers. Unlike the aristocratic conservatives, however, he viewed the state as an organization of theoretically equal individuals and not as a society of classes. Since the masses are not able to govern themselves, he believed that it was imperative for the monarch in collaboration with the bureaucracy to govern reasonably and justly. With such views as the foregoing dominating his thinking, it is easy to explain his independent and nonpartisan political attitude.

In addition to his parliamentary experience he soon found other outlets for his historical and political interests. From 1881 to 1894 he served as editor of the *Staatsarchiv,* a semiannual publication.[11] Founded in 1861 and edited for the first ten years of

9. *Ibid.,* p. 291.
10. Arthur Rosenberg, "Hans Delbrück, der Kritiker der Kriegsgeschichte," *Die Gesellschaft,* VI (1921), 245.
11. *Das Staatsarchiv: Sammlung der offiziellen Aktenstücke zur Aussenpolitik der Gegenwart* (Leipzig, 1861–1919).

its existence by L. K. Aegidi and Alfred Klauhold, it was published under the auspices of the Institute of Foreign Politics of Hamburg, the Institute of Foreign Public Law and International Law of Berlin, and the German foreign office. Each issue contained a collection of important official and diplomatic documents made public during the six months preceding publication. From 1886 to 1893 he was also editor of Schulthess' *Europäischer Geschichtskalender*.[12] Founded in 1860 and published annually, it reviewed the leading events of the preceding year, particularly those of Germany, in chronological order. It included many excerps from newspapers, speeches, and official documents. Delbrück's main task consisted of writing the concluding chapter, or summary, in which he interpreted with his usual clarity the political and international developments of the past year.

His appointment in 1883 to the editorial board of the *Preussische Jahrbücher* really marked the beginning of his most important work as a publicist. Founded by Rudolf Haym in 1858 to serve as an official organ of the political historians, the *Preussiche Jahrbücher* had advocated German unification under the leadership of Prussia and after 1871 had become a vigorous supporter of imperial orthodoxy. Until 1890 Delbrück served as coeditor with Treitschke, but thereafter he assumed sole responsibility for almost thirty years. Under his leadership the *Preussische Jahrbücher* became one of the most influential political journals of Germany and an important molder of public opinion. In its columns he sought to bind history and politics closely together, the one enriching and stimulating the other. Never succeeding in gaining a large circulation, because of the unusually high quality of its articles, it was consistently read by a small group of influential men, the élite of Germany. Among its subscribers were prominent government officials, army officers, educators, and historians. Its articles were frequently quoted in other publications.

With the expiration of his term of office in the Reichstag in 1890 Delbrück withdrew from active participation in politics. His withdrawal, however, was not caused by any diminution of interest in political affairs. On the contrary, by releasing him

12. Munich, 1881–94.

from the uncomfortable restraints of party discipline, it gave him more time for a calm and dispassionate evaluation of the political scene. Nothing pleased him more than to interpret political developments in the light of history. Unlike many other historians, whose political fervor had rapidly cooled after the unification of Germany, he retained his strong political inclinations until the end. In every issue of the *Preussiche Jahrbücher* he commented on current domestic and international affairs. Independent and courageous in his outlook, he never hesitated to express his own views, regardless of the consequences.

Like most German intellectuals of the Wilhelminian period, he became an ardent admirer of the imperial government established by Bismarck.[13] He warmly defended it against all attacks by maintaining that it would lead Germany to great heights as a nation. Perhaps his optimistic view of German political institutions can be traced to his intimate and pleasant associations with some of the higher officials of the government. In general, he was too far removed from the provinces to observe some of the disagreeable features of the bureaucracy. To his credit, however, he never permitted his unbounded confidence in the German political system to interfere with his right to criticize the policies of the government. Thus he fearlessly denounced Bismarck's unreasonable persecution of the Catholics and socialists and repeatedly condemned the oppression of the Polish and Danish minorities as morally unjustified and politically unwise.

Prior to 1914 he also viewed the course of Germany's foreign relations much too favorably. In this respect he was no more optimistic than the majority of his countrymen. With rare exceptions, he never fully grasped the extent to which the Emperor William II's foreign policies were endangering Germany's international position. For example, the seriousness of the Russian threat never dawned upon him until the spring of 1914, shortly after he had received a letter from Professor Paul Mitrofanov, one of his former students.[14] He staunchly supported the acquisition of colonies on the ground that they would offer Germany an

13. The best summary of his views on the imperial constitution is to be found in *Regierung und Volkswille* (Berlin, 1913).
14. This letter is published in *Krieg und Politik* (Berlin, 1918), I, 6–16.

outlet for her surplus of educated young people, for whom it was becoming increasingly difficult to establish a career at home. If Britain would only adopt a more sympathetic attitude toward Germany's desire for more colonies, he cheerfully predicted that the German demands for a larger navy would gradually subside, thereby removing the main source of friction between the two nations.

While supporting Germany's colonial aspirations, he constantly urged the government to exercise some degree of moderation in international affairs. He opposed the chauvinistic demands of the Pan-Germans, whom he considered a real menace, since they might plunge Germany into war at an inopportune time. During the Boer War, while many German leaders were outspoken in their sympathies for the Boers, he came to the defense of Great Britain. When the tension with England reached alarming proportions, he urged the German government to negotiate a naval agreement. In facing a hostile public opinion he favored the acceptance of Winston Churchill's proposal of a "naval holiday" as a preliminary step toward a better understanding between England and Germany.

More than any other period of his life, the war of 1914 revealed his remarkable courage and lofty patriotism. He deplored the invasion of Belgium, which he characterized as a political blunder of the most disastrous proportions, since it had hastened the entry of England into the conflict. Military strategy, he emphasized, should always be subordinated to higher political aims. When news of the military reverses on the Marne reached the German people, he advocated the negotiation of a reasonable peace settlement with the Allies, by which Germany would renounce her territorial ambitions in Europe for colonial concessions elsewhere. His proposals, of course, angered the militarists, annexationists, and other superpatriots. Led by the Fatherland party, which was generously supported by Ludendorff and Tirpitz, they bitterly assailed him for his lack of patriotism, and for the remainder of the war made life miserable for him. Unlike the other famous political historians, who had died while being admired by a grateful nation, he had to suffer unjustified abuse during his declining years.

Undaunted by the attacks that were directed at him, he quietly sought to gain a hearing for his views. With this objective in mind he helped in the founding of the *Mittwochgesellschaft* ("Wednesday Club"), which consisted of a small group of influential men from various walks of life.[15] Meeting regularly every Wednesday evening to discuss timely political and international problems, the group as a whole hoped to induce the government to enter into peace negotiations with the Allies. This organization tried to counteract the influence of the Fatherland party. Included in its membership were Count Hatzfeld and Count Hutten-Czapki; Adolf von Harnack, Wilhelm Kahl, and Max Sering, from the University of Berlin; Karl Helfferich and Paul von Schwabach, from the financial world; Schiffer, Krause, Friedberg, and Lusensky, who were representatives of the National Liberal party and members of the Reichstag; Schlutius, a representative of the Center party; August Stein, representative of the *Frankfurter Zeitung;* and high-ranking government officials. Prince Max of Baden, who later became a member, reported in his memoirs that Delbrück was the recognized leader of the group, to whom all members looked for inspiration and enlightenment. Unfortunately, the main objective of the *Mittwochgesellschaft* was never realized. After the war it continued to discuss various problems confronting the Weimar Republic.

The collapse of the Empire overwhelmed Delbrück with unspeakable grief. Thanks to his natural optimism and sense of reality, however, he quickly adapted himself to the new political situation—certainly no easy task for a man who had reached the proverbial biblical age of threescore and ten. Without sacrificing his deep-rooted affections for the old imperial government, he gave loyal support to the Weimar Republic. In 1919 he insisted that "anyone who loves the German people must serve the Republic with German faithfulness."[16] With the approval of the new government he and several other prominent historians, including Count Montgelas and Professor Mendelssohn-Bartholdy,

15. This organization is described at length by Paul Rühlmann in an article, "Delbrücks Mittwochabend," in Emil Daniels, *Am Webstuhl der Zeit* (Berlin, 1929), pp. 73 f.
16. Walter Simons, "Dauer im Wechsel," in Daniels, pp. 132 f.

were commissioned to make a formal reply to the Allied charge that Germany had been solely responsible for the war.[17] The result of their work was the publication of the German White Book, which contained new evidence to disprove Germany's guilt. Like many other German historians who had taken offense at the inclusion of Article 231 into the Treaty of Versailles, which specifically designated Germany as the nation responsible for the war, he became involved in the *Kriegsschuldfrage*, or war-guilt question. He was among the first historians to emphasize the importance of studying pre-war diplomacy as indispensable for an understanding of the fundamental causes of the war. During the next few years he contributed many articles on the origin of the war to the *Berliner Monatshefte*, in which he usually stressed the role of France and Russia in precipitating the conflict. He dealt rather sharply with Poincaré's foreign policy.

In 1919 he resigned from his position as editor of the *Preussische Jahrbücher*, with which he had been associated for thirty-six years. Two years later he resigned from active teaching at the University of Berlin. But the septuagenarian had no intention of spending his remaining years in idleness. Relieved of his heavy responsibilities as editor and professor, he now found time for other projects. Following the example of Ranke, he decided to write a world-history based on the lectures he had delivered at the University of Berlin. "There's no better way to spend your last days," he remarked to a friend.[18]

Meanwhile he engaged in a series of bitter controversies with Ludendorff, Tirpitz, Kautsky, and Harden. He boldly accused Ludendorff and Tirpitz of having destroyed the Empire by their senseless strategy. He attacked Kautsky for having exaggerated the incompetence of the imperial government and the blunders of William II, thereby giving the outside world the impression that Germany had started the war. Nor did he have any kind words for Maximilian Harden, the brilliant editor of *Die Zukunft*, whose testimony on the origins of the war before a special committee of the Reichstag he considered as totally unreliable and worthless.

17. Max Montgelas, "Hans Delbrück," *Berliner Monatshefte*, VII (1929), 730.
18. *Berliner Monatshefte*, VII (1929), 77.

## Richard H. Bauer

On his eightieth birthday (November 11, 1928) he was signally honored by many of his friends and former students. They presented him with a *Festschrift,* entitled *Am Webstuhl der Zeit,* which contained some interesting articles on a variety of historical topics contributed by Emil Daniels, General Wilhelm Groener, Major-General Ernst Buchfink, Paul Rohrbach, Paul Rühlmann, Friedrich Meinecke, and others.[19] On this occasion President Paul von Hindenburg paid tribute to him by presenting him with a shield of honor. Six months later, shortly after completing another article on the Treaty of Versailles, he was attacked by a severe case of grippe. He died on July 14, 1929, widely mourned by his numerous friends in Germany and elsewhere.

Delbrück's many writings can be divided into two groups. Some of them are primarily political; others are primarily historical. The line of demarcation between these two groups, however, is rather artificial, since Delbrück ordinarily used the historical approach in writing his political articles and unduly emphasized the political factor in his historical works.

Undoubtedly his most important political writings appeared regularly in the *Preussische Jahrbücher* under the title of "Politische Korrespondenz," in which he summarized and interpreted the current political and international situation. Always written in a clear and stimulating manner, these summaries contain intimate pictures of leading men and events. To the *Preussische Jahrbücher* Delbrück also contributed innumerable articles of a more scholarly character on a most amazing variety of topics, including biographical sketches of important political leaders, criticisms of military strategy, arguments for social legislation, condemnations of the Prussian oppression of the Poles and Danes, and discussions of constitutional questions.[20] Collections of the

19. The full title of the book is: Emil Daniels und Paul Rühlmann, *Am Webstuhl der Zeit: eine Erinnerungsausgabe. Hans Delbrück dem Achtzigjährigen von Freunden und Schülern dargebracht* (Berlin, 1928).

20. The reader's attention is called to Delbrück's article, "Die gute alte Zeit," which appeared in his *Erinnerungen, Aufsätze und Reden* (see n. 23 below). Caricaturing the human frailty of idealizing the past, it aroused widespread discussion and controversy. Another one of his more widely quoted articles, "The role of numbers in history," has been published in English as a separate pamphlet (London, 1913).

more important of these articles appear in the following volumes: *Historische und politische Aufsätze;*[21] *Erinnerungen, Aufsätze und Reden;*[22] *Krieg und Politik,* which appeared in three volumes;[23] and *Vor und nach dem Weltkrieg.*[24]

By no means are Delbrück's political works confined to shorter essays and articles. Several of his books and pamphlets are definitely political in their scope. In his *Regierung und Volkswille,*[25] which contains a series of lectures on the German constitution delivered by him at the University of Berlin during the summer of 1913, he expounded his views on the leading features of the German government. In general, this volume gives the reader an unusually favorable and optimistic picture of imperial Germany. He maintained that the constitution embraced the best features of a democracy and an autocracy without incorporating any of their glowing defects. Like the constitution of the ancient Roman Republic, he argued that it united the principles of authority and democratic self-determination by bringing the Prussian nobility into a working agreement with the democratically elected Reichstag. He summarized its merits as follows:

> Without closing my eyes to the inner defects which cling to our system of government, I must say that I see in it a much higher and better form of political organization than in any other modern state; but, be it well understood, only inasmuch as both phases of the government (i.e., the hereditary authority plus the national assembly) are recognized and exercise their right. The bills which are proposed by the representatives of the people, the control which the people exercise, the necessity of justifying oneself before the representative body, of treating with it, of dealing with this, then with that, faction, of making compromises, of concentrating the people, at least a majority of them, on one point— that constitutes the peculiarity of our strength and gives us the secure feeling that our nation is destined to a great future. . . . If one should suppress the Reichstag, or exanimate it by a violent

21. Berlin, 1887.
22. Berlin, 1905.
23. Berlin, 1919.
24. Berlin, 1926.
25. Berlin, 1914. A revised edition of this book (Berlin, 1920) has been translated into English by Roy S. MacElwee, a former student of Delbrück, under the title of *Government and the will of the people* (New York, 1923).

# Richard H. Bauer

change of the electoral law, one would bring the German Empire
to destruction just as surely as if the Reichstag should win the
powers of a so-called parliamentary government. If both government and parliament work together, they can reach the highest
aims, or at least more than do the states which are always called
upon to follow now this, now that, party; that is, to pursue politics
not from the standpoint of the whole, but of a part of the whole.[26]

In a revised edition of the book, which appeared in 1920, Delbrück stated that the war of 1914 had vindicated his former
opinions concerning the inherent strength of the empire.

Not because of any lack of parliamentary system of government
did we go down to defeat, not because we had been more militaristic in the past than our opponents, but because the militarism
of our opponents was able to win and ours was not. . . . Our curse
was not that we had a monarchical government for leadership,
but that this monarchical government was not strong enough to
counteract the chauvinistic currents of public opinion and to lead
the people against its will into the right path.[27]

Undoubtedly this book exaggerated the merits of the old imperial government and underestimated its shortcomings. While
it offered nothing new to the student of political theory, it was an
important contribution to political psychology, since it represented the views of the ruling classes in their defense of the Prussian hegemony and the privileges of the officer class. According
to Professor W. Y. Elliott,

the psychology of a very large part of the German people is reflected in these strictures of Herr Delbrück on parliamentarism
and democracy. . . . The book is full of the most interesting
personal anecdotes of political parties in the Old Germany and
of illustrations taken from the author's other works, chiefly
his *Geschichte der Kriegskunst im Rahmen der politischen
Geschichte.*[28]

Professor Elliott observed that Delbrück, as a specialist in military history, tended "to see political problems only in terms of an
efficient military machine with which to assure national power."[29]

26. *Government and the will of the people,* p. 148.
27. *Ibid.,* pp. 179 f.
28. *Political science quarterly,* XL (1925), 144–46.
29. *Ibid.,* p. 145.

No other political writing of Delbrück aroused such bitter controversy and widespread interest as *Bismarcks Erbe*.[30] Hastily written after the opening of the war of 1914, it urged the German government to make a reasonable peace settlement with the Allies at the earliest possible moment; it also attacked the annexationist designs of the Pan-Germans. By negotiating such a treaty, Delbrück boldly asserted, the German government would follow the admonitions of Bismarck, whose "main objective was to preserve peace under all conditions and whose teaching was to avoid a preventive war at all costs."[31] Germany, he insisted, should renounce her territorial ambitions in Europe for colonial concessions elsewhere. He favored the acquisition of colonies, not primarily for economic reasons or for the sake of prestige, but for the opportunities they might provide for Germany's surplus of educated young men. What Germany really needed, in his opinion, was an India, where talented and trained young Germans might go to establish successful careers for themselves. He bemoaned the fact that

> thousands of our young men of thirty and over, who have attained the full powers of manhood and whose extensive knowledge and specialized training have prepared them for larger fields of activity, are often to be found idle or partially employed among us, all of them waiting to obtain some poorly paid position. Following the example of England in India, we must send them as technicians, merchants, planters, physicians, overseers, officers, and officials to the colonies, in order that they might govern the large masses of backward races.[32]

Since Delbrück considered the African colonial possessions of Germany to be both economically unprofitable and climatically unsuited for colonization, he eagerly looked forward to the day when the Turks would grant exclusive privileges to German technicians, scientists, physicians, and other professional groups to aid in the rejuvenation and modernization of their country. Both Turkey and Germany, he predicted, would derive lasting benefits from such collaboration. Here is what he wrote in *Bismarcks Erbe:*

30. Berlin, 1915.
31. *Ibid.*, pp. 212 f.
32. *Ibid.*, pp. 193 f.

Since Africa, or any other exotic territory for that matter, will not satisfy our needs, there fortunately remains for us another type of colonization and another field of colonial activity, both of which have been opened to us and placed at our disposal by the war. Namely, there remains Turkey, whose possessions in Europe, Asia Minor, Syria, and Mesopotamia include the oldest and most fertile cultural areas of mankind. At present this country is striving to achieve closer contacts with European civilization, from which course it cannot depart, especially if it emerges successfully from the war. For this work it requires the services of European instructors, whom at present it cannot find in any other country save in Germany.[33]

*Bismarcks Erbe,* of course, aroused the anger of the Pan-Germans, who loudly demanded the annexation of Belgium and other conquered territories, without which, they insisted, Germany could never feel secure against attack. In *Wider den Kleinglauben,*[34] one of his more important political pamphlets, he denounced their annexationist designs. He was convinced that the annexation of Belgium and other regions, if anything, would embroil Germany in endless wars, because

the various nations would consider themselves threatened by our preponderance of power. Since the feeling of independence is the most cherished treasure of all peoples—in fact, their very breath of life—the ultimate realization of our demands for annexation would result in a renewal of the war within a short time. Instead of enjoying the blessings of lasting peace, we would stumble into one conflict after another, without having Austria-Hungary, Bulgaria, and Turkey on our side. . . . It is possible for us to become a great power without Belgium, as the future will teach us; but we cannot hope to become one if we proceed to annex Belgium, since our possession of that country would arouse the hostility of the entire world against us. . . . Anyone who has faith in German strength knows that we can dispense with Belgium; and anyone who has a correct insight into the world-situation realizes that we must dispense with it. . . .[35]

In order to defend the exiled emperor and the old regime against the attacks of Kautsky and Harden, Delbrück published a

33. *Ibid.,* pp. 206 f.
34. Berlin, 1917.
35. *Ibid.,* p. 23.

short pamphlet entitled *Kautsky und Harden.*[36] In this pamphlet he took occasion to assail Kautsky's book on the origins of the war, *Wie der Weltkrieg entstand,*[37] in which the author quoted freely from German pre-war diplomatic documents to expose the glaring deficiencies of the imperial government. The conclusions of the socialist leader, according to Delbrück, are untenable, since they are based on a wholly subjective interpretation of the documents. Not only does Kautsky deliberately distort the facts, but "he doesn't even make the slightest attempt to give an objective interpretation."[38] Delbrück added that Kautsky had shown poor taste in giving such widespread publicity to the emperor's marginal notes, which appeared on various diplomatic documents, while the latter was still alive. In a similar vein he denounced Harden's accusations against the old regime. In view of the fact that Harden had supported the Pan-Germans before and during the war, Delbrück felt that it was rather unbecoming of the journalist to condemn the old imperial government.

Shortly after Delbrück had been sharply reprimanded in Ludendorff's *Kriegführung und Politik*[39] for his criticisms of the diplomatic and military conduct of the war, he quickly wrote a scathing reply in self-defense. In *Ludendorffs Selbstporträt*[40] he refused to retract any of his former accusations and ridiculed Ludendorff's belated attempts to justify the military strategy of the war. Moreover, he reviewed the general's political and strategical blunders at great length, explaining how they finally led to the collapse of the Empire. The greatest blunder of all, he contended, was Ludendorff's continued refusal to negotiate a satisfactory treaty of peace with the Allies at a time when Germany enjoyed undoubted strategic advantages. He vehemently denied the charge that Germany had been "stabbed in the back" by subversive elements at home. He concluded by insisting that

> just as two great men, Bismarck and Moltke, had created the Empire, so two others, Ludendorff and Tirpitz, have destroyed it.

36. Berlin, 1920.
37. Berlin, 1919.
38. *Kautsky und Harden,* p. 6.
39. Berlin, 1922.
40. Berlin, 1922.

The senseless construction of dreadnaughts by Tirpitz and his refusal to negotiate a satisfactory naval agreement with England had forced the British to join our enemies. By converting a defensive war into one of conquest, Ludendorff committed a serious blunder.[41]

Unfortunately, Delbrück's lack of moderation in his attacks on Ludendorff seriously weakened the effectiveness of his arguments. "It would have been much better," according to Professor Johannes Ziekursch, a noted German historian, "if Delbrück had expressed himself with the greatest moderation. The bitterness of his words did not tend to strengthen his case in various influential circles."[42] Ziekursch also pointed out that Delbrück overemphasized the political role of Ludendorff, thereby leading the reader to believe that the army virtually dictated all the political policies of Germany. Obviously, this was not the case, since it had been "the intentional policy of the government to keep the officers' corps from close contacts with the political, economic, and social forces of the nation."[43]

Delbrück's views on the origin of the war are briefly summarized in *Der Stand der Kriegsschuldfrage*.[44] In this pamphlet, which the *Historische Zeitschrift* described as "a remarkably clear presentation of the war-guilt question," he endeavored to prove that Germany had not instigated the conflict.[45] After pointing out the responsibility of Russia, France, and other countries he frankly admitted that the imperial government had made three serious mistakes:

> The real political mistakes made by Germany were, first of all, the construction of large battleships which unnecessarily aroused the suspicion of the English, thereby driving them into the camp of the enemy; second, the underestimation of the magnitude and imminence of the danger of war by the emperor and the diplomats; and, third, the German plan of war, which did not take the tremendous moral and political consequences of the invasion of neutral territory sufficiently into consideration.[46]

41. *Ibid.*, p. 64.
42. *HZ*, CXXX (1924), 527 f.
43. *Ibid.*, p. 528.
44. Berlin, 1925.
45. *HZ*, CXXXII (1925), 570 f.
46. *Der Stand der Kriegsschuldfrage*, p. 32.

Delbrück's numerous political writings are important for two reasons. Besides illustrating the varied interests and journalistic activities of a typical political historian, they shed considerable light on the Wilhelminian period. Indeed, his political observations are almost indispensable for an understanding of recent German history. "They are personal and contemporary documents of the greatest interest," wrote Dr. Friedrich Luckwaldt, "since they offer a delightful and worth-while review of the years immediately preceding and following the war."[47] In general, they are rather subjective, often reflecting his political prejudices, but they are much less so than the writings of Treitschke and his contemporaries. At least Delbrück tried to be reasonably objective, as his calm and restrained style will testify.

Far more important than his political writings were his contributions to military history. More than anything else, these contributions explain his reputation as a historian. They are the result of a lifelong interest and specialization in military history. In his biography, *Das Leben des Feldmarschalls Grafen Neidhardt von Gneisenau*,[48] he made a penetrating study of the military strategy of the Napoleonic era. This book contains numerous letters of Gniesenau and constitutes a valuable addition to the literature of the Prussian reform period. By 1920 it had passed through four editions. The *Historische Zeitschrift* hailed the appearance of this biography as "one of the best publications in the field of modern history. Delbrück's careful and objective analysis and description of the military events, particularly his treatment of the campaigns of 1813, deserve highest commendation."[49]

Following the publication of this biography Delbrück wrote many articles on military strategy of ancient, medieval, and modern times, most of which were devoted to an analysis and comparison of the military strategy of Frederick the Great and Napoleon. These articles formed the basis of his most important book, *Geschichte der Kriegskunst im Rahmen der politischen Geschichte*.[50]

47. *HZ*, CXXXVIII (1928), 90 f.
48. Berlin, 1882.
49. *HZ*, LI (1885), 135.
50. In four volumes (Berlin, 1900–1920). In 1928 a fifth volume was

As a military historian he made three noteworthy contributions. First, he exploded many legends dealing with the size of armies. For example, he contended that the Persian army which confronted the Greeks at Plataea never consisted of a million men, as various Greek writers had estimated, but merely of some 15,000 to 25,000 soldiers. Nor did the army by which Charlemagne destroyed the Saxons amount to more than 10,000 men. The size of the crusading armies, often exaggerated by medieval writers, never exceeded several thousand knights. Delbrück likewise sought to destroy the legend that the discovery of gunpowder had been chiefly responsible for the decline of knighthood. To use one of his many illustrations, he pointed out that the army of Charles the Bold, which was equipped with firearms and artillery, was signally defeated by Swiss footmen who lacked such equipment.

A second contribution of Delbrück as a military historian was his interesting observation that all military strategy could be divided into two kinds—*Ermattungsstrategie,* or strategy of exhaustion, and *Vernichtungsstrategie,* or the strategy of annihilation—each of which employed different methods in dealing with the enemy.[51] The purpose of *Ermattungsstrategie* was to weaken the enemy gradually by a series of maneuvers without necessarily destroying his forces, thereby compelling him to sue for peace. The object of the *Vernichtungsstrategie* was to strike at the enemy directly in order to destroy his forces. Heretofore it had not been customary to distinguish between these two kinds of strategy. As a matter of fact, all strategy had been considered variations of the *Vernichtungsstrategie.* Delbrück characterized the strategy of the eighteenth century, particularly that of Frederick the Great, as *Ermattungsstrategie.* The strategy of Napoleon and the nineteenth century he described as *Vernichtungsstrategie.*

Unfortunately, the formulation of the aforementioned types of strategy was not accepted by the Prussian military leaders,

---

added in collaboration with Emil Daniels. Still later a sixth and seventh volume, published in 1932 and 1936, respectively, were written by Emil Daniels and Otto Haintz.

51. Konrad Lehmann, "Ermattungsstrategie-oder Nicht?" in *HZ,* CLI (1934), 48–86.

with whom he subsequently engaged in a literary feud. Led by Theodor von Bernhardi and Conrad von der Goltz, various officials of the army maintained that the *Vernichtungsstrategie* was the only recognized form of strategy.[52] They denied that the strategy of Frederick the Great differed radically from that of Napoleon. In fact, they were inclined to think of Frederick as a forerunner of Napoleon in strategical matters. Finally, they accused Delbrück of belittling Frederick by calling him an adherent of the *Ermattungsstrategie*.[53]

Delbrück, however, refused to make any concessions to his critics, and tried to strengthen his position by insisting that Clausewitz, the famous German military authority, had indicated the existence of the two types of strategy in one of his later writings. After fortifying himself with additional evidence he stood virtually alone in defending his views against the leaders of the Prussian army. Although his theories were never accepted by the military authorities, he at least emerged as the victor of the literary feud itself. He succeeded in silencing his enemies.

He made his third and greatest contribution as a military historian by weaving military history into the general pattern of world-history. In order to appreciate the significance of this contribution, it need only be recalled that heretofore the historian had treated military affairs as isolated events. He was satisfied to give the date of the battle, the size of the contending armies, and the number of troops killed or wounded. He made no attempts to fit military events into the general picture. Even the more technical descriptions of battles and campaigns by military experts were often unsatisfactory in this respect. Delbrück, therefore, made a distinct contribution to history when he succeeded in integrating military and general history.[54]

In his *Geschichte der Kriegskunst im Rahmen der politischen*

52. Friedrich von Bernhardi, *Denkwürdigkeiten aus meinem Leben* (Berlin, 1927), pp. 143 f.

53. Theodor von Bernhardi's *Delbrück, Friedrich der Grosse und Clausewitz* (Berlin, 1892) contains the chief criticisms of Delbrück's views on strategy.

54. Arthur Rosenberg, "Hans Delbrück, der Kritiker der Kriegsgeschichte," *loc cit.*, p. 249.

*Geschichte* he surveyed the development of the art of war from ancient Greece to modern times. Basing his conclusions on a profound knowledge of military sciences, he reconstructed the chief battles and military campaigns of history. In doing so he ruthlessly destroyed military legends and smashed military heroes. But at the same time he carefully analyzed the important battles and campaigns by describing the organization and leadership of each contending army, the equipment of the soldiers, the nature of the weapons, the topographical and climatic factors, the problem of supplying armies with food and matériel, the natural resources of the opposing states, and the relations of the army to the state and its political institutions. While omitting no details, he always pointed out their relationship to other important factors. In other words, he adopted the methods of Clausewitz of criticizing military events and developments. He thereby gave a new meaning and deeper understanding to military history.

In a lengthy review of the third volume of the *Geschichte der Kriegskunst,* which analyzes the military developments of the middle ages, Professor T. F. Tout, a distinguished English historian, admirably summarized Delbrück's contribution to the history of the art of war as follows:

> It [the third volume] is a wonderful evidence of Delbrück's vigour, industry, and breadth of vision. His book contains much that is interesting and important. There are many sound particular observations; there are excellent and spirited accounts of many individual battles, and there are so many shrewd statements as to the general features of medieval warfare that no student of the Middle Ages can fail to derive great advantages from its study. Professor Delbrück always tries to test the accounts of battles and campaigns by the touchstone of military possibility, and his habit of regarding medieval problems from a modern soldier's point of view saves him from the characteristic defects of that of the mere student, and gives a certain freshness and individuality to his whole work. Besides being something of a practical soldier, he is a widely read historian. Setting before himself the ideal of uniting military knowledge with military criticism, he has undertaken a task of great boldness and complexity, and often with some approach to success. . . . As a professor, even more as a writer, he has given a real impulse to the detailed study of medieval military

history. . . . I have illustrated already the arbitrary way in which some fights are singled out for treatment while others of equal significance are ignored. . . . But when all has been said against it, we must still thank the author for imparting to it a quality that is eminently stimulating and human. Its very defects are provocative of thought and suggestive of inquiry.[55]

With all of Delbrück's predilection for military affairs, it is rather difficult to think of him as a general or staff officer charged with the practical execution of military maneuvers. It is much easier to imagine him playing the role of a military theorist like Clausewitz, with whose interests and type of reasoning he had much in common. His stimulating and original observations reflect thinking of the highest order. Moreover, his formulation of the two forms of strategy proved to have great military significance. With the phenomenal growth in the size of the European armies at the close of the nineteenth century, various military authorities began to question the future possibility of crushing the enemy's forces in a few short engagements. Some of them were inclined to agree with Delbrück that future wars would last much longer than previous ones. The elder Moltke spoke of the possibility of a new "Seven Years' War" or even a "Thirty Years' War." Under these circumstances might it not have been advisable for the general staff to have adopted the *Ermattungsstrategie,* as advocated by Delbrück, in future conflicts? The general staff, however, rejected the adoption of this type of strategy in favor of the famous Schlieffen plan, which was based on a strategy of annihilation. The general course of the war of 1914, which witnessed the collapse of the Schlieffen plan, amply justified the correctness of Delbrück's observations.

Second only in importance to his military contributions was his *Weltgeschichte.*[56] Published in five volumes, it is largely a compilation of his lectures on world-history which he had delivered at the University of Berlin for many years. Since these lectures were based on his researches in military history, his

55. *EHR,* XXII (1907), 344–48.
56. Berlin, 1924–28. A revised edition of this work appears under the title: Hans Delbrück und Konrad Molinski, *Die Weltgeschichte für Alle* (4 vols.; Berlin, 1929–33).

## Richard H. Bauer

*Weltgeschichte* might be considered a by-product of his *Geschichte der Kriegskunst*. Not only does the book retain the style and characteristics of the lecture method, but it devotes many sections to the more important military campaigns and battles of history. Tremendous as was the task of writing a history of world-civilization, his work was facilitated by two factors. In addition to having taught world-history for a generation, he had the added advantage of having begun his studies in this field where there was no superabundance of monographic literature on the various periods of history.

In harmony with his opinion that one of the main functions of history is to explain the present, he attempted to bring the past into intimate relations with the present and sought to rediscover the present in the past. He conceived of world-history as the history of all peoples who have made lasting contributions to modern European civilization. Hence he excluded the ancient civilizations of America, India, and China and cast aside everything which he deemed unimportant. In general, his selection of material was largely determined by his own interests and conception of history. According to his own testimony, he borrowed heavily from Ranke's *Weltgeschichte*. In the classification and arrangement of his material he followed the traditional organization of world-history. Beginning with the history of ancient Egypt, Mesopotamia, Palestine, Greece, and Rome, he traced the growth of civilization to the close of the nineteenth century. Ancient history, he believed, ended with Diocletian, by which time the Roman Empire had fulfilled its historic mission. He concluded the middle ages with a discussion of Dante and began modern history with a study of the Renaissance and humanism, both of which he considered as forerunners of the Reformation.

Aside from the subjective selection and presentation of his material, his *Weltgeschichte* has several serious shortcomings. Underlying economic and social forces are often neglected and underestimated. Like other historians of the Ranke school, he devoted too much space to international relations and military affairs. In reviewing his treatment of ancient history in the *Historische Zeitschrift*, Professor Matthias Gelzer observed that fully

67

six pages are required to describe the battle of Marathon and only eight to discuss the importance of Hellenism! "The reader will find absolutely nothing on the intellectual influence of Hellenism on the Roman Empire or anything on the gradual orientalization of Hellenism itself."[57] Gelzer also pointed out that the analysis of the internal organization of the Roman Empire is too brief and sketchy.[58] Perhaps the chief defect of the book is that too many of its conclusions are no longer tenable in the light of recent research. With all of its shortcomings, however, the *Weltgeschichte* remains a clear and stimulating review of world-history. It stands as a tribute to Delbrück's comprehensive knowledge of history and to his indefatigable industry.[59]

A further analysis of his historical works will show that they bear a close resemblance to the writings of Sybel and Treitschke, except that his style is much more moderate in tone. Hence it is obvious that he established no new school or philosophy of history but merely continued to write as an exponent of political history. Nevertheless, he was no blind imitator of Sybel and Treitschke, since he developed some independent views concerning the nature of history. In acknowledging his indebtedness to the aforementioned historians, he confessed that he owed much more to Hegel and Ranke, for both of whom he had the warmest admiration. In his introduction to his *Weltgeschichte* he remarked that "after Goethe, German intellectual life of the nineteenth century reached its zenith in Hegel and Ranke."[60] He observed that these two famous men had more in common than they themselves had realized, in spite of Ranke's emphatic denial to the contrary.

Strangely enough, he accepted Hegel's idealistic philosophy long after it had been discarded by the majority of historians. What appealed to Delbrück was not so much Hegel's philosophy of history as his idealistic explanations concerning historical de-

57. *HZ*, CXXXII (1925), 109.
58. *Ibid.*, p. 110.
59. A lengthy summary of Delbrück's *Weltgeschichte*, written by S. Mette, appears in *Archiv für Politik und Geschichte*, X (1928), 78–85.
60. I, 10.

velopments and the nature of the state. Thus he conceived of world-history as the revelation of the Spirit in the events, institutions, and movements of mankind. Like Hegel, he regarded the state not merely as an institution but as a spiritual organism having a will and personality of its own.

> In reality man first becomes man as a member of the state; he is thereby elevated above himself. The state, therefore, exists on a higher level than does the individual; so much so, in fact, that the individual must sacrifice himself to it. This is a moral law, which mankind has recognized at all times and among all peoples. This law is empirical proof to show that there are higher objectives than the individual. The transcendental nature of man is documented in the existence of the state. The so-called "altruism" merely recognizes individuals. But why should one individual sacrifice himself for another? Obviously, there must be something transcendental, some purposes that are higher than individuals, in order that one might demand of the latter to sacrifice their very existence voluntarily. But by no means is the individual worthless or without rights on that account. While it is true that he is under the state in one sense, in still another he is above the state. Is it not the abundance of individuals that makes the state purposeful? The rights of the state and those of the individuals form a polar antithesis. Both of them make demands and both carry these demands to the absolute.[61]

It is not surprising, therefore, that Delbrück devoted so much space to the state in his writings. He was also willing to concede that historical developments might take place according to a certain Hegelian rhythm of thesis, antithesis, and synthesis. He sometimes ascribed the activities of mankind to the interaction and interplay of various antitheses, the most important of which he listed as the individual and the community, state versus state, state and church, state and society, and personality and the mass. For example, in ancient history he emphasized the struggle between aristocracy and democracy and occasionally the conflict between aristocracy and plutocracy; the more important developments of the middle ages he attributed primarily to the tension between church and state and between priest and knight; and, finally, he believed that the course of modern history was largely

61. *Ibid.,* p. 16.

determined by the interaction of many groups and institutions, such as the nobility, bourgeoisie, peasants, nationalism, Protestantism, and others. But he would never admit the existence of any laws of history.

In the last analysis, however, he mainly looked to Ranke for inspiration, whose writings and methodology he accepted as criteria by which to judge historical scholarship. In his seminar at the University of Berlin he never failed to emphasize Ranke's concepts of history, which sought to confine the historian to political history. In both his lectures and books he limited himself to a political discussion of such topics as the rise and decline of states, the relations of various states to one another, and the impact of their foreign relations on their internal political structure. Like Ranke, he urged his students to view historical periods objectively and to base their conclusions on a critical evaluation of all documents.

But in some respects he differed from Ranke. Motivated by a strong feeling of patriotism, he was inclined to interpret history from a nationalistic viewpoint. In theory he tried to be impartial in his treatment of other states, but in practice his writings displayed a definite bias in favor of his own. His nationalism, however, was much more subdued and controlled than that of Sybel and Treitschke. Moreover, by indicating the relationships of wars and military affairs to various political factors, he gave a broader interpretation to military history than Ranke. Most important of all, in his methodology he was not merely satisfied in establishing the authenticity of historical documents, but he was much more interested in trying to prove or disprove the plausibility of the actions and scenes described in them. To this second type of criticism he applied the word *Sachkritik* to distinguish it from *Quellenkritik*, or criticism of the sources. By subjecting military actions described in trustworthy Greek documents to his *Sachkritik*, he succeeded in proving that many of them were gross exaggerations and distortions of the actual happenings.

While historians in increasing numbers were attracted by the newer interpretations of history, he clung tenaciously to political history. He was not impressed or influenced by any passing fads and fancies. He bitterly lamented the fact that so many of the new historical theories had been evoked by individuals without adequate historical background and training:

> Scientists, jurists, sociologists, economists, and so-called "philosophers" have attempted to master history in order to tell the historian how to interpret history. But they lack the first and most essential prerequisite: knowledge of historical events. How can anyone dare to set up the correct theories without knowing the basic facts and without a preliminary evaluation of these facts?[62]

Delbrück contended that many of the critics of political history have no clear conception of its scope and functions. In his opinion the distinction between political and cultural history is, after all, rather artificial, since the state is not only the supreme cultural achievement of mankind but serves as the channel by which the civilization of the past is handed down to future generations. He insisted that cultural progress was inconceivable without the state. He was firmly convinced that political history furnished the best framework within which to interpret the economic, social, and cultural developments of mankind. May not another generation of historians prove him to have been correct?

In his defense of political history, however, he often underestimated the economic and social factors. At times he ignored them completely. He refused to accept Rostovtzeff's brilliant economic interpretation of the decline of the Roman Empire. He had little patience with historians who ascribed everything to economic motives. He vigorously denounced the Marxian interpretation of history. He expressed his opinion of Karl Marx as follows: "As a demagogue he was a hero; as a thinker he was a sophist; and as a scholar he was a charlatan."[63] In a lengthy article on the Marxian interpretation of history he tried to point out the fallacies in the Marxian concepts of "the class struggle," "the proletariat," "the iron law of wages," and others.[64] Unfortunately, this article revealed a none too comprehensive

62. *Ibid.,* p. 27.
63. *Ibid.,* p. 10.
64. *Preussische Jahrbücher,* CLVII ( 1920 ), 157–80.

knowledge of basic economic principles. Delbrück's tendency to minimize the nonpolitical factors of history undoubtedly constituted his chief weakness as a historian.

If he established no new school of history or left any noteworthy successors to carry on his work, he at least must be regarded as the last distinguished representative of the political historians. As his friend Friedrich Meinecke stated shortly after his death, "he is the last of the select group of political historians who had engaged in political journalism from the days of Dahlmann to Treitschke and whose scholarly writings reflected a deep interest in the affairs of the present."[65] As a brilliant professor of history and gifted editor of the *Preussische Jahrbücher,* he will be remembered primarily for his researches in military history and his many valuable political observations. But he will also be remembered for his love of truth and justice, his unfailing courage, his integrity of character, and his firm belief in intellectual freedom. Obviously, there would be no room for him in the Germany of Adolf Hitler.

65. *HZ,* CXL (1929), 703.

# IV

## George Peabody Gooch (1873–1968)

### FRED L. HADSEL

SOME historians live but one life, and setting themselves on this single course they are judged by what they did in it alone. George Peabody Gooch, however, has led many historical lives. It requires only a quick glance at the major facets of his work to illustrate this. After graduating from Cambridge University in 1895, the young scholar turned to the history of political thought and soon thereafter published his prize-winning study, *English democratic ideas in the seventeenth century*.[1] Although he did not devote himself exclusively to political thought again, his interest in the field endured. In addition to the more popular study published eighteen years later, *Political thought in England: Bacon to Halifax*,[2] his writings are sprinkled with essays relating to the history of political ideas.[3] The history of ideas and the study of historians were closely linked in both his education and his scholarly activity, and it is not surprising that a second and

1. Initially entitled *The history of English democratic ideas in the seventeenth century* (Cambridge, 1898). The shorter title is used in the second edition, which has supplementary notes and appendices supplied by Harold J. Laski (Cambridge, 1927). The work was again reprinted in 1951.
2. London, 1915. It was reprinted in 1923, 1926, 1929, 1933, and 1944. A new edition appeared in 1946 and was reissued in 1950 and 1955.
3. For example: "German theories of the state," *Studies in modern history* (London, 1931), pp. 183–207; "Hobbes and the absolute state," *Studies in diplomacy and statecraft* (London, 1942), pp. 341–73; and "German ideas from Luther to Hitler," *Studies in German history* (London, 1948), pp. 1–36.

extremely important facet of his career should reflect his interest in historiography. Beginning in the first decade of the twentieth century, with a chapter in the *Cambridge modern history*, and reaching maturity a few years later in his *History and historians in the nineteenth century*, this phase of Gooch's life witnessed perhaps his most enduring contribution to historical scholarship.[4] Having explored this area of learning, Gooch did not turn his back upon it, and historiographical essays of interest to students and scholars are scattered throughout the rest of his writings.[5]

Even before Gooch entered the field of historiography, he began writing on international affairs, as witnessed by publications at the time of the Boer War and later by his slender *History of our times*.[6] After World War I, diplomacy came to dominate Gooch's interests. His *History of modern Europe, 1878–1919* and his contributions to the *Cambridge history of British foreign policy* marked the full flow of this historical life, of which his editorship of the *Documents on the origins of the war*, his *Recent revelations of European diplomacy*, and his *Before the war: studies in diplomacy*, were the major fruits.[7] Gooch's preoccupation with diplomacy, however, did not erase his interest in general European history. His early writings in this field had appeared in the *Cambridge modern history*, to which he contributed chapters

4. "The growth of historical science," *The Cambridge modern history* (Cambridge, 1902–10), XII, 816–50; *History and historians in the nineteenth century* (London, 1913). The latter work has been reprinted many times and has also been translated into Italian, Spanish, and Japanese.

5. For example: "The study of Bismarck," *Studies in modern history*, pp. 208–32; "German historical studies since the war," *ibid.*, pp. 233–76; "Ranke's interpretation of Germany history," *Studies in German history*, pp. 210–66; "Modern historiography," *Maria Theresa and other studies* (London, 1951), pp. 207–18; and "Voltaire as a historian," *Catherine the Great and other studies* (London, 1954), pp. 199–274.

6. London, 1911. There have been numerous reprintings as well as a second edition (1946) in which the period covered was extended to 1914.

7. *History of modern Europe, 1878–1919* (London, 1923); "Continental agreements, 1902–1907," "Triple Alliance and Triple Entente, 1907–1914," and "The war and the peace, 1914–1919," *Cambridge history of British foreign policy, 1783–1919* (Cambridge, 1922–23), III, 294–538; with H. Temperley as co-editor, *British documents on the origins of the war, 1898–1914* (11 vols.; London, 1926–38); *Recent revelations of European diplomacy* (London, 1927); *Before the war: studies in diplomacy* (2 vols.; London, 1936–38).

on the impact of the French Revolution in Europe and on Anglo-Irish politics of the first part of the nineteenth century.[8] His major scholarly study, *Germany and the French Revolution*,[9] denoted the continuation of this interest, as did his *Germany*[10] and some of the essays found in *Studies in modern history* and *Studies in diplomacy and statecraft*.[11] This historical life was renewed again during World War II, when Gooch developed a major, but never exclusive, interest in the eighteenth century. The first of these studies was *Frederick the Great* in 1944. *Maria Theresa, Catherine the Great,* and *Louis XV* followed during the next twelve years. These publications were interlarded with other volumes. *Courts and cabinets* dealt with various members of European royalty from the standpoint of contemporary memoirs. *Studies in German history* picked up certain personalities of the eighteenth and nineteenth centuries, and *The Second Empire* treated the court of Emperor Napoleon III.[12]

Although these several aspects of Gooch's historical writing illustrate the remarkable spectrum of his activities, one must add still another category that is a wide miscellany in itself. Gooch's interests always were (and still are at eighty-seven years of age) delightfully catholic. Throughout his long career he was constantly inquiring into things outside his major scholarly interests. Many of these inquiries, which often first saw the light of day in speeches, were published as articles in periodicals, as parts of collaborative books, or as subsidiary chapters in his own works. Thus Gooch took part in discussions on the League of Nations and contributed to three of the publications of the Geneva Insti-

8. "Europe and the French Revolution," *The Cambridge modern history*, VII, 754–90; "Great Britain and Ireland, 1792–1818," *ibid.*, IX, 672–708; "Great Britain and Ireland, 1832–1841," *ibid.*, X, 655–84.

9. London, 1920.

10. London, 1925.

11. For example: "The political background of Goethe's life," and "Germany's debt to the French Revolution," *Studies in modern history*, pp. 153–207; "The French Revolution as a world force," *Studies in diplomacy and statecraft*, pp. 291–310.

12. *Frederick the Great, the ruler, the writer, the man* (London, 1944); *Maria Theresa and other studies; Catherine the Great and other studies; Louis XV: the monarchy in decline* (London, 1956); *Courts and cabinets* (London, 1944); *Studies in German History; The Second Empire* (London, 1960).

tute of International Relations, *Problems of peace*.[13] He wrote a
number of brochures on current diplomacy.[14] He explored lightly
the role of autobiography and historical novels in the study of
history, and he contributed to the running appraisal of civilization and public morality.[15] If these miscellaneous activities had
been undertaken by a lesser historian, they might have been considered reasonably important. In Gooch's case, however, these
essays are mainly significant because they reveal the breadth of
his interests. In a sense they were Gooch's "table-talk," but by
publishing them he opened his table to the world at large.

Gooch once remarked, when talking about his early years, that
he had been very lucky to have been born with a warm heart, an
inquiring mind, and an adequate income. This almost ingenuous
explanation casts an appropriately gentle glow upon the youth
and education of this distinguished historian. Even if one dis-
counts the nostalgia which creeps into memoirs of childhood—
and Gooch as a keen student of memoirs would be the first to
admit this possibility—it can hardly be disputed that Gooch's own
autobiography, *Under six reigns*, clearly attests to the fortunate
quality of his early education.[16]

Gooch was born in 1873 of a family which epitomized the Victorian era, for his father was a partner in a financial firm and his

13. These publications, authored by Gooch in collaboration with others,
are "1931–1932: an introductory survey," and "Some consequences of the
Sino-Japanese dispute," *Problems of peace*, 7th ser. (London, 1933), pp.
1–23, 252–63; "The growth of nationalism," *Pacification is not enough:
problems of peace*, 9th ser. (London, 1935), pp. 1–13; "1936–1937," and
"The breakdown of the collective system," *Geneva and the drift to war:
problems of peace*, 12th ser. (London, 1938), pp. 9–25, 58–74.

14. For example: *Dictatorship in theory and practice* (London, 1935),
and *British foreign policy since the war* (London, 1936), a British historical
pamphlet.

15. For example: "Political autobiography," *Studies in diplomacy and
statecraft*, pp. 227–90; "Historical novels," *Maria Theresa*, pp. 382–403;
*The unity of civilization* (London, 1924), a League of Nations Union
pamphlet; *Politics and morals* (London, 1935), based on the Merttens Lecture of 1935.

16. (London, 1958), pp. 1–14. For a general view of Gooch, see also the
admirable and friendly discussion by Felix E. Hirsch, "George Peabody
Gooch," *Journal of modern history* (hereafter cited as *JMH*), XXVI (1954),
260–71. In addition, the author had several long conversations with Gooch
in 1959–60.

mother the daughter of a clergyman. His parents' wealth and position in London opened to the young boy a variety of intellectual, religious, and cultural opportunities. When the determined physical education program of Eton proved unpalatable, young Gooch pursued his studies at King's College, a small Anglican institution in London. Home and school gave him a firm grounding in traditional studies, an active interest in religion, and a lively concern with the world at large. When he entered Cambridge, therefore, he was equipped, to use a phrase he often employed, to "warm both hands before the fire of life." He made much of his opportunity, hearing lectures on economic history by Cunningham, on constitutional developments by Prothero, and, above all, on political history by Seeley. Ecclesiastical subjects occupied his attention, as did political science. In this latter area, Gooch established his "allegiance to the thoughtful Liberalism of which Mill was the oracle," retaining this point of view the rest of his life.[17] Gooch looks back on his university years as a "sunny day in spring," not only because they were delightful but because they opened up so many doors to new thought and learning.[18]

During the years following his study at Cambridge, three events further shaped Gooch's intellectual efforts. In the autumn of 1895 he spent three months in Germany. There, intoxicated by the strong academic atmosphere of Berlin, he learned the German language, greatly expanded his knowledge of German institutions, and became a lifelong student of German history. In the spring of 1896 he met Lord Acton, whose broad grasp of history was welcomed by Gooch and whose guidance during the next five years did much to influence the young historian. In the autumn of 1896 Gooch went to Paris, where at the Sorbonne and the École Libre des Sciences Politiques he repeated the stimulating German experience. In this short span of years Gooch learned directly from such giants as Treitschke, Gierke, Acton, Lavisse, and Sorel, and the long-term result was a continental breadth to his liberal approach to history.[19]

Gooch demonstrated his attachment to a liberal interpretation

17. *Under six reigns*, p. 20.
18. *Ibid.*, p. 30.
19. *Ibid.*, pp. 32–55.

of history in his first work, *English democratic ideas in the seventeenth century*, which he wrote in 1896–97 as a counterpart to Figgis' *Divine right of kings*. Putting aside the notion that history was past politics, Gooch set out to follow in his own way Acton's classic charge that the historian's task was "to view and to command the movement of ideas."[20] In this study Gooch described the influences from both home and abroad on seventeenth-century English thought. He discussed the republicans, Levellers, Diggers, and other extremists of the revolution and then moved on to deal with the later decades of the century, when the tide flowed strongly against this radicalism. Few monographs of young scholars have survived as well as this volume, which is enthusiastic, brilliant, full of acute interpretations, and still valid in most of its conclusions. Because of his own liberalism, Gooch regarded with Whiggish tolerance even the more fanatic of the radicals. To be sure, looking back after more than a half-century of further study of the period, one notes that Gooch paid little attention to economic or social background and that he therefore discussed his thinkers in something of a vacuum. But neither this criticism nor the fact that scholars have now unearthed additional archival material detracts from the enduring quality of the volume. This view was confirmed when another distinguished political thinker of a different persuasion, Harold J. Laski, sponsored and annotated a second edition in 1927. Today, after more printings, this essay in the grand manner still continues to inspire students of political thought.

While *English democratic ideas* reflected Gooch's attitude toward history, it was by no means the only illustration during these early years of his liberal point of view. He had already been attracted to the philosophy of the Liberal party, with its emphasis on individual rights, home rule for Ireland, free trade, and anti-imperialism. It was this last issue, however, that wrenched Gooch out of a life devoted largely to research and, for more than a decade, involved him directly in politics.

20. Quoted in *ibid.*, p. 43. This attitude was also shown in his editing of the *Annals of politics and culture, 1492–1899* (Cambridge, 1901). See Hirsch, p. 260.

The South African crisis was the immediate occasion for the new direction in Gooch's life, and at the end of the century he was part of a band of young Liberals who under the leadership of Campbell-Bannerman criticized the imperialism of Joseph Chamberlain and attacked the conduct of the British government during the Boer War. In a pamphlet, *The war and its causes*,[21] which appeared at the beginning of the struggle, Gooch sought to explain the historical background and attitudes of the Boers. Two years later he contributed a chapter on imperialism to Masterman's *Heart of empire,* in which he elaborated the liberal criticisms of jingoism.[22] In 1903 he was adopted as a parliamentary candidate by the Bath Liberal organization, and in 1906, after the party as a whole regained the initiative during the dispute over protectionism, he was elected to the House of Commons. This first-hand experience during a period of major reform at home and increasing involvement abroad confirmed his liberal philosophy and broadened his knowledeg of men and issues. While Gooch was too junior to play a leading role in the Commons and was not to sit again after his defeat of 1910,[23] there can be no doubt that his excursion into politics gave him a sureness of touch, to say nothing of a direct acquaintance with leading personalities, when he came to write about this period of history.

While Gooch's parliamentary career was over, another career opened up to him the following year. In 1911, the editor of the liberal monthly, the *Contemporary review,* died. Dr. Scott Lidgett and Gooch became the new editors. Lidgett, a nonconformist theologian, dealt mainly with religious and cultural contributions, while Gooch occupied himself with political and international questions. This collaboration lasted for some thirty years, after which Gooch assumed full responsibility for the jour-

21. London, 1899.
22. C. F. G. Masterman (ed.), *The heart of empire* (London, 1901), pp. 308–97. See also *Under six reigns,* pp. 85–87.
23. Gooch tried three times between 1910 and 1914 to re-enter parliament, but the tide turned against his group of Liberals. In retrospect, he has affirmed to the author that his retirement from active political life was one of the best things that happened to him. The wealth of his writings supports this view.

nal. Only in 1960, after forty-nine years of editorship, did Gooch give up the guidance of this periodical. However, he intends to continue as one of its contributors.

Directing the attention of readers of the *Review* to a broad spectrum of interests, Gooch secured as contributors a brilliant group of diplomats, statesmen, journalists, and academicians. Only gradually, however, did Gooch himself begin to write for the *Review*. After his first article in 1915, he limited himself to an occasional book review, appreciation or essay until after the war, when the number of his contributions increased. Although Gooch considered himself a man of cool blood and, like his admired Ranke, a non-active participant in political affairs, he could not remain silent during the rise of Fascism and Nazism in Europe. During the late twenties he welcomed distinguished Italian refugees as contributors, and he spoke out editorially against the Nazi leadership of Germany in 1934.[24] During and after World War II, Gooch became a major contributor to the *Review*. Many of his essays and almost all of his more recent books first appeared there in serial form. In spite of the radical change in the times, neither Gooch nor the *Contemporary review* abandoned any part of the liberal point of view. As he once remarked to the author, the world may have changed since the heyday of liberalism, but his outlook on life had not. He espouses today the same creed he believed in fifty years ago.

While for some the editing of the *Contemporary review* might have been a major preoccupation, it was only an incidental activity for a man of Gooch's temperament and energy. The initial years of editorship were also years of intense historical scholarship. They witnessed the completion of his *History and historians*

24. Based on an address to the Sociological Society, in which he had been active since its establishment early in the century, his first article in the *Contemporary review* (CVII [1915], 743–53) is entitled "German theories of the state." A warm appreciation of Lord Morley appeared in December 1917, as did one of Lord Courtney in June 1918. Gooch later undertook as a labor of love the *Life of Lord Courtney* (London, 1920). After the war, essays on a variety of topics were increasingly frequent in the periodical he edited. For Gooch's views on Fascism and Nazism, see "Salvemini and the Fascists," *Contemporary review*, CXXIX (1926), 181–85, and "The terror in Germany," *ibid.*, CXLVI (1934), 129–36.

*in the nineteenth century,* published in 1913.[25] Gooch had first taken up the subject at the suggestion of the editor of the *Cambridge modern history,* who wished to conclude the last volume of the series with a chapter on the "Growth of the historical sciences." The young historian had done considerable research in preparing this 34-page essay, which appeared in 1910. In fact, the approach and organization which marked the article were repeated in full three years later. In this volume, which Gooch declares is his favorite,[26] he sought to assess the achievements of historical research during the nineteenth century, to portray the masters of the craft, to trace the development of scientific method, to measure the influences which contributed to outstanding works, and to analyze the effects of these writings upon their times.[27]

In pursuing this ambitious objective, Gooch dealt with some five hundred writers, ranging in his treatment from a brief and often witty comment to an entire chapter. Displaying a remarkable knowledge of German historians, he traced the emergence of the liberal and later the Prussian schools. With perhaps a bit less enthusiasm, he treated the romantic and then the national historians of France. After a sympathetic survey of English writers, Gooch passed to brief discussions of the historians of other countries. His concluding chapters dealt with various historical subjects and the historians associated with them. Gooch moved through this forest of writers and their works with consummate grace. Praising wherever possible, he gloried in the emergence of history as a scientific art in much the same manner as his great predecessors were enthralled by the particular subjects with which they dealt. He left no doubt that his hero was the man of cool detachment, Leopold von Ranke. Gooch summarized Ranke's contributions, aside from his many historical works, as threefold: in describing an event "wie es eigentlich gewesen," he sought to disregard current passions; while not the first to use archives, he

25. See note 4 above.
26. See *Under six reigns,* pp. 165–66. Gooch corroborated this in conversation with the author.
27. See the preface to the first edition of *History and historians.*

established the necessity of basing work on contemporaneous sources; he founded the science of historical evidence.[28] While not discounting Ranke's role in nineteenth-century historiography, historians today recognize that he fell short of his goal in his own works and almost naïvely minimized the subjectivity in which we are all immersed. Gooch, however, never wavered in his admiration for the great German.[29] He has remained confident that a dispassionate historian can discover the past and that this goal can be achieved without preconceived theories by the pragmatic use of historical method as it evolved during the nineteenth century.

Reviewers of *History and historians* almost all hailed the work as a major contribution to historiography, although one writer caviled at both Gooch and Ranke for thinking that scientific history could be written in the manner they advocated.[30] While queries were raised about its organization (which involved some duplication in time and country) and footnotes (which never fascinated Gooch), the work has splendidly survived the principal test of time. In reprints and new editions it continues to be the best treatment of the subject. No one else, moreover, is likely to match the author's knowledge and grasp of nineteenth-century historians. For these two reasons, *History and historians* is probably Gooch's most enduring historical contribution.

During the next four decades Gooch often returned to historiography, and from his industrious pen there came a number of essays in this general category. For example, he wrote about his mentor, Acton, and his colleague, Harold Temperley.[31] He published a survey of studies on the French Revolution and another

28. *Ibid.*, 2d ed., pp. 96–97.
29. See his "Ranke's interpretation of German history," *Studies in German history*, pp. 210–66; "Modern historiography," *Maria Theresa*, pp. 219–58. This viewpoint was also reaffirmed in conversations with the author.
30. See the reviews by James T. Shotwell, *American historical review* (hereafter cited as *AHR*), XIX (1913–14), 151–53; A. F. Pollard, *English historical review* (hereafter cited as *EHR*), XXVIII (1913), 753–58; Lord Cromer, *Spectator* (April 26, 1913), pp. 715–17; unsigned review, *Nation*, XCVII (1913), 208–10.
31. "Lord Acton: apostle of liberty," *Foreign affairs*, XXX (1952), 517–30, and "Harold Temperley," *Proceedings of the British Academy*, XXV (1939), 41 ff. Both are reprinted in *Maria Theresa*, pp. 332–47, 348–81.

on Bismarck.[32] And he wrote a series of essays on eighteenth-century writers of history, notably Voltaire, Mirabeau, and Frederick the Great.[33] The most considerable contribution in this field made by Gooch in later years was *Recent revelations of European diplomacy*, first published as a book in 1927 and revised periodically until 1940.[34] This volume, which he called a "causerie" rather than a bibliography, is both historiography, in that he discussed and evaluated authors, and bibliography, in that he surveyed the documents, memoirs, and derivative works in all the countries concerned. One of the handful of best-informed scholars on this subject, Gooch brought his charm, wit, and sympathetic understanding to bear on a survey which otherwise might have been turgid and contentious. While far more specialized than his *History and historians*, and not seriously contending with it as a work of historiography, *Recent revelations* is nevertheless in its own way indispensable to the student of pre-1914 diplomacy. This fact was recognized by distinguished historians at the time. In reviewing the first edition, B. E. Schmitt praised it highly, and in commenting on the last edition, S. B. Fay described it as a "truly prodigious accomplishment."[35] As perspectives change and interests shift, *Recent revelations* will undoubtedly become more dated. It is unlikely, however, to be replaced; for while younger scholars may know the period well, they can hardly bring to the subject either Gooch's first-hand knowledge of the people involved or his direct experience with the documentation.

*Recent revelations*, however, was only an incidental part of Gooch's work in diplomatic history, and aside from his historiographical studies he has made his most important contribution

32. "Study of the French Revolution" appeared first as a pamphlet in 1920 and later, expanded, in *Studies in modern history*, pp. 117–52. "The study of Bismarck," *ibid.*, pp. 233–67, was republished with an additional chapter as "Bismarck's table talk," *Studies in German history*, pp. 300–91.

33. "Voltaire as historian," *Catherine the Great*, pp. 199–274; "Mirabeau's secret letters from Berlin" and "Mirabeau on the Prussian monarch," *Studies in German history*, pp. 75–118. A chapter in *Frederick the Great*, pp. 298–327, deals with the Prussian ruler as a historian.

34. See note 7 above.

35. B. E. Schmitt, *AHR*, XXXII (1926–27), 879–80; S. B. Fay, *JMH*, XIII (1941), 410.

in this field. From the days of the Boer War and his active participation in British politics, Gooch had been interested in diplomacy. Almost half of his popular book, *History of our time*, first published in 1911, dealt with recent international relations. World War I deeply moved Gooch, for not only did he have personal and intellectual associations with liberal elements in Germany, but he was induced to search for an explanation of the origins of the holocaust which affronted his humanitarian outlook on life. Except for an occasional address or a lesser bit of writing during the war years, however, he stayed clear of the passionate controversy over its causes. As the war wore on, Gooch gradually identified himself with those groups which favored a league of nations and supported a moderate settlement with Germany.[36]

Gooch's major efforts in diplomatic history began after the war, when he became co-editor of the *Cambridge history of British foreign policy*, to which he contributed in 1923 three significant chapters dealing with European diplomatic history from 1902 through the war.[37] In the same year he published a general diplomatic history of Europe from 1878 to 1919, which was a projection of the standard textbook by Fyffe on European history from 1792 to 1878. The next year Gooch was invited to become the senior editor of the government's series, *British documents on the origins of the war*. In carrying out this prolonged task—the eleven volumes appeared between 1926 and 1938—Gooch not only reviewed the official diplomatic correspondence of the foreign office but also examined the personal files of the leading British participants. While reviewers of these documents commented on the problems posed by topical organization (as in this case) and chronological organization (as in the case of the French documents), or made suggestions about details, they all agreed that the editors were as impartial as humanly possible and as thorough as their high reputation would lead scholars to expect.[38]

On the basis of this rich experience, Gooch published in 1936

36. *Under six reigns*, pp. 172–83.
37. Gooch's principal diplomatic works are cited in note 7 above.
38. See the reviews by S. B. Fay, *AHR*, XLI (1935–36), 751–53, XLII (1936–37), 332–34, XLIV (1938–39), 626–27; R. J. Sontag, *JMH*, VI (1934), 215–17; and R. B. Mowat, *EHR*, LIV (1939), 148–51.

and 1938 his two volumes entitled *Before the war: studies in diplomacy,* in which he dealt in some detail with European international relations between 1898 and 1914. While the *Cambridge history,* the *British documents,* and *Before the war* represent the peaks of Gooch's work in this field, they were accompanied by a number of lesser publications. Thus half the essays in *Studies in diplomacy and statecraft* are in the area of international relations, as is one in *Studies in German history.*[39]

In examining Gooch's major diplomatic works, we need to ask two closely related questions: What was his approach to the pre-1914 policies of the European powers, and what lasting contribution did he make to the study of this period? For all of Gooch's deftness and tact—and his pen was held by a sensitive hand in a velvet glove—he was very English in his approach to the coming of World War I. As one of the editors of the *Cambridge history of British foreign policy,* he signified his intention of combining adherence to truth with "an avowed regard for the interests and above all the honour of Great Britain."[40] His own assumptions with respect to the requirements of British policy tallied with those of Lansdowne and Grey.[41] But at the same time he sought to apply Rankean standards of impartiality to the intricate diplomacy of the period.

The primary task of the historian as he saw it was to explain rather than judge.[42] Although he did make critical evaluations of the prewar figures, such as Bethmann-Hollweg and even Grey, he

39. These essays were written or rewritten between 1920 and 1940. "Franco-German relations, 1871–1914," "The diplomatic background of the First World War," "British policy before the War of 1914, in the light of the archives," "Prince Bülow and his memoirs," "Kiderlen-Wächter, the man of Agadir," and "British foreign policy, 1919–1939" appeared in *Studies in diplomacy and statecraft,* pp. 2–226. "Holstein: oracle of the Wilhelmstrasse," is in *Studies in German history,* pp. 391–512.

40. Preface to the first volume of the *Cambridge history of British foreign policy.*

41. For example, Gooch agrees with Lansdowne that the latter did not offer an alliance in May–June 1905 to France: *Before the war: studies in diplomacy,* I, 176–77. He likewise indorses Grey's reasoning on Britain's entry into the war (*ibid.,* pp. 131–33, and *Studies in diplomacy and statecraft,* pp. 103–7).

42. Gooch stressed this point of view repeatedly, e.g., in *Before the war,* II, v.

tried so conscientiously to explain the circumstances in which they acted that the net effect was one of sympathy for almost all the statesmen he dealt with.[43] Gooch emphasized the individual. In his eyes, the various foreign ministers were not mere reflections of national culture, economic interests, or psychological impulses. Rather, they were intelligent men, able significantly to affect the destinies of their countries. As a result, prewar diplomacy, in Gooch's eyes, was largely a matter of personal judgment, and his approach was almost biographical. *Before the war: studies in diplomacy* is completely cast in this mold. It gains much from its focus on the leading diplomats, but nevertheless it does give an impression of men acting in something of a vacuum. This is reinforced by Gooch's practice of letting the individual speak for himself wherever possible. On the other hand, while Gooch would not overlook a telling remark to give the portrait perspective, he was such a master at weaving the fabric of a personality that it is this tapestry which especially attracts the reader's attention.

How was the war of 1914 unleashed and who was guilty of causing it? Gooch was unwilling to condemn any one power. During the period of intense feeling over German war guilt immediately after the war, he emphasized the multiple responsibilities for the conflict. He elaborated this point of view in the *Cambridge history of British foreign policy*, before he had worked through the documents, and he continued to hold it with only slight refinements afterward.[44] Thus, while he continued to apportion immediate responsibility between Austria-Hungary and Russia, he later recognized more clearly the causal element of Bethmann-Hollweg's weakness (although not as much as some would wish). His later researches also clarified the greater share of France in creating the dangerous situation of July 1914 through encouragement of Russian designs. Gooch, however, declined to sit in final judgment on the question of exact war guilt, except to

43. This did not escape the critical notice of other authorities in the field. See for example B. E. Schmitt's review of *Before the War*, AHR, XLIV (1938–39), 627–29.

44. *Cambridge history of British foreign policy*, III, 486–508; *History of modern Europe, 1878–1919*, pp. 557–59; *Before the war*, II, v and *passim*; *Studies in diplomacy and statecraft*, p. 104.

attribute the ultimate cause of the war to international anarchy, the absence of international machinery, the doctrine of unfettered sovereignty, and the assumption that grave disputes could only be settled by the sword. His point of view was in harmony with his lifelong desire to achieve Rankean detachment. But it suggests, of course, that in the world as we know it even this ideal has its limitations.

Gooch's enduring contributions to the study of diplomacy are easily pointed out. He added in significant measure to the quality of the documentation, and he provided an indispensable guide to its use. He also illuminated the documents through his own writings. By bringing into play his insight and style, he made the principal personalities live as few writers have been able to do. At the same time, it was entirely natural that he should have been a moderate revisionist. He thought that excessive penalties on the Weimar republic would be self-defeating, and he was therefore a critic of the Treaty of Versailles.[45] In this, as in his attitude toward the war-guilt question, Gooch held throughout the following decades the views which he adopted right after the end of hostilities. It need only be observed that most of what Gooch believed in the early postwar period came to be the virtual consensus on these matters in later years.

Another of Gooch's historical lives concerns general European history. This interest first showed itself in chapters of the *Cambridge modern history* dealing with the French Revolution and the early nineteenth century. When World War I cut across his life, he found leisure to write his first full volume on the period, *Germany and the French Revolution.*[46] In this solid piece of scholarship, which still commands respect, Gooch sought to document the influence of the revolution by painting a panorama of the ferment among German intellectual and political leaders of the time.[47] Such an approach illustrated his view that history

45. *Cambridge history of British foreign policy,* III, 509–38. Gooch expressed this point of view in numerous speeches and articles as well.
46. London, 1920.
47. *Germany and the French Revolution,* pp. v–vi. Incidentally, the second portion of the work (pp. 367–514), which deals with the political effects, is less satisfactory.

includes the entire human adventure, thus again placing him among those who like Acton saw the past broadly rather than among the political historians of the Seeley persuasion. This study not only showed the results of Gooch's work on *History and historians*, for some of the early writers are discussed in both books, but it provided background for his *Germany* published in 1925.[48] The latter work, partly a history and partly a survey of the institutions of the Weimar republic, revealed Gooch's deep sympathy with the liberal tradition in Germany. Because so much of it is a description of contemporaneous conditions, it has suffered rather badly with the passage of time and the addition of perspective.

Two decades intervened before Gooch returned to general history. This period of his life, which began with the publication of *Frederick the Great* in 1944, saw him write three other studies of eighteenth-century autocrats: *Maria Theresa, Catherine the Great*, and *Louis XV*. It also saw the appearance of his *Courts and cabinets* and *Studies in German history* and concludes—perhaps only temporarily—with his latest book, published in the spring of 1960, *The Second Empire*.[49] Although none of these involved archival research—and Gooch made it clear that in no instance was he trying to produce a definitive biography of his subject—they are all based on contemporary sources, either the letters of the person concerned or the observations of acquaintances. In reviewing *Frederick the Great*, Ferdinand Schevill remarked that this approach had "the effect of making the reader a direct participant in the events."[50] These portraits are also without exception highly personal presentations in which Gooch's interest in the role of individuals found its fullest expression. As John B. Wolf said of *Louis XV*, not only did Gooch brilliantly use the memoirs of the times, but a book such as this was a "devastating response to the historical 'physicists' who attempt to explain the historical process solely in terms of abstract forces. . . ."[51]

48. Guy Stanton Ford hailed this work as the best book about Germany since 1914 (*AHR*, XXXI [1925–26], 525–26).

49. See note 12 above.

50. *JMH*, XX (1948), 167–68.

51. *Ibid.*, XXIX (1957), 263.

Moreover, Gooch set out in these volumes to entertain the intelligent reader. Those who criticize him for not writing definitive history mistakenly think that a *doyen* of historians—as Gooch undoubtedly is—must be only a dispenser of footnotes and researcher of archives. They do not appreciate the shafts of sunlight which Gooch cast into what might otherwise be a dull landscape of historical events.

Gooch's various essays and observations on the world he has lived in are scattered like odd pieces left in the studio of an artist. They were occasionally popular treatments or second looks at problems with which he had once dealt more extensively. More frequently, they were originally addresses or lectures that were later redone for publication.[52] As incidental contributions they often confirm what was indicated in other writings, but, being incidental, they do not add much to our understanding of Gooch as a historian.

One exception is "Politics and morals," which he delivered as the Merttens Lecture in London in 1935.[53] It deals with the problems posed for society by Machiavelli. Quoting with approval John Stuart Mill's view that democracy is an expression of faith in the power of mankind to learn from experience, Gooch contended that Machiavelli drew an unfair picture of man's nature and ignored the power of moral forces in the world. Moreover, he held that Machiavellian principles were no longer valid when nations had established ordered liberty in their internal affairs. While admitting that the problem was far more complex in the international sphere, Gooch argued that by recognizing the unity of civilization and the need for effective institutions to prevent aggression, it would also be possible to abandon Machiavellian principles in the relations among nations. It is indicative of Gooch's confidence in mankind that he should have elaborated this optimistic outlook at a time when the shadow of Hitler was

52. Two widely different examples are "Cambridge Chair of Modern History," *Studies in modern history,* pp. 268–89, and "German views of the state," *The German mind and outlook,* co-edited by Gooch (London, 1945), pp. 1–42.
53. Published as a pamphlet in 1935 and reprinted in *Studies in diplomacy and statecraft,* pp. 311–40.

cast across the civilization that Gooch loved and represented. It is equally indicative of Gooch's lifelong adherence to this point of view that in his reminiscences published more than two decades later he should have expressed the same confidence in his fellow men.[54]

Writing of the charity which Gooch displayed in his life and work, his distinguished colleague C. V. Wedgwood correctly affirmed that he "stood in a great humane tradition."[55] Appropriately, moreover, this comment was followed by the wistful question: who can follow in his footsteps? Gooch has established no school. To be sure, he was not a teacher. But this is not the reason. Rather, the explanation must be sought in the major change which has taken place during the past half-century in both the training of historians and the philosophic milieu in which they develop. Liberal historians such as George Peabody Gooch are no longer being produced. The fact that the times call forth a different kind of scholar should not, however, dim our appreciation of the contribution which Gooch has made to historiography or the erudition which he so gracefully displays in his many writings.

54. *Under six reigns*, pp. 327–28.
55. Review of *Under six reigns, Time and tide*, XL (1959), 77.

# V

## Gabriel Hanotaux (1853–1944)

VESTA SWEITZER VETTER

GABRIEL HANOTAUX (Albert Auguste Gabriel) was born at Beau-
revoir in Brittany on November 19, 1853. His rather discursive
memoirs, continuing through one book and a number of periodical articles,[1] give an interesting, if rambling, picture of his
boyhood and youth. His paternal ancestors were primarily of
peasant stock interspersed with an occasional artisan, such as his
great-grandfather, who was a carpenter. His father, a more intellectual type, rebelled against the bucolic life and became a notary,
with a small legal office. Hanotaux's mother was a Martin, from
a family in business. The most outstanding relative on this side,
as far as Hanotaux was concerned, was his mother's great-uncle,
Henri Martin, the historian, who served as an inspiration to the
young student, and, on occasion, rendered practical service in
arranging meetings with influential people and opening official doors.

Young Gabriel grew up happily with an older brother and a
sister in a family with a modest but adequate income, plenty of
hard work, and few conveniences. As a youth, his health was
none too good, and many vacations were spent on family farms,
where he learned to love the soil. His interest in the needs of

1. *Mon temps* (Paris, 1935); "Mon temps," *Revue des deux mondes*, 8th
period, XXXIII (May 15–June 15, 1936), 315–48, 539–72, 811–41; XXXIV
(July 1, 1936), 83–107; XXXVIII (Apr. 15, 1937), 774–800; XXXIX (May
1–May 15, 1937), 52–83, 334–70.

farmers can definitely be traced in the commercial treaties nego-
tiated while he was foreign minister, and he later boasted that he
had never disposed of his share of the family property which he
inherited.[2]

The old man looking back on his youth remembered many
impressions which aroused an interest in history. His father was
a studious man who particularly enjoyed reading historical
works, and there were always uncles and great-uncles at hand
with stirring tales of battles and great events. The Hanotaux
children played frequently in the near-by ruins of the Château
de Luxembourg, where Jeanne d'Arc had been imprisoned.[3]

"The frontier where I was born and the times in which I have
lived" are the two factors which Gabriel Hanotaux himself considered to be the determinants of his life and work.[4] Living on
the northeastern border of France, he experienced the full impact of the invasion and occupation by the Germans in 1870–71.
The Franco-German War began when he was sixteen, and his
father died in November of that year, as the Germans were
marching into the city in which he lived.[5] In May, 1871, before
the smoke of the Commune had cleared away, the young adolescent was sent to Paris to study.

Although Hanotaux had early announced his intention of becoming a professor of history,[6] much to his father's disgust, it was
not until he was about twenty-five that he really found himself.
At the age of six he attended the village school, and at nine he
entered the *lycée* at Saint-Quentin, where his brother had preceded him and where the family later moved. According to his
father's wishes, both he and his brother studied to become no-
taries. In May, 1871, he went to Paris, where he failed to pass the
Sorbonne examinations. After a summer in the country he entered the École de Droit in Paris and became a licentiate in law
before he attained his majority.

2. *Mon temps*, p. 77.
3. *Sur les chemins de l'histoire* (Paris, 1924), I, ii.
4. *Ibid.*, p. xiii.
5. *Ibid.*, p. v.
6. *Mon temps*, p. 138.

Law never really interested him, however, and he was increasingly attracted toward history. The fear of examinations caused by his earlier failure at the Sorbonne might have slowed up his formal education, but his excellence as a student counterbalanced this. He began by reading history at the École des Hautes Études.[7] Here, his knowledge of the Picard dialect enabled him to make an unusual study of one of the sources of the Fourth Crusade, which brought him to the notice of the already prominent historian, Gabriel Monod, who published the article in the newly founded *Revue historique*.[8] The publication of this monograph caused a flutter in historical circles. Henri Martin evinced an interest as his young relative gained prominence, and he introduced him to Jules Quicherat, who was at that time director of the École des Chartes. The latter encouraged Hanotaux's entrance in 1879 into that famous French institution specializing in methods of medieval history which has trained so many French historians.[9]

Gabriel Hanotaux always spoke of the École des Chartes with affection and respect. He learned method there and made contacts with such men as Quicherat, Montaiglon, Gautier, Léopold Delisle, Gaston Paris, Boislisle, and Giry. His diploma was granted on the basis of a thesis on the origins of intendants in France,[10] a subject in the field of institutions which he selected because he was not greatly interested in medieval history.[11]

Hanotaux chose Richelieu as his principal interest as early as 1878 and was prepared to devote the rest of his life to research in that field. He proposed to enter the teaching profession, despite his father's contempt for that way of earning his living. "Professor! don't think of it," his father told him. "A professor! He is only an underteacher who has made good. And you would shut yourself up for life in a *lycée* to teach classes . . . when you

7. "Mon temps," *loc. cit.*, XXXIII (May 15, 1936), 332.
8. "Les Vénitiens ont-ils trahi la Chrétienté en 1202?" *RH*, IV (1877), 74. Reprinted in *Sur les chemins de l'histoire*, Vol. I.
9. *Mon temps*, pp. 232–36.
10. Published as *Origines de l'institution des intendants des provinces, d'après les documents inédits* (Paris, 1884).
11. *Mon temps*, pp. 336–37.

could be a notary!"[12] Hanotaux's experience in this field, however, was limited by events to a little teaching in a Parisian private school, undertaken while he was still a student, to eke out
his meager allowance,[13] and the more interesting experimental
work of conducting a "conference" (the subject was not considered worthy of the designation "course") on the sources of modern
history at the École des Hautes Études.[14]

Although Hanotaux enjoyed teaching, his life lay along other
paths. Most of the young historians of his day were politicians,
and politics appealed to him. At an early age he had shocked his
father by his radical republican ideas;[15] and although he soon
lost his radicalism, he remained a devoted Republican all his life.
The assiduity of his work in the archives of the foreign office
brought him to the notice of Waddington, the foreign minister,
who was Henri Martin's colleague from the department of Aisne
in the National Assembly. After refusing, because of bad health,
a diplomatic assignment which would have involved his leaving
France, Hanotaux accepted a position as "attaché without pay"
to the foreign office.[16] This in February, 1880, became "attaché
with pay" on the archives staff, and he was soon given an increase
in salary because of an article on Greece.[17]

Gambetta, one of his political heroes, encouraged Hanotaux
in his growing desire to make history alive by presenting it in an
interesting manner and by bringing the lessons of the past to bear
on the decisions of the present. When the former became prime
minister he appointed the young historian co-chief of the office
assisting the cabinet in foreign affairs, a position which he assumed again under Challemel-Lacour and Ferry. In 1885, after
a few minor missions, he became counselor of the French embassy in Constantinople; and in the following year, as chargé
d'affaires, he was French delegate at the conference charged with
regulating the Bulgarian question.

12. *Ibid.*, p. 38.
13. *Ibid.*, pp. 332–35.
14. *Ibid.*, p. 341.
15. *Ibid.*, p. 138.
16. "Mon temps," *loc. cit.*, XXXIII (May 15, 1936), 326–28.
17. *Ibid.*, pp. 346–47.

That same year he was elected to the chamber of deputies at a special election but served only one term, being beaten by a royalist in 1889. He returned at once to the foreign office as a functionary in charge of the countries held under French protectorates. In 1890 he was a member of the French delegation to the conference relative to the delineation of the spheres of influence in Africa, and two years later he assumed the direction of consulates and commercial affairs. This steady progress was crowned in 1894 by the offer of the portfolio of foreign affairs, a position which Hanotaux accepted and held for four years, with the exception of a short interval in the beginning of 1896. As foreign minister he was particularly interested in the development of the Franco-Russian alliance and the expansion of French interest in the countries bordering on the Mediterranean, especially Africa. After the fall of the ministry in June, 1898, Hanotaux renounced politics to devote himself to the writing of historical works.

Although he later spoke with scorn of those who liked the security of government positions[18] and claimed that the "taste for retreat, for silence, for intellectual independence" caused him to abandon public life,[19] this was hardly the whole truth. As the years went by, Hanotaux had identified himself completely with that section of the Republican party which disliked factionalism and believed, above all, in getting things done. In order to accomplish its ends, this group manifested a tendency to split more and more from the Left and draw closer and closer to the Right through the policies of "appeasement" and "rallying." The high point of this policy was reached in the nineties in the series of ministries under Dupuy, Ribot, and Méline (1894–98), which came to a sudden end amid the violent controversies of the Dreyfus case. The coming into power of the more radical republicans put an end willy-nilly to the political careers of their predecessors. The fact that Hanotaux stood as candidate for the senate in the Aisne in 1904, where he was badly defeated, indicated that public life still had its attractions. For the remainder of his life, how-

18. *La fleur des histoires françaises* (Paris, 1911), pp. 270–71.
19. *Mon temps,* p. 297.

ever, he was restricted to serving as delegate on occasional missions and making innumerable public speeches.

Hanotaux had not neglected history even in the midst of his diplomatic labors. The concentration upon the restoration of France after the Franco-German War was general, and most of the young historians studying in Paris in the seventies were ardent patriots. They were affected by the current belief that superior German intellectual methods and scientific techniques had won the war. *Ergo,* they studied German historical method assiduously, hoping to demonstrate to the intellectual world that they could be as scientific as their conquerors and in that way do their part in helping their country.

Hanotaux was not the least of these, and for his own research he proposed to concentrate on the period of Richelieu. When he entered political life he inevitably had less time for study. He did not abandon history, however; he simply enlarged his conception and technique to include his new activities. In fact, he came to consider his writings and his political career as inseparable parts of one whole, and he felt that his contribution to French life as a writer of history was just as significant as his contribution to the development of the French colonial empire and the restoration of French influence in the concert of the European powers.

This combination of historian and politician was not unusual in France. Guizot, the minister of Louis Philippe, and Thiers, the first president of the Third Republic, were notable historians in their day who occupied the highest state positions. Henri Martin, always a model for Hanotaux, played a significant part in the political events of his time, and nearly all living French historians took sides publicly in the agitation of the Dreyfus case. Hanotaux, however, was more conscious and specific in his approach than were his contemporaries.

The role which he assigned to historians was no mean one. "Sciences, arts, techniques, all the productions of human activity flowed into history,"[20] he thought. But more than that, history

20. *De l'histoire et des historiens* (Paris, 1919), p. 8.

is the "mistress of princes and of peoples; she works without cessation to distinguish good from evil; she passes the acts of man through the sieve and separates the bad from the good grain. She judges and is the tribunal where sits the conscience of future generations."[21] In consequence of this,

> when a man decides to write history, no matter how feeble and slender the subject he selects, he becomes the instrument of Destiny; as he is responsible for his narrative and his judgment, so he is responsible for their consequences. According to the fashion in which he exposes the affairs of the past, the affairs of the future will go well or ill.[22]

Thus, history became for him not merely an exposé of the past but a way of life for the future. His ideal was not the scholar, publishing pedantic works which no one would read, but the man of action,[23] even the prophet.[24] Underlying all his writings is his conviction that history is definitely a moral force.[25]

Although his conception seems very grandiose indeed, the inevitable result of this kind of thinking is a very personal sort of history written around its author's own experiences and interpretations. That, in the case of Hanotaux, these should be concentrated on his country was natural, for the significant events of his impressionable adolescent years centered around the Franco-German War. "I have seen frightful things," he wrote many years later, "and the most frightful of all is defeat."[26]

Thus nationalism dominated all of his historical writings. He became interested in the causes of the greatness of France in the past and concerned himself with trying to analyze and interpret those causes in a manner which might help those who were trying to rebuild the nation. By revealing the past glories of their coun-

21. *Ibid.*, p. 10.
22. *Ibid.*, p. 42.
23. *Ibid.*, pp. 39–41; *L'énergie française* (Paris, 1903), p. 329.
24. *Sur les chemins de l'histoire*, II, 239, 248–49; *Histoire et historiens*, p. 11.
25. I.e., *Histoire du cardinal de Richelieu* (3d ed.; Paris, 1899), I, vii; *Histoire de la nation française* (Paris, 1929), I, 11.
26. *Sur les chemins de l'histoire*, I, vi.

try to the French people, particularly the youth, he hoped he was inspiring his countrymen to renewed efforts at restoring these glories and perhaps even increasing them.[27]

Love of one's country, to him, was a most commendable quality; but when that country was France, devotion was inevitable,[28] for it was a country "so worthy of being loved."[29] It possessed nearly everything to make men happy. "To speak of France, what an undertaking!"[30] and it was to this that Hanotaux devoted his life and his vision.[31] He was a sentimental nationalist. France, "so lovely,"[32] was to him almost a living person, beautifully proportioned, smiling, full of grace, hard working, vivacious, ardent, yet restrained, reasonable, the good sister of all those in trouble, loving and seeking to be loved.[33] He admitted generously that France was not the largest nor strongest power in the world, but balanced his admission by his claim that the moderation of French riches was more desirable and more permanent.[34] French thrift, he insisted, was due not to miserliness but to a desire to save for investment, and thus was a potent factor in spreading French civilization throughout the world[35]—an end much to be desired. Above all, he admired French spirit and morale.

His works can be divided into two parts. As a young man, he published a number of scholarly works such as might be expected to come from the pen of any well-trained historian of promise.

27. "Mon temps," *loc. cit.*, XXXIII (May 15–June 15, 1936), 315–16, 337–38, 822; XXXIV (July 1, 1936), 106; *Sur les chemins de l'histoire*, I, viii, xi–xiii; *Histoire de la France contemporaine* (Paris, 1903–8), I, viii; *La fleur des histoires françaises*, pp. i, 280; *L'énergie française*, p. 329; "Défense de l'histoire," *Revue des deux mondes*, 8th period, V (Oct. 15, 1931), 772–73.
28. *La fleur des histoires françaises*, pp. 93–94.
29. *L'énergie fançaise*, p. 5.
30. *Ibid.*, p. 6.
31. In the introduction to his *Histoire de la France contemporaine* (I, vii) he states that all the works he has begun or published have but one object: France.
32. His dedication of *L'énergie française*, title-page, also pp. 33, 199.
33. *Ibid.*, p. 199; *La fleur des histoires françaises*, pp. 312–13.
34. *La fleur des histoires françaises*, pp. 310–11.
35. *Ibid.*, p. 281; *L'énergie française*, p. 150.

These include a few monographs on various subjects of the middle ages; his dissertation on intendants; the collections published as a result of his association with the commission on diplomatic archives;[36] and his studies on Richelieu. After 1900 his works are less erudite and cover various phases of contemporary French life.

The earlier works on medieval topics can be ignored here, for they were the product of his student days. Hanotaux was always a little proud of them; but, while they indicated merit, they were written before his ideas matured and played only an introductory part in his development as a historian.

The other writings in this earlier period were concentrated around the subject of Richelieu or were the by-products of his research in that field. Unquestionably Hanotaux's claim as a scholarly historian rests primarily on these works, which include a large number of articles and the famous *Histoire du cardinal de Richelieu,* of which four volumes had appeared. His interest in the past glories of France had, to a considerable extent, determined his selection of the seventeenth century—France's *grand siècle*—as his special field of interest.[37]

His conception of his task was immense.

> My idea was to write a history of the great century. But the history of a century is the accumulated knowledge of all that the men of this century have done during the hundred years it has lasted, of all the meeting and crossing of the passions, the acts, the illusions, the disillusions throughout its course; I say that the history of a century includes the knowledge of the centuries which have followed in order to judge its accomplishments. It is, then, a world, it is the universe, it is mankind! To know all, that is the program![38]

Limitation was necessary, however, and he decided to concentrate on Richelieu in particular because he felt that that statesman gathered up and perfected the work of Sully and Henry IV

36. See below, p. 113.
37. *Histoire du cardinal de Richelieu,* I, viii; *Mon temps,* pp. 312–13, 317; "Mon temps," *loc. cit.,* XXXIII (May 15, 1936), 331–33; *La fleur des histoires françaises,* p. 187.
38. *Mon temps,* p. 312.

and prepared the way for the culminating magnificence of Louis XIV.

Hanotaux considered that Richelieu's great work was the unification of the kingdom. The cardinal, to him, "set the seal on French unity, consecrated religious tolerance, and established the rules of a language destined to serve the spokesman of nations in making more precise, formulas of justice and treaties of peace."[39] The adequate portrayal of these contributions meant a tremendous undertaking. It involved a knowledge of the work of Richelieu's predecessors and successors; an understanding of developing French institutions and all the complex relationships between royalty, nobility, bourgeoisie, and common people; a clarification of the religious problem and its entanglements with the political and economic situation; and a study of foreign affairs, including all the complications of the Thirty Years' War. It was a task which, indeed, required a lifetime.

The personality of Richelieu interested Hanotaux. In the introduction to the first volume, published in 1893, fifteen years after he began his research, the historian states his conviction that he has added to the accuracy of the portrait of Richelieu the statesman.

> I have found in Richelieu a genius, accessible, with a psychology rather simple and easy to decipher. . . . I have seen a French statesman, in the practical and positive sense, with a glance cold and certain, and a rough hand. I have added his name with no effort to the series of our great political leaders with Philip the Handsome, Charles V, Louis XI, and the men of the Revolution. What distinguishes him is his clarity, his logic, the measure of his energy, and, it is necessary to add, his marvelous agility. This thin and delicate man maintained himself in power for so long a period only by *tours de force* in which he demonstrated his great patience and his adroitness. . . .
>
> There was in him a priest, believing, as did all the world in his day. But there was, above all, a man of action. . . . He retained always . . . something of the cavalier, which shows clearly in his face with its pointed beard. He had his romances. . . . But his real passion, the flame which devoured and consumed his entire life, was his ambition. He wished power, he wished to keep it

39. "Mon temps," *loc. cit.*, XXXVIII (April 15, 1937), 782–83.

until his death; once minister, his ambitions identified themselves with the well-being of the state; he consecrated himself to a great work: the achievement of French unity by the definite establishment of the absolute authority of the king and by the ruin of the Spanish royal house. This man lived only for that.[40]

Hanotaux proposed to recount the "drama" of the life of this man in detail. The early volumes are undoubtedly the best. The first is excellent in plan and treatment, describing the background and early life of Richelieu and the geography, the institutions, and the people of France in 1614. With the concluding summary the stage is carefully and completely set for the incidents presenting themselves when Richelieu achieved supreme power. Hanotaux never again reached the standard set by this book.

The second volume, published in 1896, treats of the early political problems confronting Richelieu and his method of handling them. By its nature, this volume is not as perfect in outline as its predecessor. It was at this point that active political work interrupted Hanotaux's concentration upon his cardinal, and the third volume was not published until thirty-seven years later (1933). It was written with the collaboration of the Duc de La Force, as was the fourth volume, which appeared in 1935; together they complete the story of the internal unification of France.

These four volumes are far from fulfilling the original plan of Hanotaux. They do not represent a complete story of Richelieu's career chronologically. Moreover, while foreign affairs are not ignored, the emphasis is definitely on the internal situation. The latter volumes are not as heavily documented as the earlier, and they are of less significance in the field of historical writing.

After he abandoned active public life, contemporary events absorbed more and more of his time, and Hanotaux never returned single-heartedly to the study of the seventeenth century.

> To join the past to the present, such was the work of the time and the situation in which destiny placed me. It was not a question of enclosing myself in the seventeenth and eighteenth cen-

40. *Histoire du cardinal de Richelieu*, I, vi–vii.

turies, or even in the nineteenth, which was passing; it was necessary to consider the totality of the work of the nation and of the
world.[41]

The breadth of his interest soon defied specialization.

Hanotaux's works on his own period are prolific and cover
nearly all aspects of contemporary life. By their nature they are
personal books, the expression of his own beliefs on current
topics, often arising from his practical experience. Because that
experience has come primarily in the field of politics, his political
writings constitute his major contribution.

Politically, as we have seen, he was a conservative republican.
He believed in democracy, but he felt that the masses needed
rulers. He admired most those prime ministers who tried hardest
to overcome the party quarrels which so complicated the early
life of the Third Republic and to accomplish a definite program.
Thus Gambetta,[42] Jules Ferry,[43] Jules Méline,[44] and Poincaré[45]
became his political heroes. He supported the moderate and
conservative republican groups in the crises besetting the Third
Republic, opposing General Boulanger, whose supporters wished
to make him dictator,[46] blaming the Panama financial scandals
on a weak government and an uncontrolled press[47] and supporting the position of the Méline cabinet which considered the
Dreyfus case closed.[48] The maintenance of order and a vigorous
government policy seemed vitally necessary to Hanotaux, and
such a program always won his support. Unity, frequently absent from French politics, seemed to him the most admirable and
desirable trait.[49]

He wrote innumerable articles on political questions, but the
best expression of his ideas and his methods can be found in his

41. "Mon temps," *loc. cit.*, XXXVIII (April 15, 1937), 777–78.
42. *Ibid.*, XXXIII (June 15, 1936), 838; "Gambetta," *ibid.*, 6th period,
XX (Nov. 1, 1920), 5–23.
43. "Mon temps," *ibid.*, 8th period, XXXIX (May 15, 1937), 348–49.
44. "Jules Méline," *ibid.*, 7th period, XXXI (Jan. 15, 1926), 440–53.
45. *Raymond Poincaré* (Paris, 1934), pp. 59–60, 85, and *passim.*
46. *Histoire de la nation française* (Paris, 1929), V, 642–48.
47. *Ibid.*, p. 631.
48. *Ibid.*, p. 641.
49. *Joffre* (Paris, n.d.), p. 72.

interesting and readable four-volume *Histoire de la France contemporaine* (1903–8), which treats of events from 1870 to 1878, and in his *Histoire politique de 1804 à 1926*, included in the *Histoire de la nation française* (1929). The first of these is, by its nature and concept, more scholarly than the second and ranks second to *Richelieu* as a contribution to historical writing. It covers a less ambitious field than that earlier work, and Hanotaux had the advantage of having lived through the events of the period about which he was writing. This study comes closer to fulfilling Hanotaux's original conception; but it is, of necessity, despite its basis on actual documents, a source rather than a definitive treatment. No student of the founding of the Third Republic can afford to ignore it, but it is colored by the views and experiences of its author.

Admittedly a popular history,[50] Hanotaux maintained that it was based upon accurate historical methods. He proposed to "present to democracy a sufficient quantity of precise information, of documents which were checked, and proceedings which were verified."[51] While he strove to be impartial, he averred his republicanism;[52] had he been strictly accurate, he would have added "conservative" republican.

The four volumes portray in an interesting manner the events incidental to the firm establishment of the Third Republic. They present a touching picture of the tragic events of the war and the Commune and an eloquent analysis of the struggles to bring to an end the German occupation. Thiers is treated with great sympathy. The general lack of bitterness toward the Right may be explained not only by Hanotaux's "impartiality" but by his own political position.[53] Incidentally, this is the only title of Hanotaux's that has been translated into English,[54] but the translation shows evidence of haste and is not too well done.

Hanotaux's career in the foreign office developed as a result

50. *Histoire de la France contemporaine*, I, ix.
51. *Ibid.*
52. *Ibid.*
53. See above, pp. 94–95.
54. *Contemporary France* ( 4 vols., London, 1903–9 ).

of his interest in foreign affairs, and he definitely believed that it was necessary to study international relationships in order to arrive at a proper understanding of history.[55] Specifically he was interested in the restoration of France as a great power in Europe, which he believed could best be accomplished by close association with the Mediterranean countries. His book on the diplomacy of the years 1907–11[56] adequately illustrates his ideas. It is true that France had played no insignificant part in world-history from the time of the Crusades, but Hanotaux regularly extolled this influence to the point of gross exaggeration.[57]

As an ardent nationalist, it was natural that he should hate Germany, and he disliked everything about not only that nation but the northern countries and their Teutonic background in general. Materialism, diabolical sophism, the worship of brute force, he felt, were the attributes of their philosophers and their rulers,[58] and he would have none of them. He rebelled not only against their politics and philosophy but against their historical method. His *Histoire de la nation française* disavowed the significance of German influences in the life and culture of medieval France.[59] Moreover, the entire conception of the fifteen volumes aimed at discarding German historical method and setting up a new kind of history, more vital and more true, he believed, than the stodgy German method of documentation alone.

Hanotaux was an Anglophobe as well; he thought the English just as bad as the Germans,[60] and his anti-English policy in the foreign office was not insignificant as a contributing factor in the development of the Fashoda incident in 1898, which nearly led to serious trouble between France and England.

55. *Histoire et historiens,* pp. 82–83.
56. *Études diplomatiques: la politique de l'équilibre, 1907–1911* (Paris, 1912).
57. See particularly his introduction to the *Histoire des colonies françaises et de l'expansion de la France dans le monde* (Paris, 1929), Vol. I, *passim;* and *Jeanne d'Arc* (Paris, 1911), *passim.*
58. *Sur les chemins de l'histoire,* I, 342.
59. In the introduction he boasts that the first volume on literature (Vol. VI of the series) proved that the *chansons de geste* were Latin and not German in tradition (p. xv) and that the volume on the Frankish invasion put Teutonic influence in its "proper" light (pp. 1, li).
60. *Sur les chemins de l'histoire,* I, 343.

On the other hand, he revered the Latin tradition and Mediterranean culture. He never tired of comparing the clear sunny weather and brilliant coloring of the south with the gloomy fogs of the north. Latin reasonableness and the generally gentler way of life (his description) he always contrasted with the brutality and ferocity of the Teutonic countries.[61] The religion of the south—Catholicism—appealed to him,[62] as did the Latin language.[63] His collection of sketches in *La paix latine*[64] was the result of his travels in the Mediterranean area. He always emphasized the inheritance which France had received, sometimes carrying it to rather ridiculous extremes.[65]

The high spot of his writings on international relations can be found in his works on the war of 1914, which include a dozen books and many periodical articles, of which the outstanding is the set of fifteen volumes of his *Histoire illustrée de la guerre de 1914* (1915–23), "the passionate subject of his supreme efforts as a patriot."[66] To him, the Allied victory, due primarily to France[67] with a little help from the United States,[68] represented the defeat of brute force, the triumph of good over evil. During the war he constituted himself an ardent agent of French propaganda, writing constantly, both to keep up French morale and to interest the United States in the conflict. The only hope for the future of the world lay, for him, in the complete and total crushing of Germany. Once the war was ended, he continued his polemical writing against that country, and there was no more vigorous supporter of the French policy of keeping Germany down.

Hanotaux had had extensive and close contact with the colonies during his office-holding days, and he believed wholeheartedly in the development of the French colonial empire not only because it was of benefit to France but because he felt that it

61. E.g., in *L'énergie française*, pp. 72–74.
62. *Ibid.*, p. 73.
63. *Ibid.*, p. 74.
64. Paris, 1903.
65. As, e.g., when he claimed that it was the Mediterranean tradition which won the war of 1914 for France and the Allies (*Histoire et historiens*, preface).
66. *Sur les chemins de l'histoire*, I, xxv.
67. *Poincaré*, pp. 20–21.
68. *Le secours américain en France* (Paris, 1915).

helped the countries where French influence spread. There was nothing mercenary in his attitude, for he was contemptuous of those who spoke in terms of money and wanted to know only how much the colonies cost and what they were worth.[69] For him, France had a world-task to perform: spreading the benefits of French language, customs, laws, and civilization as far as possible and creating new Frances wherever opportunities presented themselves.[70] He felt that this was a vital part of French tradition, a special role which Providence had assigned to France since the days of Julius Caesar.[71] As he personified France, he personified her colonies. "For peace, for war, internally, externally, for the present, for the future, colonies are to people as children are to families. A nation without a colony is a sterile power: all the praise and all the applause of history will go always to colonizing countries."[72]

He begrudged the loss of the French colonial empire in the eighteenth century, particularly in America, and always maintained a deep interest in the entire western hemisphere. He boasted of the strong French traditions which still persisted in sections of both Canada and the United States; and South America, he thought, possessed a close sympathy with France because of her Latin traditions.[73] Hanotaux was one of the moving figures and first president of the Comité France-Amérique established in 1909 to promote a cordial relationship between France and the Americas, particularly through educational means.[74]

In keeping with his ambition of inspiring the French people with descriptions of their glories, Hanotaux presented his ideas in books. L'affaire de Madagascar[75] and Fachoda,[76] covered events with which he had had actual experience. But these were

69. L'énergie française, pp. 292–95.
70. La fleur des histoires françaises, p. 128.
71. Histoire des colonies françaises, I, xlviii.
72. Sur les chemins de l'histoire, I, 296.
73. La politique de l'équilibre, p. 239.
74. Ibid., pp. 240–41. For a general summary of his interest in North America see his La France vivant en Amérique du Nord (Paris, 1913).
75. Paris, 1896.
76. Paris, 1909.

not enough. Publication of the impressive *Histoire des colonies françaises et de l'expansion de la France dans le monde,*[77] in six volumes, began in 1929 under his editorship, and the general introduction to this series gives us the best exposition of his ideas on colonial development.

Although Hanotaux was at his best in the fields of political and international relations, he came increasingly to feel that history concerned more than politics. He felt that earliest origins should be considered, as well as soil, climate, and the customs of daily life.[78] Religion and human passions were also vitally important.[79] In fact, it was really necessary to consider the ensemble of national and worldly accomplishment,[80] for only in that way could a complete picture of an age and a country be rendered. This interest led to the publication of his *Énergie française,* in 1903, and *La fleur des histoires françaises,* in 1911, both comprising sketches of various phases of French life from notes taken on his travels in the late nineties in the course of his research for his studies of Richelieu. The culmination of this idea came with the publication of the fifteen volumes of the *Histoire de la nation française,* for which he acted as editor, wrote the general introduction, and contributed the volume on nineteenth-century history. Although Hanotaux had conceived the idea and planned the collaboration in 1914, the war postponed publication until the twenties.

The study of geography always appealed to him, and he felt that French geography, particularly her location as a "crossroad" of European travel, had played an important part in the development of French history.[81]

The rise of interest in economic and social history did not leave him untouched. On one occasion he even stated that political

77. 6 vols.; Paris, 1929–33.
78. "Mon temps," *loc. cit.,* 8th period, XXXIII (May 15, 1936), 315; *Histoire de la nation française,* I, ii.
79. *Mon temps,* p. 317.
80. "Mon temps," *loc. cit.,* 8th period, XXXIX (Apr. 15, 1937), 778.
81. *La fleur des histoires françaises,* pp. 30, 47, 63; *L'énergie française,* p. 6. The first two volumes of the *Histoire de la nation française* treat of geography.

history is nothing other than economics,[82] but this is little more than lip service, for he never penetrated more deeply than generalization. In nearly all of his works he devoted sections to the life and customs of the time of which he writes. These are interesting and often valuable, but they are descriptions of local and national life rather than analyses of social and economic forces.

In his economic ideas he represented, as he did in politics, the best of the middle class. The bourgeoisie, he felt, were "the most enlightened and most sensitive part of the nation."[83] His youthful experiences as a witness of the last agonies of the Commune colored his ideas for life; the chief crime of the Communards to him lay in their platform of decentralization and their disruption of French unity in the face of the German occupation rather than in their social ideas.[84] He disliked socialism in all its forms[85] and Marxism in particular, for not only was the latter based on materialism, with which Hanotaux had little sympathy, but it bore the stigma of a German origin.

Hanotaux did not dislike the masses; on the contrary, he had great faith in them, but, as we have seen, he felt they needed rulers and control. These rulers should devote themselves to the welfare of all the people,[86] and society should do its utmost to create equality of opportunity.[87] He believed profoundly in the sanctity of private property, but he did not like parasites;[88] he felt that work was necessary to all,[89] and that all work was honorable. His book *Du choix d'une carrière* (1902), in which he describes the great variety of occupations possible in France, was addressed to French youths. Laws tending to ameliorate the conditions of the working class won his support as a parliamentarian

82. *Histoire et historiens,* p. 27; see also *Histoire de la France contemporaine,* III, 474.
83. *Histoire de la France contemporaine,* III, 76.
84. *Mon temps,* p. 182; *Histoire de la France contemporaine,* I, 157–59.
85. See his *La démocratie et le travail* (Paris, 1910), for his ideas on socialism.
86. *Poincaré,* pp. 89–90.
87. *La fleur des histoires françaises,* p. 292.
88. *Ibid.,* p. 270.
89. *Ibid.,* pp. 269–70, 293, 295; *L'énergie française,* p. 30.

and as a writer, for he felt that the laborer ought to receive a fair wage[90] and that no one ought to go hungry.[91]

In the field of education Hanotaux's ideas were modern. He believed in making it less formal and more vocational. Character, rather than an accumulation of useless knowledge, should be the aim of education; and life was a better teacher than books. "To know is a little thing; to will, to act, that is what matters. To give man this character, this certainty of judgment, and this power of decision which are everything in life, what is the best teacher? Books? No. Life itself."[92]

Religion and philosophy were closely associated for Hanotaux. His mother had followed the current bourgeois practice of being a good but not ardent Catholic.[93] Like most students of his time, he himself ignored the church after making his first communion and went through the gamut of all the nonreligious fashions which prevailed.[94] As a middle-aged man, however, he became affected by the religious revival in France and adopted an increasingly spiritual approach.

Catholicism was in keeping with his general philosophy. Its unity, language, and Mediterranean inheritance all appealed to him. France, of course, was also traditionally Catholic, the "eldest daughter of the church." He wrote no special book on religion; his *Jeanne d'Arc*[95] comes closest to it and was a vital factor in his religious development. Despite his interest in Catholicism, he was never intolerant and always definitely liberal in his religious views.

All this had an effect upon his historical writing in so far as his ideas on causation were concerned. He claimed that it was the enigma in history which attracted him,[96] but he made little contribution to its solution. His thinking in this direction was obscure and never carefully developed. He was essentially an ideal-

90. *La fleur des histoires françaises,* p. 293.
91. *Ibid.,* p. 295.
92. *Du choix d'une carrière,* p. 6 and *passim.*
93. *Mon temps,* p. 64.
94. *Ibid.,* p. 292.
95. Paris, 1911.
96. *Mon temps,* p. 231.

ist rather than a materialist in his philosophy; beyond that there was nothing concrete. The "soul" of what he was studying always interested him, whether he was working on a person,[97] an institution,[98] or a country.[99]

A few lines might be devoted to a consideration of *Jeanne d'Arc*, published in 1911, as a step in Hanotaux's development as a historian. He spent considerable time on this work, both in collecting material and in preparing it for the press. Its illustrations and format are admirable; that is more than can be said for the contents, for it represents some of its author's most ambiguous thinking and his most ambitious claims for his country and for the subject of his selection.

The problem of the source of Jeanne's inspiration interested him, and he proclaimed her as a combination of the human and divine approaching each other "in a mysterious collaboration to work in a common cause, the safety of France."[100] Her accomplishments were nothing short of marvelous! She saved France and the monarchy. She established the principle of freedom of belief and preserved the thought and culture of antiquity, of Catholicism, and of the Mediterranean countries (against the encroachments of Germanic Burgundy and England). She prevented the spread of the Reformation to France and prepared the way not only for the absolutist kings but for the Revolution. She was

> the "angel" of the Renaissance, the messenger of the new order, the "annunciatrix" of a freer and better humanity; her virtue, her patriotism, her religion, can be designated as purity, courage, and sacrifice. This is the teaching she leaves us. We are only at the dawn of the days which will see her mission accomplished without limit.[101]

97. Such as Richelieu, Jeanne d'Arc, Poincaré, etc.
98. "L'esprit de l'Académie," *Les quarante, 1635–1935: trois siècles de l'Académie française* (Paris, 1935), p. 33.
99. *L'énergie française*, p. 331; *Mon temps*, p. 340; *La fleur des histoires françaises, passim*. See also his description of France in 1614 in the last chapter of his *Histoire du cardinal de Richelieu*, Vol. I.
100. *Jeanne d'Arc*, p. 38.
101. *Ibid.*, pp. 420–21.

It is no wonder that one reviewer felt Hanotaux was heading toward the clouds;[102] and it is needless to say that this book, while popular in certain circles, added little to its author's prestige as a scientific historian.

Although he frequently wrote about individuals, and even went so far as to state that "explaining an epoch through its heroes is a task to which one can worthily devote one's entire life,"[103] and, again, that "without heroes there is no progress and no history,"[104] he had little of the concept of heroes as the determining factors of historical movements. He made those statements when he was writing about individuals; when he wrote more generally, it was to the people as a whole, he felt, that France owed her greatness.[105] He attributed more to Providence than to anything else. For example, he stated definitely that Jeanne d'Arc was sent by divine intervention to save France[106] and that Poincaré's leadership during the war of 1914 was the gift of Providence.[107] Frequently he was more vague, as when he stated that a country had the historians,[108] the generals, and the rulers that it deserved.[109] This can scarcely be called profound thinking.

Science interested Hanotaux, and he thought it important; but he felt that as a philosophical basis of life it was insufficient and inadequate.[110] History to him possessed the attributes of science in its methods of research and criticism of facts, in its attempt first to analyze and then to synthesize.[111] But "as a daughter of action, history reached heights that science did not know."[112]

Art in all its phases also interested Hanotaux. He was fond of

102. Charles Petit-Dutailler, *RH*, CX (May, 1912), 83.
103. *Mon temps*, p. 317.
104. *Histoire et historiens*, p. 35.
105. *La fleur des histoires françaises*, p. 269; *Histoire de la France contemporaine*, I, ix; *Joffre*, p. 6.
106. *Histoire des colonies*, I, xxvi.
107. *Poincaré*, pp. 26, 65.
108. *Histoire et historiens*, p. 48.
109. *Joffre*, p. 5.
110. See his article on "Monsieur Taine et Monsieur Pasteur," *Sur les chemins de l'histoire*, Vol. II, *passim*.
111. *Histoire et historiens*, p. 23.
112. *Ibid.*, p. 43.

architecture[113] and constantly extolled the French language and literature. He was particular about his books, choosing, when he had the opportunity, the type and paper and deciding the format himself.[114] He preferred to have his works illustrated and, when that was possible, selected the illustrators and subjects with great care.[115] His *Jeanne d'Arc, Histoire des colonies françaises, Histoire illustrée de la guerre de 1914,* and *Histoire de la nation française* are all profusely, interestingly, and even beautifully illustrated.

He felt that history was an art, because the story gave pleasure and aroused emotion. It attempted to attain beauty by an animated recital of events, harmony of proportions, clearness of deductions, descriptions of persons, and the illusion of life.[116] History should be well written, more than a literal copy of details, and selective like art, indicating significance by throwing important things into relief.[117]

But history is not an art alone; rather art is the instrument of history. The historian is a story-teller, but his stories are true.[118] Truth must always be the first law of history, he thought,[119] and he believed that he followed it implicitly. It is difficult, however, for a man with a thesis to be sure that he is following the truth, particularly when his thesis is based on patriotism acquired in adolescence through the unhappy experience of his country's conquest by a foreign power. He wanted to tell the truth, and he tried by the best means in his power, but the odds were against him.

The development of his historical thought naturally affected his historical method. Early in his career he made a great contribution to French historical writing by sharing with Albert

113. *L'énergie française,* pp. 77–80.
114. *Histoire et historiens,* preface; "Mon temps," *loc. cit.,* 8th period, XXXIX (May 1, 1937), 72.
115. *Jeanne d'Arc,* pp. ix–xi; *Histoire de la nation française,* Vol. I, introduction.
116. *Histoire et historiens,* pp. 13–14.
117. *La fleur des histoires françaises,* p. iii; *Histoire et historiens,* pp. 18–19.
118. *Histoire et historiens,* preface.
119. *Ibid.,* pp. 22, 43; *Sur les chemins de l'histoire,* I, 4.

Sorel, historian of the French Revolution, the privilege of being the first of the students allowed to enter and use the archives of the French foreign office.[120] Hanotaux considered this opening of the archives to be a "veritable revolution in the history of France."[121] It was an accomplishment befitting the Third Republic, giving the reality of the facts of the past back to the French people. In March, 1880, he became the secretary of the commission newly created to consider the means of communicating these documents to the public, and when the first volume of the analytical inventory appeared in 1882, his name was on the title-page. In 1888 he published the *Recueil des instructions données par les rois de France à leurs ambassadeurs près du Saint-Siège*, another task assigned to him by the commission on diplomatic archives. He worked with this group for more than fifty-five years. His volume of *Maximes d'état et fragments politiques du cardinal de Richelieu*, published in 1880, won universal praise as a work of scholarship.

It is not surprising, however, that this work of erudition, limiting itself to the publication of texts, did not suffice for him. He stated again and again that documents were the basis of all historical writing[122] but added that this did not mean the confusion of documentation with history; rather, it was the anatomical construction or skeleton of historical writing.[123] As a statesman himself, he knew how much was left out of written documents, and he believed that a dependence on them alone might easily result in false interpretation.[124] Dates, he thought, were insignificant except to establish a relationship between events.[125]

Hanotaux was conscientious by nature and had spared no pains to perfect his education, even taking a course at the Paris Conservatoire des Acteurs to get rid of his Picard accent and

120. *Mon temps,* p. 328; *Sur les chemins de l'histoire,* II, 294; "Mon temps," *loc. cit.,* 8th period, XXXIII (May 15, 1936), 318–19.
121. "Mon temps," *loc. cit.,* 8th period, XXXVIII (April 15, 1937), 782.
122. *Histoire et historiens,* p. 24; *Sur les chemins de l'histoire,* II, 240.
123. *Histoire et historiens,* p. 24.
124. *Histoire de la France contemporaine,* III, 61–62; *Histoire des colonies françaises,* I, xx.
125. *Histoire et historiens,* p. 31.

learn to speak pure French.[126] He knew Latin, Greek, German, English, and Italian but, like most of his countrymen, never cited a reference to a foreign book if a French translation existed. He knew the French archives and libraries intimately and studied occasionally in foreign countries. His studies on Richelieu are heavily documented, but the very concept of his later works meant the elimination of footnotes. His *L'énergie française*, he almost boasts, "has nothing scientific about it. Neither figures, nor tables, nor statistics; it says only what has appeared to me to be amiable in a country so worthy of being loved."[127]

The necessity of making an income from his historical writings was a problem which Hanotaux had to face from the beginning. He began writing historical sketches for newspapers early in his career, and his most common procedure was to write a series of articles on the subject on which he was working and later collect them in a book. Thus, a not inconsiderable part of his research on Richelieu, much of his work on Jeanne d'Arc, and most of the essential portions of his writings on contemporary events and historical criticism appeared first in current periodicals.[128] Gambetta's newspaper, the *République française*, was his earliest medium, but that gave way to others, particularly the *Revue des deux mondes*, for which he wrote during most of his active life.

As his interests broadened, he found his individual efforts at writing inadequate to cover the vast field of his curiosity and the message which he wished to give to all Frenchmen. He wrote voluminously and prolifically; but as he tried conscientiously to have some basis of research or experience at the foundation of all of his works, he could not do as much as he desired. To achieve his ends, he used secretaries and collaborators. He secured the help of the scholarly Duc de la Force for his third and fourth volumes on Richelieu and of Lieutenant-Colonel Fabry for his studies of the generals of the war of 1914.[129] Even these methods proved inadequate, and Hanotaux conceived the idea of com-

126. *Mon temps,* pp. 258–59.
127. *L'énergie française,* p. 5.
128. E.g., *La Politique de l'équilibre* was originally published in the *Revue hébdomadaire,* 1907–12; *Histoire et historiens,* in the *Revue des deux mondes,* 1914; etc.
129. I.e., *Joffre.*

pilations, whereby a large subject could be covered by dividing it into a number of volumes and the exigencies of research satisfied by assigning each volume or subject to an expert in that particular field. He used this method most successfully in the fifteen volumes of his *Histoire de la nation française,* which he felt developed "the complete meaning of his life as a historian."[130] He selected his collaborators with care and supervised their work closely. He demanded expert knowledge, but he also insisted upon a clear, interesting presentation and a good style.[131] Above all, he required that the men he chose agree with his ideals. The result of this is evident if the series is compared with the compilations of Ernest Lavisse.[132] The latter's work is more scholarly, but it is less readable, more valuable to the historian than to the general reader, and less broad in its scope. Lavisse was more interested in history for its own sake; Hanotaux considered his series a "task of national piety."[133]

History as a subject appealed to him. He discussed it frequently in all his works and devoted several books to the presentation of his ideas.[134] He considered that the greatest historians had lived in Greece and Rome.[135] His own debt to many modern historians he admitted; Fustel de Coulanges came closest, of all the nineteenth-century writers, to his ideal.[136] Contemporary historical writers of other countries were ignored.

Hanotaux's style is almost always interesting, often eloquent, and occasionally brilliant. His picture of Richelieu, already quoted,[137] is typical of his best work. The vigor and picturesqueness of his language is particularly effective for the kind of popu-

130. *Sur les chemins de l'histoire,* I, xv.
131. *Histoire de la nation française,* I, ix.
132. Ernest Lavisse, *Histoire de France depuis les origines jusqu'à la Révolution* (Paris, 1900–1911) and *Histoire de France contemporaine depuis la révolution jusqu'à la paix de 1919* (Paris, 1920–22).
133. *Histoire de la nation française,* I, ii.
134. *Histoire et historiens; Sur les chemins de l'histoire* (2 vols.); *Henri Martin, sa vie—ses œuvres—son temps, 1810–1883* (Paris, 1885); see also "Défense de l'histoire," *loc. cit.,* pp. 768–73.
135. *Histoire et historiens, passim.*
136. "Fustel de Coulanges," *Revue des deux mondes,* 7th period, XIV (Mar. 1, 1923), 34–56.
137. See above, pp. 100–101.

lar writing at which he aimed. He wrote appealingly and persuasively, particularly when he was discussing his work or his country.

> The professor raises future generations and transmits to them the gains of the past; the writer and the philosopher apply themselves to the soul, nourishing the sacred flame of idea, and exhaust themselves, seeking, in the shadows of the future, the beacon toward which humanity should direct its route.[138]

> [France] is a living person: her body is slender and well proportioned, her bearing supple, her face lights with a smile in which there is ecstasy; her glance is straight, high, and far. As the fairies in the tales of Perrault, she has, despite her age, the privilege of being always young. Through her smiling optimism, through the limpid vivacity of her thought, through the light which emanates from her, she radiates upon humanity.[139]

One is almost convinced.

Hanotaux could write with delicacy as well as with ardor. He used figures of speech effectively, and his wide vocabulary aided him in description in which he was particularly adept. "Sky, soil, water, fauna, and flora,—all these co-operate, harmonize, and adapt themselves to play the magnificent symphonies of nature which are the traditional renown of our provinces."[140] A munitions factory is described with as much sensitiveness and color as that used in depicting a French rural scene,[141] and the man who first developed water power was "the poet who baptized the new industrial force" which he called "white oil."[142] While his style was often flamboyant, it could be concise, even epigrammatic. "Do you understand what the expression 'My property' [*Mon bien*] means to [the peasant]? Work, honor, dignity, profit, savings, independence. . . . His property is liberty itself."[143]

As he grew older, he became more discursive and rambling,

138. *La fleur des histoires françaises,* p. 280.
139. *Ibid.,* p. 285.
140. *Ibid.,* p. 47.
141. *L'énergie française,* pp. 153–61.
142. *Ibid.,* p. 172.
143. "Mon temps," *loc. cit.,* 8th period, XXXIII (June 15, 1936), 812.

and the number of books he wrote and the breadth of the subjects he selected were conducive to repetition.

In appearance he was the scholar rather than the politician. He was tall and distinguished, with a high forehead, curly hair, and fine hands. His health, which was bad during his youth, left him always a little delicate. His mother, a good manager of the modest sum left her by her husband, came to Paris to live with her children while they went to school. She continued to make her home with the historian, exercising a considerable influence upon his life until her death at a ripe old age. She was a practical sort of person, never experiencing a thrill over the political honors accorded to her son and refusing to visit him at the foreign office during the four years he was in charge. She did attend his reception by the Academy, however, the only satisfaction his public career ever afforded her.[144] Hanotaux did not marry until late in life.

The historian was pleasant and unassuming in his manners, appealing personally to all who met him. He enjoyed society moderately but was naturally of a retiring disposition and had no great social ambitions. He was on familiar terms with most of the outstanding people of his day. Journeys on foot and bicycle were, with hunting, his favorite sports.[145]

Hanotaux was always particular about his personal surroundings. He was a bibliophile with a collection which reached over a third of a million books and included many notable items. He also collected autographs, documents, and reproductions of the Annunciation.[146] He tells us that when he was working on a book like *Richelieu* or *Jeanne d'Arc* he tried to surround himself with physical mementos of the life of the period he was studying.

Great honor was accorded to Hanotaux in France. Just before Gambetta's death, that statesman procured the young historian's nomination to the Legion of Honor for the first volume of the inventory of the foreign-office archives. The early volumes

144. *Mon temps,* pp. 62–63.
145. *Ibid.,* p. 282.
146. "Mon temps," *loc. cit.,* 8th period, XXXIX (May 1, 1937), 68, 72–73.

of *Richelieu* won for him, in 1896, the Gobert Prize, the highest honor bestowed by the French Academy, and his election into that institution itself the following year. Hanotaux was proud to identify himself with that group for the remainder of his life.

The unquestionable attainment of his earlier works assured re-viewing-space for all his later productions. Because of the defi-nitely personal nature of their ideas, however, the character of the review depended upon whether or not the reviewer's opinions coincided with those of the author. Thus the more scholarly re-views, such as the *Revue historique* and the *Revue des questions historiques,* were restrained and even skeptical, while the *Revue des deux mondes* was always full of praise and respect. The only significant article on Hanotaux's work is a very favorable one by Imbart de la Tour, a historian of the medieval period.[147]

In summary, Hanotaux's early contributions to history stand unchallenged. His later works are important for the vigor, elo-quence, and breadth of their ideas rather than for their originality or profundity. Some of them will long be read for the picture they give of French life and for their point of view, for they represent a close association with the conservative intellectual group of his time. They are more important, perhaps, as source material than as definitive historical writing.

Advancing age did not put a stop to Hanotaux's activity. De-spite frequent reiteration of an optimistic view of the future of France, there was an undercurrent of fear present in all his writ-ings. He protested a little too much. This fear came into the open with the outbreak of the war with Germany in September, 1939, when he was nearly eighty-six years old. His polemical writings against his old *bête noire,* published regularly in the *Illustration,* urging an economic federation for Europe and the moral supremacy of the pope as the only possible safeguards against the menace of Naziism, were stopped in the spring of 1940 only by the new German occupation of France.

147. Imbart de la Tour, "L'œuvre historique de M. Hanotaux," *Revue des deux mondes,* 7th period, XXIII (Sept. 1, 1924), 166–86.

# VI

## Karl Gotthard Lamprecht (1856–1915)

Annie M. Popper

Karl Gotthard Lamprecht was born in 1856 in Jessen, a small town near historic Wittenberg in the province of Saxony. His mother was of German and Wendish descent. She was a devoted wife and mother upon whom, however, the deeper conceptions of the world and of religion did not dawn until after Karl, her youngest son, had reached the age of manhood.

His father, of Kur-Saxon stock, was a Lutheran minister in Jessen, with the reputation of being an expert in biblical interpretation. He was a man of truly Christian spirit but was averse to all doctrinal discussions and controversies. He even refused to help clarify his son's conceptions when the latter found himself troubled with religious doubts. All the comfort he ever gave his son was to say that he considered all religious doubts as happy symptoms of the development of a stronger personality out of which they would also clarify themselves.[1]

Perhaps the example of his father's religious liberalism, combined with a truly pious spirit, later encouraged Lamprecht to pursue his historical and psychological studies regardless of the conclusions he might reach. There actually was a time when he was denounced as an atheist, though later even opponents de-

---

1. Most of the remarks on Lamprecht's childhood and his early environment are based on his *Kindheitserinnerungen* (Gotha, 1918).

clared this accusation unwarranted.[2] Moreover, Alfred Doren, an intimate friend of Lamprecht, recorded that in his "biblical faith"[3] Lamprecht found comfort again and again in the storms of his life. Like his father, Lamprecht avoided talking about controversial theological questions, and similarly he shunned partisan politics.[4]

Lamprecht seems to have resembled his father in more than one way. Like him, he became a man highly above the average, endowed with a versatile mind, a vivid imagination, tenacity of purpose, and an indestructible optimism. In his *Kindheitserinnerungen* he tells us how impressed he was by some of the strange tricks his imagination played upon his boyish mind, how he loved to watch nature closely and collect many of its treasures. He also speaks of his ever present urge to explore the country beyond the limits known to him. All these traits we find again in the man and his writings, but particularly the last one. Never was he satisfied with the knowledge gained; it merely served him as a gateway to new fields of exploration.

At the age of ten he entered the *Gymnasium* in Wittenberg. Three years later he was sent to the *Gymnasium* in Pforta (Schulpforta), famous for its discipline and thorough humanistic training. During his five years of education in Schulpforta, Lamprecht, like other great men before him, such as Ranke, received impressions which greatly influenced his later life. He once confessed that the seed for his principal work, his *Deutsche Geschichte,* had been planted in Schulpforta, where Rector Herbst, a historian, had opened his mind to the mutual relationship between individuals and their times.[5]

2. O. Hintze, "Über individualistische und kollektivistische Geschichtsauffassung," *HZ*, N.F., XLII (1897), 62.

3. Alfred Doren, "Karl Lamprechts Geschichtstheorie und die Kunstgeschichte," *Zeitschrift für ästhetische und allgemeine Kunstwissenschaft,* XI (1916), 386; cf. Rudolph Kötzschke, "Karl Lamprecht," *Deutsches bibliographisches Jahrbuch, 1914–1916,* p. 148.

4. It is easy, though, to detect passages in his writings and speeches betraying his Lutheran background and his nationalism and cultural imperialism nourished by the significant developments in Germany of which he was an eager eyewitness from 1866 to 1915.

5. As the first-fruit of his historical outlook, some notes may be considered

Lamprecht received his university training in Göttingen, Leipzig, and Munich (1874–79), where he studied history, political science, economics, and the history of art. Among his professors were J. Weizsäcker, E. Bernheim, E. V. Noorden, W. Arndt, and W. Roscher. Of these men, Bernheim and Roscher, the latter the head of the historical school of economics, fascinated him most. The influence of Roscher can be detected in Lamprecht's Ph.D. dissertation: *Beiträge zur Geschichte des französischen Wirtschaftslebens im elften Jahrhundert.*[6] Based on primary sources, it was intended by its author to be a contribution of *Kulturgeschichte,* thus foreshadowing the main interest of his later life.

The early death of his father, in 1879, obliged Lamprecht to earn his living. He therefore became a tutor in a well-known banker's family in Cologne and at the same time did his required years of practice teaching at the Friedrich Wilhelm Gymnasium. In 1881 he habilitated himself in Bonn, where he became professor extraordinarius in 1885. Five years later he accepted a call as professor in Marburg, and in 1891 he became a professor at the University of Leipzig, where he remained active to the end of his life in 1915.[7]

Lamprecht owed his freedom from financial cares in Bonn to the civic spirit of Gustav von Mevissen, leader of the Rhenish National-Liberal party. Mevissen, wishing to promote the intellectual life of his country by furnishing the means for historical research, engaged Lamprecht to work for him on Rhenish history for a period of three years. One of the early results of Lamprecht's activities was the publication of the *Westdeutsche Zeit-*

---

which he wrote as early as 1878, without any intention of publication at that time: "Über Individualität und Verständnis für dieselbe im deutschen Mittelalter," printed in his *Deutsche Geschichte* (1st and 2d eds.; Berlin, 1909), pp. 3–48.

6. Leipzig, 1878. Ten years later it was translated into French, which seems to speak well for the dissertation.

7. Lamprecht visited the United States in 1904 and gave lectures in St. Louis and New York which were published under the title *Moderne Geschichtswissenschaft* (Freiburg, 1905; English trans., *What is history?* [New York, 1905]). His impressions of the visit were recorded in *Americana: Reiseeindrücke, Betrachtungen, geschichtliche Gesamtansicht* (Freiburg, 1906).

*schrift für Geschichte und Kunst,*[8] to which he contributed numerous articles. The following year he founded the Gesellschaft für Rheinische Geschichtskunde, which became the very center for thorough research in Rhenish history and for the collection and publication of valuable primary sources.

As in Bonn, so throughout his later career, Lamprecht not only collaborated with existing learned societies, journals, etc., but also became the inspirer and even founder of various new ones. In Leipzig the Sächsische Kommission für Geschichte, which became the model for similar commissions in other parts of Germany, owed its origin to Lamprecht and enjoyed his active support from 1896 until his death. He also became editor of various collective works, such as Heeren-Uckert's *Geschichte der europäischen Staaten, Leipziger Studien aus dem Gebiet der Geschichte,* and various others.[9]

His organizing activities, much frowned upon by his opponents, found a large field at the University of Leipzig. There, in 1909, he became the founder of the independent Institut für Kultur- und Universalgeschichte, which was to breathe his very spirit and to remain his favorite creation. Later it was mainly he who inspired the founding of the Friedrich August Stiftung for the establishment of various institutions for research in intellectual sciences, though in matters of organization his suggestions were rejected by his colleagues.

In view of the active part Lamprecht had been taking in the agitation for a reform of the German universities, it goes without saying that he tried to introduce various innovations when he held the annual office of rector, 1910–11.[10] However, most of his suggestions were strongly opposed by his colleagues.[11]

8. Trier, 1882. This was a joint undertaking with another author (Hettner), who had already planned it; Lamprecht was an editor from 1882 to 1891.

9. See Rudolf Kötzschke, "Verzeichnis der Schriften Karl Lamprechts," *Berichte über die Verhandlungen der Königlich Sächsischen Gesellschaft der Wissenschaften zu Leipzig,* Philologisch Historische Klasse, LXVII (1915), 105–19.

10. See, e.g., his article "Zur Fortbildung unserer Universitäten," *Internationale Wochenschrift für Wissenschaft, Kunst und Technik,* Dec. 4, 1909.

11. During his rectorate he and President Butler of Columbia University

Lamprecht's capacity for work was astonishing. He was a prolific writer. His main work, the *Deutsche Geschichte*, finally comprised twenty-one volumes.[12] Not counting these or his collected works, Kötzschke lists one hundred and eighty of his writings.[13]

As early as 1885, while still in Bonn, Lamprecht published his *Deutsches Wirtschaftsleben im Mittelalter*.[14] It was a voluminous work on the development of the material culture of the country-side (*plattes Land*) of the Moselle region which was to serve as a preliminary study for his *Deutsche Geschichte*. Perhaps stimulated originally by Nitzsch's stress on economic factors in the shaping of constitutional developments in medieval Germany and France, Lamprecht's own investigations led him beyond Nitzsch. Lamprecht used his economic findings in his own way, to show the interdependency of seemingly unrelated phases of development in the history of his country. Winter praised this as a great achievement on the part of Lamprecht, attained by new means, namely, by applying the statistical method to his historical materials.[15] Instead of using each document only for the sake of its individual information, Lamprecht compared a great many documents on related events and transactions in order to arrive at the laws that might have governed them. Winter's enthusiasm for Lamprecht's *Deutsches Wirtschaftsleben im Mittelalter* apparently was not entirely shared by Lamprecht's professional col-

---

tried to bring about the establishment of an American-German exchange professorship at the University of Leipzig, such as there was already at the University of Berlin. Unfortunately, their efforts had only temporary success. (*Rektoratserinnerungen*, ed. Dr. Arthur Köhler [Gotha, 1917]).

12. *Deutsche Geschichte* (12 vols. in 16 parts; Berlin, 1891–1901); *Deutsche Geschichte zur jüngsten deutschen Vergangenheit* (2 vols. in 3 parts; Berlin, 1905–11); *Deutsche Geschichte der jüngsten Vergangenheit und Gegenwart* (2 vols.; Berlin, 1912–13). Before Lamprecht's death a third edition of most volumes was published, a fourth of some, and a fifth of the first.

13. This is the most complete bibliography of Lamprecht's writings available (Kötzschke, *loc. cit.*, pp. 139–49).

14. 3 vols.; Leipzig, 1885–86.

15. Georg Winter, "Die Begründung einer sozial-statistischen Methode in der deutschen Geschichtsschreibung durch Karl Lamprecht," *Zeitschrift für deutsche Kulturgeschichte*, N.F., I (1894), 196–219.

leagues. Particularly, the soundness of his theories about landlords was questioned. Certain parts of his work, they said, showed signs of hurried composition and too hasty conclusions. Schmoller, by no means blind then to Lamprecht's weaknesses and still less so later, admits that when reviewing the book in 1888 he had remarked, in all sincerity, that it had raised Lamprecht to the ranks of the older German agrarian historians, such as Hanssen, Maurer, Nitzsch, Arnold, Inama (Sternegg), Meitzen, and Schroeder.[16]

Although genuinely interested in economic questions, Lamprecht did not fail to turn with like eagerness to the investigation of the intellectual and spiritual forces in life and particularly to those of the imagination. An early fruit of such studies was *Die Initialornamentik des 8.–13. Jahrhunderts*.[17] To him the science of history (in the broadest sense of the word) was the science of the psychic changes[18] of the communities of man.[19]

With this conception of history forcing itself upon his mind more and more, Lamprecht wrote his *Deutsche Geschichte*, fully expecting sharp criticisms from the historians of the influential "political school." However, not until after the publication of the fourth and fifth volumes of his great work in 1891 and 1894 was a controversy opened that was to become most heated in the period from 1896 to 1900 and was not to abate entirely for nearly twenty years.

From a historiographical standpoint Lamprecht's publications during those stormy years are most revealing of all. Their great number makes it impossible, within the frame of this essay, to go into a detailed critical analysis of his views as they formed and transformed themselves during the progress of his work and the

16. Gustav von Schmoller, "Zur Würdigung von Karl Lamprecht," *Schmollers Jahrbuch für Gesetzgebung, Verwaltung u. Volkswirtschaft im Deutschen Reiche,* XL (1916), 1113. Schmoller was for years an intimate friend of Lamprecht, but later they became estranged; this obituary is impartial enough.

17. Leipzig, 1882.

18. This included economic factors, for Lamprecht thought any economic activity as much determined psychologically as any other "mental" activity (*Alte und neue Richtungen in der Geschichtswissenschaft* [Berlin, 1896], pp. 11, 17.

19. *Die kulturhistorische Methode* (Berlin, 1900), p. 15.

crossfire of the literary guns.[20] For our purposes it seems best to limit our attention to a selected few of his articles and to some passages in certain volumes of his *Deutsche Geschichte*. From the beginning of the controversy Lamprecht maintained that the differences between his historical approach and that of his opponents were indicative of still existing "contrasts" between the newer tendencies in the science of history and the older, between the collectivistic school of historians and the individualistic.[21] In fact, Lamprecht believed his time to have practically reached the turning-point in a movement the faint beginnings of which he ascribed to Herder, the originator of the concept of *Volksseele*.[22] Lamprecht hoped that his *Deutsche Geschichte* might help to strengthen the existing tendencies in that direction.[23]

Seen through Lamprecht's eyes, the main diversities between the newer school and the older may be reduced to a few essential points. Investigations of the older school are hemmed in by Ranke's "ideas," with their roots in metaphysics; those of the younger school can pursue freely the inductive method. The older school is prevailingly artistically descriptive and directed teleologically; the younger, genetic and causal. The former restricts its studies mainly to the leading individuals and their actions as reflected in the life of the state; the latter extends them to conditions as reflected in all phases of life of a given human group. The one is concerned with what is unique in history, the other with what is typical; thus one leads to political history (hero history) and the other to *Kulturgeschichte*. Since the latter

20. A bibliography of the polemical and methodological literature that had already appeared in connection with his *Deutsche Geschichte* by 1901 is to be found in the first volume of that work (2d ed., and 3d rev. ed.). It lists over a hundred contributions, including some from foreign publications.

21. "Was ist Kulturgeschichte?" *Deutsche Zeitschrift für Geschichtswissenschaft*, N.F., I (1896–97), 77. The writer feels justified in speaking henceforth of a collectivistic and an individualistic "school," though Lamprecht frequently uses the term *alte und neue Richtungen* ("old and new tendencies").

22. However, Bernheim and Lamprecht were the first German historians to consciously distinguish between individualistic and collectivistic historical writing. See Paul Barth, *Die Philosophie der Geschichte als Soziologie* (Leipzig, 1915), I, 502.

23. Vol. I (2d rev. ed., 1894), p. viii.

is mainly concerned with what is typical, it stands for a more scientific method; indeed, Lamprecht, as Comte had done before him, maintains that it alone can raise history to the rank of a genuine science.[24]

Lamprecht was convinced that history should be rewritten ever so often in order to reflect the prevailing *Zeitgeist*. In his own time he sensed a tendency not to content itself any longer with research for the sake of research. There appeared to be a demand for higher criteria for purposes of an analysis and an eventual synthesis of the uncountable phenomena of life.[25] Besides, like Buckle before him, Lamprecht was deeply impressed by the great progress the natural sciences had accomplished with their exact methods. He, too, felt that history had fallen behind and

24. Auguste Comte has been considered the founder of so-called "French positivism" through his work *Cours de philosophie positive*, the fourth volume of which (1839) contained the foundations of a scientific sociology and at the same time the fundamentals of his philosophy of history.

Bernheim regrets that Comte's thoughts for a long time became known to a wider public, particularly in Germany, only indirectly and frequently in a somewhat distorted reproduction, as, for instance, in Henry Thomas Buckle's *History of Civilization in England*. Moreover, Comte's views were spread through so many writers that, as in the case of Hegel, they were frequently adopted with no consciousness of their origin. See Ernst Bernheim, *Lehrbuch der historischen Methode und der Geschichtsphilosophie* (5th and 6th newly rev. and enl. ed.; Leipzig, 1908).

Perhaps this was true also with Lamprecht, who vigorously denied any dependence whatsoever on Comte and, as proof of this contention, published his private notes of the year 1878 (see above, n. 5).

Writers do not agree to this day whether Lamprecht was a positivist or not. Thus Rachfahl, Bernheim, and Spiess take the affirmative; Kötzschke, Doren, and Kuhnert, the negative. However, while Rachfahl speaks of positivism as "disguised materialism," Bernheim maintains that "Lamprecht is no more a materialist than Comte."

25. Hintze, *loc. cit.*, pp. 60–67, charges that the craving for a historical synthesis was in Lamprecht's own personality. Perhaps so, but this does not alter the fact that such a tendency was characteristic of his time. Alfred Doren (*loc. cit.*, p. 385) remarks as follows: "The aesthetic convention at Berlin, 1913, has revealed, perhaps surprisingly to many, how very deeply rooted a longing there is in the historically orientated sciences of art for critical methodological self-reflection on their own field of work and its limits . . . , the demand for simplification, synthesis, methodological clarification, pressing toward the last principles was distinctly discernible with the historians [of art] too. . . ."

should be raised to a genuine science by a study of the laws behind it. To Lamprecht it seemed a psychological necessity that the intellectual sciences should follow the lead of the natural sciences.

The thought of raising history to the rank of a science winds itself like a red thread through practically all of Lamprecht's discussions of historical theories and methods.[26] It is true, he emphasized again and again, that historical writing as such, because of its very nature, would always remain a piece of art,[27] but he maintained that this was equally true of any description of scientific phenomena.[28] Sciences, according to Lamprecht, are systems of judgments.[29] Like so many others in his day, he believed that the sciences focused their attention exclusively on what was typical, regular, determined by law. This assumption became of great significance for his historical thought.

> Working scientifically means to determine not what is singular but what is general, not to ascertain in things what separates them but what connects them; it means to grasp the endless world of the singular—for what exists in nature and history is singular—in general concepts and thus classifying, master it. This concept of science holds for history as well as for any other science.[30]

Lamprecht maintained that the "political" historical school could not fulfil the scientific prerequisite of a comparative method to detect what was "typical" in the historical phenomena because of the peculiar individualistic origin of their "ideas" and the important role as historical forces which they were ascribing

26. *Zwei Streitschriften den Herren H. Oncken, H. Delbrück, M. Lenz zugeeignet* (Berlin, 1897), p. 37; "Die historische Methodes des Herrn von Below," *Beigabe zur HZ*, LXXXII (1899), 48; *Die kulturhistoriche Methode,* pp. 27–30, 38. In the article mentioned last, Lamprecht suggests for the study of the cultural periods (see p. 19) the founding of a "historical ethnology,'" i.e., of a discipline taking the same place in its relation to historical writing as ethnography does to ethnology.

27. *Die kulturhistorische Methode,* pp. 6, 25, 29.

28. *Ibid.,* pp. 8, 29.

29. "Die historische Methode des Herrn von Below," *loc. cit.,* p. 15.

30. *Zwei Streitschriften den Herren H. Oncken, H. Delbrück, M. Lenz zugeeignet,* p. 37.

to them as disciples of Ranke.[31] Thus Lamprecht became the champion of *Kulturgeschichte*, as contrasted with "political history."[32] Since the days of Voltaire the term *Kulturgeschichte* has been interpreted in many different ways.[33] Lamprecht defined it as follows:

> *Kulturgeschichte* therefore is the comparative history of the factors of sociopsychic development; and its relation to the histories of language, economics, art, etc., is the same as that of other comparative sciences to those subordinated to them. It too, therefore, operates—of course with application to its peculiar material —with the specific methods of the comparative sciences: with inductive synthesis, comparisons, generalizations.[34]

Lamprecht emphasized that his history-of-civilization method was not determined by any particular Weltanschauung.[35] He did not think it a contradiction to this statement, however, to presuppose the application of the principle of causation to all phenomena of history.[36] In fact, he considered this the very strength of his system—if "system" it may be called.

Allegedly, Lamprecht had arrived at his history-of-civilization method purely empirically. While studying the source materials

31. *Die kulturhistorische Methode,* pp. 21–25. It should be noted here that in the course of time Lamprecht considerably modified both his interpretation and his evaluation of Ranke's historical concepts. One is temped to consider Lamprecht as the very personification of evolutionism; his philosophy of history never became static. Toward the end of his life he seems to have stood much closer to Ranke, perhaps closer than he himself realized (Emil J. Spiess, *Die Geschichtsphilosophie von Karl Lamprecht* [Erlangen, 1921], p. 17).

32. "Was ist Kulturgeschichte?" *loc. cit.,* p. 142.

33. Georg Steinhausen, "An den Leser," *Archiv für Kulturgeschichte,* VIII (1910), 1; Walter Goetz, "Geschichte und Kulturgeschichte," *ibid.,* p. 6.

34. "Was ist Kulturgeschichte?" *loc. cit.,* p. 145.

35. *Alte und neue Richtungen,* p. 8.

36. Lamprecht is occasionally guilty of a rather loose use of terms, such as "laws," "causality," etc. They occur with different meanings in his various writings. In one of his pamphlets he protested vigorously against the assumption that he had used the term "causality" in the sense of "absolute causality." He wished it to be understood that what he meant was "subjective causality," which was a necessity of our thinking due to the peculiar structure of our mind (psyche). ("Die historische Methode des Herrn von Below," *loc. cit.,* pp. 21–22.)

of German history, as well as those of church history of the tenth century, he was struck by the psychic distance, i.e., the difference between the psychic attitudes of men of those days and of his own. On the other hand, he was impressed by the great similarity of psychic tendencies in the two fields. Such a psychic homogeneity he discovered also in the realms of art, literature, manners, etc. In other words, he found a common dominant for that particular period. Thus he arrived empirically at a concept of *Kulturperiode* as an all-prevailing sociopsychic condition of a particular period, as a diapason that diffuses all psychic expressions and hence all historical phenomena.[37]

The concept of cultural periods itself was not new. Lamprecht remarked that it might be traced as far back as the end of the eighteenth century and that applications of it in historical writings might be found at least since the middle of the nineteenth century.[38] He frankly stated that he had adopted the term "age of individualism" for the corresponding period in German history from Jacob Burckhardt's *Kultur der Renaissance* and that a precedent for periodization had been established, too, by political economists. But he justly claimed originality for his finding of a uniform principle of orientation for all periods.[39] It was his pride that his *Deutsche Geschichte* was the first practical application of the so-called *kulturhistorische Methode,* for in it he had disposed almost of the entire subject material from the viewpoint of those sociopsychically determined cultural periods.[40]

37. *Die kulturhistorische Methode*, p. 26.
38. *Ibid.*, p. 31.
39. For details see *ibid.*, p. 21.
40. In the preface to the third edition of Vol. I of his *Deutsche Geschichte* (1902) Lamprecht makes the illuminating statement that he would now permit himself to indicate also in the outward appearance of the book (by respective subtitles) the sequence of those periods of psychic developments of the nation on the assumption of which he had already based the very first edition (1891). He had made one great exception to this, however. Although he had early acknowledged the principle that economic factors were psychic, the need of an enormous amount of preliminary work prevented him from applying it systematically until he wrote the supplementary Vol. II, *Zur jüngsten deutschen Vergangenheit* (1st ed.; Berlin, 1903). Lamprecht saw the "soul" of economic life in sensations of wants and the will to satisfy them. Cf. *Einführung in das historische Denken* (Leipzig, 1912), p. 105.

As indicated above,[41] to ascertain the characteristics of a cultural period Lamprecht endeavored to study various forms of expression of the human soul. He gave special attention to sociopsychic utterances of man's intellect, will, and feeling as reflected in language and sciences, in economic life, in law and morals, and in arts.[42]

Lamprecht stated that theoretically an analysis of all component sociopsychic factors of a cultural period would have to be made to arrive at sound conclusions. But this would obviously take more than a lifetime. In practice, at least for the present, this was made unnecessary by what he considered the legitimate device of applying the laws of physiological and psychic relations to the phenomena of history.[43] Just as according to Cuvier, we can determine the character of a whole skeleton from an examination of but a few of its parts, it would be possible in the field of human psychogenesis to gain not an entirely perfect, but nevertheless a first, view of the total course of the historical life of a period by a study of merely a selected few of the countless relations of its psychic phenomena.[44] Experience had taught Lamprecht to start an analysis of the psychic factors in the field of art.[45] The plastic arts, because of their three-dimensional nature, had proved even more revealing to him than paintings. When the "diapason" for a given period of art had been ascertained he

41. See above, p. 125.
42. "Was ist Kulturgeschichte?" *loc. cit.*, p. 118; cf. Spiess, pp. 146, 185.
43. Lamprecht based his law of psychic relations on Wundt's law of historical relations (Spiess, pp. 63–65).
For years Wundt was Lamprecht's main authority as to psychological theories. Later he was also influenced by those of Theodor Lipps. But when Lamprecht applied their principles, he frequently did this in such a sweeping fashion that the philosophers themselves could not follow him. "But as a psychologist," writes Wundt, "he went his own way. . . . The psychology in which he lived simply was not one which seeks to explain connections between psychic phenomena through an analysis of them but it was the intuitive psychology of the artist . . ." (Wilhelm Wundt und Max Klinger, *Karl Lamprecht* [Leipzig: S. Hirzel, 1915], p. 17). See also Adolf Kuhnert, *Der Streit um die geschichtswissenschaftlichen Theorien Karl Lamprechts,* inaugural dissertation, Universität Erlangen (Gütersloh, 1906), p. 13.
44. *Einführung in das historische Denken,* p. 70.
45. *Ibid.,* p. 127.

would search for a similar dominant in the other realms of human imagination. The outcome of his investigations was, according to his own statement, that all the factors involved could easily be subsumed under the specific periods realized through a study of the evolution of art. They appeared to form a psychic unit.[46] After further research Lamprecht finally convinced himself of the existence of five main cultural periods in German history, each governed by its peculiar "diapason":[47]

1. Symbolism: early historical days
2. "Typism": early middle ages
3. Conventionalism: late middle ages
4. Individualism: modern times
5. Subjectivism: more recent days, approximately since the eighteenth century[48]

Correspondingly, he found the following economic states in German history:

1. Primitive economy: *occupatorische Wirtschaft*
2. Natural economy, collectivistic: the community of the mark
3. Natural economy, individualistic: landlordism
4. Money economy, collectivistic: guilds, etc.
5. Money economy, individualistic: capitalism

He deliberately chose connotations for the great cultural periods broad enough to serve as highest concepts to which all psychic developments of human communities of a given period could be subordinated—hence all historic phenomena.[49]

A study of the history of other nations led Lamprecht to find evidence of cultural periods similar to those listed above for Germany. He maintained that they could be proved, too, by the application of the logic of statistics based on calculations of prob-

46. *Ibid.*, pp. 71–72, 127–30; see above, p. 129.
47. "Was ist Kulturgeschichte?" *loc. cit.*, p. 129; *Einführung in das historische Denken*, p. 310. A brief survey of their evidence in German history may be found in *Moderne Geschichtswissenschaft*, pp. 22–50.
48. At the end of the nineteenth century Lamprecht became conscious of the dawning of a second period of subjectivism (*Deutsche Geschichte der jüngsten Vergangenheit und Gegenwart*, I, iv). A table of the characteristics of each period is given by Spiess, pp. 166–67.
49. See *Die kulturhistorische Methode*, pp. 28–29.

ability and the law of great numbers. While the periods there-fore did not partake of the nature of an absolute law, they were of "the eminent heuristic value of any statistical rule."[50]

Lamprecht admitted that some psychic factors appeared to be stronger in one cultural period than in another and that it was impossible to separate the periods with any chronological preciseness.

As the underlying principle common to all sociopsychic, as well as to all individual-psychic, life, Lamprecht detected a tend-ency toward an increasing psychic intensity, expressing itself in a growing differentiation in every field of psychic development, in a movement from a stage of bondage of the soul to greater and greater freedom. Thus, money economy was a more intensive form of economic life than the natural economy of the preceding period. Painting in the age of individualism was more intensive than in that of conventionalism.

Lamprecht tried to prove the correctness of his findings by the application of the principle of the creative synthesis, by Wundt's law of psychic resultants, about as follows: A chord is not just the sum of the individual tones of which it is composed but is something qualitatively new. Similarly, if a majority of people feels, conceives, and wills the same, their common feelings, con-cepts, and volitions are not identical with the mere sum of the in-dividual factors involved. Owing to an immanent psychic causal-ity, there has been created an element of a qualitatively different nature which finds expression as public opinion, patriotism, etc. If, therefore, numerous sociopsychic factors exist side by side, each with a continuous effect—as they do in any normal course of historical development—these must keep the surplus of psychic energy increasing; hence the historical life must be evolving into ever increasing intensity (psychic differentiation).[51]

Thus Lamprecht believed he had found the causal connection between his cultural periods. To confirm this theory he cited two

50. "Was ist Kulturgeschichte?" *loc. cit.*, pp. 133–35.
51. *Ibid.*, pp. 94, 114–32.

other laws taken from the realm of individual psychology and applied by him to the sociopsychic phenomena.[52]

In the first place, no concept (*Vorstellung*) can entirely disappear: it must continue to be effective. Therefore, the living concepts of one generation can never become extinguished; they must, consciously or unconsciously, influence succeeding generations.

In the second place, all psychic life is change, acquiring of new contents, in the case of the individual as well as the group. The new contents cannot gain exclusive mastery because of the persistence of the old. The necessary result is a synthesis of the old and the new.[53]

The psychic processes that eventually bring a new cultural period into being have been described by Lamprecht at great length.[54] He based his "psychic mechanic of transitions" mainly on Lipp's psychology. Lamprecht distinguished, as in cases of individuals, the following psychic phenomena of transition in the normal course of human communities: strong new stimuli, coming from without or from within,[55] penetrate the psychic life of contemporaries, or at least of their leading portion,[56] and cause a sort of a psychic storm during which the old dominant is destroyed; a new naturalism is gained, which is finally replaced by

52. According to Lamprecht, the law of psychic resultants applies to the sociopsychic factors gained from the past (*das Gewordene*), just as it does to those of the present (*Das im Werden Begriffene*). Thus Lamprecht claimed to have ascertained sociopsychic causality for those factors, too, and to have proved that all so-called "conditions" (*Zustände*), apart from the natural factors, such as climate, etc. (and even they were not absolutely static), were psychic mass phenomena, hence creative forces, mightier than the strongest influence of any individual historical personality. This served him at the same time as another argument in favor of the collectivistic historical method ("Was ist Kulturgeschichte?" *loc. cit.*, pp. 109–15; also *Zwei Streitschriften den Herren H. Oncken, H. Delbrück, M. Lenz zugeeignet*, pp. 50–51).

53. *Die kulturhistorische Methode*, p. 28.

54. *Moderne Geschichtswissenschaft*, pp. 76, 80–88; *Einführung in das historische Denken*, pp. 42–46, 146–49.

55. Lamprecht held that they appeared very frequently in connection with economic and social life (*ibid.*, pp. 46, 145).

56. "Was ist Kulturgeschichte?" *loc. cit.*, p. 138.

the victorious new dominant in an unprecedented climax of idealism; this stage is followed by a rationalization of the dominant, ending in a period of decadence until new stimuli appear and start the whole series of processes anew.[57]

Lamprecht explained that not every single psychic phenomenon of one period of transition in German history would be found in the others, and still less so in those of other countries. Great similarities, but not identities, were to be expected. The same was true of the great cultural periods themselves. Their applicability to the course of any normal national history could be considered as having been empirically proved.[58] Yet the boundary lines might have to be changed here and there after further investigation. Moreover, only a universal history, i.e., a comparison of the cultural developments of a greater number of nations—in principle, of all great communities—could ascertain whether certain factors, now considered typical, were not, in reality, merely characteristic of Germany or the Germanic nations.[59] He frankly admitted that, seen from this angle, his cultural periods had only tentative validity. However, before they could be determined with any claim to finality many a problem would have to be solved that had hardly been touched yet. Among others, he mentioned questions regarding the psychic scope (*Seelenweite*) and the rules, if not laws, behind the transmissions of cultures in the various forms of renaissances ( revivals of past cultures) and of receptions (influences of one contemporary culture upon another).[60]

---

57. One of Lamprecht's illustrations in German history: from 1750 to 1870, first period of subjectivism; since about 1850, owing to new and strong stimuli largely connected with the economic and social life, elements of disintegration; this stage of *"Reizsamkeit"* ( "neurosis") leading to new naturalism in the seventies and eighties. During the nineties slight indications of the newly arising idealism, ripening into full evidence in the first decades of the twentieth century. This psychic scheme Lamprecht used as the foundation for his *Deutsche Geschichte der jüngsten Vergangenheit und Gegenwart*. See also *Einführung in das historische Denken*, pp. 42–51; for the development of historical concepts ( "historical sense") during the periods of subjectivism see *ibid.*, pp. 42–45.
58. See above, p. 131.
59. *Moderne Geschichtswissenschaft*, pp. 87–88.
60. *Einführung in das historische Denken*, pp. 160–62.

Practically nothing could be said, as yet, about the factors determining national decadence. For the present he gave a rather interesting warning against mistaking temporary nervous and psychopathic symptoms for signs of national decline, for they might reveal themselves later as nothing but psychic growing-pains.[61]

While in principle it would take generations to do the necessary comparative research work to arrive at a universal history, in practice he hoped he might accomplish this task himself, in a tentative form, with the aid of his history of civilization method, i.e., with the short cuts already discussed. At one time he was even optimistic enough to think it possible, theoretically at least, that after the necessary research of generations historians might be able to take the last step and arrive at a history of mankind which he considered as the ultimate end of the science of history. Later, however, he saw obstacles that seemed insurmountable even to him, and he confessed his belief that the last origin of historical development would probably forever remain unfathomable to the human mind.[62]

Let us pause here and restate briefly Lamprecht's fundamental viewpoints as discernible from his writings and, within the necessary limits, from our presentation above. Lamprecht assigned to history a task similar to that which Comte and Wundt ascribed to philosophy.[63] It is not surprising, therefore, that Lamprecht's philosophy of history and his Weltanschauung coalesced. They might be expressed as follows: Mind and nature are one.[64] History is human psychogenesis. The sociopsychic forces are stronger than the individual ones; hence they determine the course of history to a greater extent. Among all psychic stimuli, the economic ones seem to play not an exclusive but a most prominent role.

61. As an example in the past he mentions Germany's periods of sentimentality and of *Sturm und Drang* (*ibid.*, pp. 138–39).

62. "Was ist Kulturgeschichte?" *loc., cit.*, p. 137; Doren, "Karl Lamprechts Geschichtstheorie und die Kunstgeschichte," *loc. cit.*, p. 78.

63. The task of joining the last generalizations of all sciences into a well-ordered harmonious whole (Spiess, p. 85).

64. Cf. Spiess, p. 51. Kuhnert (p. 12) draws attention to similarity with Herder's thought.

All historic phenomena are subject to causality—at least they appear so to the human mind. They are in a constant evolutionary flux.[65] All being is at bottom a becoming, the ultimate origin of which is beyond the scope of history; in fact, beyond the reach of the human mind, it will remain "God's Secret."

A summary of Lamprecht's essential views on historical methodology, like that just given of his philosophical thought, might be useful here. He proposed to raise history to the level of a science. The historian should approach his materials without any preconceived metaphysical concepts. For the ascertainment of any laws that might govern the historical forces he recommended his history-of-civilization method. The latter emphasized factors typical rather than individual, applied biological and psychological laws to the sociopsychic phenomena of history, and purported to follow closely the scientific devices of induction, isolation, comparison, analogy, classification, statistics, and hypothesis.

Innovations of Lamprecht, or at least partly such, were: his isolation of the artistic elements as a starting-point for an analysis of a cultural period of a nation, the choice of a uniform principle —the growing sociopsychic intensity—for the distinction of cultural periods, the contention of their inwardly determined chronological order, the claim of their general validity, not to speak of the application of his scheme to his voluminous *Deutsche Geschichte*.

While even most of his antagonists have given Lamprecht credit on some score, it seems no exaggeration to say that almost every one of his propounded views has been weighed and found wanting by one historian or another. Because of limits of space only a few particularly relevant criticisms will be added to those already made or mentioned in passing. Bernheim attacks the narrow definitions of science with which Lamprecht justifies his

65. "And how much time has entered into eternity since man's first attempts, with hesitating steps, to pass from stimulus and association to the beginnings of that tremendously complicated process which enters into the simplest conclusions of our thinking today" (*Moderne Geschichtswissenschaft*, p. 120).

one-sided collectivism.[66] What Lamprecht sometimes characterizes as individual, as irrational, and therefore as an object of
artistic but not of scientific perception[67] is, for Bernheim, the very
factor ("the differentiating plus") which determines a development.[68] He admits that the latter is unpredictable, but he refers
to the fact that after it has come into being it can be explained by
regressive analysis on the basis of the laws of psychic and physical
causation involved.[69]

Worth mentioning also are observations made by Eulenburg,
one of Lamprecht's most objective and, at the same time, penetrating critics. He remarks that the history of the Jews shows
that artistic ability does not always hold pace with that in other
fields. Even so, he does not actually object to Lamprecht's starting with an examination of the elements of arts in order to facili-
tate an analysis of the cultural factors involved. What he criticizes most is Lamprecht's shifting from this original basis when
he justifies the choice of his point of departure with the contention
that the very flowers[70] of a civilization should be taken as criteria

66. Many passages in Lamprecht's articles undoubtedly confirm the
weakness referred to by Bernheim, while others do not convey this impression. In theory Lamprecht overstressed his point in order to show the difference between the individualistic and collectivistic tendencies and to bring
about a shift of emphasis. He pronounced himself to be neither a pure
individualist nor a pure collectivist but a universalist, i.e., one who combines
the methods of the two. He maintained that the universalist did not under-
estimate the importance of the genius but considered also "the many," who,
because of the power of their historical effects, after all domineered over
the genius. The moral value of the latter should, in principle, not be estimated differently from that of any other person ("Der Ausgang des geschichtswissenschaftlichen Kampfes," *Die Zukunft*, XX [July 31, 1897], p.
207; "Ältere und neuere Richtungen in der Geschichtsschreibung," *Deutsche
Zeitschrift für Geschichtswissenschaft*, N.F., II [1897–98], p. 125; cf.
*Moderne Geschichtswissenschaft*, pp. 117–18.

67. "Die historische Methode des Herrn von Below," *loc. cit.*, p. 17.

68. Bernheim, pp. 115–17, 154.

69. Like Wundt and Bernheim, Lamprecht himself emphasizes that in
history no results can ever be predicted, because like causes do not necessarily have like results according to the law of contrasts. ("Was ist Kulturgeschichte?" *loc. cit.*, pp. 14–95).

70. *Moderne Geschichtswissenschaft*, p. 119. It might be mentioned that
Lamprecht thought that an examination of the flowers of a civilization would
enable the historian to distinguish also its roots.

for its nature.[71] Eulenburg points out that expressions of the human imagination thus become a standard of values with Lamprecht and are ranked above those of the intellect. It means that in the last analysis he answers the question, "How can a scientific universal history be established?" with an aesthetic evaluation.[72]

Like other critics, Eulenburg rejects Lamprecht's analogies between the psychic attitudes of the individual and those of the group (nation).[73] He takes the stand that there is an essential difference between the individual soul, tied to a biological unit which fulfils certain physical and psychic functions, and the "social soul," not connected with a real substratum, neither with the nation nor with any other. According to him, it is merely an auxiliary concept, artificially created, and therefore without a sociopsychic development. Nor is the nation a biological unit, sharply separated from other nations as one individual is from another. Similarly, he judges Lamprecht's analogy between the stages of development of an individual and the various cultural periods of a nation as untenable, as a comparison between two incommensurable factors—between the individual that has a reality and the cultural periods that have none—are but concepts. Hence Eulenburg holds that a proof for a succession of cultural periods determined by necessity has not been produced. In fact, Eulenburg ends with the contention that the law of increasing psychic differentiation (Lamprecht's sociopsychic mechanic) is, in reality, not a specific psychic law but a general biological one,

71. For further inconsistencies involved see Franz Eulenburg, "Neuere Geschichtsphilosophie," *Archiv für Sozialwissenschaft*, N.F., XXV (1907), 135.

72. *Ibid.*, pp. 334–35. Eulenburg draws attention to two earlier attempts of using aesthetic standards, the one for philosophy by Zorschammer (*Imagination as fundamental principle of the world process*) and the other for history by Moritz Carrière (*Art in connection with the development of civilization*).

73. Lamprecht considered a nation the most regular of human communities. As one of the exceptions he named the United States, because her nationhood began with people already possessed of a high civilization (*Moderne Geschichtswissenschaft*, pp. 87–88; *Die kulturhistorische Methode*, p. 27). Since nations do not live in isolation and Lamprecht himself attached importance to their mutual influence, it is difficult to conceive of a "normal nation." See also Bernheim, p. 116.

in accordance with Spencer's principle of the "change from an incoherent homogeneity to a coherent heterogeneity."[74]

So far we have directed our attention to Lamprecht's theories rather than to his practices in historical research and writing. Only a few comments on these will be necessary, since various reviews of individual volumes of Lamprecht's *Deutsche Geschichte* are available.[75] These contain both high praises and severe criticisms, the latter coming chiefly from German scholars.[76]

It may be said that Lamprecht did not—and perhaps could not—come up to modern standards of historical research because of the immense range of the task he had set for himself. It was because of this circumstance that he avowedly availed himself, for the time being, of secondary sources on a larger scale than otherwise justifiable. However, he often used them without sufficient discrimination, which caused specialists in the field to discover numerous mistakes taken over from unreliable sources.

As mentioned before, Lamprecht also became guilty of applying analogies and drawing conclusions without a proper basis for them;[77] of ignoring certain factors as irrelevant that did not fit into his history-of-civilization scheme; and of insufficient restraint of his imagination in cases of missing links.[78]

Lenz's accusations of plagiarism were disproved by Lamprecht. The latter might have saved himself some insinuations of this kind if he had used more footnotes with references to specific

74. *Loc. cit.*, pp. 320, 332–37; for relations between Lamprecht's thought and Spencer's see also Spiess, p. 39.

75. They may be found in the leading periodicals, magazines, etc., professional and popular, of Germany as well as of English- and French-speaking countries. For English-speaking readers who have no access to the German literature on Lamprecht, the following references to *AHR* may prove useful: E. W. Dow, "Features of the new history apropos of Lamprecht's *Deutsche Geschichte*," III (1898), 431–48; reviews of individual volumes by W. E. Dodd, VII (1902), 789–91; IX (1904), 394–97; and Camillo von Klenze, XII (1907), 633–36.

76. For a long time he was more appreciated abroad than among scholars in Germany. He received honorary degrees from Columbia University in New York (1904), St. Andrews University in Edinburgh (1911), and the University in Kristiania (1911).

77. See above, p. 138.

78. Spiess, p. 21.

authorities and had not restricted himself to such a great extent to rather general bibliographical acknowledgments.

When Lamprecht plagiarized, he did it unwittingly, perhaps as a result of careless note-taking, as Schmoller suggests, or because he assimilated thoughts of others so readily and later presented them as his own, unconscious of their real origin.

Spiess criticises Lamprecht for giving broad space to some cultural phases—economics and arts—but comparatively little to others—religion, morals, and sciences. He proves his point with a reference to the striking lack of balance in the first volume of Lamprecht's *Zur jüngsten deutschen Vergangenheit*.[79] Yet it would be an error to assume this weakness to be evident throughout his voluminous work to any such extent. We know that Lamprecht himself regretted that no more preliminary studies of moral forces had been available. To religion he ascribed great importance in German history well into the modern period, but he believed it to have lost some of its driving-power in the twentieth century.

When the shortcomings alluded to above, and others, were revealed in often lengthy reviews Lamprecht usually made light of them. When his opponents had used insulting language he would occasionally answer in like coin. He repeated again and again that all criticisms of detail missed the real issue, that because of the scope of his task his work was more of the nature of a first draft and should not be expected to have been written with the exactness of a little monograph.

Nevertheless, there was little excuse for as many inaccuracies regarding facts, dates, etc., as have been found, for instance, in Lamprecht's account of the peasant revolt of 1525, in his *Deutsche Geschichte*, Volume V.[80] Also, his style showed signs of too hurried composition. Certain passages ought to have been

79. *Ibid.*, p. 173.
80. Max Lenz published an unusually detailed review of this volume in *HZ*, N.F., XLI (1896), 358–477, but it was far from impartial, for Lenz was one of Lamprecht's bitterest opponents and wrote the article with the avowed aim of ruining Lamprecht's reputation as a historian.

polished, and numerous clumsy and vague terms might have been avoided. On the whole, though, his language was rather fluent and powerful. Lamprecht availed himself amply of rhetorical aids, such as contrasts, satires, etc. His *Deutsche Geschichte* was not written in the usual scholarly form, and he was therefore sharply criticized. Yet he succeeded in arousing the historical interest of the educated middle class,[81] and no work of his critics ever reached the large number of readers that were fascinated by Lamprecht's *Deutsche Geschichte* and his historical articles. Contemporary historians, such as Lenz and Bernheim, began to speak in all seriousness of a Lamprecht "danger."

Although Lamprecht did not found a school and deservedly received many criticisms during his lifetime and later, he seems entitled to a place in German historiography. The broad historical interest he succeeded in kindling among his devoted students, many of whom have made a name for themselves and show his influence in their writings, has often been attested even by his enemies. As a merit, too, it may be considered that Lamprecht's writings were largely the expression of the age in which he lived. With some exaggeration,[82] it is true, Kuhnert remarks of him: "We value him because he has turned the full illuminating power of our own time upon the past and has thereby restored to history its soul."[83]

To us, most credit seems due to Lamprecht for having deliberately caused a controversy among historians which roused many of them from a tendency toward self-complacency and decadence to a careful reexamination of their own historical tenets. Al-

81. Schmoller, *loc. cit.*, pp. 1124–27, 1137, admits that the great success of Lamprecht's *Deutsche Geschichte* rested, after all, primarily on its intrinsic merits. Of Vol. V, Schmoller writes: "I do not feel competent to judge the greater part of its contents . . . but I wish to emphasize how much I admire this volume. There is not another German economist or historian who could write it. The amount of his knowledge of art and literature is amazing."

82. Even so, there is some truth in Kuhnert's statement, and it may partly explain the unusual appeal Lamprecht's writings had to the public at large.

83. P. 50; cf. Schmoller, *loc. cit.*, p. 1137.

though many of Lamprecht's views have been rejected, the cultural factors of history, as well as mass phenomena, have received far more attention ever since than they would have been accorded—at least in Germany—without him.[84] In the last analysis, his merit rests perhaps less with his writings as such than with their challenging force.

84. Cf. Bernheim, p. 717; see also Walter Götz, "Geschichte und Kulturgeschichte," *Archiv für Kulturgeschichte*, VIII (1910), pp. 4–5.

# VII

## Ernest Lavisse (1842–1922)

Donald F. Lach

Ernest Lavisse was born in the small northern French village of Nouvion en Thiérache in December, 1842. In his later years he recalled most clearly his summers at home: the green fields and sloping hills stretching far around the town and encompassing it in the quiet noises of the countryside. He recalled the thrifty farmers, their industrious wives, and the lonely chapel bell which called them home at the first long shadows of evening.[1] His memories were not of domestic hardship. The father, a small merchant, managed to provide well and to give his oldest son the advantages of education which he himself had never had. Of his mother, Lavisse remembered but little, except that she was a sturdy peasant by origin and that she always remained a little in awe of the son whom she had borne and could not understand. In recalling his father Lavisse recollected best the kind modulation but firmness of his tone. It was a voice which brooked no disobedience but rewarded with kindly encouragement.

His father's teachings were supplemented by the historical recollections of his grandmother. He sat on her knee while she told of Napoleon's campaigns and of "Brother Theodore," who never returned from Russia; and then he shivered as she described the horrors brought to France by the Cossacks and by invasion.[2] She vaguely remembered Robespierre and had even

1. *Souvenirs* (Paris, 1912), pp. 1–8.
2. *Ibid.*, pp. 103–6.

heard tell of Danton, and she believed they were wicked men, not brave and gentle like the emperor.

From his grandmother's history lessons he rapidly moved on to the village school, where Father Matton taught all subjects. There he read, learned to write and to figure. Six times nine was torture until it was learned; nine times six was even worse. Father Matton was kind but strict, even excessively so. The child liked especially the saints' holidays and religious pageants, but he definitely could not understand the logic of the Old Testament, although he enjoyed the many battles, and the story of Samson was always an attraction.

Then shortly after his tenth birthday he was required to put aside his friends and playmates at Nouvion and go off to Laon, where the ambitious father felt his son might receive more adequate instruction in the *collège*.[3] Despite his first fears, Lavisse later recognized these as his happiest years. Many of his teachers he only vaguely remembered, while insignificant incidents remained in his memory as milestones. These years of apprenticeship gave him the necessary techniques for further study. Here he learned Latin and Greek, the teaching of which he later defended. Not only did he study foreign tongues, but for the first time he learned to be at home in his own. For practice in style he described the beautiful forest of Nouvion, using the masters as background for his work. He learned to appreciate Lamartine and to take pride in the intellectual heritage of his country. The "battle stage" in his historical studies was extinguished here, never to be revived again.

After three years' stay at the *collège* Lavisse left for Paris, in October, 1855, where he entered the Lycée Charlemagne.[4] At this institution he had men as teachers who were prominent figures in the life of Paris, and certain of the students were sons of eminent Frenchmen, among whom Albert Duruy was outstanding. History was a *spécialité* to both Duruy and Lavisse. The latter chose for himself the field of history, since it was a pleasure for him

3. Cf. *ibid.*, pp. 129–78, for a complete account of his life at the *collège* of Laon.
4. Cf. *ibid.*, pp. 179–230.

"to see men act and to hear them speak and to watch life move along." Michelet was his great master. The introduction to Michelet's *Universal history* appealed to the young student as "a poem of humanity." He admired in Michelet "the gift of reliving life with the vision of a poet and of expressing in the words of a poet the feelings of sorrow, hate, and love."

With his mind made up, young Lavisse left the *lycée*, in November, 1862, and enrolled in the École Normale Supérieure. After three years' study at this institution, he was appointed a fellow in history and at the same time renewed his connections with Albert Duruy. In the Latin quarter he met certain radical students like Gambetta and Clemenceau, and he himself became a Romantic in literature and a Republican in politics. This strain of radicalism did not last long. By the end-years of the sixties he was once more a good Bonapartist. He had used to good advantage his friendship with Albert Duruy, the son of Victor Duruy, Napoleon III's minister of education. In 1868 Lavisse was recalled from Nancy, where the year before he had accepted a position, to assume the post of secretary to Victor Duruy.[5]

Through his connections with Duruy he became interested in the minister's designs for revamping the French educational system. Shortly thereafter, however, he was appointed as private tutor to the Prince Imperial, the future Napoleon IV, even as Michelet had tutored the son of Louis Philippe. His teaching days were cut short by the war of 1870, but he maintained a steady stream of correspondence with the prince until 1878, meanwhile remaining an active and even a belligerent Bonapartist.[6] He chided the *Journal de l'Aisne*, his departmental newspaper, for expressing Republican sympathies and did not hesitate to advance by devious means the cause of his erstwhile student.

Not only did the war of 1870 throw Lavisse out of a job, but it created in him a realization that there must be some basis for Germany's victory. Fitting action to the thought, he left for Ger-

5. *Un ministre, Victor Duruy* (Paris, 1895).
6. Cf. Charles L. d'Espinay de Briort, "Une correspondance inédite: le prince impérial et Ernest Lavisse, 1871–79," *Revue des deux mondes*, 8th period, L (1929), 55–91.

many to study with Waitz and other Germans of the Ranke school. From 1873 to 1875 he observed carefully the diverse features of the German educational system in Berlin and concluded that it was from these splendid organizations that Germany derived amazing technical and intellectual progress. He also wrote articles for the *Revue des deux mondes* on such contemporary topics as the Reichstag, the German workers' movement, and the Hohenzollern family.[7]

His more profound researches were in the medieval and early modern history of Brandenburg and Prussia. After his doctoral dissertation, entitled *La marche de Brandenbourg sous la dynastie ascanienne*,[8] he published his *Études sur l'histoire de Prusse*,[9] which continue the story after the Ascanian dynasty. In these works Lavisse does not attempt to contribute anything to the data of Brandenburg-Prussian history; he presents, rather, the thesis that the Prussian state owes its basic formation to the border peoples who have colonized it. He stresses the importance of the early Slavic infiltrations from the east and the conquests of the knights of the Teutonic order in Prussia. In the turmoil of the Thirty Years' War, Lavisse asserts that other foreign groups, especially Bohemians, were forced to seek refuge in Brandenburg. He contends that the general depopulation occasioned by this war was met by the Great Elector through importation of Dutch engineers and scientists. In maintaining his thesis Lavisse naturally plays up the importance of the French Huguenot refugees who emigrated to Brandenburg after the revocation of the Edict of Nantes (1685). He argues that it was not until the time of Frederick II that deliberate governmental steps were taken to supplement the population by the encouragement of immigration.

7. See in the *Revue des deux mondes:* "Les élections au parlement d'Allemagne," 3d period, II (1874), 158–77; "Une visite au parlement de l'empire d'Allemagne," 2d period, CVIII (1873), 187–206; "Les partis socialistes et l'agitation ouvrière en Allemagne," 2d period, CVII (1873), 442–64; "La crise économique en Allemagne," 3d period, XVIII (1876), 373–402; "Les prédécesseurs des Hohenzollerns, d'après un historien allemand," 3d period, XII (1875), 407–31; "Un livre français et un livre allemand sur l'Allemagne," 3d period, XXI (1877), 924–39.
8. Paris, 1875.
9. Paris, 1879; reviewed by Karl Lohmeyer, *HZ*, LIX (1875), 318–20.

Lavisse contends that from this mosaic of foreign peoples the Prussian state received its laborers, artisans, scholars, and scientists who formed the backbone of its rise to power and distinction.

In his lengthy comments on these works, Ernst Berner, the German historian, wrote:

> The emigration of the Protestants who had been driven from their homeland, especially the French, certainly contributed much profit and many blessings to the Prussian people, and the colonization of west Prussia through the efforts of Frederick the Great remains one of the outstanding feats of his career; but despite these considerations . . . it is impossible to see in them the founders of the Prussian state. Within the series of wise measures taken by the Hohenzollerns colonizing activity has rightly a place of honor, but to try to understand the history of the Prussian state on this basis alone results in a complete misinterpretation of history. Ingrafted branches on the tree of a great state Lavisse sees as the roots of the tree itself.[10]

Upon returning from Germany, Lavisse taught at the Lycée Henri IV until 1878, when he was appointed professor at the École Normale. One of the most famous of his students, Charles Seignobos, writes of this period:

> I was in the first class when Lavisse arrived at the École Normale, as the *maître de conférences* of history. He had no experience in teaching and had only a very meager command of historical data; but he had courage, intelligence, and a love for history and education. He told us of everything he had studied and to what a degree he had penetrated it. He never tried to impress us . . . with his erudition; on the contrary, he always remained the virtuous master and historian, and scientific investigator. He always pointed out to us his sources and his working tools.[11]

Hardly was the young professor established in his new post than he launched out vigorously against the French system of education. On the public platform and in the contemporary pe-

10. Ernst Berner, "Neuere französische Forschungen zur preussischen Geschichte," *Forschungen zur brandenburgischen und preussischen Geschichte,* II (1889), 316.

11. C. Seignobos, "Ernest Lavisse," *Revue universitaire,* XXXI (1922), Part II, 260.

riodicals he urged much-needed reforms in elementary, second-ary, and advanced schools. He not only made recommendations, but he acted. He wrote histories of France for school children from a purely patriotic-nationalistic point of view in which he begged the children not to forget the huge indemnity imposed upon the fatherland by Germany and also to remember that the Alsatians and Lorrainers loved France but were forced to live under German rule.[12] In the universities he advocated the adop-tion of Ranke's system of historical research. He was willing always to take the best of Germany for the good of France.

With his reforms in education only in the first stages, Lavisse was called in 1883 to act as assistant to Fustel de Coulanges at the Sorbonne. From this vantage position he was able to crusade even more advantageously for reform. The anticlerical attitude of Jules Ferry and the Republican government won Lavisse over to their camp, so that he became as rabid a Republican as he had been a Bonapartist. With the winning of free and compulsory primary education in 1882 Lavisse was able to concentrate his attention more on the secondary schools.

When he went to the Sorbonne there was no organization in that great institution for initiating the advanced student of his-tory into the mysteries of scientific research. His first point of attack had to be made on the government and especially on the Committee for Reform in Education. To these people he had to justify the study of history from a practical point of view. In this attempt Lavisse conveniently outlined his reasons for studying history:

> The principal purpose in the teaching of history is to aid the intellectual and moral education of the students.
> The teaching of history develops the intellect by exercising the

12. See his *Histoire de France: cours élémentaire* (Paris, 1875), p. 175. In 1926 his *cours moyen* went through its twenty-fifth edition and the year before his *cours supérieur* went through its second edition. The *cours élé-mentaire* has also gone through more than one edition, for it was repub-lished in 1925. Lavisse also edited patriotic readings for classes in civic training: *Les récits de Pierre Laloi* (Paris, 1925) and "Tu seras soldat," *Histoire d'un soldat français* (Paris, 1916). See Carlton J. H. Hayes, *France, a nation of patriots* (New York, 1930), pp. 350–51, 363–64, 374.

memory, by cultivating the imagination, by creating an ability to discern, appreciate, and evaluate facts, persons, ideas, periods, and countries, and by placing intellectual data, literature, and art in their proper places from the social and political perspective.

The teaching of history helps moral education, but it is necessary to say in what ways and to what degrees. . . .

It is not always true that the virtuous are rewarded or the guilty always punished; unhappily, evil and violence often succeeded. It is no more true that the destinies of a nation can be justified and explained solely by its virtues and vices: there also enter the elements of the energy and wealth of the country.

The design to make history serve as a sort of moral sermon is laudable, but a teacher must always be sincere above all else. . . . That is to say, he is not to doubt that historical instruction may be and ought to be used as a stronghold of moral consciousness.

From the very first he is a searcher after truth; he makes every effort to uncover it; and he proclaims it without reserve. The professor is an impartial judge of facts and of doctrines; his personal beliefs and his patriotism do not influence his judgment, which must be absolute. All historical instruction thus practiced is a moral object lesson. . . .

The professor of history then has the right to be a moralist; in fact, it is his duty. He will shun dogmatism, declamation, and evangelism, but he will pause before the good men whom he will encounter. He will expound at length on the charity of a Saint Vincent de Paul. He will minimize the details of Louis XIV's campaigns and expend the time necessary to delight in the persons of Corneille, Molière, Turenne, and Vauban.[13]

Professor Lavisse carried the fight for reform still further. He upheld classical education, for he claimed that the "youth of a generation should study the adolescent period of humanity" before approaching more mature contemporary problems. Into the Sorbonne he introduced the German seminar, having as some of his first students such eminent scholars as Langlois and Seignobos. Besides the introduction of the seminar, he insisted that less attention be paid to chronology and political history and that more stress be laid on proper research methods and on other technical phases of historical activity. He insisted that his students should be well grounded in the arts and literature and that

13. "Du rôle de l'enseignement historique dans l'éducation," *À propos de nos écoles* (Paris, 1895), pp. 77–78.

they should have an understanding of contemporary social and political problems as well as a profound knowledge of their respective fields of specialization.[14]

In the spring of 1886 Lavisse journeyed again to Berlin, after being away from the German capital for over nine years.[15] While in Germany he worked at the archives in Berlin and Königsberg. Meanwhile he published a series of articles under the general title *Études sur l'histoire de l'Allemagne*.[16] These essays deal with medieval Germany and are noteworthy contributions because of the skillful manner in which the machinations of church and state are interwoven. In 1887 he published a book of essays dealing with nineteenth-century Germany, entitled *Essais sur l'Allemagne impériale*. These were followed by a comparative study of the backgrounds and lives of the three German emperors of 1888: Wilhelm I, Frederick III, and Wilhelm II.[17]

In the early nineties Lavisse produced his famous biography, *La jeunesse du grand Frédéric*,[18] which is still generally acknowledged as a historical classic. The clear delineation of the character of the young Frederick, the love for illuminating details and anecdotes, coupled with incomparable simplicity and directness of style, served to enhance the beauty of Lavisse's biographical masterpiece. Even the German scholars were forced to admit that he shed new light on Frederick and especially on the relations between father and son. Only one major criticism could be offered, namely, that his reliance on memoir accounts was too evi-

14. Cf. his speech given before the Faculté des Lettres of the Sorbonne on Nov. 3, 1885, as recorded in his *Études et étudiants* (Paris, 1890), p. 114.
15. See "Notes prises dans une excursion en Allemagne," *Revue des deux mondes*, 3d period, LXXV (1866), 903–21.
16. Includes the following articles in the *Revue des deux mondes:* "Les préliminaires de l'histoire d'Allemagne," 3d period, LXX (1885), 390–417; "La foi et la morale des Francs," 3d period, LXXIV (1886), 365–97; "L'Entrée en scène de la papauté," 3d period, LXXVIII (1886), 842–81; "La conquête de la Germanie par l'église romaine," 3d period, LXXX (1887), 878–902; "La fondation du Saint-Empire," 3d period, LXXXVII (1888), 357–93.
17. *Trois empereurs d'Allemagne* (Paris, 1888).
18. Paris, 1891.

dent.[19] The French scholars hailed the *Youth of Frederick* as a classic of French historical literature.[20] This work, probably more than any of his others, won for him in 1892 election to the French Academy.

In 1893 he continued his biographical study of Frederick by publishing *Le grand Frédéric avant l'avènement*.[21] This work is not comparable in organization or style to its predecessor. The author in his preface states that if the work makes any real contribution to Frederican studies it is largely because of the minute detail with which the prince's life is surveyed. Probably the most important contribution from the point of view of foreign observers is the carefully edited letters preserved in the appendixes. These were found in the French archives of foreign affairs and were written by contemporary Frenchmen living in Berlin. They cover the period from 1732 to 1740.

In 1888 Lavisse had succeeded Henri Wallon as professor of modern history at the Sorbonne. In the nineties he reached the pinnacle of his triumph as a public lecturer. One of his American students, Othon Guerlac, later of Cornell University, recorded the following remembrances of Lavisse's lectures:

> Those who studied in Paris in the last decade of the last century may remember an unsightly brick structure temporarily erected in the inner court of the Sorbonne. It served as a shelter for public lectures while the main wing of the old building was being demolished and the masons were tearing down the historic amphitheater to which, for eighty years, some of the most renowned orators from Guizot to Brunetière, had attracted vast throngs.
> At the door of this provisional shack one could see, every Thursday morning, at half-past nine, an eager crowd waiting for the opening. Then they would climb up the narrow stairs leading to the amphitheater, and, in an instant, the whole room would be full. Down in front, a few benches were occupied by registered students, while the rest of the hall was filled by the usual public of

19. This opinion was expressed in *Jahresberichte für Geschichtswissenschaft*, 1891, sec. 62, Part II, p. 21.
20. Cf. Gabriel Monod's appreciation in *RH*, XLVI (1891), pp. 90–92.
21. Paris, 1893.

Sorbonne public lectures: old gentlemen, mature ladies, pretty young girls, serious-looking and spectacled old school teachers, Russians, Englishmen, Americans, Swiss, Swedes, even Frenchmen—all ages, all nationalities. At ten o'clock sharp the doors were shut. Coming from a little side office, the lecturer would appear, preceded by the traditional glass of water and three pieces of sugar on a tray. He was a man in the fifties, tall, vigorous, with a big head slightly inclined, a gray beard, sharp blue eyes, a strong, sonorous, well-modulated voice. With his commanding stature, the rosette in his button-hole, his somewhat abrupt delivery, he reminded one of a colonel in citizen's clothes more than of a professor. At the beginning of every year he would explain to his public two rules that were special to his course: the doors were closed after the beginning of every lecture, so that no one could, in the midst of it, come in or go out. This was to discourage idle curiosity, which has a way of entering anywhere simply because there is a door open. Likewise, applause was discountenanced as foolish and insulting to the speaker, for this was not an operatic performance but a university lecture by Ernest Lavisse, professor of modern history.[22]

Many of his other students record with what quiet dignity he unceremoniously began to talk. He did not launch into great flights of eloquence, but he soberly described the varied careers of Louis XIV or Colbert. His audiences at the Sorbonne were well aware of his scholarly interest in the era of the Sun King, for not only his lectures but also his articles in the contemporary periodicals betrayed his field of concentration.

Despite his unquestioned scholarly abilities, Lavisse had not that type of mind interested in delving into a minutiae of detail to seek for a solitary fact or idea.[23] He did not despise such work, for he encouraged and aided his students in every way possible to perceive the unsolved historical problems and to employ the scientific method in their solution. Such problems, however, held little personal appeal for him. He visualized history not from the

22. Othon Guerlac, "Ernest Lavisse, French historian and educator," *South Atlantic quarterly,* XXII (1923), 23–24.

23. On this interesting part of Lavisse's historical outlook see especially C. V. Langlois, "Ernest Lavisse," *Revue de France,* V (1922), 472: "M. Lavisse, who was a great historian in every sense of the word, was not a scholar."

Donald F. Lach

point of view of specialized topics but as an integrated picture in which the layman, as well as the scholar, might indulge.

His great work in universal history, the *Histoire générale du 4ᵉ siècle à nos jours*,[24] was produced in editorial collaboration with Alfred Rambaud. He did, however, little of the actual work connected with this endeavor, for he was too preoccupied with his regular work and with the *Revue de Paris*, the editorship of which he had assumed in 1894.[25]

At the dawn of the new century he began to edit the massive *Histoire de France depuis les origines jusqu' à la Révolution*,[26] which was to gain for him a place of pre-eminence as a historian of his own country. This work was a survey of French history from the most ancient times to the Revolution of 1789. Various experts in the different periods of French history wrote sections. For himself, Lavisse retained the era of Louis XIV. At last his many lectures and articles were compiled in a single manuscript which appeared in 1906. The American historian, James Westfall Thompson, stated definitely that no man was so capable of writing an adequate study of the era of Louis XIV and that no other historian could have done an adequate job so well and with so much beauty.[27]

The one thing Lavisse set out to do, and a thing which he accomplished successfully, was to "debunk" the standard accounts of the era of Louis XIV which took seriously the versions of Voltaire and Michelet. Lavisse deprived the Sun King of many of his rays by showing him in his later years as a weak and stubborn old man who refused to acknowledge that his day was past. Louis XIV was reduced from "the state" to the man.

He divided the work on the era of Louis XIV between two volumes of the *Histoire de France*. The first of these two, Volume VII, was divided into two parts. In these parts he attacks the era of Louis XIV primarily from the point of view of institutional de-

24. 12 vols.; Paris, 1893–1901.
25. Cf. Charles Pfister, "Ernest Lavisse," *RH*, CXLI (1922), 317.
26. 9 vols.; Paris, 1900–11. Condensed version in one volume *Histoire de France illustrée depuis les origines jusqu'a la Révolution* (Paris, 1911).
27. *AHR*, XII (1907), 130–33.

153

velopment. The first book, on the period from 1643 to 1661, remains one of the most concise and understandable histories of the Fronde. In the simple and direct style characteristic of his works, Lavisse analyzes the Fronde in the following words:

> France was torn apart by persons with no high ideals, no benevolent sentiments, except for certain high-minded parlementarians and members of the middle class. Nothing is sadder or more scandalous in our history than these four years of war. . . . The history of the Fronde reveals the immaturity of the state and the country. It discloses a dreadful inability to work and act together, to find the means and ideals to oppose the power of the king. Finally, the young king's observation and comprehension of the Fronde explains in part the political ideals and opinions of Louis XIV.[28]

As Lavisse recognized the influence of the Fronde in Louis XIV's development, so also did he observe the effects of Richelieu's policies on the young king. Especially did he stress the evolution of government interest toward such institutions as finance, commerce, agriculture, industry, the press, laws, police, justice, religion, and the various strata of society, not to mention his outstanding analysis of the effects of autocratic government in intellectual development. Volume VII, Part II, concluded with an analysis of foreign policy from 1661 to 1685 and a general survey of the period.

The epoch from 1685 to Louis's death in 1715 was done with the collaboration of Saint-Léger, Sagnac, and Rebelliau. Lavisse wrote only the last book of this Volume VIII, in which he studied Louis in relation to the court. This chapter gives the reader the feeling that he is visiting an art gallery in which he finds word pictures of such characters as the Duc de Bourgogne, the Duc de Chartres, and Madame de Maintenon. The other writers in this volume concern themselves primarily with internal politics and diplomacy, although an adequate survey of institutions is also given.

When Lavisse was not occupied with his work in teaching and research, he studied further the groundwork of French educa-

28. *Histoire de France,* VII, Part I, 44.

tion. When the École Normale was joined to the University of
Paris in 1904, he accepted the post as director of the new organization. These early days of the twentieth century saw Lavisse at
the prime point in his career—at the point where he engaged in
active living, where he confronted problems of administration
and settled student quarrels. It was in this prewar period that he
most enjoyed returning to Nouvion each spring to give a little
talk to the graduating class of the local school and to gossip about
"old times" with the white-haired men he had known as schoolboys. Each year he also spoke to the *collège* at Laon, which had
since become one of the outstanding *lycées* of northern France.
Gradually the rugged fighter of earlier days assumed the calm
security of a life well spent, and the mellow philosophy of three
score and ten found its way in 1912 into a little volume of *Souvenirs.* Here the historian had, of necessity, to give way to the
aged artist, who paints in glowing colors, and with no attempt at
objectivity, the triumphs and discouragements of boyhood and
youth.

Hardly had his pen formed the last hopeful words of these
memories when reality in the guise of war drove sweet remembrances from the old man's mind. Once again the ancient
hatreds and prejudices were revived. In Lavisse no thought remained of quiet meditation and mellow contemplation. War, as
in 1870, directed his attention once more to the people across the
Rhine who again had invaded his beloved France. Even the
quiet countryside of Nouvion was forced to play host to the enemy. Two great swords he had to fight with: the sword of an
enviable reputation as an objective historian of Germany and
the agile pen of an experienced journalist.

No magazine in France issued more propaganda than the *Revue de Paris,* and no historian distorted history more than Ernest
Lavisse.[29] Perhaps his position was understandable in that the

29. Although this accusation is grave, ample evidence of such distortions
may be found in his articles in the *Revue de Paris* for the war period. Such
articles as "La Prusse" were mere compilations of excerpts from his earlier
works proving the "brutality of the Germans." From these partial truths he
drew his conclusions. In 1923 Georges Demartial, French political writer
and "revisionist," first published a denunciation of Lavisse's war activities in

Germans had burned his home at Nouvion and indirectly killed his brother, who died, as contemporary accounts say, of a "trench disease."[30]

In the years of war Lavisse wrote no fewer than fourteen propaganda articles for the *Revue de Paris*.[31] In these he argued that public opinion should be manipulated for nationalistic purposes. He damned the Germans for rape and pillage and for their ideas on the "necessity of war." In March, 1914, he had organized, with the aid of General Pau, the Ligue Française, which favored country over party, intensive exploitation of colonies, and hostility toward Germany. At the same time he argued that wars in a general sense are harmful but that the war of 1914 would be beneficial since it would spell the end of German militarism.[32] His denunciations of Germany included a terrific outburst against a system of education which creates "efficient bandits"—against that selfsame system which he was so instrumental in giving to France.

At the conclusion of peace he was chosen chairman of the committee investigating territorial questions[33]—he who, with Charles Pfister, had written a pamphlet on Alsace-Lorraine during the

---

his *La guerre de 1917: comment on mobilisa les consciences* (Paris, 1923). This denunciation is repeated in H. E. Barnes, *The history of historical writing* (Norman, Okla., 1937), p. 278.

30. Pfister, *loc. cit.*, p. 318.

31. "La guerre," XXI (November, 1914), 1–9; "L'état d'esprit qu'il faut," XXII (January, 1915), 5–12; "La Prusse," XXII (February, 1915), 673–93; "Trois idées allemandes," XXII (May, 1915), 225–35; "Bonne année," XXIII (January, 1916), 5–14; "Un sincère témoignage sur la guerre," XXIII (April, 1916), 673–80; "La direction de l'opinion publique," XXIII (July, 1916), 5–10; "Si la guerre est bienfaisante?" XXIII (October, 1916), 669–76; "Lettre à une normalienne," XXIV (December, 1917), 779–90; "Seconde lettre à une normalienne," XXV (January, 1918), 65–75; "Comme dans un rêve," XXV (November, 1918), 449–52; "Réflexions pendant la guerre," XXV (December, 1918), 702–8; "Réflexions pendant la guerre II," XXVI (January, 1919), 225–34; "Réflexions pendant la guerre III," XXVI (June, 1919), 449–62.

32. See his *German theory and practice of war* (Paris, 1915).

33. J. T. Shotwell, *At the Paris Peace Conference* (New York, 1937), p. 14.

war denouncing all German claims as lies. He did not confine his activities to investigation of territorial claims, for he spoke to the German delegates at the Paris Peace Conference with all the venom of four years' hate:

> You are here before your judges, to answer for the greatest crime in history. You are going to lie, for you are congenital liars. But, beware, lying is awkward when you know that those who are listening to you and are looking at you know that you are lying.[34]

It is hard to reconcile the tender sentiments of 1912 with this vicious hate of 1919. It is less difficult to understand that by 1921–22 war clouds had cleared, and Lavisse was able to publish perhaps the greatest monument to modern French history, the *Histoire de France contemporaine depuis la Révolution jusqu' à la paix de 1919*.[35] In writing his conclusion to these ten great volumes he expressed with unforgettable simplicity the faith and hope he felt in the future of France and the republican form of government.

> Let me recapitulate: From 1800 to 1814, the parliamentary régime; from 1814 to 1830—except for the Hundred Days—a divine-right kingdom; from 1830 to 1848, a constitutional kingdom; from 1852 to 1870, the Second Empire, which endured longer than any preceding form of government. Since then, we have had a republic for more than half a century.
>
> It remains to be said that a republican government is never a perfectly harmonious government. A republic must be extremely tolerant. We are told that liberty of the press and of assemblage, that the free right to protest and demonstrate against the acts of the government, are fertile seedbeds of trouble. But I fancy that no one of us expects to live an absolutely untroubled life. Liberty has this beneficent quality: popular passions wear themselves out, so to speak, in experiments. The leaders of the most violent factions are sobered by sharing the responsibilities of the government. They are flattered by the honors of office. Public debates are better than secret conventicles, where men conspire to do violent deeds. Imprudent speakers and writers involuntarily dis-

34. Quoted in Barnes, p. 278.
35. 10 vols.; Paris, 1920–22.

close the hidden purposes that animate them. They enlighten public opinion, which is, after all, the supreme and final judge.[36]

Hope was always a characteristic element in Lavisse's more philosophic works. Although he recognized the difficulties of the present moment, he was always optimistic enough to believe that humanity and France, despite the awful interlude of the war, would emerge, by natural bounty and by human strength, into the full sunlight of prosperity. His thoughts did not include the human race as a whole, for he lived and died a nationalistic liberal of the nineteenth century who felt that man's destiny must be worked out on national lines established by war and tradition.

Although he was a product of nineteenth-century liberalism and a firm believer, in his later years, in the virtues of a nationalistic-republican-capitalistic system, his later historical writings were definitely tinged with that flavor to which the name "new history" has been ascribed. He used all the technical means at his command not to ferret out the details of political and diplomatic history but rather to give meaning to epochs by describing customs, manners, commerce, religion, literature, art, and science.[37] He was not a conscious follower of the theory of economic determinism, but he gathered about himself a group of men who were fully aware of the importance of that theory.

His writings were models of Rankean technique written with that simple and grand style peculiar to masters of French. He went back to the sources but contented himself with picking out the summits of interest, leaving the valleys to be explored by those students and followers of his who possessed such patience and time. His works were usually arranged with deference to chronology, but from time to time he found a topical arrangement more suitable. His writings were always narrative, with philo-

36. These conclusions of the *Histoire contemporaine* were also published under the title "Raisons de confiance en l'avenir," in *Revue de Paris*, XXIX (May, 1922), 225–41. The English translation was published in the *Living age*, CCCXIV (July 15, 1922), 137. Charles Andler wrote an appreciation of the work entitled "La dernière œuvre d'Ernest Lavisse," *Revue de Paris*, XXX (January, 1923), 303–40.

37. This is admirably illustrated in his little *Vue générale de l'histoire politique de l'Europe* (Paris, 1890).

sophic bits interspersed. His only limits were geography, for he confined himself to the study of Prussia, Germany, and France, although he did limit his most intensive researches to the middle ages on one side and the eighteenth century on the other. The most characteristic feature of his writings was the sunny optimism he always felt for the future. He never studied a period for itself but endeavored always to connect it with the present. He was a greater editor than a scholar.[38] In this role he gave to history three monumental works.[39] He gave further to France that technique known as "scientific history." His influence in educational reforms was great and has been of lasting consequence.

In August, 1922, his wish of seventy years was granted, for he returned then to Nouvion, and he was buried in his native soil with all the honors due a distinguished member of the French Academy. Nowhere does he express his outlook on life more clearly than in the closing sentences of his *Souvenirs:*

> Oh, I see very well all the imperfections of men and of things. I have known, and I know many hours of fear and anxiety; but, never, have I despaired and I shall never give up to despair. The feelings of my youth, intact and strong, command in me hope. I am hoping.[40]

38. Philippe Sagnac, "Ernest Lavisse," *Encyclopaedia of the social sciences,* IX, 199–200.

39. In addition to the three *Histoires,* he edited *La vie politique à l'étranger* (Paris, 1889–91), *Album historique* (Paris, 1897–1907), and *Le monde contemporain, 1870–1900* (Paris, 1905).

40. *Souvenirs,* p. 287.

# VIII

## Georges Lefebvre (1874–1959)

### GORDON H. McNEIL

GEORGES LEFEBVRE was born in Lille, in the Nord Department, in 1874, and here he spent the first half of his life.[1] His father was a commercial employee, and it was thanks to a series of scholarships to the newly established Ferry school system and the University of Lille that the young Lefebvre received his education. It is interesting to note that he made his first trip to Paris, less than 150 miles away, at the age of twenty-four, for the oral examination for the *agrégation*. There then followed a long period, from 1898 to 1924, of teaching in various lycées in the provinces and finally in Paris. It was, as he frankly recorded it, a life of poverty, with both a family and relatives to support. It was also a life of obscurity. Even after he began to teach in Paris, he had no contacts with intellectual circles; and Jaurès, whom he so admired, he never saw except from a distance at a public meeting.

If it was a life of obscurity, and undoubtedly of frustration, it

1. Biographical details may be found in the following sources: *Annales historiques de la Révolution française* (hereafter cited as *Annales*), No. 102 (1946), pp. 185–86; No. 106 (1947), pp. 188–90; No. 159 (1960), *passim* (this is a memorial issue consisting of articles on Lefebvre by students and colleagues); Georges Lefebvre, *Études sur la Révolution française* (Paris, 1954) (hereafter cited as *Études*), "Notice biographique"; R. R. Palmer, "Georges Lefebvre: the peasants and the French Revolution," *Journal of modern history*, XXXI (1959), 329–42; Marcel Reinhard, "Un historien au XXᵉ siècle: Georges Lefebvre," *Revue historique* (hereafter cited as *RH*), CCXXIII (1960), 1–12; Beatrice Hyslop, "Georges Lefebvre, historian," *French historical studies*, I (1960), 265–82.

nevertheless was also a life of sober, serious scholarship, which was to continue for the rest of his life. There were the long years spent laboriously gathering the data from hundreds of local archives and writing his impressive thesis, *Les paysans du Nord pendant la Révolution française,*[2] which earned him the doctorate at Paris in 1924 and the notice of his colleagues.[3] The supplementary thesis was his already published *Documents relatifs à l'histoire des subsistances dans le district de Bergues (1789–an V).*[4] In the long introduction to this work he antedated the contributions of Mathiez to the history of the impact of economic regulation during the revolution. He was to return to the subject of the history of the peasants in 1932 with his *Questions agraires au temps de la Terreur.*[5]

On receiving the doctorate at Paris, he held successive appointments at the universities of Clermont, Strasbourg, and Paris; and in 1937, at the age of sixty-three, he followed Sagnac in the chair of the history of the French Revolution at Paris, which he held until, having reached the age of sixty-seven in 1941, he was retired. But he continued to lecture, almost without compensation, during the Vichy regime, until his final retirement after the war.

Lefebvre's scholarly activity never ceased. His first interest as a student had been in medieval history and, since early in his career (when he had already shifted his interest to the revolution) he had need of the additional income it offered, he found time to prepare a three-volume translation of Stubbs's *Constitutional history of England,* and he wrote sections of his own for the third volume. This of course was simply a diversion, and his promotion to university lecturing foreshadowed a more consequential field of publication. The first result was his collaboration with Guyot and Sagnac in writing *La Révolution française* for the "Peuples et civilisations" series.[6]

2. Two vols.: Paris, 1924. A one-volume edition, minus the documentation and statistical material, was published in Bari, Italy, in 1959.

3. For an account of the reception and critical analysis of this book from the perspective of a generation later see the article by Palmer.

4. Two vols.: Lille, 1914, 1921.

5. Strasbourg, 1932; 2d ed., La Roche-sur-Yon, 1954.

6. Vol. XIII, Paris, 1930.

There was also more yet to come on the peasants and the revolution. The year 1932 saw off the presses both his *Questions agraires au temps de la Terreur,* already mentioned, and *La Grande Peur de 1789,*[7] which represents an unprecedented fusing of the author's prior interest in the status of the peasants, as revealed in the local documents, with a newer interest in what may be called social-psychological history. In later years he referred to this as the work with which he was most pleased.[8]

Three years later there appeared his *Napoléon* in the "Peuples et civilisations" series,[9] which was outside the range of his immediate interest, but which was a skillful synthesis of existing knowledge and the insights which he brought to the Napoleonic era from his knowledge of the preceding period. There followed the small volume, *Les Thermidoriens,* in the popular Colin collection,[10] which provided a continuation of the three volumes on the revolution in that series by Mathiez. It in turn was followed after World War II by *Le Directoire,*[11] which completed the series.

Just prior to the outbreak of World War II, for the celebration of the one hundred and fiftieth anniversary of the revolution, Lefebvre contributed—literally, for he accepted no royalties—his *Quatre-vingt-neuf,*[12] a brilliant summary of the events and larger significance of that fateful year, which in the translation by Robert Palmer,[13] widely circulated in a paperback edition,[14] is undoubtedly his best known work in this country. The final volume in the long and distinguished list, which was published in 1951, was a new edition of *La Révolution française.* The work was now his alone, reflecting on the one hand his long years of personal research and extensive reading in the monographic literature,

7. Paris, 1932.
8. Letter to author, September 10, 1946. See the comments of Reinhard on this (p. 7).
9. Vol. XIV, Paris, 1935. For a detailed review, which is quite laudatory, see Pieter Geyl, *Napoleon, for and against* (New Haven, 1949), pp. 421–49.
10. Paris, 1937.
11. Paris, 1946.
12. Paris, 1939.
13. *The coming of the French Revolution* (Princeton, 1947).
14. New York: Vintage Books, 1957.

particularly in the social and economic area, and on the other his deeper insight into such subjects as, for example, the psychological origins of the Terror.[15]

In the meantime there had appeared numerous articles and periodic bibliographical essays on the revolutionary and Napoleonic periods in the *Revue historique,* plus a steady stream of book reviews in the *Annales historiques de la Révolution française* (which he edited from 1932 until his death), many of which were in the Macaulay tradition, presenting more of Lefebvre's conclusions than of the books themselves.

Lefebvre always conceived of himself as a research scholar who might advance hypotheses and write surveys but whose starting point and solid foundation were always the primary sources, the indispensable documents.[16] For him history must be based on *érudition*—a word he used frequently—and, echoing the aphorism of Seignobos, "No documents, no history," he maintained that "without scholarship, there can be no history."[17] Thus he was bluntly critical of history which was not firmly based on the sources[18] and also of historians who had slighted scholarly research in favor of interpretative writing no matter how well done, even if they were as eminent as Carl Becker.[19]

A more distinctive and personal contribution to the historiography of the revolution was his use of the statistical approach to social and economic history. His thesis had been solidly based on numerous statistical analyses of the sources concerning such matters as landownership and transfer, and class distribution. If in

15. See for example the admirable analysis of the European economy and society on the eve of the Revolution (chaps. ii and iii), and the discussion of the origins of the Terror (pp. 401–9: compare pp. 249–53 of the earlier volume).

16. For a discussion of Lefebvre's conceptions of historical method, see Jean Suratteau, "Georges Lefebvre, historien politique," *Annales,* No. 159 (1960), pp. 32–46, which is based in part on several articles and lectures which the present author was not able to see.

17. "Recherche et congrès," *RH,* CCVI (1951), 2.

18. See for example his review of a book which presumed to present proofs concerning the supposed Masonic conspiracy on the eve of the revolution, in *Annales,* No. 101 (1946), p. 73.

19. *Ibid.,* No. 117 (1950), 82–85.

social history one is to study large groups of the population, instead of merely the relatively few who compose the upper classes, as he insisted one should,[20] the statistical method, he maintained, was the only way of arriving at reliable conclusions. "Il faut compter" was a familiar refrain in his discussions of method.[21] Of course he also wrote that all history cannot be recorded in curves on a chart, and that there is always the unique and imponderable; but he repeatedly urged that wherever appropriate the statistical methods of the natural sciences be used.[22]

This certainly applied to the study of social structure, which he realized was the least developed field of history. He was personally aware of the inability of any one person to study more than a single locality and class, and he therefore concluded that significant results could be arrived at only as such methods were used in carefully planned, cooperative efforts.[23] This had been seen at the beginning of the century by Jaurès, who had organized in 1903 a cooperative project for the study of the economic history of the revolution, and Lefebvre contributed to it his study of the food supplies of the district of Bergues already mentioned, as well as his subsequent work on agrarian problems during the Terror. When he assumed the chair of the history of the French Revolution at the Sorbonne he actively encouraged cooperative research. He directed the reorganized Institute for the History of the French Revolution[24] and played a leading part in promoting a cooperative program of research and publication, sponsored by the commission founded by Jaurès, on the French bourgeoisie from the end of the old regime to the Restoration. By the time of his death—twenty years, another world war, and a number of national and international conferences later—some

20. "Avenir de l'histoire," *Études,* p. 3.
21. "Une colloque pour l'étude des structures sociales," *Annales,* No. 147 (1957), pp. 100–101.
22. Remarks of E. Labrousse in *Bulletin de la Société d'Histoire Moderne,* 12th ser., No. 11, p. 6.
23. "Recherche et congrès," pp. 1–3; Albert Soboul, "Georges Lefebvre, historien de la Révolution française," *Annales,* No. 159 (1960), pp. 12–13.
24. *Annales,* No. 102 (1946), pp. 185–86.

progress had been made.[25] At these conferences Lefebvre had dis-cussed methods and problems, he had encouraged any and all cooperative efforts in the columns of the *Annales,* and he had participated in the work himself, having at the time of his death written a few chapters for a pilot study of the bourgeoisie of Orléans.[26]

In any historiographical study one is concerned not only with the methods used by the historian being studied, but also with his particular viewpoint and biases, and his philosophy of history. In the case of Lefebvre, this is no simple matter, for his phi-losophy and viewpoint can best be called pluralistic or eclectic.[27] There is in his writings and lectures a refreshing absence of dogmatic assertion, for he was no system builder, and he firmly resisted the temptation to simplify when actually writing history. He was critical of oversimplified doctrines of historical causation, and even the much admired Jaurès came in for censure for pre-senting what Lefebvre considered to be an overly simple explana-tion of the causes of the revolution.[28] Lefebvre's eclecticism and his lack of dogmatism are neatly illustrated in his conclusion to a review of the various theories concerning the origins of Napole-onic imperialism: "In each of these interpretations, one finds a part of reality, but reality is something more than all of them."[29]

One element of the reality that was Lefebvre was the fact that he was a Frenchman. There was an earnest patriotism which ap-

25. Reports of progress and future plans, together with extracts from Lefebvre's contributions, appear in *ibid.,* No. 91 (1939), pp. 86–88; No. 94 (1939), p. 374; No. 97 (1940), pp. 56–61; No. 102 (1946), p. 186; No. 105 (1947), pp. 73–82; No. 142 (1956), pp. 104–5; No. 144 (1956), pp. 328–31; No. 147 (1957), pp. 99–105; No. 148 (1957), pp. 278–80; No. 153 (1958), pp. 1–13. See also Marc Bouloiseau, "De Jaurès à Georges Lefebvre: la Commission d'Histoire Économique de la Révolution," *ibid.,* No. 159 (1960), pp. 57–66.

26. MM. Schneider, Braudel, Labrousse, and Renouvin, "Les orientations de la recherche historique," *RH,* CCXXII (1959), 39.

27. His approach to these topics was summarized in a series of lectures at the Sorbonne in 1946 on "Notions d'historiographie moderne" and in several additional articles which the author has not seen.

28. "La Révolution française et les payans," in *Études,* p. 247.

29. *Napoléon,* p. 144.

peared in his lectures and writings, and in 1945 he wrote with old-fashioned bluntness of his having continued to lecture at the Sorbonne during the Vichy period in order to prevent "treason" from placing one of its adherents in his place.[30] One detects the same sense of earnest nationalism two years later when he quoted in a very emotional passage the statement by Robespierre opposing the appointment to the Committee of Public Safety of a man who had participated in the surrender of Valenciennes to the enemy.[31] But his most eloquent statement was the final paragraph in his *Quatre-vingt-neuf,* which was addressed to the youth of France. It invoked the glorious tradition of the revolution and closed with a "Vive la Nation."[32]

This of course is loyalty to the France of the revolutionary tradition, and more specifically for him, to the Jacobin democratic and social republic of 1793–94.[33] On the occasion of the centennial of the revolution of 1848, Lefebvre proudly affirmed that he was a Jacobin, if one wished to call him that, but certainly not the last, for he hoped there were others less old; and he ended the speech with an emotional apotheosis of the republic.[34] It should be noted, and it is not unimportant, that this republic meant to him both the equality implied in the ideal of social democracy, and also liberty; and he took the occasion just before his death to remind his readers in the Russian-controlled zone of Germany of the perennial problem of providing institutional safeguards for personal liberty in the face of recurring attempts to deny it.[35]

30. Letter to author, October 11, 1945.

31. *Annales,* No. 106 (1947), p. 190.

32. Pp. 246–47. This was omitted from the translation. See also his extremely nationalistic analysis of the "Marseillaise" in his Sorbonne lectures ("La chute du roi," "Les cours de Sorbonne," pp. 88–91).

33. "Sur la pensée politique de Robespierre," *Études,* pp. 95–98.

34. "Le 24 février 1848," *1848 et les révolutions du XIXᵉ siècle,* XXXVII (1946), 15–17.

35. "A la mémoire de Maximilien Robespierre," in *Maximilien Robespierre 1758–1794: Beiträge zu seinem 200. Geburtstag,* ed. Walter Markov (Berlin, 1958), p. 13. Palmer (p. 334) has called attention to the interesting fact that Lefebvre's essay is the only one of the many written by non-Germans for this volume which was not translated into German.

Lefebvre never wrote a biography, and his preference for groups rather than individuals as the subjects of his study was quite definite.[36] His *Napoléon* was the history of an era, not of a man; but his treatment of the "great man" par excellence of modern history gives us insight into his conception of the role of the individual in history. His analysis of Napoleon's personality and character is a classic of balanced historical interpretation,[37] the theme of which is that "before all, Napoleon is a *tempéra-ment.*"[38] The basic explanation, although not the complete explanation, for his foreign policy, for example, lies in his ambition, in the irresistible promptings of his character.[39] In the conclusion, Lefebvre presents a carefully weighed analysis which balances the impersonal factors in prior historical developments against this basic *tempérament,* but he makes no attempt to assess the relative importance of these two forces—saying simply that the man had had considerable influence, but only to the extent that he operated in the mainstream of European history.[40]

Lefebvre was much intrigued throughout his career by the psychological element in history, but it was social-psychological rather than biographical history which was of particular interest to him. In his article, "Foules révolutionnaires," published in 1934,[41] he urged historians to study the collective mentality. This to him was the connecting link between antecedent conditions and resulting events. In the case of the French Revolution, analysis of the mental *contenu* of each class has been recognized as a notable contribution to this scarcely explored field of history. Such of course was his *La Grande Peur,* together with the not very well-known case study entitled "La meurtre du comte de Dampierre."[42] What interested him particularly, and it is a pity he did not write a general study of the subject, was what he called

36. Suratteau, pp. 43–44.
37. Pp. 60–66.
38. P. 62.
39. P. 145.
40. P. 565.
41. Reprinted in *Études,* pp. 271–87.
42. Reprinted in *ibid.,* pp. 288–97.

"le complexe révolutionnaire."[43] By this he meant the specific psychological pattern associated with the "complot aristocratique." It included first a fear of an aristocratic conspiracy against the revolution, a defensive reaction, and then a "volonté punitive" which, he insisted, was one of the keys to the history of the revolution.[44] He makes no attempt to apply some of the newer psychological insights and theories to this pattern, and he has been criticized for this. Having defined the phenomenon, as he saw it in the documents, he simply noted its persistence throughout the revolution until, as he wrote, the "fever" subsided with the military victories of 1794.[45] For Lefebvre this was the basic psychological pattern, and it is a frequent theme in his books, lectures, and reviews.

For one as closely concerned with social and economic history as Lefebvre was, the economic interpretation of events was inevitably a large part of historical reality. But as we have seen, it was only part of the total reality in his pluralistic conception of history. He had no sympathy for the doctrinaire economic determinist, yet in his eclectic philosophy of history there was a prominent place assigned to economic factors, and he was constantly alert to see their influence on the political, social, and cultural story, and quick to criticize those who failed, in his opinion, to see their significance.[46]

He acknowledged the influence on his early thinking of French Marxists, notably Jaurès;[47] he took for granted a Marxian "dialectical march of history," for example in the conclusion to *La Révolution française;*[48] and he applied this particular theory to various topics of revolutionary history. Time and again he assumed that the class struggle was a fundamental factor in history,

43. He referred once to his dossier on this subject in *Annales,* No. 101 (1946), p. 84.
44. *La Révolution française,* pp. 131–33.
45. *Ibid.,* p. 409.
46. See for example his sharp criticism of Herman Wendel's *Danton* on this point in "Sur Danton," *Études,* p. 30.
47. "Pro Domo," *Annales,* No. 106 (1947), p. 189; Soboul, p. 3.
48. P. 638.

168

that it was "the principal motive force in history."[49] But in spite of this terminology, he was actually quite free, when describing the course of events and the interplay of multiple causes, from the dogmatism of the extreme Marxist; and in his personal politics he could, so his friends have reported, support the Communist party while not joining it.[50] When one recalls his family background and early life, one can understand his sometimes sharp and acid feelings on the subject of class,[51] as well as such phrases in his writings as the "harsh egoism of the bourgeoisie" and the "cascade de mépris." He sought in this way to characterize the bitter consciousness or sense of class.[52] On occasion he could be quite blunt on the subject of the interests of the well-to-do—for example, in explaining the lenient treatment of hoarders by bourgeois jurymen during the Terror. As he put it in one of his postwar lectures, when hoarding is a current problem, wolves do not eat one another.[53] He was similarly harsh in his criticism of Tocqueville for sharing the fear and rancor of his class.[54] Several years before his death he went so far as to state that certain reinterpretations of the French and English Revolutions, such as the suggestions of Professor Cobban concerning the "myth of the French Revolution," reflected the reaction of a dominant class which felt menaced by the upsurge of democracy and the Russian Revolution.[55]

Such distortions are not, however, typical. Much more typical is his cautious and scholarly analysis of social class structure, and

49. *Annales,* No. 117 (1950), 81, 85; "À propos d'un centenaire," *RH,* CC (1948), 6–7.

50. See the interesting analysis in René Garmy, "Georges Lefebvre et l'homme (Souvenirs)," *Annales,* No. 159 (1960), p. 83.

51. See for example the analysis in his preface to *Die Sansculotten von Paris: Dokumente zur Geschichte der Volksbewegung 1793–1794,* ed. Walter Markov and Albert Soboul (Berlin, 1957), p. ix.

52. *Quatre-vingt-neuf,* p. 52; *Le Directoire,* p. 147.

53. "Le gouvernement révolutionnaire (2 juin 1793–9 Thermidor II)," "Cours de l'École Normale Supérieure de Sèvres," p. 140.

54. "Le 24 février 1848," p. 11; "Introduction" to Alexis de Tocqueville, *L'ancien régime et la Révolution, Œuvres complètes,* II (Paris, 1952), 15.

55. "Le mythe de la Révolution française," *Annales,* No. 145 (1956), p. 344.

of the role of social class in shaping the course of events during the revolutionary era. Herein lies one of his most important contributions to the historiography of the French Revolution. Students of the revolution in the nineteenth century were aware of the importance of class considerations. Occasionally they were too aware of it, and Marx, as every schoolboy at least in Russia knows, defined all history as the history of class struggles, thus sorely complicating the task of subsequent historians with his oversimplification of the class structure and its significance. Non-Marxists had other ideas concerning class, but they and the Marxists both lacked the facts which only detailed research could provide.

It was Lefebvre who, brushing aside the verbiage about the "dialectical march of history," and following the lead of Loutchisky and several others, really inaugurated the scholarly study of class structure in the revolutionary period with his research on the peasants. Years of archival work made him particularly alert to the complexities of class structure, the wide variations from region to region, and the fact, often forgotten, that social structures change. His detailed work on the peasants of the Nord Department is a classic case study in complexity and change, even though it is confined to the peasants of a single department in a single decade. In *Le Directoire* he presented in just a few pages— in sharp contrast to the study of the Nord peasants—a fascinating summary of the class structure at that time, indicating the extreme state of flux which prevailed as a result of the impact on society of the revolution and the many changes which had accompanied it.[56] As a historian he showed little interest in the contributions of sociologists and social anthropologists to an understanding of social class; perhaps he was not aware of the work being done. On the complicated and much discussed subject of the criteria for determining class, his mind was made up. The basic consideration in determining social class, within what had been the third estate, was wealth and income, and therefore the class distribution in a particular community was to be reconstructed from

56. *Le Directoire*, pp. 144–47.

fiscal records concerning income and property.[57] He recognized, however, that a document recording contemporary opinion concerning class status in a particular city might be of value.[58]

His conclusion concerning the rural class structure, in summary, was that the peasant population (leaving aside the nonpeasant residents) consisted of a "dominant class"—the "cock of the village" category of well-to-do *fermiers* and *cultivateurs;* a midde class or *petite bourgeoisie paysanne,* which together with the first category comprised the rural bourgeoisie; and at the bottom of the scale the rural proletariat, consisting of *ménagers* and *journaliers.*[59] When he suggested a classification of urban society, he proposed a four-part structure: a dominant class, a middle class, a popular class, and a proletariat of manual laborers.[60] These classifications of the population are a healthy corrective to the oversimplified distinction between bourgeoisie and proletariat which, he repeatedly said, distorted the history of the revolution, and which he found exemplified in two recent works on the period.[61] Conversely it is one of his chief claims to a prominent place in the historiography of the revolution that he analyzed its course in the light of the complexities of class interest, going more deeply than his predecessors had into the actual class considerations which influenced events. When he repeats a familiar theme, such as that of the bourgeois victory of 1789, he does so with a sense of nuance and insight which is a welcome contrast to Jaurès and Mathiez, for example.[62] But the more significant contribution is twofold: (1) his identification of the *sans-culotte*

57. Soboul, p. 16. He was continually alert to evidence of this sort. See for example the long review of a brief article based on such documentation for Toulouse in *Annales,* No. 122 (1951), pp. 198–202.

58. *Annales,* No. 138 (1955), pp. 80–82.

59. *Les paysans du Nord pendant la Révolution française.* pp. 40, 321; *Questions agraires au temps de la Terreur,* p. 69. Cf. "La Révolution française et les paysans," *Études,* pp. 250–51.

60. "Un colloque pour l'étude des structures sociales," pp. 104–5.

61. *Annales,* No. 106 (1947), pp. 175, 177; No. 156 (1959), p. 171.

62. See his discussion of the community of interests, in spite of antagonism on other matters, between aristocracy and bourgeoisie in the capitalistic organization of agriculture ("La Révolution française et les paysans," *Études,* p. 258); and *La Révolution française,* pp. 155–62.

group as consisting not only of the urban and rural proletariat but also of the much more politically important popular category of artisans and shopkeepers in the cities and the *petite bourgeoisie* in the villages; and (2) his explanation of how class considerations within this pattern had a definite but limited effect on the course of events.

Once a united third estate in the cities and a "bloc paysan" in the countryside had overthrown the old system of privilege in 1789, there then arose conflict within this victorious "popular front." In the villages, the mass of small proprietors and modest *fermiers* and *métayers* were strongly attached to the traditional communal pattern of collective rights and regulations, with all of the advantages these had for the little man; while the rural bourgeoisie was oriented, by economic interest, toward the modern pattern and legal concepts.[63] The resulting economic conflict was reflected in the political story. The rural, upper bourgeoisie, at outs with the poorer peasants on this and other issues, was uneasy over the threats to its economic dominance,[64] and rightly so, for during the Jacobin republic of the year II the ruling Mountain followed a policy of conciliating the poorer peasants.[65] But then came a reaction which brought the dominant group back into authority in the villages.[66]

A similar conflict developed in the cities over the economic policies made necessary by the impact of revolution and war, ranging the *sans-culottes*—the proletariat plus the popular category of artisans and shopkeepers—against the more well-to-do bourgeoisie, or *notables*. In Lefebvre's opinion numerous controversies of the period stemmed from this conflict, for example the opposition of the *sans-culottes* in Lyons to the insurrection, which they saw was an upper bourgeois enterprise.[67]

63. *Les paysans du Nord pendant la Révolution française,* pp. 70–71, 110–11, 254, 425 ff., 906; "La Révolution française et les paysans," *Études,* pp. 250, 263.
64. *Les paysans du Nord pendant la Révolution française,* pp. 321–24, 798–803.
65. *Ibid.,* pp. 430, 477–78, 863.
66. *Ibid.,* pp. 695, 865.
67. *Annales,* No. 101 (1946), pp. 74, 76.

The theme of his books on Thermidor, the Directory, and the Napoleonic period is that the urban and rural upper class reasserted itself, with a heightened consciousness of class as a result of its experiences; and that it did so in a social hierarchy which eventually united the *notables,* the old upper bourgeoisie, the *nouveaux riches* of the war years, and the former aristocracy.[68] This was the group which finally completed the bourgeois revolution and took possession of the French government in 1830.[69]

Mention should be made of still another aspect of Lefebvre's scholarly and eclectic approach to the history of the social class. While he sees class considerations as affecting such varied decisions as those that fixed the fate of the king and the details of the voting system, he nevertheless disagreed at times with the class interpretation of events. Thus he differed with Mathiez on the economic policies of the year II, and specifically the Ventôse decrees. These, according to Lefebvre, were only a "mesure de circonstance" and not a plan to reorganize society.[70] He contended that the Convention, although a bourgeois body, sometimes worked against the interests of its class because its primary concern was not to defend those interests but to win the war.[71]

May one, less than a year and a half after Lefebvre's death, attempt an assessment of his place in the historiography of the French Revolution? Such an evaluation at this early date is risky. Yet certain conclusions seem to be evident.

Lefebvre was the leader in the twentieth-century movement in the direction of the scholarly study of the social and economic history of the French Revolution, and of the peasants in particular; and by both example and exhortation throughout his long career as scholar, professor, and editor he gave a strong stimulus to the careful, professional, and analytical work which so clearly distinguishes his own writing (and that of those who have fol-

68. *Les Thermidoriens,* pp. 12–13, 54, 107, 198–200, 212–213; *La Révolution française,* pp. 420–29; *Le Directoire,* p. 195; *Napoléon,* pp. 4, 68, 119, 134–38, 408, 412; *Les paysans du Nord pendant la Révolution française,* pp. 695, 865.
69. *La Révolution française,* p. 637.
70. *Ibid.,* p. 398.
71. *Ibid.,* pp. 546–49.

lowed his example) from earlier attempts to describe social and economic developments during the revolution. Yet he had no idea that he had achieved a definitive understanding of French society during that period, and the theme of tentativeness—that more work must be done, that new insights and hypotheses would and should appear—runs through all his work. Hence also the cordial reception he accorded to the recent studies of writers in the area of social history who further refined his work on class.[72]

Belonging to an older generation, he himself made very little use of the insights of the various social sciences which were developing during his lifetime. He thought that perhaps psychoanalysis would some day make a contribution to historical understanding, but he felt that that day had not yet arrived.[73] His own characterization of Napoleon as a *tempérament* was a first step, in his opinion, in the direction of a sort of biological-psychological approach to history, but he was careful to say that this was just a hypothesis.[74] His work on the Great Fear and his emphasis on the "complot aristocratique" during the revolution, as well as his studies of class structure, took him to the borders of social psychology and sociology, and also, when he studied the peasant village, to the borders of social anthropology as well. He affirmed that history in the future should join forces with these related disciplines,[75] but he himself was cautious. He was reluctant to stray very far from his documents, and he avoided easy formulas.

Lefebvre united the caution of the research scholar, ever aware of his dependence on his documents, with a willingness at least to consider new methods, whether they be statistical or psychoanalytical. This combined approach he applied both to economic and social history on the one hand, and to a newer category of social-psychological history on the other. Herein lies his significance in the historiography of the French Revolution.

72. See for example his reviews of recent books by Soboul and Rudé in *Annales,* No. 156 (1959), pp. 164–73, 174–77.

73. *Ibid.,* No. 120 (1950), p. 392.

74. *Ibid.,* No. 136 (1954), p. 268. See also his comments on this in "Quelques réflexions sur l'histoire des civilisations," *ibid.,* pp. 102–3.

75. "Avenir de l'histoire," *Études,* p. 6.

# IX

## Sir Richard Lodge (1855–1936)

John H. Davis

When Sir Richard Lodge, full of years and of honors, addressed the Royal Historical Society, of which he had just been elected president, upon the subject "Thomas Frederick Tout: a retrospect of twin academic careers," he closed with an unexpected note of humility in comparing his accomplishments with those of his predecessor:

> It was inevitable that two men starting from very much the same point, with similar interests, aims, and occupations, should regard themselves as having run a race against each other for over half a century. And over the long course he had won. I may have gained certain advantages at the outset, but he had superior grit and staying power. He kept his gaze more firmly fixed upon the finishing post, whereas I had allowed my eyes and even my steps to wander too often by the way. He accomplished solid and lasting work, mine so far has been scantier and more fugitive. . . . He overcame all obstacles, he lived a gallant life, he was in many ways a great man, and he will go down to posterity as a great teacher and a great historian.[1]

The statement gives a clue to the speaker's career, and the final sentence might well have been used as his own epitaph, for Lodge has been justly called "a signal and outstanding example of the combination of the scholar and the man of action."

Brief though it was, the address, which was far more auto-

1. *Cornhill magazine*, N.S., LXVIII (1930), 126.

biographical than biographical, revealed its author as a remarkable man who twice did not hesitate to break with what seemed to be a successful career for the greater glory of history. And few who heard it expected their septuagenarian president to live to produce works which rivaled, if they did not surpass, the sum total of his previous productions in quantity as well as in quality. Indeed, the life of Sir Richard holds an interest which his writings do not invariably display, and in that time-honored dichotomy of "life and work" one is tempted to dwell upon the former at the expense of the latter.[2] If further justification for this were needed, it might be found in the following reasons: his long career formed a connecting link between the age of Stubbs, Creighton, and Freeman and the organized research of today; he was intimately associated with the development of historical study in three important universities and a messenger of the gospel of history to Scotland; finally, an understanding of his activities makes clearer the trends of his writing and explains the long gap in his productivity.

Family influence played an indirect and minor role in making a historian of Lodge, although he guided his sister Eleanor's footsteps in pursuit of the muse. It must have been, nevertheless, an unusual family which could produce in one generation four such outstanding scholars as Sir Oliver, the scientist, spiritualist, and one-time principal of Birmingham University; Alfred, a famous mathematician; and two historians, Sir Richard and Eleanor Constance, vice-principal of Lady Margaret Hall, Oxford, and later principal of Westfield College, London.

A remote ancestor of the Lodges migrated to Ireland from Yorkshire in the time of Charles II, and the family remained there until the beginning of the nineteenth century, when Richard's grandfather, the Reverend Oliver Lodge, returned to En-

2. I wish to acknowledge my great indebtedness to Miss Margaret Lodge for her extraordinary kindness in sending me the typescript copy of her very interesting unpublished biography of her father. I am dependent on it for many unacknowledged facts and quotations. I must also express my gratitude to Dr. D. B. Horn for his valuable assistance, his unpublished bibliography, and other inaccessible material; to Sir Francis Wylie for his help; and to many other English and American scholars who took time to answer requests for information.

gland and finally settled in Cambridgeshire. As he was the husband of three wives and the father of twenty-five children, it was natural that the family should scatter; so Lodge's father, another Oliver, settled and then married in Penkhull, Staffordshire, in the eighteen-forties. Here, as agent for the sale of blue clay to the neighboring potteries, he did a flourishing business, which later necessitated a move to Wolstanton, but business remained a family affair, with the children frequently taking a hand in clerical tasks.

Richard, the fourth son, was born at Penkhull on June 20, 1855, and grew up in the smoky atmosphere of the "five towns" under the stern Victorian discipline of his business-like father. Literary tastes were instilled by the mother's side of the family. Partly because of the father's belief in rigorous treatment and partly because of family connections with the school, Richard was sent to Christ's Hospital, an ancient foundation of Edward VI in Newgate Street, London. For nine years he wore the traditional blue coat and yellow stockings of the school.[3] Here he attained his enormous height of six feet, four inches, which so distinguished his physical appearance and which was characteristic of his family. The parental philosophy (that support would be freely forthcoming for sons who adhered to the family business but that anyone who wished to pursue the career of learning must help himself) led Richard to seek the Brackenbury historical scholarship at Balliol College, Oxford. This launched his historical career.

The long interval of years which elapsed from the day he entered Oxford as a shy, angular schoolboy in ill-fitting, borrowed clothing until he was returned to Oxford to be laid to rest in Holywell cemetery with dignitaries from several universities and learned societies in attendance, may conveniently be divided into three periods—geographically, Oxford, Scotland, and Harpenden; or, occupationally, undergraduate and don, professor and man of action, and researcher and scholar.

Oxford left an indelible impress on Lodge. Friends, ideas, and

3. Mr. G. L. O. Flecker, headmaster of Christ's Hospital, wrote a letter to the *Times*, Aug. 6, 1936, enumerating Lodge's many activities in behalf of his old school. He was almoner twice and later president of the council.

affections of his Oxford days remained with him through life; and he became, as it were, an amalgam of the spirit of his two colleges, Balliol and Brasenose. He made his first assault on the Brackenbury in 1873 and always retained a vivid memory of that ordeal: the portrait-lined hall, the self-assured, gowned undergraduates, and the two awkward and timid London schoolboys, himself and Tout, writing furiously.[4] He failed in the first attempt but secured an unexpected exhibition which enabled him to enter Balliol the following autumn, and he succeeded on the third try. Oxford in the seventies was an exciting place. Ruskin was leading his "diggers" (of whom Lodge was to be one) to work on the Ferry-Hincksey road. Balliol, enjoying its golden age under the mastership of Benjamin Jowett, was the nursery of many outstanding men of the next generation. Observe the historians alone: slightly senior to Lodge were Richard Prothero, Herbert Warren, C. H. Simpkinson; his own year was a veritable *annus mirabilis,* for among his contemporaries were W. P. Ker, R. Lane Poole, Horace Round, T. F. Tout, Arnold Toynbee, and F. C. Montague; and C. H. Firth was one year junior.[5]

At the time, Balliol had no regular fellow of history. Lodge and some of his friends took their first essays to J. Franck Bright, of University College. In mid-career, however, he came under the instruction of the great Stubbs, thanks to the bargaining-power of Benjamin Jowett, who, in obtaining the services of the regius professor as chaplain of the college, required that he teach four selected undergraduates in history.[6] As an under-

4. *Cornhill,* N.S., LXVIII (1930), 117. For this examination Lodge spent three weeks cramming Hallam's *Middle ages,* Robertson's *Charles V,* Macaulay's *Essays,* and the *Institutes* of Justinian.

5. *The collected papers of Thomas Frederick Tout* (3 vols.; Manchester, 1935), I, 3. Charles E. Mallet, *History of the University of Oxford* (3 vols.; London, 1924–28), III, 457.

6. *Cornhill,* N.S., LXVIII (1930), 119. Sir Charles Oman (*On the writing of history* [London, 1939], pp. 221–35) gives an interesting account of the development of the Oxford history school. Lodge frequently mentioned Stubbs's influence—e.g., *History,* XVI (1931), 188, where in a book review he condemned the study of contemporary history and remarked: "I am fortified by the recollection that my eminent teacher, Dr. Stubbs, always maintained that recent history was wholly unsuited for educational purposes."

John H. Davis

graduate, Lodge won all the available history laurels: the Stanhope prize (1875), with an essay on Cardinal Beaufort, and in the next year the Lothian, on the subject "The causes of the failure of parliamentary institutions in Spain and France." Then came the expected "first" in a class which included G. E. Buckle and Arthur Hassall. He had just resumed his interrupted study of the classics when Brasenose College "startled Oxford" by announcing a fellowship in both ancient and modern history. Lodge, one of thirteen applicants, entered the contest and won.

Later he confessed a regret that he had not followed Jowett's advice to continue with "greats" (Latin, Greek, and philosophy) or to proceed with advanced study; but, weary of examinations and "satiated with success," after a brief stay at the University of Vienna, he plunged, as he said,

> into the absorptive life of college lecturer, tutor, librarian, vice-principal, as promotion came to me. I also took a number of other occupations, including the game of golf which left me sadly little time for the serious study of history. . . . It is true that like Tout I wrote text books, but unlike him I did little else.[7]

Little else, if one is to except his wide interest in games, the boat club, Vincent's; his editorship of the nascent *Oxford magazine* (1883); his famous Sunday breakfasts—all of which endeared him to the undergraduates and made the attractive don and his charming wife outstanding in the life of the college.[8] His influence, however, was felt beyond its walls. He, A. L. Smith, and

7. *Cornhill*, N.S., LXVIII (1930), 121.
8. Mallet, III, 461; *Oxford magazine*, LV (October, 1936), 81. Lodge is described at the time by a younger Brasenose colleague, F. J. Wylie, in an obituary notice in the college magazine, as follows:

"Lodge too, was a lovable man. He might easily have been formidable, with his great height, somewhat truculent moustache, and eyes that looked so very straight at you. 'Sometimes when Lodge looks at me,' a fellow of the college once said to me, 'I have an uneasy feeling that he wants to kick me.' And he *could* look like that on occasions. But he couldn't go on being formidable, he had too much humor, and too much kindliness. Anything brusque was on the surface, a thin cover to a warm humanity. His manliness, his broad judgement, his dislike of anything affected or pretentious, whether in behavior or in writing—these fitted him well for the business of a Brasenose don, and it was as that that he spent what must have been among the happiest and most satisfying years of his life."

179

Arthur Johnson were the leading members of the Association of History Tutors, which did so much to formulate the program of the school of modern history (recently divorced from law) and to complete the system of intercollegiate lectures, or "lecture pool," inaugurated by Mandell Creighton in the sixties. This "history ring," or "gang" (as their opponents dubbed them), became so powerful that on many occasions it did not hesitate to thwart the plans and ignore the lectures of successive regius professors.[9] Meanwhile Lodge's own lectures were crowded, and his ability as examiner and tutor was acknowledged by all; but a growing sense of dissatisfaction haunted him. "I was beset," he wrote, "by the thought that I was dissipating my energies and that I was getting into a groove from which there was no obvious exit except a complete change of scene."

Many old Balliol friends in Scotland urged him northward, and so, when a Royal Commission finally forced the establishment of chairs of history in the Scottish universities (1894), he applied first for Edinburgh; but when Prothero was chosen, he transferred his candidature to Glasgow and was successful.[10] The Scottish phase had begun.

The subject of his inaugural lecture at Glasgow was "The study of history in a Scottish university." As champion of a newcomer to the curriculum, especially one which was forced from the outside, Lodge felt "impelled . . . to advertise the wares which I have to submit for your approval or consumption." He de-

9. Oman, pp. 221–35. The Creightons interested Lodge in the Association for the Education of Women, and after 1882 he took two women pupils a year.

10. In his article, "History in Scottish universities: reminiscences of a professor" (*University of Edinburgh journal*, IV [1931], 97–109), Lodge enumerated the problems, associates, pupils, departmental changes, etc., of his long residence in Glasgow and Edinburgh. His chief competitors at Edinburgh were P. H. Brown and G. W. Prothero. At Glasgow he won over Oscar Browning, H. A. L. Fisher, and W. J. Ashley.

Sir Charles Firth ("Dates and anniversaries," *History*, N.S., XVI [1931], 97) gives this anecdote: "I remember being asked in 1894, when a professorship of history was vacant at Glasgow, which of the numerous candidates was likely to be appointed. I said, 'Lodge.' My friend replied, 'Well, he is the right man for the place. He has more lectures concealed about his person than any man in Oxford.'"

veloped three propositions: that history deserves to be studied, that it should be studied in universities, and that it had especial claim to the attention of a Scottish university. He based his apologia upon the experience of other universities; upon the thesis of Sir John Seeley that history offers excellent training in morals and citizenship; upon the necessity of observing the continuity of history; and upon the idea that practical discipline of the reasoning faculties is provided by "the sifting of evidences, the comparison of authorities, and the judicial decision between conflicting views." It is impossible to judge a structure from a few bricks, but to quote *obiter dicta* from the address may reveal some of Lodge's ideas on history. "It is true," he said, "no success has attended the attempt to formulate general laws of history, or to find a scientific basis for the actions of states so that men can prophesy the future from the past"; or "Nothing is more misleading than a partial or a pedantic knowledge of history," which is able to supply arguments for the most opposite political views. He held that "it is not the business of a professor . . . to make proselytes to any particular view: it is his business to supply knowledge rather than convictions; to furnish his students with the means of forming their own judgments, and not to force down their throats his own opinions." Or again, "Few things are more likely to contribute to the stability and prosperity of a democratic state than the training of its members by an intelligent study of history." After sketching his own plans and praising the work of Scottish historians and historical societies, he concluded:

> If any exertions on my part can create or extend an interest in the study of history in general; still more, if they can induce any student to devote himself to historical research, and especially to the history of his own country . . . I shall feel that the modest hopes with which I commence my teaching in this university will have been more than fulfilled.[11]

The stay in Glasgow proved brief. Even before he journeyed to Scotland a siege of illness necessitated a long vacation abroad.

11. *The study of history in a Scottish university; an anaugural lecture delivered on October 22nd, 1894* (Glasgow, 1894).

Since he suffered most of his life from bronchial asthma, the murky, foggy atmosphere of the west proved too severe for him. When Prothero resigned at Edinburgh in 1899, Lodge gained that appointment.

In both Glasgow and Edinburgh the professor lectured five days a week to an "ordinary class" during the short Scottish term (October to April) on a general survey of British history which broadened out to include England's European relations. Less frequently he met smaller "honours classes." Here he specialized on his favorite topics: the eighteenth century, the British Empire, or the importance of sea power. These courses were designed less for research than to furnish lucid outlines of a period; to show the chain of cause and effect; and to enable a student to master other periods by independent work. The numbers in his ordinary classes grew rapidly: in Glasgow from an original nineteen to over fifty, while in Edinburgh, especially after the new Arts Ordinance (1908) placed history on an equality with older subjects, the number of students increased from fifty to well over two hundred.[12]

In Scotland the friendly don developed gradually into the more isolated and austere Scottish professor. In his new surroundings the old links with the students—the coachings, the breakfasts, and playing-fields—were gone. His method of lecturing also underwent a change. At Oxford he spoke rapidly, often from notes, and moved about on the dais; but in Scotland his tempo slowed, he became less dependent upon notes, more formal and formidable. Students spoke of him as "the most com-

12. See *University of Edinburgh Journal*, IV (1931), 101–6, for departmental struggles and changes at Edinburgh during Lodge's tenure. Some research was possible in Scottish history, but it was more difficult in his field. Dr. D. B. Horn writes: "If an exceptional student wished to continue work on history after graduation Lodge was always ready to give generous advice and assistance, but post-graduate work in European history meant months or years reading at the P.R.O. and B.M. Few Scottish students could afford to do this. . . . . When the Institute of Historical Research was founded in London, Lodge did everything in his power to encourage post-graduate students to work there and shortly before he retired he arranged for the University to pay the fees of students from Edinburgh who went to the Institute."

petent and masculine lecturer I have heard," or "the finest lecturer of my time, the perfection of form, charm, delivery."

In Edinburgh, since history was already firmly established, Lodge chose as his inaugural subject, "How should history be studied?"[13] In his lecture he compared two views of history: one history as a means of general education, the other history as training in research (he called them the "approach" of Oxford and of Paris). He maintained that an ideal school should secure the benefits of both by combining with a broad general knowledge the minute study of one particular field. For he held that the student, "by tracing his knowledge back to original sources and subjecting them to the most minute examination," would gain an insight and surety of judgment unattainable in any other way. And he voiced violent disagreement with an American professor who had told him: "Don't bother yourself with all that grubbing among mouldy records, leave that to the Stubbses and Freemans, they are the hewers of wood and the drawers of water for us whose business is to expound the lessons of history to the world."

In the Scottish years Lodge developed into a great administrator, a civic figure, active in national and local politics but more especially in various forms of social and educational betterment. At Edinburgh he became assessor of the *senatus* on the university court and dean of the faculty of arts, and many expected that he would be made principal—but, as he later told a friend, his colleagues thought he had too much power already. Under his guidance the department expanded enormously, both in numbers, and in the range of subjects offered.

Always a believer in the close connection between history and politics, he plunged, soon after his arrival in Edinburgh, into the activities of the Liberal League. These "imperialistic" Liberals, under the leadership of Rosebery, Haldane, and Grey, condemned the "labby and flabby" wing of the party at the time of the Boer War. As president of the eastern Scottish branch, Lodge presided at numerous meetings, made many speeches, and

13. *How should history be studied?* (Edinburgh, 1901).

formed an enduring friendship with Lord Rosebery. Seeley's influence may have led him into politics, but the Balliol of Jowett, Green, and Toynbee taught him to believe that every man was bound to give some social service to the community. He wanted to prove to himself "whether a university professor . . . was altogether the feckless and rather incompetent person in practical life which he was often perhaps justifiably considered to be." Thus he took a leading part in organizing and directing such social services as the University Settlement, the Charity Organization Society, and the Distress Committee. A natural leader of men, these organizations brought out his fighting qualities, whether with the government in behalf of the unemployed or against refractory workers. He was also drafted by his old pupil, Lord Askwith, to act as arbitrator during the era of strikes which preceded the war, an employment which sometimes found reflection in his books.[14]

The war of 1914 only increased Lodge's activities and burdens. In addition to his other work he was made secretary of the Scottish Committee of the Prince of Wales' Fund for Relief of Distress. With two sons in the army he went abroad himself on two occasions to lecture to troops, and in the final year of the war death took three of his seven children. Honors, as well as sorrows, came to him, for during the Edinburgh years he was knighted (1917), made honorary fellow of Brasenose, and received honorary degrees from Glasgow, Manchester, and Edinburgh.[15] But old qualms of discontent again assailed him. "Extraneous activities" were making him neglect the study of history, "which at the outset," he said, "I had taken as my life's work."

14. E.g., in *Great Britain and Prussia in the eighteenth century: being the Ford Lectures delivered in the University of Oxford* (Oxford, 1923), p. 36, he speaks of Lord Hyndford's acting "very much as a conciliator in a modern industrial dispute." In *Studies in eighteenth century diplomacy, 1740–1748* (London, 1930), p. 47, he says of the Convention of Turin that it "reads more like a labour agreement than a political convention."

15. See *Times*, Feb. 13, 1917, for an account of the knighthood. Two other historians, Julian Corbett and Paul Vinagradoff, were knighted at the same time. Lodge's honorary degrees were: LL.D., Glasgow (1905); Litt.D., Manchester (1912); LL.D., Edinburgh (1926).

184

I trusted too long to past accumulations of knowledge, and it was necessary to replenish the store. This could not be done if I stayed in Edinburgh. . . . So after thirty-one years of service in Scotland and seventy years of life I quitted Edinburgh and migrated to the neighborhood of the Public Record Office and the British Museum in the hope of rejuvenating myself by becoming once more a student of history.[16]

With this valiant statement he retired into activity. How well he succeeded during the Harpenden period will be seen from the discussion of his work.

His historical writing falls into two uneven divisions. During the forty-five years of teaching in Oxford and in Scotland the register of his writings is relatively small. Indeed, in Dr. Horn's unpublished bibliography titles from the years 1878 to 1923, including books, reviews, and articles, take up only three pages; whereas seven are required to enumerate the work of his last twelve years. Another sharp difference is that, whereas the books of the earlier period are entirely textbooks, the latter work represents more specialization and research.

In England the final quarter of the last century and the early years of the present one were a veritable "age of text books," ranging from simple manuals, designed to meet the needs of the new historical instruction in schools and universities, to the elaborately planned series, such as the Cambridge histories, the Oman, or the Hunt and Poole multiple-volumed histories of England, which were designed to embody the latest results of "scientific" scholarship. Lodge and most of his well-known contemporaries in the field of history took an active part in laying this solid foundation of political texts. On this proclivity of the English for texts, the French reviewer of Lodge's *Richelieu* remarked: "Le petit livre . . . fait honneur à la collection qu'il a inaugurée et qui vient de s' ajouter à toutes celles que le goût de vulgarisation historique a suscitée chez nos voisins, nos précurseurs dans un genre qui convient particulièrement à leur esprit positif et *matter of fact.*"[17]

16. *University of Edinburgh Journal,* IV (1931), 109.
17. G. Fagniez, *RH,* LXIII (1897), 379.

SIR RICHARD LODGE

During his years of teaching he produced: "a pioneer work," *The history of modern Europe, 1453–1878*,[18] more familiarly known as *The student's modern Europe; Richelieu*,[19] in the "Foreign statesman series"; *The close of the middle ages, 1273–1494*,[20] in the Rivington series "Periods of European history"; and *The history of England from the Restoration to the death of William III, 1660–1702*,[21] for the "Political history of England" series. In addition to these books he contributed chapters on eastern diplomacy to the *Cambridge modern history:* "The European powers and the eastern question," "The extinction of Poland, 1788–1797," and "Austria, Poland, and Turkey";[22] three articles for the ninth edition of the *Encyclopaedia Britannica,* on the Hanseatic League and on medieval and modern Spain; numerous articles for the three volumes of *Palgrave's dictionary of political economy;* a translation of two chapters of Bluntschli's *Theory of the state;* and about an average of one review a year for the *English historical*

18. London, 1885. This became a standard text in schools and colleges in Great Britain for over forty years and went through many editions. Revised in 1927 under the title *History of Europe, 1789–1920,* the section from 1871 to 1920 was written by Lodge's "brilliant pupil," D. B. Horn. His own section remained virtually unaltered, and he took no cognizance of changes in information and interpretation. In the preface of the new edition he tells of writing the original text at the request of Mr. Strachan-Davidson, of his desire to exploit his new-found knowledge, of the unpleasant task of curtailing the proofs and cutting out all the "purple passages."

19. London, 1896. T. Kükelhaus (*HZ*, LXXIX [1897], 325–27) speaks of it as "die beste moderne Biographie Richelieus." G. Fagniez (*loc. cit.*, pp. 379–81) is more critical. He carefully notes Lodge's contributions but points out the need of revision. Short notice in *AHR*, III (1898), 384–85.

20. London, 1901. J. H. Robinson (*AHR*), VII [1902], 396) is critical; J. P. Whitney (*EHR*, XVII [1902], 819–20) is complimentary. In the *Guide to historical literature* (New York, 1931) R. A. Newhall says of the series: "After the lapse of a generation these books are probably the most useful handbooks of political history in English" (p. 68). Other contributors to the series were: C. Oman, T. F. Tout, A. H. Johnson, H. O. Wakeman, A. Hassall, H. M. Stephens, W. A. Phillips—all prolific textbook-writers.

21. London, 1910. Critically reviewed by W. C. Abbott in *AHR*, XV (1910), 853–55. Other analytical reviews: *EHR*, XXVI (1911), 791–94; *RH*, CVI (1911), 146–47; *Scottish historical review*, VIII (1911), 203–4.

22. Also contributed chaps. xi and xvii to *Cambridge modern history,* VIII (Cambridge, 1904), 306–37, 521–52; and chap. xii to *ibid.*, V (Cambridge, 1908), 338–71.

*review,* many of which were on successive volumes of the famous French *Recueil des instructions données aux ambassadeurs et ministres de France, depuis les traités de Westphalie jusqu'à la Révolution française,* though occasionally the work reviewed reflected the subject of the book he was engaged upon at the time.

This condensed bibliography of the early period indicates interest in an extensive range of subjects, a gradually increasing concentration on more limited but more amply treated periods, and a definite fondness for political and diplomatic history. The author also showed a progressive improvement in the manipulation of subject matter. Trained at the hands of Stubbs, an intimate friend and disciple of Creighton, a lifelong admirer of Ranke, "whom," he said, "I was brought up to regard as perhaps the greatest all round historian of the nineteenth century," his work naturally reflects their characteristics—their sober, cautious, analytical style. One reviewer expresed it in these words:

> Professor Lodge is of the school of Ranke rather than Macaulay. His volume has none of the premeditated brilliance of the great Whig historian. It is free from that "stamping emphasis" of which Lord Morley once complained. But the style fits the subject, being concise yet supple; it is laudably free from needless rhetoric, being set rather in the scientific key.[23]

Another spoke of his books as "without ornament, but judicious and compact."

It would be a work of supererogation to attempt to enumerate the many changes and discoveries made by research since the publication of these texts. At the time they were written they incorporated the results of the best available secondary work. They have been through many editions and are still useful. To condemn them as severely political, tending to be compendiums of names and facts presented in an almost chronological order, is merely to call them typical of the "new history," the vulgarizations of their time. James Harvey Robinson, prophet and propa-

---

23. *Scottish historical review,* VIII ( 1911 ), 203. When Lodge addressed the newly formed Glasgow Historical Society on the subject of great historians he particularly praised Thucydides, Tacitus, Gibbon, Macaulay, and Robertson ( *ibid.,* I, 224 ).

gandist of the succeeding brand of "new history," which has emphasized economic, social, and intellectual developments at the expense of the political, took this ironic thrust at the type of writing represented by Lodge and his generation in the following short notice of Lodge's *Close of the middle ages:*

> Professor Lodge has added . . . another somewhat dreary sketch of political events to the somewhat juiceless series known as "Periods of European history." . . . His chronicle is but slightly more philosophic than one of the ninth century, and he shows that extreme partiality for proper names which one finds in the Catalog of the Ships or in an Icelandic Saga. To judge from the index, Professor Lodge has found occasion to mention within the modest compass of his volume upwards of a thousand proper names. Obviously if the capture of the fortresses of Elna and Girona, "both after an obstinate resistance" by Philip le Hardi, and the fact that Giovanni, the third son of Sixtus IV's brother married the daughter of Federigo de Montefeltro—if all events of similar importance must at least be mentioned in a small volume covering over two centuries of European experience, no wonder that there is no room to say anything of European progress except in a most perfunctory chapter upon the Renaissance at the end of the volume, entirely uncorrelated with the rest of the book. Those familiar with Professor Lodge's gloomy *Modern Europe* will find that his conception of the functions of an historian has been in no way modified by the current discussions in France and Germany as to the proper scope of general history, nor by the recent contributions to economic history.[24]

This assault, though containing elements of truth, is unfair. Lodge knew, as well as any, that each generation must rewrite its texts and had himself expressed that idea ten years before in his Glasgow inaugural:

> History is a progressive and not a stationary subject. The books which satisfied and instructed one generation have to be rewritten, altered, and added to, the next. There is a constant bringing to light of new evidence . . . which compels students to reopen what seem to be settled questions and to reconsider verdicts which appeared final and conclusive. . . . The process is both

24. *AHR*, VII (1902), 396. For an interesting modern defense of the political approach see Miss Violet Barbour's review of G. N. Clark, *The later Stuarts, 1660–1714* (Oxford, 1934), in *AHR*, XL (1935), 728–31.

necessary and stimulating; without it history would still be instructive, but it would be lifeless and dull; to borow a simile from a Scottish game, it would be like playing golf forever on a course that contained no hazards, no bad lies. It would be exercise, but it would be a poor game.[25]

Indeed, in his review of G. N. Clark's *The later Stuarts*, which superseded his own best text, Lodge graciously pointed out the shift in emphasis and Professor Clark's successful blending of economic and social history into the political narrative, explaining that his own "rather perfunctory chapter on literature and kindred topics" was added to a volume "somewhat ostentatiously called the 'Political history of England'" because of an afterthought on the part of the editor.[26]

*Great Britain and Prussia in the eighteenth century*,[27] the Ford Lectures delivered at Oxford in the spring of 1922, marked a turning-point in Sir Richard's career. He said:

> The preparation of the Ford lectures . . . reawakened old enthusiasms, and convinced me that I must free myself from other business and establish a closer connection with the Record Office and the British Museum. So at last I cut the Gordian knot, by resigning my chair and came south in the hope of becoming once more an historian rather than a factotum.[28]

Its preparation was somewhat hasty. As its author was too engrossed in manifold activities during the preceding years to keep *au courant* of contemporary literature on the subject, the book has been criticized for shortcomings in documentation and for certain dubious conclusions,[29] but it inaugurated the long line of

25. *The study of history in a Scottish university* (Glasgow, 1894), p. 17.
26. *EHR*, L (1935), 717–19. Several reviewers had censured Lodge for this "inadequate postscript."
27. Oxford, 1923.
28. *Cornhill*, N.S., LXVIII (1930), 123. His return for the lectures was a personal triumph. He had a large audience, which included old associates and friends, and so impressed the undergraduates that they broke tradition in applauding the performance. He gave the same lectures on the following days at Westfield College for his sister Eleanor.
29. W. L. Dorn, "Frederick the Great and Lord Bute," *JMH*, I (1929), 529–61, defends Bute against Lodge's strictures. In his *Competition for empire, 1740–1763* (New York, 1940) Dorn contends that Sir Richard

articles and studies on the eighteenth century which did much to throw light on that period of which Carlyle declared "not dismal swamp under coverlet of London fog could be uglier."

The bibliography of the final years (1924–36) may be summarized as follows: one full-length book (his best), *Studies in eighteenth century diplomacy, 1740–1748;*[30] two volumes of diplomatic correspondence, edited with introductions and explanatory notes, *The private correspondence of Chesterfield and Newcastle, 1744–46*[31] and *The private correspondence of Sir Benjamin Keene, K.B.;*[32] chapters in four books of collected essays or lectures;[33] two articles for the *Dictionary of national biography* (on Sir William Turner and Sir James Henry Ramsay); five documented articles and twenty reviews for the *English historical review;* eight articles or addresses for the *Transactions of the Royal Historical Society;* and five articles, forty-five reviews, and almost as many short notices for *History*—a formidable total.

Some of the articles were based directly upon archival research; others were simplifications of his own findings which often took the form of "historical revisions" or lectures to learned societies. With two exceptions—a lecture on Sir Robert Peel and his first presidential address to the Royal Historical Society on Machiavelli's *Il principe*[34]—they were devoted to the early eighteenth

---

interpreted Frederick's actions of 1756 too much in the light of the *Politische Correspondenz;* see especially chaps. iv, vii, and viii and his able bibliographical essay. Reviews of *Great Britain and Prussia: AHR,* XXIX (1924), 325–26, by B. E. Schmitt; *EHR,* XXXIX (1924), 292–93, by Basil Williams; and *RH,* CXLVII (1924), 250–52, by A. Waddington.

30. London, 1930.

31. Camden series, Royal Historical Society, 1930.

32. Cambridge, 1933.

33. "Sir Robert Peel," *Political principles of some notable prime ministers of the nineteenth century,* ed. F. J. C. Hearnshaw (London, 1926), pp. 43–104; "The Anglo-French alliance, 1716–1731," *Studies in Anglo-French history during the eighteenth, nineteenth and twentieth centuries,* ed. A. Coville and H. Temperley (Cambridge, 1935), pp. 3–18; "Sir Robert Walpole," *From Anne to Victoria,* ed. B. Dobrée (London, 1937), pp. 108–29; and "The Methuen treaties of 1703," *Chapters in Anglo-Portuguese relations,* ed. E. Prestage (London, 1934).

34. *Transactions of the Royal Historical Society,* 4th ser. (London, 1918——), XIII, 1–16. This lecture derived from his Oxford teaching and from his admiration of Ranke.

century and dealt primarily with three fields: the War of the Austrian Succession, Anglo-French relations prior to that war, and some aspects of England's relations with Spain and Portugal. On the first of these, in addition to the *Studies,* Lodge wrote four well-documented articles for the *English historical review,* which give a fairly complete picture of England's diplomatic maneuvers at the Russian court between 1739 and 1748; undoubtedly he intended to collect them later into a volume. These were: "The first Anglo-Russian treaty, 1739–1742"; "The Treaty of Abo and the Swedish succession," "Russia, Prussia and Great Britain, 1742–1744"; and, in two instalments, "Lord Hyndford's embassy to Russia, 1744–1749."[35] Within the same field were: "An episode of Anglo-Russian relations during the War of the Austrian Succession"; "The mission of Henry Legge to Berlin, 1748"; and two simplifications, "The continental policy of Great Britain, 1740–1760," and "The maritime powers in the eighteenth century."[36]

The two other periods were covered much less technically. On Anglo-French relations prior to 1740 one should mention: "English foreign policy, 1660–1715," "English neutrality in the War of the Polish Succession," "The Treaty of Seville, 1729," "The Anglo-French alliance, 1716–1731," and "Sir Robert Walpole"; on Spain and Portgual, two addresses to the Royal Historical Society, "Sir Benjamin Keene, K.B.: a study in Anglo-Spanish relations" and "The English factory at Lisbon: some chapters in its history," and two historical revisions, "The Spanish succession" and "The Methuen treaties of 1703."[37]

The devotion to one period and to one type of writing called forth occasional apologies from Sir Richard:

> But a shoemaker must stick to his last, and I own that I myself take such pleasure in fitting together the jig-saw puzzle of diplo-

35. *EHR,* XLIII (1928), 354–75, 540–71; XLV (1930), 579–611; XLVI (1931), 48–76, 387–422.

36. *Trans. Roy. Hist. Soc.,* 4th ser., IX, 63–83; XIV, 141–73; *History,* N.S., XVI (1932), 298–304; XV (1930), 246–51 (historical revision No. 55).

37. *History,* N.S., XV (1931), 276–307; *Trans. Roy. Hist. Soc.,* 4th ser., XIV, 141–73; XVI, 1–43; *Studies in Anglo-French History,* pp. 3–18; *From Anne to Victoria,* pp. 108–29; *Trans. Roy. Hist. Soc.,* 4th ser., XV, 243–69; XVI, 211–47; *History,* N.S., XII (1928), 333–38; XVIII (1933), 33–35 (historical revisions Nos. 44 and 65).

matic relations I find myself impelled to assume . . . a similar enthusiasm on the part of listeners and readers. I have tried to remember that diplomacy is carried on by human beings and not by labelled machines.[38]

This delight in constructing coherent pictures from scattered diplomatic correspondence, this almost personal interest in the "humbler agents of diplomacy," gave to his later work a freshness and immediacy lacking in the textbooks. Not that it was without a certain tediousness, for diplomatic history is a field of which Professor Temperley truly said: "Some parts are as technical and difficult as chess or mathematics and cannot be treated artistically at all." But Lodge's work was clear, and clarity was his aim.[39]

No English historian since the days of the "industrious" Archdeacon Coxe read such "acres of despatches" or soaked himself more thoroughly in the papers of the politicians of the mid-eighteenth century. He utilized the letters of Newcastle, Carteret, Hyndford, Chesterfield, Bedford, Sandwich, Keene, and many others—whether from the Record Office, the British Museum, private collections, or printed versions—for a work which Professor Muret called "si probe, si consciencieusement documentée, et si utile."

The approach was somewhat unique. Even on the brief period which Sir Richard considered preeminently his own he never produced a comprehensive magnum opus, one in which an attempt was made to weave together all the complex threads of diplomacy into a single pattern. Instead, he attempted to throw light upon certain important negotiations, certain selected diplomatic landmarks. This method, described as "quelque peu ar-

38. *Trans. Roy. Hist. Soc.*, 4th ser., XVI, 43. In *ibid.*, XIV, 1, he says: "I have written a good deal about diplomacy during the war of the Austrian succession in defiance of Carlyle who calls it 'an unintelligible huge English and Foreign delirium . . . a universal rookery of diplomatists whose loud cackle and cawing is now as if gone and mad to us; their work fallen putrescent and avoidable, dead to all creatures.' "

39. In reviewing an epigrammatic historian, Lodge remarked: "But it may be doubted whether his frequent allusive and enigmatic sentences, reminiscent of Lord Acton in his occasional moods of suggestive obscurity, are really suited to diplomatic history, which requires above all things clarity" (*History*, N.S., XV [1931], 299).

bitraire," allowed him to avoid the dangers of overaccumulation (as in the work of J. F. Chance) or the accusations of being incomplete. In this detailed work his "researches among the trees enriched his presentation of the wood." In the *Studies in eighteenth century diplomacy*, which is typical,[40] he demonstrated the vital position of the Dutch, the predominant part England and France played in the War of the Austrian Succession, and the way in which their diplomacy conditioned the actions of the other powers. He rescued from obscurity and neglect politicians and diplomatists like Lord Cartaret and Lord Sandwich (whose papers at Hinchingbrooke he was permitted to use); and from the Duke of Newcastle he scraped the mud of previous detractors. He clarified the policies of the "professor in politics," the Marquis D'Argenson, and of St. Severin, pointing out incidentally the mistakes of older historians of the period, like Arneth, Broglie, and Droysen. Finally he gave a much clearer insight into the *concilabulum* than many constitutional historians, for as a background to the diplomatic negotiations at Hanau, Worms, Breda, and Aix-la-

40. The chapter headings indicate his topical method: (chap. i) the so-called "Treaty of Hanau," 1743; (chap. ii) the Treaty of Worms, September 13, 1743; (chap. iii) D'Argenson's relations with Germany and Sardinia; (chap. iv) D'Argenson and the Dutch; (chap. v) Breda and Lisbon, August, 1746—January, 1747; (chap. vi) Sandwich and Macanaz at Breda, January–May, 1747; (chap. vii) Between Breda and Aix-la-Chapelle; (chap. viii) the Treaty of Aix-la-Chapelle. In his books Lodge followed the chapter heading with an analytical table of contents, or outline. For a complete analysis of the *Studies* see P. Muret, "L'histoire diplomatique du milieu de XVIIIe siècle d'après les travaux de Sir Richard Lodge," *Revue d'histoire moderne*, VII (1932), 77–83. He says: "Ils constituent certainment la contribution la plus étendue et beaucoup la plus critique que nous possédons aujourd'hui sur cette période si confuse." On the early part of the war, especially on the Bavarian phase, his book is superseded by Fritz Wagner, *Kaiser Karl VII und die grossen Mächte* (Stuttgart, 1938). Favorable reviews of the *Studies:* P. Vaucher in *History*, N.S., XV (1931), 371–73; W. F. Reddaway in *EHR*, XLV (1930), 653–55; G. Pagès in *RH*, CLXXIII (1934), 384–85; C. Perkins in *AHR*, XXVI (1931), 805–7.

Of the *Studies*, Lodge's friend and pupil, C. R. L. Fletcher, wrote: "I feel it is the best thing you have ever done. You have really made state papers tell their own story, so consecutively, so humanly, so unlike the style in which nearly every other 'scientific historian' makes them tell it. Gardiner and Ranke will, when you meet in Valhalla, hold out a hand of welcome to you as one of their own true breed" (Miss Lodge's manuscript).

Chapelle he revealed the intrigues of the shifting groups within the inner circle of cabinet ministers.[41]

Most of the detailed work will survive and form an incentive for further study of the period. Its sins are rather of omission than of commission. A conspicuous flaw pointed out by Pierre Muret in his study "L'histoire diplomatique du milieu du XVIII$^e$ siècle d'après les travaux de Sir Richard Lodge" is his failure to give adequate consideration to the pressure of public opinion, or of the royal will, in influencing the decisions of cabinet members in regard to foreign policy. Some contend that Lodge's work is too nationalistic, too much an English counterpart to that of J. G. Droysen;[42] but this criticism applies rather to the Ford Lectures than to the *Studies,* and even here the "nationalism" consists rather in the employment of English sources than in a chauvinistic defense of English policy. More unfortunate, from the student's point of view, is the fact that Sir Richard, who had such a thorough knowledge of the English documentation, never saw fit or took the time to produce an "étude d'ensemble" of his sources or to include a bibliography of any sort in his later work. Instead, one must scan footnotes which include explanatory material on the text, supplementary quotations, pungent critical remarks on historians, as well as bibliographical information and standard documentary references, some of which are far too abbreviated.[43]

41. In the *Studies,* as in the introduction to the *Private correspondence of Chesterfield and Newcastle,* one gains a clearer insight into the workings of the "inner cabinet," or "closet," than from the recently published posthumous article of E. R. Turner on that subject (*AHR,* XLV [1940], 761–76). Lodge was so convinced of the need for an understanding of foreign policy that he took Professor Namier severely to task for his "conspicuous omission" in this respect and for his resultant unfairness to Newcastle in his interesting review of *England in the age of the American revolution,* Vol. 1 (London, 1930), in *History,* N.S., XVI (1931), 172–76.

42. W. L. Dorn, *Competition for empire,* p. 401. In the preface of his book, Lodge contends that he was struggling against this very thing. "I was impressed by the danger that the retrospect of the past might be colored by the hostility aroused during the conflict. Against this danger—already conspicuous in the course of the war—and against the degradation of history to be the handmaid of political passion I could, at any rate, offer a passive protest."

43. For illustration: In *Great Britain and Prussia* the first four chapters

In addition to articles of pure research, Sir Richard wrote many summaries. Some were prefatory sketches to a situation he was about to describe in detail; some were historical revisions; some appeared as reviews of books or of documents. These historical *coups d'œil* furnished students and others who might have been intimidated by his technical work an opportunity to observe his conclusions with less effort. Take, for example, the article "The Treaty of Seville, 1729"; in it he devoted thirty of his forty-three pages to a sketch of the succession problems and of the conflicting commercial interests which confronted each of the major powers in the early eighteenth century. In discussing the "Polwarth papers" he reviewed at length the relations of England with the northern powers; in "Sir Benjamin Keene," with Spain; in the "English factory at Lisbon," with Portugal—all before approaching the real subject of his discourse.[44] Some simplifications oversimplified. In the articles in *History*—for example, on "The continental policy of Great Britain, 1740–1760" and "The maritime powers in the eighteenth century"—he attempted to differentiate between Whigs and Tories on the basis of foreign policy (the former, "interventionists"; the latter, "isolationists"), in contrast to the caution and the qualifications with which other recent historians have applied party tags during the mid-century.

"Although a reviewer is bound, in the exercise of his trade, to lay stress upon what he considers the defects of a book, he is equally bound to point out its merits."[45] This was Lodge's reviewing creed. It was an occupation which interested him, which he

---

contain thirteen explanatory notes, sixty references to published documents (mostly Frederick II's *Politische Correspondenz*), and sixty-three references to manuscript sources—nearly all bare references with no comment. In the later *Studies* notes are much fuller; e.g., chap. i contains thirty-three notes, of which only two are simple explanations and only four are bare references to books or documents. The remaining twenty-seven contain ten references to published and twenty-four to unpublished sources and include three discussions of books or historians, as well as one German, six French, and seventeen English quotations. Nearly all contain explanatory remarks of some kind.

44. *Trans. Roy. Hist. Soc.*, 4th ser., XV, 243–69; XVI, 1–43; 211–47. There was a good deal of repetition, especially on Anglo-French relations, prior to 1740.

45. *History*, N.S., XVI (1932), 356.

enjoyed, and at which he excelled. As he approached his eighties the trips from Harpenden to the Record Office and the Museum became increasingly difficult, but he could sit in his garden and do reviewing "with a promptness not usual with scholars" (as the editor of the *English historical review* remarked). What a number of them he produced! In his seventy-sixth year, for example, he turned out fourteen reviews and short notices for *History* and three for the *English historical review*. It is impossible to analyze all and difficult to make generalizations applicable to all. He was perhaps at his best on foreign documentary publications or foreign books. Over a period of years he followed such series as the *Recueil des instructions données aux ambassedeurs et ministres de France*, or the *Politische correspondenz* of Frederick II. In reviewing these collections he presented with great clarity the general story, any new discoveries, and any suggested revisions of interpretation provided by the documents. In considering the work of foreign historians or of solid scholarship he usually subordinated any tendency to discover peccadilloes to the larger purpose of explaining important findings.[46] But he could be scathingly critical, as when he tore apart the editing of the Polwarth manuscripts in an address to the Royal Historical Society.[47] He had a passion for correct dates and correct genealogies, and time and again he was annoyed by the work of amateur historians, "whose blemishes might have been easily got rid of if some expert had been induced to revise the proofs,"[48] while his lifelong career as an examiner often made him mention new discoveries in the

46. See reviews of P. Vaucher, *Robert Walpole et la politique de Fleury* (Paris, 1924), in *EHR*, XL (1925), 438–41; of P. Geyl, *Willem IV en England tot 1748* (The Hague, 1924), in *ibid.*, pp. 616–21; or of J. F. Chance, *The alliance of Hanover* (London, 1925), in *ibid.*, XXXIX (1924), 293–97.

47. "The Polwarth papers and the Historical Manuscripts Commission," *Trans. Roy. Hist. Soc.*, 4th ser., XV, 1–43. He attacked the editor for translating French documents, for an inadequate introduction, and for a poor index. His enthusiasm for published documents led him to defend the "excerpt method" followed by the Royal Historical Society in editing the *British diplomatic instructions* (*EHR*, XLIII [1928], 433–38), in contrast to Professor Temperley's outspoken condemnation (*ibid.*, XLI [1926], 603–4).

48. *History*, N.S., XII (1928), 335; XVIII (1933), 55.

form of possible examination questions. Special *bêtes noires* were errors on details of the Spanish Succession, confusion in such dual personalities as the ruler of Austria and the Holy Roman Empire or of England and Hanover, oblique allusions to contemporary political conditions, and the lack of footnote references or their consignment to the rear of chapters or books in any serious work of scholarship. "Pemmican" history and the "contemporary craze for journalism in history and biography" also came in for condemnation.

Indefatigable to the end, from his suburban retreat Sir Richard descended almost daily upon London to do research in the archives, to assist in the work of his old school, to take part in historical meetings. He had a passion for organization, and one friend remarked that he should have been the governor of an Indian province rather than a historian. He helped to found the Historical Association (1906) and later to develop several of its branches. In addition to his presidency of the Royal Historical Society, he was active on the committee of the Institute of Historical Research and a keen organizer of those "academic jaunts," the Anglo-French and the Anglo-American historical conferences.[49] At the same time he maintained an interest in the accomplishments of old pupils and younger scholars. "He worked at my edition [of Chesterfield's letters] as hard as I did myself and seemed to grudge no labor in teaching me the things I ought to have known," said Professor Dobrée. But years crept on apace. The old passion for lecturing, even on a pleasure cruise, brought on a collapse in 1935; and, though he recovered, it was the prelude to the end. He died August 2, 1936, with a book at his bedside for review and with a card asking that certain books be laid out for him at the British Museum.

49. He visited Canada and the United States in 1924, for the Richmond meeting of the American Historical Association.

# X

## *Erich Marcks (1861–1938)*

GORDON M. STEWART

WHEN Erich Marcks came to this country in 1913 to lecture on history at Cornell University he was told by an American colleague to be thoroughly German in his presentation of the subject. He was not to speak down to his students but to make them aware of their cultural deficiencies by showing them those aspects of the historical nature of personality, society, and the state which were typically German in their age and complexity. The assignment was a happy one. Marcks said later that he had never before rejoiced so completely in being a German. These were not the sentiments of a narrow patriot. He was sincerely interested in American life and was generous in his praise for our schools. He could not, however, avoid feeling that he was the product of a high civilization bringing light to a promising but immature new world.[1]

A review of Marcks's career down to the time when he came to America shows him to have been admirably well fitted to represent those elements in German scholarship which the world prior to 1914 had learned to admire. His training in method had been in the rigorous tradition of classical studies. When he began to write and teach he joined the group of historians who, after the war of 1870–71, had returned to Ranke's ideal of objective his-

1. *Männer und Zeiten* (5th ed., Leipzig, 1918), I, 407–35.

tory written from a broad, supranational point of view. Thus, his first works were on the French wars of religion. Although later studies dealt with German subjects, they were considered notable for their lack of bias. His published works revealed him as a master of a rich and flowing style. Finally, he was endowed with a genuine enthusiasm for history, which made him an engaging and stimulating lecturer.

As he spoke to his American students of Germany's development in the nineteenth century, Marcks made no effort to conceal his pride in her military power and in the leadership of Bismarck. The army, he explained, owed its importance in Germany's constitutional framework to the country's geographical position in Europe.[2] These remarks, he noticed, were met with friendly incredulity. Prussian militarism and the ideals of the Bismarckian state were hardly part of the Cornell tradition. But this was to be expected, and it added something to the joy of teaching in a foreign country to be able to talk about matters which were generally taken for granted at home.

The pleasure which Marcks took in justifying the old Reich before a critical audience was to return to him in an unexpected way. When the German monarchy fell in 1918 and the republic was formed at Weimar, the nation's leadership throughout most of the preceding century appeared to have been discredited. Bismarck's policy of building the state around a powerful and militaristic Prussia was no longer accepted generally as a model of political wisdom. Particularist, liberal, and pacifist writers found a wide market for their attacks on the old regime. To defend the great chancellor's policy against such criticism was to adopt the program of the "political historians," of whom Treitschke, Häusser, and Sybel were the greatest. This was the task which Marcks set for himself in 1920. He brought it to completion with the publication of *Der Aufstieg des Reiches*,[3] a book which glorified the Bismarckian empire. Thus it was that within his lifetime he had been an exponent of the two dominant schools of nineteenth-

2. *Ibid.*, p. 425.
3. 2 vols.; Stuttgart and Berlin, 1936.

century German historiography, the school of Ranke and that of the "political historians." The study of his development reveals a gradual but steady shift from the former to the latter.

There was a serenity and balance to Marcks's early life which gave tone to his whole career. He was born in 1861, the year before William I called Bismarck to Berlin. His father was a successful architect; his mother, a descendant of the Huguenots who had settled in Germany.[4] As he grew up in Magdeburg he was introduced to the world of classical culture at the *Gymnasium*.[5] This led him into the study of ancient history, which he pursued at the universities of Strassburg, Bonn, and Berlin under Heinrich Nissen and Theodor Mommsen. His thesis for the Ph.D. degree, based on a study of Greek and Latin sources, was an evaluation of the classical accounts of Drusus' tribunate and the civil war of 91–89 B.C.[6] He graduated *summa cum laude* in 1884.

In addition to his work in ancient history, Marcks studied under Jacob Sturms and Hermann Baumgarten.[7] It was through the influence of these men that he developed an interest in modern history. He was especially impressed with the teaching of Baumgarten, who, though he had been a strident publicist in the days of unification, had returned to the ideals of Ranke.

Shortly after receiving his degree Marcks entered the field of Reformation history. An inherited interest in the fate of the Huguenot party took him to London and Paris to study the materials on the French wars of religion. In a letter dated Easter, 1886, he gave a charming account of his experiences in France.[8] He told of his dislike for the dusty archives, the noisy streets, and the cold, damp weather. The miserable little stove in his room was quite unequal to the task of keeping him warm. But what a change when spring came and the gay crowds thronged the Champs Élysées! The superintendent of the archives had the

4. Arnold Oskar Meyer, "Erich Marcks Nachruf," *Forschungen zur brandenburgischen und preussischen Geschichte,* LI (1939), 168.
5. K. Stählin, "Erich Marcks zum Gedächtnis," *HZ,* CLX (1939), 496.
6. *Die Überlieferung des Bundesgenossenkrieges 91–89 v. Chr.* (Marburg, 1884).
7. Stählin, *loc. cit.,* p. 496.
8. *Männer und Zeiten* (3d ed.; Leipzig, 1912), I, 85–93.

good sense to declare a six-day holiday during Easter week, and so, with Baedeker in hand, Marcks set out for the Huguenot towns of Orléans and La Rochelle. His enthusiasm for history, dampened, perhaps, by the arduous work and bad weather of Paris, flamed anew when he visited the buildings which had once housed the characters of his study. Standing in the Gothic hall at Amboise, he could picture Francis II and Mary Stuart trembling before the threatening Huguenots and nobles. From the documents in Paris he had reconstructed an hour-by-hour account of the conspiracy. Now he could complete the picture of the event which he had formed in his mind.

In view of what he saw in the provinces, Marcks was forced to revise his estimate of the French. They were not, he decided, the frivolous, nervous, and overcivilized race pictured by most of his compatriots who knew only the capital. Their clean towns and solid farms showed them to be honest and unaffected folk.[9]

In his study of the wars of religion Marcks became involved in the general problems of French diplomacy during that period. Finding that the meeting between Catherine de Medici and the Spanish representatives at Bayonne had never been treated satisfactorily, he interrupted his work and produced a three-hundred-page monograph on the subject, *Die Zusammenkunft von Bayonne*.[10] In it he traced the origins of the meeting, gave an analysis of Catherine's motives, and offered the thesis that its influence in French affairs had been obliterated by April, 1566. His zeal was rewarded by a very favorable review from the pen of Theodor Schott.[11] In France a somewhat less friendly view was taken of the work.[12] The author's conclusions were considered well reasoned and plausible, but it was felt that he had failed to offer sufficient evidence in their support.

Three years later, at the age of thirty-one, Marcks published the first volume of a biography of Gaspard de Coligny.[13] That he

9. *Ibid.*, p. 88.
10. Strassburg, 1889.
11. *HZ*, LXIV (1890), 306.
12. *RH*, XLI (1889), 418.
13. *Gaspard von Coligny* (Stuttgart, 1892).

considered himself to be a full-fledged historian can be seen in the boldness of his plan. Along with the life of the Protestant hero, he set out to include a history of the Huguenot party "organically conceived."[14] Moreover, he rejected the timid practice of biographers who simply recounted the external history of their subject. His work was to be a deep introspective study.[15]

The first part of the volume deals with Coligny's life down to the year 1559. The second part, almost two-thirds, is devoted to a description of French society and a history of Calvinism. This division of the material met with enthusiastic approval in Germany.[16] In France the objection was raised that the method of including a general survey of society in a biography disrupted its unity and deprived it of any logical limits. Why, it was asked, does the author neglect the intellectual history of the Crusades and church history in the days of the early popes?[17]

While engaged in research and writing, Marcks had begun his career as a teacher. In 1887 Heinrich von Treitschke sponsored his application for the position of lecturer in modern history at Berlin.[18] Six years later he was called to Freiburg as Privatdozent, the advancement coming partly because of the success of his *Coligny*. In 1894 he moved on to Leipzig.[19]

In his formal acceptance of the post at Freiburg, Marcks addressed the university on the subject of Philip II. The reception given this address and others on subjects related to his work encouraged him to cultivate the form of the historical essay. When, some years later, a collection of these was published under the title *Männer und Zeiten*, it proved to be his greatest popular success.[20]

Marcks next wrote a small work called *Königin Elisabeth von England*.[21] Although somewhat longer than his essays, it, too, was intended for the general public. Accordingly, he employed a new

14. *Ibid.*, p. vi.
15. *Ibid.*, p. v.
16. *HZ*, LXXV (1896), 522.
17. *RH,*, LII (1893), 391.
18. Stählin, *loc. cit.*, p. 497.
19. *Ibid.*
20. 1st ed.; Leipzig, 1911.
21. Bielefeld and Leipzig, 1897.

technique in composition. After months of intensive study he wrote the whole book in eleven days.[22] The result was a broad and lively account molded into a firm unity. Without limiting himself in the choice of subject matter, he had solved the problem of synthesis.

The ten years which Marcks had spent studying and writing about the age of the Reformation had been a period of rapid development. Endowed at the outset with unusual talents—Mommsen had valued him highly as a student of ancient history[23]—he had applied himself industriously to the problem of mastering historical material and presenting it. His proved ability as a historian was recognized when he was asked to write a life of William I for the *Deutsche allgemeine Biographie*.

The request came while his work in the field of the Reformation was still unfinished; yet he welcomed the chance to move into nineteenth-century German history. His interest in the period had been developing since childhood. The great events of 1866 and 1870 had been among his earliest memories.[24] As a student he had known and admired the publicist-historians Baumgarten and Treitschke. When he began teaching, his closest friends on the faculty at Berlin—Koser, Schmoller, Meinecke, Hintze, and Naudé—were all students of Prussian history.[25] Finally, he had grown up with the name of Bismarck ringing in his ears.[26] He had caught a glimpse of the "sad but mighty" face of the chancellor at the funeral of William I.[27] Two years later he pushed through the crowd at the Stettiner Bahnhof and watched the old gentleman as he sat talking in a coach. Never had he seen such grandeur in nature or in man.[28] An interview with Bismarck in 1893 impressed him with the tragedy of the passing of such a figure from national life.[29] In the years that followed, Marcks could not avoid a feeling of uneasiness about the

22. Meyer, *loc. cit.*, p. 172.
23. *Ibid.*, p. 169.
24. Stählin, *loc. cit.*, p. 502.
25. *Ibid.*
26. *Männer und Zeiten* (1912), II, 34.
27. *Ibid.*, pp. 34–35.
28. *Ibid.*, p. 35.
29. *Ibid.*, p. 52.

course of German affairs.[30] He became convinced that the country needed to capture and preserve the memory of its great leaders as a guarantee for the future.[31] Thus the biography of William I gave him the opportunity to perform what he considered to be a patriotic act.

The directors of the Bavarian Historical Commission had originally called upon Heinrich von Sybel to produce the account of the emperor's life. When Sybel died in 1895 they turned to Marcks. It was the article for the *Deutsche allgemeine Biographie* which formed the basis for his *Kaiser Wilhelm I*.[32] His research was restricted to a survey of the published sources,[33] much of his material coming from Sybel's *Begründung des deutschen Reiches durch Wilhelm I*.[34] For this reason he presented the account without footnotes. It made, nonetheless, a great impression. A French reviewer pointed to the author's psychological insight and his loyalty to the tradition of Ranke.[35] Munroe Smith, an American biographer of Bismarck, was especially impressed with the frank treatment of the less favorable side of William's character.[36] In Germany the modification of Sybel's account of the origins of the war of 1870 was looked upon as a marvel of objectivity and candor.[37] It can be said to have been his most successful book up to this time.

Marcks once wrote that every day which passed after Bismarck's death proved over again how great was the need for a biography of the chancellor.[38] In order to fill this need he had begun collecting materials for such a work around the turn of the century. In the spring of 1901 an official of the foreign office in-

30. *Geschichte und Gegenwart* (Berlin and Leipzig, 1925), p. 148.
31. *Männer und Zeiten* (1912), II, 28.
32. Leipzig, 1897.
33. Stählin, *loc. cit.*, p. 505.
34. Munich and Leipzig, 1889.
35. *RH*, LXXI (1899), 394.
36. *AHR*, III (1898), 725.
37. *HZ*, LXXXII (1899), 316.
38. *Bismarck: eine Biographie*. Vol. I, *Bismarcks Jugend 1815–1848* (Stuttgart and Berlin, 1909), p. vii. A second volume has appeared posthumously but could not be obtained for the preparation of this article: *Bismarck und die deutsche Revolution 1848–1851* (Stuttgart, 1940).

troduced him to Prince Herbert Bismarck.[39] The prince gave him invaluable help in his work: collecting documents, making available the family papers at Schönhausen and Friedrichsruh, and sending for information from numerous other sources. Other members of the family and friends of the chancellor were equally cooperative in supplying material for the biography. Because the documents took years to master, it was not until 1909 that the first volume appeared.

In his introduction Marcks stated that again his aim had been to write a well-rounded biography.[40] By this he meant that the materials had been integrated and related so as to present a portrait rather than a simple narrative. In no other work did he succeed so well in realizing this ideal.[41] Although the volume ends with Bismarck's entry into public life in 1848, Marcks's profound analysis of his formative years illuminates all his later life.

While compiling and writing his great biography Marcks had moved from Leipzig to Heidelberg, and finally to Hamburg, where, in 1907, he became one of the first appointees of the Scientific Foundation. These were his happiest and most successful days as a teacher. His lectures are said to have been "models of clarity and elegance."[42] It was his practice to read from a prepared text, but in such a way as not to lose contact with his auditors.[43] His voice was controlled, his delivery appropriate to the material.[44] Much as he admired the fire and passion of Treitschke, he remained true to himself, infusing his polished sentences with that warmth of feeling which is to be found in all of his works. Each lecture had a beginning and end; many of them were considered memorable for their unity and force.

The age of the Counter Reformation was his favorite topic.[45] The four-hour lecture which he devoted to this period has, fortu-

39. *Ibid.*, p. x.
40. *Ibid.*, p. viii.
41. Cf. *AHR*, XVI (1910), 127; *EHR*, XXV (1910), 622; *HZ*, CIV (1910), 322.
42. *AHR*, XLIV (1939), 479.
43. Meyer, *loc. cit.*, p. 172.
44. Stählin, *loc. cit.*, p. 496.
45. Meyer, *loc. cit.*, p. 172.

nately, been printed.[46] It begins with a brilliant description of the two opposing forces of the age—Calvinism and Catholicism. Calvin and Geneva are given as symbols of the first; Loyola and Trent, as symbols of the second. A survey of the international scene is followed by discussions of the internal affairs of Spain, France, the Low Countries, and England. Here the narration of the actual course of events begins. The unfolding of the struggle is interspersed with character sketches in the style of Ranke. Cultural, economic, and social developments are introduced into the account. As the lecture draws to a close, the material takes on a new form. The political forces active in Europe have replaced religion as the center of interest. The sweeping syntheses which appear at the beginning of the lecture are repeated at the end, but with special regard for the new state system. Religion and politics are thus balanced almost perfectly, and through the study of their mutual interplay the diverse aspects of the age are molded into a unified whole.

The students who chose to work under Marcks found him to be a master craftsman, more concerned with the development of their talents and interests than with the founding of a new school of history. The variety of subjects in the *Festschrift* dedicated to him on his sixtieth birthday bears witness to this.[47] They found, moreover, that he made it a point to be accessible to them and to cultivate them as his friends. Many of them came to know the hospitality of his home. Throughout the latter part of his career he spent hours answering letters from his former students, giving advice and encouragement and keeping alive that feeling of loyalty and friendliness which it was his genius to inspire.[48]

Marcks was extremely conscientious in upholding the standards of history. A good scholarly book called forth his warmest

46. "Die Gegenreformation in Westeuropa," *Propyläen Weltgeschichte* (Berlin, 1930), V, 217–314. For another excellent example of his pedagogical skill see also "Bismarck und die Bismarck-Literatur des letzen Jahres," *Deutsche Rundschau*, LXXXXIX (1899), 37–66, 240–80.
47. *Vom staatlichen Werden und Wesen* (Stuttgart, 1921).
48. Stählin, *loc. cit.,* p. 531.

praise.[49] He could be appreciative of sincere and honest work of the second rank, although he was outspoken in pointing to its shortcomings.[50] When he felt called upon to deal with an author whom he considered unqualified to handle the subject under review, Marcks was most direct in his criticism. "I know," he wrote of Guilland's *L'Allemagne nouvelle et ses historiens*, "that my demands are high, but historiography requires that one who undertakes to generalize about such difficult and intricate things must have a sound knowledge of facts, not just a nodding acquaintance with them."[51]

It appears that Marcks rarely became involved in academic quarrels. His was an irenic disposition. This was fortunate, for he grew up in a world famous for its bitter disputes. Baumgarten and Treitschke had been at each other's throats over the question of the latter's disregard for truth in writing his great history. Mommsen had stood out against Bismarck after the unification of Germany had swept most of the historians into the chancellor's camp. In writing about these disputes Marcks displayed a high degree of tact and good will.[52] It was perhaps this quality, along with his ability as a teacher and author, which won for him the position he held in academic circles. Years ago Guy Stanton Ford wrote that "no other living German historian with the possible exception of Professor Schmoller is so universally respected by his colleagues, to whatever school they may belong."[53] There is no reason to believe that this opinion changed in later years.

Marcks was apparently as fortunate in his private life as he was in his career as a historian. His wife, the former Friederike von Sellin, bore him three sons and a daughter. Their home was

49. See review of Paul Herre, *Papstum und Papstwahl im Zeitalter Philips II.* (Leipzig, 1907), in *HZ*, CIV (1910), 151.

50. See review of Baron Alphonse de Ruble, *Le traité de Cateau-Cambrésis* (Paris, 1899), in *HZ*, LXIV (1890), 303.

51. *Männer und Zeiten* (1912), I, 320.

52. Cf. Marcks's introduction to Hermann Baumgarten, *Historische und politische Aufsätze und Reden* (Strassburg, 1894). See also *Männer und Zeiten* (1912), I, 305–13.

53. *AHR*, XVII (1912), 834.

far more than a mere adjunct to the university. A lively interest in contemporary painting led them to cultivate the artists Leopold von Kalckreuth and Ludwig von Hoffmann, in addition to the many friends they had in the academic world.[54]

An interest in world-affairs led Marcks to contribute to the public discussion of the issues facing Germany in a number of speeches and articles. The statesman, he believed, must be left to make decisions in specific instances. As a historian, he sought merely to "connect the past with the present and illuminate the one with the other."[55]

He expressed the uneasiness which he felt about the course of German development in an address entitled *England and Germany, their relations in the great crises of European history, 1500–1900*, which he gave in London in 1900 and which was subsequently printed both in German and English. In the introduction to the German edition he spoke of a "lack of moderation in our public discussion."[56] The strained relations with England caused him concern, for he believed that "a certain historical and intellectual, and perhaps also political community," existed between the two countries.[57] These views did not, by any means, lead him into a liberal or pacifist position. He was proud of the "decidedly monarchical"[58] constitution of Germany and saw imperialism as the path of glory and strength to be followed in the future.[59] He knew the dangers involved in challenging the position of England in the world; and, though he hoped for a peaceful issue in the coming competition for lands and markets, he advised his countrymen to give full support to the army and navy.[60]

54. Karl Alexander von Müller, *Zwölf Historikerprofile* (Stuttgart and Berlin, 1935), p. 18.

55. *England and Germany, their relations in the great crises of European history, 1500–1900* (London, Edinburgh, and Oxford, 1920), pp. 5–6. This essay, along with others dealing with British foreign policy since the time of Elizabeth, has recently been reprinted in *Englands Machtpolitik: Vorträge und Studien* (Stuttgart, 1939).

56. *Ibid.*, p. 6.

57. *Ibid.*, p. 4.

58. *Ibid.*, p. 42.

59. *Männer und Zeiten* (1912), II, 313.

60. *Ibid.*, p. 282.

After the outbreak of the war of 1914 Marcks charged England with having entered the conflict in cold blood.[61] Russia, Germany, Austria, and France had legitimate historical reasons for war. The issue would be decided by earnest and serious fighting, but it would not involve the terrible hate which Germany felt for England. Her entry into the war was a crime committed in the name of selfishness and pride. She was close to Germany in race, institutions, cultural heritage, and religion. How could such action be explained? There was but one answer: the war on England's part was attempted fratricide.

Marcks believed that the war was the final stage in Germany's growth.[62] In 1866 Prussia had become dominant in Germany; in 1870 Germany had become a European power; and in the war of 1914 she would become a world-power.

The sacrifices demanded of his countrymen, and perhaps the loss of his eldest son during the first months of fighting, convinced Marcks that merely to understand the nature of the conflict was not enough. It was, of course, necessary to "connect the past with the present," and he sought to do this by speaking in public and writing for the periodical press. He was certain, however, that in turning to the past one could find inspiration as well as understanding. Germany, in her life and death struggle, must be led and encouraged by the memory of her greatest leader, Otto von Bismarck. The long, contemplative biography which he had begun would not be finished for years and could hardly be expected to command a very wide audience. Marcks decided, therefore, to write a "report" (*Bericht*) of Bismarck's life.[63] After years of study he was steeped in the materials relating to the chancellor's career. Thus it was that he was able to complete his famous "report" in six weeks, almost entirely from memory.[64] It was entitled *Otto von Bismarck, ein Lebensbild*, and was published in 1915.

In some respects the "report" is the most remarkable book he

61. *Ibid.* (1918), II, 293.
62. *Ibid.*, p. 289.
63. *Otto von Bismarck, ein Lebensbild* (Stuttgart, 1915), p. vii.
64. *Ibid.*

ever wrote. The flamboyant and leisurely style of his earlier and later works is nowhere in evidence. It is an outpouring of information. The sentences are short; the paragraphs, tightly knit. Yet there is a satisfying completeness about it. Although the narration of the chancellor's career moves on at a headlong pace, it is supported by a simple but adequate outline of the history of the period. It apparently gave Marcks great satisfaction to be able to create a truly popular work about Bismarck. He is said to have regarded it as the best book he ever wrote.[65]

The war stimulated Marcks. Hard as it was to witness the terrible loss of life and the growth of prejudice and hate, he was, in a way, prepared for it. The peace which brought defeat, revolution, and privation found him, at first, unprepared. A new world had sprung up around him. In presenting his views he was prone to refer to himself as a member of the older generation, as a man who had not changed with the times.[66] "I am a historian," he said, "who in his personal feelings is accustomed to live in the days of Bismarck, that is, in the glorious heights of our past."[67] The great biography, which was from his point of view a confession of faith, lay unfinished, for it required a sympathetic audience. Writing about it to a friend, he said: "My deepest emotions have not changed. Can they find expression in a changed world?"[68]

Although Marcks's longing for prewar Germany was doubly strong, since he was both a monarchist and a creative writer who identified himself with the period, this did not lead him into the camp of the pessimists. In the darkest days of the breakdown, when the productive machinery of the country was crippled and France threatened invasion, he counseled patience and, above all, elasticity.[69] Recovery, he believed, would be slow.[70] The disloy-

65. Stählin, *loc. cit.*, p. 513.
66. *Geschichte und Gegenwart*, p. 3.
67. *Ibid.*, p. 83.
68. Stählin, *loc. cit.*, pp. 512–13.
69. *Geschichte und Gegenwart*, p. 167.
70. *Ibid.*, p. 87.

alty of the workers, political particularism, and pacifism, "the most baneful of all social forces,"[71] stood in the way. There were, however, more encouraging elements in the picture which were not to be overlooked. The political structure bequeathed by Bismarck was still intact. Economically the nation was unified as never before. The rising generation impressed one with its keenness.[72] Finally, no nation with a past as great as Germany's could be thoroughly disheartened. Even in her darkest hours Germany had reason to be proud of her record.[73]

Turning to the past, Marcks dwelt on the days of the Great Elector, Frederick II, the War of Liberation, and Bismarck. Prussia and Germany, he declared, owed their greatness to a successful foreign policy.[74] If the nation would rise again, it must look abroad for its opportunities. These were not far to seek. England's grip on the continent would relax, for her chief interest was in her empire and the unsolved social problems at home.[75] France, "the real Napoleon of the twentieth century,"[76] would split the entente by her policy of ruthless aggression.[77] If Germany could but find a ruler to embody the unified will of the nation, she could again assume her rightful position in the affairs of Europe and the world.[78]

It was with such thoughts in mind that Marcks began his last great work, *Der Aufstieg des Reiches*, in 1920. The very title suggests its pertinency to the times. In it he hoped to trace the history of Germany from 1807 to 1890.[79] Although the material was by no means new to him, he went about his task with painstaking care. After his retirement in 1928 he worked under severe

71. *Ibid.*, p. 99.
72. *Ibid.*, p. 101–2.
73. *Ibid.*, p. 107.
74. *Ibid.*, p. 111.
75. *Ibid.*, p. 112.
76. *Ibid.*, p. 79.
77. *Ibid.*, p. 163.
78. Erich Marcks and Karl Alexander von Müller (eds.), *Meister der Politik* (Stuttgart and Berlin, 1923), I, vi.
79. Müller, p. 20.

pressure. His strength was declining, and he was forced to disregard bodily pain in order to continue his research and writing.[80] As it was, he was unable to carry the main body of the account past the year 1871. His treatment of the period 1871 to 1878 was handled in a single chapter, and the remainder of Bismarck's official career was omitted.

The book which cost Marcks the enjoyment of a restful old age has been called his greatest contribution to historical literature.[81] If anything could fill the gap left by his unfinished biography of Bismarck, it is probably the second volume of *Der Aufstieg,* which covers the period from 1862 to 1871. Bismarck holds the center of the stage throughout the whole account. The treatment is not that of the biography, since the personal side of the chancellor's career is almost entirely omitted. Yet one may safely say that the two books, taken together, present the complete Bismarck. The period of formation, described intimately, is balanced by an account of the period of greatest activity, treated as history.

The question naturally arises why Marcks did not simply continue the biography. It has already been suggested that he found it difficult to express his deepest feelings in the uncongenial atmosphere of the Weimar Republic; and that, as a monarchist, he turned to history to defend the unification of the nation under the Prussian crown. It may well be that the most compelling reason for leaving the biography and starting work on *Der Aufstieg* was his concern for the future. The "political historians" had hoped to inspire and direct action by writing the nation's history at a time when they looked forward to a fundamental change in the constitution. It is the writer's opinion that Marcks accepted their program and ideals after 1918 because he considered the republic unsatisfactory and ephemeral and hoped for the establishment of a more unified state.

The publication of Heinrich Ritter von Srbik's *Deutsche Einheit* in 1935 naturally invited comparison between the two books. Srbik wrote from the *gesamtdeutsch* point of view, making out a

80. Stählin, *loc. cit.,* p. 529.
81. Meyer, *loc. cit.,* p. 168.

better case for Austria than is customary in the writing of German history. The reviewers seem to agree that Marcks differed from Srbik more in approach than in spirit.[82] He was fair to the Austrians; but since he regarded the Bismarckian empire as fully justified in its time, his choice of materials was naturally different from that of the Austrian historian.

Except for two lines in the introduction which state that the Third Reich is carrying on the traditions of the past, there is nothing in *Der Aufstieg* to suggest that it was completed in the time of Hitler.[83] Marcks bore somewhat the same relation to Nazi historiography as Hindenburg did to the dictatorship. He accepted the idea of authoritarianism, but he was not certain that the National Socialists were the right people to lead Germany. In 1932 he penned a fulsome sentence describing them as

> the raging and unstemmed current; the offspring of all the political, cultural, economic, and social maladjustment which has bedeviled Germany during the last decade; growing at a mad pace in reaction against these conditions; motivated by patriotic feeling and social bewilderment; fed and strengthened by privation and wrong; increased by a fighting enthusiasm for Germanism, fatherland, and unity; enlarged beyond bounds by the fall of the middle class; pushed on to the extreme by anger and scorn, by radical will to reform and naïve utopianism; a movement of noble passion, but not without dregs, full of youthful drive, sacrifice, and hope; noble and wild forces shoulder to shoulder; a wonderful organization of the masses, ready to give and ready to act, but undisciplined and, from the point of view of the state, dangerous.[84]

Hitler he regarded as a pure-minded agitator and a gifted party politician, unqualified to lead the nation in such a time of stress.[85] The formation of the *Junker* cabinet under Franz von Papen greatly pleased him, for he believed that the dynamic forces of

82. *Historisches Jahrbuch,* LVIII (1938), 463; *Historische Vierteljahrschrift,* XXXI (1939), 787; *JMH,* IX (1937), 523.

83. *JMH,* IX (1937), 523.

84. Erich Marcks and Ernst von Eisenhart Rothe, *Paul von Hindenburg als Mensch, Staatsmann, Feldherr* (Berlin, 1932), p. 65.

85. *Ibid.,* p. 69.

National Socialism could, under strong leadership, be brought into the service of the nation.[86]

This was Marcks's last printed statement before the Nazis came into power. There is reason to believe that after January, 1933, he accepted Hitler as the true leader of Germany.[87]

In the fall of 1938 Marcks died. With the exception of the biography of William I, not one of his major works was completed. He left the study of Coligny's life to begin his *Wilhelm I.* and *Bismarck*. The latter was dropped after the war when he undertook the writing of *Der Aufstieg*. In each case the new work that he took up bore a distinct relation to his view of the world around him. The general trend of his development suggests two elements in his character which may be mentioned in partial explanation of the fact that he wrote history appropriate to the times. One was an increasing patriotism. As long as he lived, he remained loyal to the Germany he had known in his youth. As he saw conditions change, he felt compelled to do what he could to maintain the old order of society and, after 1918, to bring Germany back to the position of a great power in Europe. The other was a profound artistic sense. In his historical writings Marcks expressed his innermost feelings. As these became clarified under the pressure of a changing world, he shifted from one subject to the next in order to give them adequate expression. In reviewing his career one is impressed with the fact that, although his greatest works are unfinished, he fulfilled himself to a remarkable degree in his writings.

The academic career which he began in Berlin took him to Freiburg, Leipzig, Heidelberg, Hamburg, Munich, and finally back to Berlin. In addition to writing and teaching, he served from time to time as an editor and was a member of several commissions and boards.[88] The ultimate importance of his busy and

86. *Ibid.*, p. 73.
87. Stählin, *loc. cit.*, p. 526.
88. Marcks founded the *Heidelberger Abhandlungen zur mittleren und neuen Geschichte*. He edited: *Deutsche Zeitschrift für Geschichtswissenschaft; Leipziger Studien aus dem Gebiet der Geschichte; Karl August, Darstellungen und Briefe zur Geschichte des weimarischen Fürstenhauses und Landes* (Berlin, 1915——); *Meister der Politik* (with K. A. von Mül-

productive life cannot be estimated. An analysis of his method and thought may, however, throw some light on the matter.

The foundation stones upon which good history rests are the documents. Marcks was thoroughly trained in their use. As some of his books are without footnotes, it is impossible to know in every instance what sources he used. It is said, however, that he never considered his ability as a writer to be an excuse for poor workmanship. In all his books, according to those competent to judge, the evidence of careful research is to be found.[89]

The limitations of his sources are usually indicated. When he made use of noncontemporary documents, their nature and degree of reliability were frankly stated. If an apocryphal story was worth telling, he told it as a story, not as a fact. When conjecture could suggest what might have occurred, he gave his opinion but made clear that no historical material could be found to bear him out.

The greatest feat that he performed in finding and marshaling information was in the writing of his *Bismarck*. Every imaginable type of material was used: stories, legends, newspapers, letters, and records. The truly amazing element in his work is not the amount of the material but the way in which it was used. At no time does the reader feel that the order, emphasis, or tone of the text is dictated by the sources.

In writing, Marcks generally adhered to the narrative form of arrangement. Periodization is based upon what seem to be the epochs in the development of the subject. One chapter may deal with a period of two years, another with twenty. The narrative, from time to time, is dropped in order to introduce explanatory material or to summarize and interpret an intricate course of events. In his scholarly works he never sacrificed completeness for the sake of simplicity; nor did he, on the other hand, forget

---

ler) (3 vols.; Stuttgart and Berlin, 1923–24). He was a member of the historical commissions of Saxony and Baden and of the Berlin Academy of Science, secretary of the historical class of the Bavarian Academy of Science, president of the Munich Historical Commission, and Prussian historiographer.

89. Meyer, *loc. cit.*, p. 170.

the reader who is finding his way through the material for the first time.

In determining the emphasis to be placed on the various aspects of the subject, Marcks used a technique as a biographer which differed considerably from that which he employed as a historian. In *Bismarck, Coligny,* and *Wilhelm I* he attempted to do four things: to give a sound account of the subject's life, to penetrate into his psychology, to relate him to the period in which he lived, and to show his historical importance.

The narrative is the form around which the other elements of the biography are grouped, but it is not of first importance. Facts are included more for their significance in the interpretation of the character than because they were considered of some consequence at the time they occurred. Sometimes, indeed, there is almost a scarcity of factual material. In the case of *Bismarck,* Marcks assumed a fairly complete knowledge of the period on the part of the reader and felt free to allude to episodes and stories without recounting them. Something is doubtless lost to one whose store of information is inadequate; yet the effect of familiarity, the very boldness of such a procedure, lends great vitality to the portrait.

His chief interest as a biographer was in presenting a psychological study of motivation. That he was considered highly successful in this has already been indicated. Certainly he was far from timid in what he attempted. "I demand of the biographer," he wrote, "that he have the courage to go beyond the external and visual aspects of his subject and present completely and without restraint the vivid picture of the personality which has come to him intuitively."[90]

The best illustration of Marcks's method is in the famous description of Bismarck's religious conversion. This was not an easy task. One need only recall the widely varying interpretations of Luther's early life to realize the extreme difficulty an author encounters in presenting this most elusive element in man's emotional and intellectual constitution. In the case of Luther one can choose between the certainty of the believer in spiritual deter-

90. *Coligny,* p. v.

minism, the unction of the institutionalist, the analysis of the intellectual historian, and the findings of the psychologist. Marcks shunned any of these approaches in his treatment of Bismarck and chose to present a warm introspective study. First, the spiritual difficulties of the young Junker are described in detail: his restlessness and lack of adjustment; his loneliness after a number of unsuccessful love affairs; his interest in Spinozistic rationalism and his feeling of its inadequacy as a philosophy of life. Thus the stage is set for the entrance of Blankenburg and Maria von Thadden, who were to introduce him to pietism. So delicate and penetrating is the account of Bismarck's relations with these earnest people that one almost feels transplanted into the dreamy world of Wilhelm Meister. For a time the masterful young aristocrat gives way to the romantic German. The experience was a profound one. In presenting it in its full intensity and beauty, Marcks has shed light on all of Bismarck's subsequent career. That the chancellor was a man of faith can be discovered in any account of his life, but the quality of his religious experience has never been so ably described.

Although Marcks was invariably impressed with the uniqueness of a great personality, he did not neglect the less distinguished persons who lived close to the giants of history whom he chose to study. There is breadth and fulness in all of his works. Brilliant portraits abound in the *Coligny* and *Elisabeth*. The intellectual and spiritual struggles of Bismarck's contemporaries are introduced to balance the section dealing with his own inner life. Indeed, the claim has been made that the biography is a significant contribution to the history of romanticism.[91]

The historical importance of the subject is suggested by references to the past and the future and to the political framework of the contemporary world. The biographer never completely eclipses the historian. The continuity of historical development in time and the interplay of forces across the face of Europe are never forgotten. Marcks mastered the history of a period as a prerequisite to writing biography.

The range of materials which he included in his history fol-

91. Meyer, *loc. cit.*, p. 174.

lows the pattern set by Ranke and Treitschke. Political and intellectual phenomena, supported by numerous biographical studies, make up the bulk of his history. The emphasis which he placed on the various elements in society was dictated by three considerations. First, the state was looked upon as the highest form of social organization, and therefore his whole account is built around political history. Second, the period itself determined, to some extent, the relative importance of the other elements included. In the age of religious wars the church looms large in the account; later it assumes a position of less importance. Never, however, does he reflect the characteristics of a period in perfect balance. This is because of his third criterion, an organic and generic conception of society. As in the case of his biographical works, in which the child and the schoolboy are treated in the light of the author's understanding of the man, so, in his history, the various forces at work in any one period are seen in the perspective of their later development.

There is no evidence in any of Marcks's scholarly works that he skimmed over or slighted material simply because it was difficult to grasp or hard to explain. Indeed, from the point of view of content alone, Marcks is heavy reading. Yet, the presentation of intricate phases of diplomatic, constitutional, military, and theological history is rarely pedantic. In describing either the defense of St. Quentin in 1557 or the theology of Calvin, he does not struggle along with the obvious help of secondary sources. He is sure-footed, free, and opinionated. His reasoning is forceful, and his summaries clear. For pure elegance of thought and exposition his complicated passages are by far the most enjoyable.

Karl Alexander von Müller has called Marcks the greatest artist of his generation of German historians.[92] It is true that in his works he strove for fine effects and a polished style. His sentences, except in the "report" of Bismarck's life which he wrote during the war, bear the mark of the older German academic idiom. They are often massive, full of ideas packed into a succession of clauses. His paragraphs would do as chapters in a novel,

92. Müller, p. 17.

some of them running for five or six large pages. Yet, if the framework is heavy, the content is, at times, lively. The epigram and the well-turned phrase appear frequently, especially in his later works. There is sly humor in his description of the town of Kassel, in which he listed its characteristics as "poetry and humility, purity and narrowness."[93] Flashes of this sort stand in sharp relief, for the general tone of Marcks's text is mellow and serious. It is impossible here to quote at sufficient length to give the impression one gains from reading *Der Aufstieg*. The paragraphs, huge as they are, have an organic unity. It is not uncommon for them to begin with a long recitation of facts and then gradually to gain in freedom as the interpretative passages are introduced. By a skilful selection and arrangement of details Marcks is able to command the reader's attention at the outset and, indeed, to create a degree of suspense regarding his comments on the material. The full richness of his prose is displayed, however, in the purely interpretative sections. Working within the frame of reference which he has carefully constructed, he is able to use a suggestive and allusional style and to attain a striking intensity and warmth.

At times he was obviously carried away with his subject. It was then that he employed extravagant phrases which recall the great period of romantic literature in Germany. Hegel, for instance, "carried his banner from Heidelberg to Berlin";[94] the music of Schubert and Weber expressed the "restless yearning of the German heart."[95] Philip II "embodied the tragedy of his warm-blooded southern people," and his influence was "more a power of death than of life."[96]

Certain words, high in emotional content, appear often in his works. They were not chosen merely for effect. Marcks confessed that he could not write on some subjects with a feeling of inner coldness.[97] The question naturally arises whether he was able to

93. *Der Aufstieg des Reiches*, I, 112.
94. *Ibid.*, p. 117.
95. *Ibid.*, p. 115.
96. *Männer und Zeiten* (1912), I, 22.
97. *Der Aufstieg des Reiches*, I, xvi.

combine his warmth of feeling with accuracy and reliability. The answer, in part, is that his works show careful research and a high degree of professional integrity. In this matter he followed his old teacher Herman Baumgarten, who was noted for his "passionate sense of justice."[98] A conservative, a Protestant, a monarchist, and a Prussian partisan, he described the limitations of William I without hesitation and praised the achievements of Philip II, Friedrich Ebert, and Stresemann. In reading *Der Aufstieg des Reiches* one is impressed with the fact that Marcks is more than just in treating characters with whom he disagreed fundamentally. His deep feeling for Germany made it impossible for him to hate or scorn any part of it. The two negative acts which combined to make the Bismarckian empire possible—the frustration of the hopes of 1848 and the exclusion of Austria from Germany —are treated with firm loyalty to the victorious parties but with deep sympathy for the defeated.

In the field of biography Marcks's bias is perfectly evident. He admired Bismarck intensely. As a historian he tried to be frank about his subject's shortcomings. There are certain aspects of the chancellor's career, however, which he treated lightly because they did not seem to represent the true Bismarck. Eberhard Gothien pointed with keenness to Marcks's description of the Aachen period as an illustration of this type of writing.[99] On the other hand, his defense of Bismarck in the matter of the Ems dispatch comes close to special pleading. One feels that his practice of writing introspective and highly interpretative biographies led him of necessity into a type of distortion.

Marcks did not base his writings upon a systematic philosophy of history. He rejected the title of *Geschichtsphilosoph* emphatically and claimed that he was merely a historian who interpreted the past on the basis of documents.[100] As an artist, he disliked theorizing. At one time, indeed, he refused to talk about the nature of history because, he said, too many of his colleagues had become entangled in the problem of analysis.[101] Although he felt

98. Meyer, *loc. cit.*, p. 169.
99. *HZ*, CIV (1910), 329.
100. *Geschichte und Gegenwart*, p. 111.
101. *Männer und Zeiten* (1912), I, 3.

a certain sympathy for those who sought evidence of supernatural forces acting in human affairs, he was certain that the discipline of history had nothing to do with such explanations.[102]

It is possible, nonetheless, to discover a number of ideas about the nature of history which he developed in the course of his studies and used in explaining the past. They occur most frequently in his essays, in which he achieved a level of abstraction not common to his more scholarly works. For the sake of clarity they will be presented in a simple and straightforward form, which must, of necessity, do violence to the author's fine shadings of emphasis and meaning.

In the first place, Marcks believed that the future could be regarded as undetermined. Man is free, but he is free only within certain bounds. Geographic and economic factors limit his activity. The great deeds of history cannot, however, be explained in purely materialist terms. For an understanding of them, one must grasp the nature of the state and its rulers.

Marcks treated the state as an animate being. The characteristics of the national state are those of the race, and the race is closely rooted to the soil. The life of the state is like the life of the individual. Some states are vigorous; some are inert. Some have the enthusiasm of youth; others, the timid hesitancy of old age. A tired state wants peace; a restless one demands war. It is in an aggressive foreign policy that the state expresses its personality and brings to itself the greatest blessings of internal progress. The very essence of the state is the will to power. Because he believed this, Marcks feared any form of weakness. The liberals of 1848 carried their policy beyonds the limits of patriotism and endangered the future of the state. Thus it was right that they should fail. Labor politics, pacifism, and communism are diseases which must be cured in order that expansion and healthy progress may continue. When war comes, the individual, in sacrificing his life for the state, loses his small individuality and passes into a higher union with the totality. The state, then, has a mystical quality, not unlike the church.

In times of stress men lay hold of the spiritual powers of the

102. *Ibid.*, p. 161.

state, and in doing so they find within themselves the moral strength of the great leaders of the past. Frederick II was not far from the battlefields of Saxony in 1813, and Bismarck stood close to men during the last years of the war of 1914. Such leaders are able to influence and guide the future, for in their days of greatest activity they embodied the state itself. Marcks believed that they themselves were conscious of this and that the highest interests of the state became identified with their own interests.[103] He did not mean that they saw into the future or served some remote goal. The Hohenzollern rulers who were obsessed with greed for power showed great statesmanship, for their interests were those of the state. Those who wished to rule in peace were statesmen of the second rank.

Since the leader and the state do, in fact, become identified, it is not possible to understand the former by viewing him simply as a man. In his biography Marcks dealt with the day-to-day life of Bismarck. He insisted, however, that the true meaning of the Iron Chancellor is not to be grasped by visiting him at Friedrichsruh and seeing what he ate and drank and how he read his newspaper during a conversation. The heroic statue which dominates the port of Hamburg shows his real significance. The details of his features are indistinguishable; the man recedes; and the massive bulk of the leader, the symbol, alone remains.[104]

The race must cherish and preserve the memory of its great, for in their lives the direction of the future has been given. Marcks believed in the power of ideas. A good part of *Coligny* and *Der Aufstieg* is given over to intellectual history. The greatest ideas, however, are those which carry the strength of the nation's leaders into the life of the people. Goethe and Bismarck are, for Germany, the supreme guides. Similar in some respects, but essentially antagonistic, they represent the two basic components of the nation's glorious future.[105]

Marcks had a low opinion of the "scientific" type of analysis in the study of social phenomena. "True reality," he wrote, "more

103. *Ibid.*, p. 172.
104. *Paul von Hindenburg*, p. 75.
105. *Männer und Zeiten* (1912), II, 28.

real than any types we may construct, is still the individual. Woe unto that concept of human things which forgets this."[106] Whether actually he has freed himself from types and categories may be questioned. His books are studded with brilliant character sketches. Movements are understood in terms of their leaders, and nations epitomized by their rulers. It is not a far cry from the classifications of the sociologist to the use of representative men. One feels, at times, that history is a play in which the symbolic significance of the characters is of more importance than their given parts. Roon is the embodiment of traditional aristocratic Prussianism; Wellington and Hindenburg are the great conservatives who carry the ways of the past into a changing world; and David Hansemann is the smart, aggressive, middle-class capitalist. Junkerdom, conservatism, and liberalism are not referred to as movements so often as they are introduced in the persons of their leaders. It must, in justice, be pointed out that, although Marcks did not escape a type of implicit classification, he did avoid the mistake of transferring categories uncritically from one discipline to another. His categories are the creations of his own mind and carry the full force of his thought and imagination.

The very personal nature of Marcks's history is, perhaps, its best guarantee for survival in the future. Its scientific value is, of course, high. Much of the research which he did will not have to be done over again for a long time. Even his *Wilhelm I.*, which was written before the opening of the archives, is said to be unequaled to the present day. Yet it is true that eventually more accurate history will be written. When that time comes Marcks will be read for his fine imaginative insight and for the ideas and feelings which he expressed at a given stage in German history.

In writing about Friedrich Schlosser, a liberal historian of the first half of the nineteenth century, Marcks made the comment that he approached the discipline of history with preconceived ideas.[107] On the basis of the Kantian categorical imperatives

106. *Ibid.*
107. "Ludwig Häusser und die politische Geschichtsschreibung in Heidelberg," *Heidelberger Professoren aus dem 19. Jahrhundert* (Heidelberg, 1903), I, 292.

Schlosser damned the rulers and aristocrats of the preceding generation to the inferno of his works. In reading of such a feat, one cannot avoid the feeling that, although history should be more than an uncritical and universal damnation, the old liberal did exhibit a certain crude dignity in performing his task. His personal convictions in the realm of ethics and philosophy rendered him independent of the standard set by the world. It is exactly this element of independence which is lacking in Marcks's treatment of nineteenth-century German history. He regarded Bismarck as the greatest teacher historians could have. "If we do not learn from him," he wrote, "we are hopeless."[108] To judge the chancellor in the light of historical knowledge would be presumptuous. To Marcks's way of thinking, it appeared far more seemly to judge history in the light of a knowledge of Bismarck. It would be foolish to claim that there is not much to be learned from the great German statesman. There is, however, much which must be repudiated. In omitting to do the latter, Marcks displayed the one great weakness in his history. As an artist he was able to re-create the past as few have done it. As a diligent historian he based his works on sound and extensive research. Had he been able to free himself sufficiently from the past to render an independent and unique judgment of it, his works might well have ranked with the greatest in historical literature.

108. *Männer und Zeiten* (1912), II, 34.

# XI

## Albert Mathiez (1874–1932)

FRANCES ACOMB

ALBERT MATHIEZ was born of peasant stock on January 10, 1874, at La Bruyère in Haute-Saône. If he left memoirs they have not been published and the more personal and private aspect of his life has yet to be reconstructed by some diligent researcher. Friends and associates have, however, furnished us with some record of his career and some testimony regarding his personality and his interests.[1] The record begins with adulthood. Mathiez, after attending a series of provincial *lycées*, entered the École Normale Supérieure in 1894 and left it as *agrégé* in 1897. Following a short interlude in the provinces, he was admitted to the Fondation Thiers, remaining there from 1900 until 1902. At this time he became a student of Alphonse Aulard and under Aulard's direction wrote the theses for which in 1904 he received the degree of *docteur ès lettres* from the Sorbonne. The major thesis was *La théophilanthropie et le culte décadaire, 1796–1801: essai sur*

1. For biographical material see the *Annales historiques de la Révolution française*, Vol. IX (1932), especially the following articles: Henri Calvet, "Albert Mathiez, professeur en Sorbonne," pp. 264–70; Louis Gottschalk, "L'influence d'Albert Mathiez sur les études historiques aux États-Unis," pp. 224–29; letter of Mathiez to Louis Gottschalk, Nov. 23, 1930, pp. 218–20; Georges Lefebvre, "Albert Mathiez," pp. 98–102, and "L'œuvre historique d'Albert Mathiez," pp. 193–210; Georges Michon, "Albert Mathiez et les événements de 1914–1920," pp. 247–51; Albert Troux, "Albert Mathiez à Nancy (1908–09) et à Besançon (1911–1920)," pp. 240–46; and Hermann Wendel, "Albert Mathiez vu par un 'Dantoniste' allemand," pp. 235–39. See also J. M. Thompson, "Albert Mathiez," *EHR*, XLVII (1932), 617–21.

ALBERT MATHIEZ

*l'histoire religieuse de la Révolution;*[2] the minor one, *Les origines des cultes révolutionnaires (1789–1792).*[3] Mathiez then became a teacher in the Lycée Voltaire, where he remained until 1911, with two short interruptions during which he was substitute instructor (*suppléant*) on the faculties of Caen and Nancy, respectively. Meantime he had broken with Aulard and founded the Société des Études Robespierristes, becoming editor of its journal, a new organ, the *Annales révolutionnaires*. In 1924, by amalgamation with the *Revue historique de la Révolution française*, it became the *Annales historiques de la Révolution française*. This journal was, in its earlier years, almost a single-handed enterprise, and Mathiez himself always remained one of the principal contributors, as well as editor. In 1911, in consequence of his now growing reputation, Mathiez was appointed to the faculty of the University of Besançon, where he remained until the close of the year 1919. He was not drafted for service during the war, it is said, because he had lost the sight of one eye.[4] His interest in scholarly output was not diminished by the war; indeed, it was stimulated. The *Annales* and the Société des Études Robespierristes were suspended for a while, but in 1916 they were revived. A vigorous critic of the war dictatorship, although not an opponent of the war, Mathiez only narrowly escaped the censorship.[5] This activity as critic, coupled with his defense of Bolshevism, is generally believed to have been the reason why, when Aulard resigned from his chair at the Sorbonne in 1924, Mathiez was passed over in favor of Philippe Sagnac.[6] To Mathiez it was always a cross that so much of his life had to be spent in the provinces and that he could work in the great Pari-

2. Paris, 1903.
3. Paris, 1904.
4. Troux, *loc. cit.*, p. 243. I have not seen any other reference to this disability.
5. *Ibid.*, p. 244.
6. Michon, *loc. cit.*, p. 250; Thompson, *loc. cit.*, p. 619. In an article, "Le Bolchévisme et le Jacobinisme" (*Scientia*, XXVII [1920], 52–65), Mathiez held that the analogy between the Bolshevist and Jacobin phases of the Russian and French revolutions, respectively, was very close. This article exists also as a separate publication under the same title (Paris, 1920).

226

sian archives only during the vacations.[7] But he was to receive his reward. Professor at the University of Dijon from 1919, he was, in 1926, called to the Sorbonne as *suppléant* for M. Sagnac, who was to be absent in Egypt. When Sagnac returned, Mathiez was retained as assistant lecturer (*chargé de cours*). He had little more than five years in Paris. Suddenly, on February 25, 1932, in the course of delivering a lecture, he was stricken and died.

Not long afterward there appeared in *La Révolution française*, organ of the late Alphonse Aulard and of the Société de l'Histoire de la Révolution Française, the following curious eulogy, spoken at the annual assembly of the society by Pierre Caron, its general secretary. Caron said:

> Another name upon our lists is to be marked with the obituary cross—that of Albert Mathiez, assistant lecturer at the Sorbonne, deceased February 25th last. In truth, actually estranged from us since 1908 because of incidents it would be out of place to recall today, he had ceased to be a colleague to become simply a subscriber, and I might omit any allusion to the sudden stroke which carried him off under the dramatic circumstance of which you are aware. But I am loath to maintain a silence which could be attributed to a lack of serenity. Death must efface personal injuries. Questionable as have been and remain certain of the theses which he defended with so much ardor, the man who has just gone from us played for thirty years, in the realm of our studies, a role of the first rank, the importance of which only prejudice could deny. We give to the memory of Albert Mathiez the homage due to that of a relentless worker, a great inspirer [*remueur*] of ideas and of minds, entirely devoted to his self-assigned mission of revisionist [*animateur*], and fallen while acquitting himself of it.[8]

Here, in these few words, one senses the peculiar bitterness of the schism which for upward of twenty years divided French scholars of the Revolution, a bitterness which was in no small part due to the personality of Mathiez himself. There was apparently no trace of urbanity in his spirit. It is evident not only from his writings, which are generally polemical in tone, but from the

7. *Autour de Danton* (Paris, 1926), p. 7.
8. *La Révolution française*, LXXXV (1932), 98.

testimony of both foe and friend, that he neither asked nor gave quarter. From one academic post to another, a fearsome reputation preceded him. After he had arrived and had become known, the greater part of this evaporated. There were, according to Louis Gottschalk, two Mathiez—the one brusque and aggressive, the other genial and friendly.[9] Yet his friends would seem to have been disciples rather than persons chosen without reference to their opinions. To his students, writes Georges Lefebvre, he was a master, not only because of the trouble he took with them, but because of his vigor and enthusiasm: "He not only awoke minds; he enlisted wills and called forth vocations."[10] His work was, in a very complete sense, his life; and he could not easily separate professional differences from personal ones. Was he ever guilty of the converse fault, that is, did he ever elevate a personal hostility into a professional one? There is no shadow of accusation that this was ever the case in his relations with his equals or his inferiors, but it is possible to suppose that his quarrel with Aulard had some personal motivation. Aulard was originally his master and virtually the official revolutionary historian to the Third Republic. Mathiez was ambitious; and Georges Lefebvre, who was closely associated with Mathiez professionally, suggests that the feud may in part be laid to Mathiez' ambition.[11] Mathiez himself said, not that he was jealous of Aulard, but that Aulard was jealous of *him*. But the dispute arose in the first instance, he insisted, for scientific reasons,[12] and very likely this is true. For it is hardly to be conceived that Mathiez, from the very outset, envisaged a great battle with his teacher as the likeliest way to fame. It seems more probable that he discovered only gradually that neither his interpretations nor his ambition would brook subordination to Aulard, of whom he had formerly been the admirer.

What were the "scientific reasons" which were the original cause of the break between the two? It has been pointed out by

9. Gottschalk, *loc. cit.*, p. 228.
10. Lefebvre, "Albert Mathiez," *loc. cit.*, p. 99.
11. Lefebvre, "L'œuvre historique d'Albert Mathiez," *loc. cit.*, p. 198.
12. Mathiez to L. Gottschalk, Nov. 23, 1930, *loc. cit.*, pp. 218–19.

M. Lefebvre that Mathiez' initial interest in religious history was inspired by Aulard.[13] But, although Aulard praised the "irreproachable documentation" and the "personal and original" gifts shown by Mathiez in the presentation of his doctoral theses,[14] he was unable to accept Mathiez' interpretation. It was Aulard's opinion that the revolutionary cults were simply expedients of revolutionary defense, whereas Mathiez held that they were related profoundly to the whole thought of the revolutionaries on the role of religion in society. Other elements of difference in religious history appeared[15] about the same time that Mathiez came under the influence of Jean Jaurès.[16] One could not do better than to let Mathiez speak for himself here. He wrote:

> It is true that in this period of beginnings, the idea of associating the historical movement with the class struggle was not, with me, a dominant conception to which I subordinated other explanations. But already, as you notice, the social conflict was attracting me. . . . But I should like you to be convinced, my dear friend, that I do not adhere to systematic views on philosophy and on the world. I have a horror of abstract constructions. It is because the former explanations (political or religious, etc.) of the revolutionary crisis did not satisfy my mind that I abandoned, completed, rectified them. It would be a mistake to catalogue me in a classification, in a herbarium. I am a devotee of life [*J'ai le culte de la vie*], and I love to picture to myself its complexity in the mass and in detail. . . . Nothing systematic, but as complete a description as possible in order to show the concatenation of facts and situations which dominate men and parties and involve them in spite of themselves. If I had the time and space, I would explain

13. Lefebvre, "Albert Mathiez," *loc. cit.*, p. 99.
14. Thompson, *loc. cit.*, p. 617.
15. Mathiez to L. Gottschalk, Nov. 23, 1930, *loc. cit.*, pp. 218–19.
16. Lefebvre, "L'œuvre historique d'Albert Mathiez," *loc. cit.*, p. 198. In a review of his own edition of Jaurès' *Histoire socialiste de la Révolution française* Mathiez later wrote: "For myself, who have had the honor to append my name [as editor] to the reprinting of this work, I humbly declare that I have drawn from it not only the stimulation without which my researches would have been impossible but many suggestions which served me as governing ideas [*lignes directrices*]" (*Ann. hist.*, II [1925], 76). Mathiez admired particularly Jaurès' analysis of class interests in the earlier stages of the revolution (*Annales révolutionnaires*, XIV [1922], 256).

to you why history such as Aulard understood it is a polemical history for the profit of a party and why I rose little by little, while freeing myself from his influence, to a more objective view of things. . . . Thus I embarrassed the republican defense politics of Aulard and of his Radical friends, who, systematically, did not wish to draw attention to the primordial role of the bourgeoisie and to the misery of the people, who played the role of dupe. In other words, I departed early from the apologetical theses of the master as soon as I perceived whither they led.[17]

Mathiez has here indicated what an extended reading of his works would only confirm in regard to the salient points of his notions on the subject matter of history and its interpretation. He has so frequently been thought of as a Marxist that it is worth inquiring just how far this is true. Certainly he found the conception of the class struggle profoundly illuminating. He carried his belief in economic motivation to the point of entertaining a low opinion of human nature, at least in its political manifestations—Robespierre and a few others excepted. But these ideas were merely tools, not dogma. Mathiez did, in fact, at one time (as we shall see in a later connection) almost abandon the thesis of the class struggle for that of nationalism. He might upon occasion invert the Marxian order by showing that economic results had political causes, as he did, for example, when he analyzed the crisis of the spring of 1792.[18] Despite his assertion, quoted above, that men are influenced by circumstances against their wills, he elsewhere had disowned determinism: "I do not believe in Destiny, in the existence of an irresistible force of things which drags men along and dominates them, blind instruments for unknown ends."[19] Certainly Mathiez always wrote as if his characters must be judged responsible for their acts. The two statements seem, at first sight, difficult to reconcile; but probably the truth is that it appeared to Mathiez, as it does to many people, that sometimes men are free and sometimes they are not. For the

17. Mathiez to L. Gottschalk, Nov. 23, 1930, *loc. cit.*, pp. 219–20.
18. *La vie chère et le mouvement social sous la terreur* (Paris, 1927), p. 56.
19. *Rome et le clergé français sous la Constituante; la constitution civile du clergé, l'affaire d'Avignon* (Paris, 1911), p. 1.

distinctly accidental, also, he found a place. The death of the dauphin was a "fortuitous event"; yet Mathiez said that it postponed the Restoration for twenty years.[20]

In his own words, Mathiez did not have a "systematic" approach. He adopted the notion of the class struggle. Likewise he had earlier adopted Durkheim's definition of religion as any body of beliefs and practices which are obligatory for all members of a group[21] and made it the basis of his doctoral theses. But apparently he took no other ideas from sociological theory; indeed, he distrusted sociology as an adjunct to history.[22] His approach is quite aptly summarized in his words: "J'ai le culte de la vie." This is probably what J. M. Thompson, the English historian and biographer of Robespierre, implies in his appraisal of Mathiez: "Mathiez remains a 'pure' historian of a distinguished and unusual kind, who has reverenced facts as facts, and understood men as men."[23] If in regard to individuals Mathiez allowed his prejudices to obstruct the subtlety of his valuation, his characters are, nonetheless, human beings.

Although Mathiez will be best remembered for having done the most to supply a social and economic basis for the political superstructure of French Revolutionary history, nevertheless he was not primarily a social or economic historian. He was not, for instance, a historian of institutions per se. Lefebvre complains that Mathiez devoted too little attention to the feudal and agrarian problem and that in his study of opinion he did not pay sufficient attention to the mentality of the popular classes. Furthermore, he was not an economist.[24] Certainly he did not write economic history as such, divorced from the political milieu. Mathiez' major interest was the history of parliamentary parties and opinion. Lefebvre sees in this a survival of the influence of Aulard,[25] but such a judgment seems somehow inadequate. And if Mathiez inherited anything here from Aulard, the legacy was not com-

20. *La réaction thermidorienne* (Paris, 1929), p. 271.
21. *Les origines des cultes révolutionnaires*, p. 11.
22. Lefebvre, "L'œuvre historique d'Albert Mathiez," *loc. cit.*, p. 196.
23. Thompson, *loc. cit.*, p. 621.
24. Lefebvre, "L'œuvre historique d'Albert Mathiez," *loc. cit.*, pp. 208–9.
25. *Ibid.*, pp. 195–96.

plete, for Mathiez, unlike Aulard, was not much interested in constitutional history. One could not say that he denied the significance of constitutional history, for it finds a place in his writing, but his interest in it was distinctly minor. In the fact that Mathiez' synthesis was political, the primary influence would seem to have been not Aulard but Rousseau—the Rousseau of the *Contrat social,* wherein political society becomes the ultimate good and finds its justification in the semimystical concept of the general will. There is a good deal of the general will in Mathiez, for, cynic though he was, the notion of the transcendental transformation of personal into public interest was to him of real and passionate concern, the very core of the democratic way of life. This is primarily why he attacked Danton and glorified Robespierre. The rehabilitation of Danton, he wrote, "is not only an outrage to the truth but the indication of a policy which is equivocal and dangerous for democracy."[26] Of Robespierre, he said: "We love him for the teachings of his life and for the symbol of his death."[27] A rather curious declaration this, wherein Mathiez, anticlerical and unbeliever, resorted to a kind of figure of the incarnation to express his almost religious conviction.

It cannot be denied that Mathiez used history as a text from which to preach an ideal—a social-democratic ideal. During the period of the war of 1914 and its aftermath, Mathiez' idealism so affected his scholarship as to lead him into certain aberrations of historical judgment. In a lecture entitled "Pourquoi nous sommes Robespierristes," delivered in 1920 and published in *Robespierre terroriste,* Mathiez declared that the death of Robespierre left such a breach in the ranks of the Revolutionary leadership that the republic was shaken to its foundations.[28] But in neither *La Révolution française*[29] nor *La réaction thermidorienne,*[30] both written subsequently to the *Robespierre terroriste,* did Mathiez

26. Wendel, *loc. cit.,* p. 236.
27. *Robespierre terroriste* (Paris, [1921]), p. 188.
28. *Ibid.,* pp. 169–70.
29. 3 vols.; Paris, 1922–27. References in this essay will be to the excellent translation by Catherine A. Phillips entitled *The French revolution* (New York, 1929).
30. See above, n. 20.

imply any such complete adherence to the great-man theory of historical causation. In these other works there can be discerned, rather, the interpretation that what really shook the republic to its foundations was not the death of Robespierre but the break at that time within the Committee of Public Safety and the consequent collapse of its dictatorship.[31] That is, the death of Robespierre was more properly effect than cause. Again, in order to excoriate the exceptional regime that was imposed upon France from 1914 to 1918, Mathiez painted an idyllic picture of the Terror of 1793. He did not argue that war should not involve a degree of "regimentation"; quite the contrary. What he did contend was that, since France in 1914 was united and republican, there was no excuse for censorship and the general suspension of civil liberties. The revolutionaries of 1793, said Mathiez, never organized a preventive censorship, never delivered civilians up to a military justice, never closed the rostrum of the Convention or of the clubs.[32] Well, one may answer, the tribunals were no doubt civil tribunals; but what of that in view of the Law of Suspects? And as for opinion, it was doubtless legally free, if one dared to express it! In another place, again with the object of attacking the internal policy of the French government during the war of 1914, Mathiez wrote:

> Far from being a cause of weakness, liberty was for Revolutionary France the instrument of salvation. The divisions, the factions, even the risings, are only surface incidents. Feuillants, Girondins, Montagnards, Dantonists, Robespierrists, succeeded each other in power. But it was the patriot people who judged their differences. . . . Never did it exercise such an influence in public affairs; never was it to such a degree a sovereign people, master of its destinies.[33]

The reader may well wonder whether he is reading Mathiez or Michelet. How far this democratic mysticism, which, indeed, is latent in all Mathiez' work, has carried him away from the thesis

---

31. *The French revolution*, Book III, chap xiv; *La réaction thermidorienne*, pp. 2–20.
32. *Robespierre terroriste*, p. 6.
33. *La victoire en l'an II, esquisses historiques sur la défense nationale* (Paris, 1916), p. 279.

of the class struggle as reflected in the party history of the national assemblies is here strikingly evident. It is true that Mathiez had not at this time set forth all his evidence for the existence of the class struggle, but it can hardly be maintained that he had not yet made up his mind that it really did exist and that the conflict of the parties was of fundamental importance.

But if, under the influence of emotion endangered by wartime conditions, Mathiez was guilty of diverging from his own more sober judgments in order to plead a case, he ought not to be too harshly judged. Others have done as much and more. And, furthermore, if Mathiez quite consistently preached an ideal of social democracy, he had too high a regard for the sacredness of historical facts to write history in the interest of a particular party. This is how he himself put it:

> If history is past politics, that is no reason . . . why it should become the humble servant of the politics or rather of the politicians of the present. It has a reason for existence only if it says in complete independence what it believes to be the truth. . . . I do not write in order to catechize, to recruit adherents for this or that party, but to instruct and inform. I should be lowered in my own eyes if I concerned myself, in taking up my pen, with how politicians of the day, in France and abroad, will use my writings. That these men of action—red, black, or white—should concern themselves with exploiting my books to the profit of their cause is a vexation [ennui] that I must endure with patience.[34]

Now if Mathiez believed that the past is not the servant of the present—that is, in historical writing—what did he hold to be the uses of the present in historical interpretation? Here, again, he was explicit:

> My whole effort has consisted in withdrawing myself as much as possible from our present ways of thinking and judging in order to find again those of the men of the eighteenth century. . . . The historian ought not to interrogate the past with the formulas of the present. His task is more modest but more difficult. It consists in rediscovering the formulas under which the eternal problems of humanity are posed at different epochs and in showing what varied solutions they have received.[35]

34. *La réaction thermidorienne*, pp. vii–viii.
35. *La Révolution et l'église; études critiques et documentaires* (Paris, 1910), p. viii.

Again: "The fundamental problems are always the same, but their aspect changes, and their solutions depend on those multiple factors which can be grouped under the general denomination of 'spirit of the age.'"[36] Mathiez quite successfully lived up to his theory of the universal problem and the particular solution. For example, he insisted that, contrary to the prevailing practice among liberal historians, the religious conceptions of the revolutionaries could not be read in the light of the modern ideal of the completely neutral state, for such an ideal was then unknown, it being deemed that some form of religion was an essential bulwark of the state. Yet Mathiez was extremely sensitive, as a historian, to present events. They were always suggesting analogies that became the basis of his work. M. Lefebvre indicates a probable relationship between the failure of the Radical party, in the first decade of the twentieth century, to institute social reforms and Mathiez' disparagement of Danton.[37] He also points out the coincidence between the war of 1914 and Mathiez' studies on the economic foundations of the Terror, on the status of foreigners in France during the Revolution, and on the organization of the Revolutionary army.[38]

Mathiez' interest did not stray much beyond the confines of the Revolution and its immediate antecedents. The number of his publications outside that field is almost negligible. But from the summoning of the estates-general to the coup d'état of 18 Brumaire, there was no period in which he had not done spadework and contributed to its reinterpretation. His last book, *Le Directoire*,[39] did not extend in time beyond September 4, 1797, but he had planned to carry his work to the advent of Napoleon. Mathiez' interest in the post-Thermidorian period led him to make a characteristic observation, apropos of the fact that historians have often revolted from this period in disgust. "The historian," he remarked, "has no right to choose from what is to be the object of his studies, to accept what pleases him, to reject

36. *La Révolution et les étrangers; cosmopolitisme et défense nationale* (Paris, [1918]), p. 1.
37. Lefebvre, "L'œuvre historique d'Albert Mathiez," *loc. cit.*, p. 199.
38. Lefebvre, "Albert Mathiez," *loc. cit.*, pp. 99–100.
39. *Le Directoire, du 11 brumaire an IV au 18 fructidor an V*, publié, d'après les manuscrits de l'auteur, par Jacques Godechot (Paris, 1934).

what is repugnant to him. . . . Reality is a whole."[40] His devotion to synthesis was only equaled by his power of achieving it. Mathiez' work as historian has a remarkable unity. None of the threads he had once picked up were ever dropped, and he ended his career as he had begun it, with the policies of the Directory. Furthermore, he never really reversed his essential judgments. There is a development in his interpretation, but it is one of expansion rather than of change. In part, this consistency was probably due to method, to the fact that Mathiez was not in the habit of running after theories; but no doubt it was primarily the consequence of a strong inner consistency of viewpoint and personality and of an early intellectual maturity.

In spite of what has just been said about the unity of Mathiez' work, it can rather easily be divided into successive, if overlapping, phases.[41] His principal doctoral thesis, the reader may be reminded, was *La théophilanthropie et le culte décadaire*, the minor one a suggestive sketch entitled *Les origines des cultes révolutionnaires*. The idea set forth in these books has already been stated. It is, in brief, that there was a close relation between the Revolutionary cults and the view of their propagators, anti-Christian though they were, that society must have a religious sanction. Mathiez' first interest in Robespierre arose out of the study of the part played by him in connection with the de-Christianizing campaign and the festival of the Supreme Being. There followed a battery of articles dealing with various aspects of religious history. A number of these were collected into two books, entitled, respectively, *Contributions à l'histoire religieuse de la Révolution française*[42] and *La Révolution et l'église; études critiques et documentaires*.[43] These Mathiez followed with a significant work entitled *Rome et le clergé français sous la Constituante*,[44] which successfully maintained that the break with Rome was at least as much the fault of the papacy as of the

40. *La réaction thermidorienne*, p. 4.
41. This has been pointed out by M. Lefebvre in "Albert Mathiez," *loc. cit.*, pp. 99–100.
42. Paris, 1907. Preface by Gabriel Monod.
43. See above, n. 35.
44. See above, n. 19.

Constituent Assembly. In the same year Mathiez also published a short study, *Les conséquences religieuses de la journée du 10 août 1792: la déportation des prêtres et la sécularisation de l'état civil*,[45] in which he held that the legislation of this moment of the Revolution was probably not intended to secure the separation of church and state, although, in fact, it constituted a step in this direction. It might be added here, in connection with Mathiez' reading of the religious history of the Revolution, that the real separation between the church (i.e., the constitutional church) and the state dated, he insisted, from the beginning of the campaign of violent de-Christianization in the fall of 1793, rather than from the date of the legal and financial separation in the fall of 1794, after Thermidor.

From religious history Mathiez passed to the task of destroying Danton's reputation and recreating Robespierre's. This involved extended studies in parlimentary corruption and foreign policy, especially under the Convention. As usual, Mathiez published his work first in the form of short articles. Some of these were collected into two volumes, entitled *Études Robespierristes: La corruption parlementaire sous la terreur* and *La conspiration de l'étranger*.[46] Then came *Danton et la paix*,[47] a new study devoted to Danton's intrigues with foreign governments, and *Un procès de corruption sous la terreur; l'affaire de la Compagnie des Indes*,[48] an exposé of a case of graft in which the documents are published and practically allowed to speak for themselves. *Robespierre terroriste*[49] was again in part a reprinting of hitherto published articles but contained also Robespierre's notebook and his notes on the Dantonists, critically edited. *Autour de Robespierre*[50] was a collection chiefly of articles published between 1910 and 1924 and bearing on the policies of Robespierre and his relations with the Committee of Public Safety, the Committee of

45. Paris, 1911.
46. 2 vols.; Paris, 1917–18.
47. Paris, [1919].
48. Paris, 1920.
49. See above, n. 27.
50. Paris, 1926. Translated into English as *The fall of Robespierre and other essays* (New York, 1927).

General Security, and the Convention in the last months before the events of 9 Thermidor. *Autour de Danton*[51] was, on the other hand, a study published completely and for the first time in 1926, covering Danton's entire career. But it was not a biography. Mathiez never wrote a real biography of either Danton or Robespierre. *Girondins et Montagnards*[52] was Mathiez' last volume on the history of parliamentary struggles under the Convention. The outcome of what he himself referred to as "this great lawsuit,"[53] that is, Robespierre versus Danton, has undoubtedly been that Danton's reputation has been rather badly damaged, and Robespierre's enhanced. But it is generally agreed that Mathiez' prejudices led him to judgments in this matter beyond what his evidence would warrant.

The judgment on Robespierre is closely related to a third line of investigation that Mathiez began pursuing in the course of the war of 1914, namely, the origin and development of the policy of the "maximum." Some of this work was published in *La victoire en l'an II*,[54] but the culmination of Mathiez' research and writing along this line was *La vie chère et le mouvement social sous la terreur*.[55] A brief summary of the argument of this book will not, perhaps, be out of place. Under the old regime, said Mathiez, the state pursued a policy of intervention in the interest of the consumer. Toward the end of the period there were experiments in laissez faire, but they were not popular. Economic liberalism had captured only the thinking élite and the capitalist classes. The great majority of the *cahiers* demanded a policy of intervention and regulation, but the bourgeois Constituent Assembly nevertheless adopted a free-trade policy. Since the year 1789 produced a good harvest, there was acquiescence. But when times were bad again, in 1792, there was a widespread and profound, if unorganized, class movement in favor of regulation. Some slight concession in the direction of price-fixing was made following the

51. See above, n. 7.
52. [Paris], 1930.
53. *Robespierre terroriste*, p. 169.
54. See above, n. 33.
55. See above, n. 18.

August revolution, but it was soon withdrawn. The year 1793 witnessed a continuation of the economic crisis, intensified by invasion and the provincial revolts which were themselves a class movement centering in the bourgeois departmental administrations. Now Montagnards, as well as Girondins, were free-traders; but to save the Revolutionary republic the Montagnards, after the fall of the Gironde, entered into an alliance with the Hébertists, the demagogues of the sans-culottes, who demanded the maximum and the Terror to enforce it. The Revolutionary Tribunal was made competent for all cases of fraud and illicit profits. Mathiez did not attempt to estimate how great a proportion of the total number of executions was decreed for economic reasons directly, although he gave examples of such cases. Nor did he insist that the maximum was the only reason for the Terror, for, although the severity of the maximum was somewhat relaxed after the fall of the Hébertists, the severity of the Terror increased. What Mathiez did demonstrate was that there was a definite relationship between the instigation of the Terror of 1793–94 and the admission into the government of the popular and terrorist faction and that the Terror was an integral part of the policy of the maximum demanded by that faction. This is perhaps the most notable single contribution made by Mathiez to the history of the Revolution.

It will have been observed that the work of Mathiez is like a mosaic, built up out of small pieces of research. But one does not have to read through all the fragments to reconstruct the picture, for Mathiez did partly succeed in writing one continuous narrative of the Revolution. In 1922 he published the first volume of *La Révolution française*, entitled *La chute de la royauté (1787– 92)*. The second volume, *La Gironde et la Montagne*, appeared in 1924; and the third, *La terreur*, in 1927. *La Révolution française* was designed for the general reader as well as the student, and this fact, beside the limited space allotted by the publishers, precluded documentation, a restriction which Mathiez deplored. In *La réaction thermidorienne*, which Mathiez intended to be a continuation of the synthesis, he reverted to the more detailed type of study, thoroughly footnoted. *Le Directoire, du 11 brumaire an*

*IV au 18 fructidor an V,* edited by Jacques Godechot from Mathiez' notes, is the last volume of the synthesis and is on the same extended scale as *La réaction thermidorienne.*

Pre-eminently a research historian, Mathiez ransacked the archives—those of Paris especially, since he wrote about the Revolution from the viewpoint of Paris. In addition, he examined the contemporary journals (the *Moniteur* being the chief source for parliamentary proceedings), memoirs, and correspondence, and for the study of public opinion he used pamphlets extensively. In fact, there is apparently no type of source which escaped his scrutiny. His synthesis for the Revolution is not a summary of the monographic studies of the subject, though it is hardly permissible to doubt that Mathiez, whose listed book reviews total around six hundred, had an unrivaled knowledge of that sort of literature. His footnote references to secondary works are generally given either because such works contain source material or because Mathiez is examining the opinions therein expressed. His method of dealing with the documents has not been without criticism. M. Lefebvre, for example, hovers between rebuke and admiration. Mathiez, he says, was likely to apologize for the *témoinage unique* (reliance upon which is, of course, against one of the canons) simply because it is often the only available evidence, but, on the other hand, the boldness of his imagination in the interpretation of the documents was, M. Lefebvre implies, a quality of the first order.[56]

Mathiez distinguished scholarship from history. The one, he said, searches for and criticizes the evidence; the other reconstructs and expounds. That is, one might say, history is the more creative and is akin to literature. In writing *La Révolution française* Mathiez said he was attempting to perform the function of the historian.[57] Perhaps he would have agreed that in a rather considerable portion of his work he does hardly more than the scholar's task. This reflection may be illustrated by reference to Mathiez' practice of publishing archival material along with a more or less extensive commentary demonstrating some particular contention, with the result that the reader is somewhat in

56. Lefebvre, "L'œuvre historique d'Albert Mathiez," *loc. cit.,* pp. 201–2.
57. See Mathiez' preface to *La Révolution française.*

doubt whether to classify the production as book (or article) or as documents. *Un procès de corruption sous la terreur* is one example of this sort of hybrid; another is *Le club des Cordeliers pendant la crise de Varennes et la massacre du Champ de Mars*,[58] a study not hitherto mentioned.

Probably Mathiez did not intend to give a great emphasis to literary construction as one of those attributes of history which distinguish it from scholarship. Yet it is none the less true that *La Révolution française*, which is prefaced with the explicit statement of Mathiez' determination herein to transcend scholarship and to write history and which is the most broadly "reconstructive" of all his works, is likewise the most finished from a literary standpoint. Here there is the same terse and often mordant vocabulary which distinguishes his other writing, but displayed with a greater economy of languages. Antitheses, of which Mathiez was fond, are carefully worked out and effectively employed. The narrative is extremely detailed, without, however, any sacrifice of smoothness of style and without any obscuring of interpretation. Indeed, Mathiez manages to impart a distinctly dramatic quality to the presentation of both issues and situations. Although he wrote always with clarity—and, above all, with vigor—he wrote too much, one may infer, to take such pains habitually.

With all his passion for archival research and his not infrequent exposition of bits of evidence uncovered thereby, Mathiez was not primarily interested in the systematic publication of documents. This task he left to others. His editorial activity consisted chiefly in the publication of the *Annales révolutionnaires* and its successor, the *Annales historiques de la Révolution française*. Besides this, there was the new edition of Jean Jaurès' *Histoire socialiste de la Révolution française*.[59] Finally, with Léon Cahen, he prepared a small elementary source book of French laws and treaties entitled *Les lois françaises de 1815 à nos jours*.[60]

58. Paris, 1910. A *Supplément* was published in 1913.
59. 8 vols.; Paris, 1922–24. See above, n. 16.
60. Paris, 1906. The second edition (Paris, 1919) was entitled *Les lois françaises de 1815 à 1914*. A third edition with the same title as the second was published in 1927.

The eulogy of Mathiez by Pierre Caron quoted earlier in this essay indicates something of the effect of Mathiez' influence in France upon studies of the Revolution, despite the mutual antipathies of the schools. The quality of his contributions has been widely recognized abroad. Translations of *La Révolution française* exist in English, Russian, and Norwegian.[61] Perhaps nowhere outside of France has his work been more generally appreciated than in the United States, where the younger historians of the French Revolution well-nigh universally acknowledge their indebtedness.[62] Mathiez is still, as it were, a contemporaneous influence. The interpretations which he set forth are alive in a very immediate sense; they have not yet had time to become venerable and classic.

61. Ricardo R. Caillet-Bois, *Bibliografía de Albert Mathiez* (Buenos Aires, 1932), p. 17. Reprinted from the *Boletin del Instituto de Investigaciones Históricas* [de la Facultad de Filosofía y Letras], XIV (1932), 268–453. This useful compilation purports to be a complete bibliography of Mathiez' writings. Its principal divisions are books, articles (about 475), and reviews (about 600).

62. See Gottschalk, *loc. cit.*, pp. 224–29; also his article, "The importance of Albert Mathiez," *Nation*, CXXVII (July–December, 1928), 619–21. For an English estimate of the significance of Mathiez' work see J. M. Thompson, *loc. cit.*, pp. 617–21. For German estimates see, respectively, Hermann Wendel, *loc. cit.*, pp. 235–39, and Hedwig Hintze, "Die französische Revolution, neue Forschungen und Darstellungen," *HZ*, CXLIII (1930), 298–319. An Italian appreciation is that of Corrado Barbagallo, "Albert Mathiez," *Ann. hist.*, IX, 221–23. The best of the French critiques is contained in the two excellent articles by Georges Lefebvre, *loc cit.*, pp. 98–102 and 193–210.

# XII

## *Pierre Renouvin (1893–     )*

S. William Halperin

The career of Pierre Renouvin, professor at the Sorbonne and member of the Institut, has been one of the most brilliant in the recent annals of French historical scholarship. He first vaulted to fame with the publication of *Les origines immédiates de la guerre (28 juin–4 août 1914)*,[1] when he was thirty-two years old. Since then, thanks to a succession of outstanding works, his reputation has continued to grow. Today he is regarded as one of the foremost diplomatic historians of our time. Diplomatic history is of course an area in which Frenchmen have traditionally excelled. Renouvin thus represents one of the latest in a long chain of illustrious names that have given his country so eminent a place in this domain. He has received many marks of recognition. One of these is honorary foreign membership in the American Historical Association. Since the death of Georges Lefebvre in August 1959, Renouvin has been the only Frenchman to enjoy this distinction.

Not by his writings alone has Renouvin served the cause of historical scholarship. In 1928 he was named one of two secretaries assigned to a newly appointed national commission headed by the well-known historian Sébastien Charléty. The task of this commission was to arrange and supervise the publication of a monumental series which has since become famous the world

1. Paris, 1925. In this essay no effort is made to discuss all of Renouvin's writings. Only the most important ones are dealt with.

over as the *Documents diplomatiques français, 1871–1914.* In addition to his secretarial duties, Renouvin shared with his friend Charles Appuhn responsibility for the preparation of the eleven volumes covering the period from 1911 to 1914.[2] This assignment, which of course called for careful selection and editing, he completed in 1939.[3] Six years later, following the return to a normal rhythm in scholarly activity as in everything else, Renouvin was appointed to fill the vacancy created some time before by the death of Charléty.[4] While serving as president of the commission, he directed the preparation of the volumes for the years 1894–1900 and 1907–1911.[5] In 1959 he had the satisfaction of seeing the last instalment of the series go to press. Thus a project of incalculable value to scholars everywhere was finally brought to completion. Should the French government undertake a sequel to it by publishing the diplomatic correspondence for the period between the two world wars, Renouvin will in all likelihood be invited to direct such an enterprise.

Despite the claims of research, writing, and teaching, Renouvin has accepted heavy editorial responsibilities. From 1923 to 1939 he served as *rédacteur en chef* of the *Revue d'histoire de la Guerre mondiale.* Throughout the greater part of this period he also handled the documentary section of the *Esprit international,* a periodical published in Paris under the auspices of the European Center of the Carnegie Endowment for International Peace. In 1941 he took over the direction of France's leading historical journal, the *Revue historique.* This enabled him to play a central role in the scholarly life of his country.

Renouvin has likewise been active in the field of educational administration. From 1955 to 1958, without giving up any part of his teaching duties at the Sorbonne and at the Institut d'Études Politiques, where he lectures on the history of international relations, he served as dean of the Faculty of Letters of the University of Paris. In this capacity he devoted his efforts mainly

2. Renouvin to author, May 2, 1960.
3. *Ibid.*
4. *Ibid.*
5. *Ibid.*

to organizing the so-called "third cycle" of higher education.[6] Although the task took much of his time and energy, it did not interrupt or slow the rhythm of his productivity as a historian. On the contrary, it coincided with an accelerated tempo of publication and the appearance of his best work.

Renouvin was born and educated in Paris. He attended the Lycée Louis le Grand. His professors were impressed with his interest in history and urged him to go into teaching. At the Sorbonne he followed their advice. Under the direction of Alphonse Aulard, the celebrated historian of the French Revolution, he did his first bit of original research. The subject chosen was one aspect of the work of the French provincial assemblies of 1787. In 1912, before he was twenty, he successfully passed the examination for the *agrégation* in history. However, he began to feel that the life of a lycée professor might not be entirely to his taste. He turned to the study of law and won his licentiate in 1913.

At this point he experienced another change of heart and reverted single-mindedly to his interest in history. Resuming his research under the direction of Aulard, Renouvin planned a comprehensive study of the origins, development, and accomplishments of the provincial assemblies of 1787. The outbreak of hostilities in the summer of 1914 interrupted these labors. Renouvin served as an infantry officer. He was severely wounded in 1917. Unable to discharge his military duties because of the handicapping injuries he had sustained, he returned in 1918 to the project on the provincial assemblies. Three years later the work was completed and published as a doctoral dissertation.[7] Based on a tremendous amount of archival research and betraying the author's thorough familiarity with the printed sources, it constituted a well-nigh definitive treatment of the subject. In preparing it Renouvin had received advice and encouragement not only from Aulard but from two other distinguished scholars:

6. *Ibid.* For the genesis of the "third cycle" see Renouvin's article, "Le troisième cycle de l'enseignement supérieur des lettres," in *Revue de l'enseignement supérieur*, No. 3 (1959), pp. 113–29.

7. *Les assemblées provinciales de 1787: origines, développement, résultats* (Paris, 1921).

Camille Bloch and Marcel Marion. He treasured their help; they welcomed him into their well-tilled field. But already the eighteenth century had ceased to monopolize his attention. He forsook it for a new and absorbing interest: the history of the recent war. He never regretted this shift. It paved the way for his debut as a diplomatic historian.[8]

The change of direction came about as a consequence of the French government's decision in 1921 to create at the University of Paris a program of study focusing on the critical examination of sources pertaining to the years 1914–18. The Sorbonne wished to entrust this program to an *agrégé* in history who was a war veteran and who had earned the *doctorat ès lettres*. It chose Renouvin, and he promptly inaugurated the program with a seminar on the sources for a study of the crisis of July 1914. He repeated this seminar during the next few years. In devoting his attention to the origins of the war, Renouvin was expressing not only a new and genuine professional interest. He was also, like so many other young Frenchmen who had spent years in the trenches, seeking for purely personal reasons to learn more about the conflict which had so profoundly affected the course of their lives.[9]

This professional and personal concern, together with encouragement from many of his colleagues, led Renouvin to prepare a monograph on a delicate, thorny, but extremely popular subject. Controversy over the question of responsibility for the outbreak of war in 1914 had raged without interruption ever since the early days of the struggle. Germany's enemies pointed an accusing finger at her. She denied the charge and accused her accusers. In the course of the dispute a great many diplomatic documents were published. To be sure, they shed light on the convolutions of

8. It also resulted in his being asked to write *Les formes du gouvernement de guerre* (Paris, 1925). This excellent monograph formed part of a monumental series on the history of the recent war sponsored by the Carnegie Endowment for International Peace. Renouvin's contribution was an analysis of the operation of the French wartime government. It began with a sketch of the regime on the eve of the struggle and concluded with a résumé of the new trends that had sprung from the war.

9. Renouvin to author, August 2, 1960.

the July crisis. But the story they were made to tell by the interested parties who pieced the evidence together was never quite the same; it tended to vary with the nationality of the narrator. Thus the controversy remained not only unsolved but more heated than ever. Scholars had entered the fray. As a consequence it developed into an erudite free-for-all, a battle fought with the paraphernalia of learning in which the object more often was to defend or attack rather than to ascertain the truth for its own sake and to follow it wherever it might lead.

To this controversy Renouvin brought a refreshing degree of judiciousness and *sangfroid*. In his introduction to *Les origines immédiates de la guerre*, which he completed in March 1925, he faced up to the problem of trying to be objective about so touchy a subject. Having noted the rabid partisanship that still dominated the discussion, he declared his intent to proceed differently. But even if it were true that the methods of the research historian could be applied to a subject of this kind, how could anyone be certain, Renouvin wondered, that he was in fact approaching it in the proper frame of mind? During the war, of course, impartiality had been out of the question. The interests and prestige of the belligerent powers had been too much involved. But even now, almost eleven years after the start of the war, it seemed quite impossible to carry on research without taking sides. Yet the attempt had to be made. This, Renouvin explained, he had tried to do. He had sought, before reaching any conclusions, to study the facts in an entirely critical spirit.[10]

But even with the best of intentions, did not the investigator make himself vulnerable by looking for the truth at a time when the available evidence was still incomplete and, worse yet, open to suspicion? To be sure, as Renouvin pointed out, the documents published since 1919 by the republican governments of Austria and Germany had greatly facilitated the task of the researcher. Helpful too, if used with the utmost caution, were the memoirs of statesmen and ambassadors and the reams of testimony—sworn affidavits—gathered by a committee acting at the behest of the

10. *Les origines immédiates de la guerre*, pp. vi–vii.

German national assembly. Needless to say, the historian would have to rely mainly on the diplomatic correspondence; but the rub here was that France and England had not yet followed the example of Austria and Germany. So far the two Western powers had merely announced their intention of doing so. However, the lacuna was really not too serious: the Russian correspondence revealed a good deal about the attitude of Paris and London. But there was still another difficulty, and it constituted the principal reason for anxiety: even the invaluable official publications could not be trusted unreservedly. Important or useful documents might have been left out of them. Renouvin cited in this connection the case of the German collection assembled by Karl Kautsky. Renouvin was satisfied that Kautsky, an ardent foe of William II, had omitted nothing that was damaging to the imperial regime. But he called attention to sworn testimony indicating that some compromising documents might have been destroyed before Kautsky was given access to the files of the Wilhelmstrasse. While thus making the point that the published correspondence did not merit absolute confidence, Renouvin also warned against exaggerated distrust. The important thing, given the incomplete and uncertain character of the available evidence, was to assume that any conclusions reached would have to be tentative. Yet this was scarcely a reason for avoiding the subject. Most of the actors and witnesses were still alive. So long as they were, a historical inquiry into the July crisis would not prove fruitless. But it must be undertaken at once, not deferred until some later date.[11]

In keeping with the self-imposed attitude of the historian who sought to explain rather than to argue or judge, Renouvin drew no invidious distinctions between the powers when he assessed the underlying origins of the war. All of them without exception were caught in a web of cause and effect from which they could not or would not break out. Thus Renouvin noted that after 1871, when Germany established her hegemony in Europe, a prolonged counterreaction set in which eventually produced the Entente Cordiale of 1904, the Anglo-Russian rapprochement of 1907, and

11. *Ibid.*, pp. vii, viii–x, xi–xii.

S. William Halperin

the Anglo-French conventions of 1912. The Germans saw in this
a threat of "encirclement." The two Moroccan crises of 1905 and
1911 rekindled the long-standing animosity which France and
Germany felt toward one another and led both of them to in-
tensify their military preparations. The Balkan crisis of 1912–13,
following that of 1908–9, brought the interests of Austria and
Russia to the point of direct confrontation. Because the Treaty
of Bucharest of August 10, 1913 represented a setback for them,
the Austrians were determined not to accept the resultant situation. The Germans had refrained from egging Vienna on while
the crisis was in progress. However, they came away feeling that
they had lost ground. Russia, in the meanwhile, had expanded
her armaments and tightened her military ties with the French.
In the latter she sensed a new firmness.

> The idea that war was inevitable tended to spread. The cir-
> cumstances of European politics, the armaments race, the grow-
> ing rivalry between the two groups of powers, seemed unavoid-
> ably to lead to this idea. The conflict was expected; when the
> statesman arrived at this conviction, he reasoned and acted as
> if the trend were invincible. He would have to be able to prepare
> for the struggle without believing in it; how could he escape
> from this fatality?
> Such was the moral situation that dominated the decisions of
> the statesmen in July 1914 and explained the evolution of the
> crisis.[12]

All this was impartial enough. But when Renouvin began his
microscopic examination of the July crisis, he lost little time taking a stand. Without departing from the fair-minded, judicious
approach he had promised to adopt, he made no bones about the
fact that, according to his reading of the evidence, the Germans,
together with the Austrians, were largely responsible for the
transformation of the original Austro-Serb quarrel into a European struggle. His reconstruction of what happened naturally
centered on the first days of July, when Austria queried the Germans. Powerful elements in Vienna wanted to make war on the

12. *Ibid.*, p. xiii.

Serbs in retaliation for the assassination of Archduke Francis Ferdinand at Sarajevo. But first they had to know the attitude of Germany. There were influential people in the Dual Monarchy who wished to defer the settling of accounts with Serbia. Germany, by the stand she took, would decide. Did she advise caution, restraint, or delay? On the contrary, she decided to utilize the Austro-Serb crisis to bolster the prestige of her ally. This was to be achieved by immediate Austrian action against Serbia. The Germans, to be sure, wished to keep the hostilities confined to those two countries—which of course would have meant throwing tiny Serbia to the Austrian wolves. The trouble might not spread. The Germans had no desire to attack or involve Russia. Neither they nor the Austrians wanted a general war. But they knowingly and willingly accepted that risk:[13] this was the crucial, decisive point. By the 27th of July, the Germans, in concert with the Austrians, had created the "conditions" of a conflict that was to engulf the great powers.[14]

While by no means blind to the considerations that could be adduced in defense or extenuation of Germany's behavior—notably the fear of alienating her only remaining ally and thus finding herself completely isolated vis-à-vis the "encircling" powers of the Triple Entente—Renouvin saw little merit in the line taken by some of her apologists. Indeed, but still in the spirit of the truth-seeker rather than the polemicist, he even went so far as to accuse them of distorting the meaning of certain facts. Thus they sought to draw attention to the secret intentions of the powers in order to suggest that if Germany had been clumsy, the Entente had been too adroit. Renouvin objected that an approach of this kind would not contribute to a clarification of the main problem.[15] He readily acknowledged, in discussing the general, underlying causes of the conflict, that mutual distrust and the system of alliances affected the diplomacy of *all* the powers. He also pointed out that the already drafted plans of the military exercised an even greater influence on the course of the July crisis

13. *Ibid.*, p. 27.
14. *Ibid.*, p. 256.
15. *Ibid.*, p. 265.

and that they played a role in Russia as well as in Germany.[16] But he insisted that the question of responsibility could be properly understood only by assessing the conduct of the powers at the very beginning of the crisis, when they were still in a position to decide freely what they proposed to do. Later their freedom would be gone. From the available data on the initial phase of the drama, it was reasonably clear to him that the Central powers betrayed an aggressive intent by refusing any solution other than force in dealing with the Serbs. Germany and Austria took this stand with their eyes wide open, after coolly envisaging all the possible consequences. "Within the context of the *immediate* origins of the conflict," Renouvin concluded, "the position they assumed proved to be the predominant factor.[17]

As he moved through the successive phases of his analysis, Renouvin continued to maintain the detachment of a scientific historian even though by his judgments he identified himself with the anti-German camp. In addition, he handled the evidence, which of course admitted of more than one interpretation, with extraordinary skill and finesse. Not the conclusion, which obviously contained nothing new, but the nuanced, fair-minded, masterly way in which it had been reached, made *Les origines immédiates de la guerre* a landmark in the historiography of July 1914. To be sure, it had its flaws. One of these, and it was undoubtedly serious, was the relative paucity of attention given to the much disputed subject of Franco-Russian relations during the crisis. But in comparison with all preceding studies, the book represented a giant step forward.

The long-awaited British documents on July 1914 were published in 1926. Renouvin, who had been planning to bring out a second edition of his book, wisely waited until the new collection was available. Leaning heavily on it, he went over the ground again and wrote a considerably augmented version.[18] He was

16. *Ibid.*, pp. 266–68.
17. *Ibid.*, p. 268.
18. It was published in Paris in 1927 under the original title. Shortly afterward an English translation appeared: *The immediate origins of the war* (New Haven, 1928).

able to clarify several important points, but the general lines of the original treatment remained unchanged. Other writers took note of what he had done when they proceeded to construct accounts of their own. Although his own interest shifted toward subjects of larger chronological scope, he followed with close attention the fantastic growth of the literature on July 1914 and occasionally composed an article on it. He was of course familiar with such distinguished works as *The origins of the World War* by Sidney B. Fay, *The coming of the war: 1914* by Bernadotte E. Schmitt, *Der Ausbruch des Weltkrieges* by Alfred von Wegerer, and *Le origini della guerra del 1914* by Luigi Albertini. In subsequent books he himself returned, but only briefly, to the events of the crisis. Each time he reaffirmed in substance the position he had taken in 1925.

*Les origines immédiates de la guerre* received widespread acclaim. In the United States, where the question of war guilt had precipitated a lively controversy among diplomatic historians, leading experts were at one in paying tribute to the signal nature of Renouvin's contribution. Schmitt described Renouvin as a "fair-minded" man who, like certain writers in other lands, was "animated by an honest desire to ascertain the truth" and to state his case "dispassionately."[19] Furthermore, Renouvin neglected "none of the nuances"[20] and maintained "excellent proportions" in the construction of his narrative.[21] For the developments that followed Germany's "blank check" to Austria, Renouvin's treatment, because of its superior organization which enabled the reader to follow the chronological sequence without difficulty, surpassed even so splendid an account as Fay's.[22] Charles Seymour also gave it high praise. In the preface to the English translation of Renouvin's book, he eulogized the Frenchman as belonging to the select company of "objective scholars" who had succeeded in freeing themselves from the thrall of "national prejudice" and "wartime

19. Bernadotte E. Schmitt, "The origins of the war," *Journal of modern history,* I (1929), 112, 119.
20. *Ibid.*, p. 113.
21. *Ibid.*, p. 116.
22. *Ibid.*

emotion" and who were consequently able "to approach the task of investigation in a scientific frame of mind."[23] Renouvin's research was marked by "strict adherence to the canons of historical scholarship,"[24] and his conclusions were "framed with judicial care."[25] Very appropriately Seymour added: "It is notable that the critics of his work, whether among the advocates of the cause of the Entente, or those of the cause of Germany, have confined their objections to details and have acknowledged their confidence in his capacity for handling diplomatic documents and in his desire to evaluate the evidence impartially."[26]

This allusion to the unanimous applause which greeted *Les origines immédiates de la guerre* found partial confirmation in the reaction of Fay. Both Schmitt and Seymour belonged to the circle of scholars who held that Germany was mainly responsible for the outbreak of the war. Fay, on the other hand, was a leading "revisionist" who claimed that at least some of the charges leveled against Germany in connection with the question of war guilt were either baseless or exaggerated. Consequently, particular interest attached to his judgment of Renouvin's work, which presented a balanced but nonetheless critical estimate of Germany's role. In his review of the first edition, Fay showed himself to be second to no one in extolling its merits. He wrote:

M. Renouvin is a cautious objective scholar. He has sifted carefully all the evidence on the diplomatic crisis which followed the assassination of the Archduke at Sarajevo. He has written by far the best account of the immediate causes of the war which has appeared from the hand of a Frenchman. He establishes, day by day and hour by hour, the exact sequence of actions. This is the kind of book which makes a real advance toward the truth. He sweeps away most of the legends which have fed upon prejudice, propaganda, and ignorance, and which led the Versailles Peace Commission presided over by Mr. Lansing to make the untrue charge that Germany and her allies deliberately plotted the war.[27]

23. *The immediate origins of the war*, p. xiii.
24. *Ibid.*
25. *Ibid.*, p. xiv.
26. *Ibid.*
27. *American historical review*, XXXI (1925–26), 354–55.

Thus, while praising the book, Fay was careful to stress the impossibility of squaring Renouvin's account with the extreme Allied position on war guilt. However, the fact remained, as Fay himself hastened to note, that "even after clearing away the falsifications and legends which have too long passed current in the Entente countries, M. Renouvin still has serious charges against the Central Powers which throw on them a large share of the responsibility."[28] Not all of these accusations were sound, Fay insisted. Furthermore, Renouvin's treatment of certain points was too brief. But he predicted that historians would indorse Renouvin's conclusion that the general as distinguished from the immediate causes of the war "were at work more or less in all countries in Europe."[29] The American scholar thus gave a boost to his own contention that special responsibility could not be ascribed to any one power or combination of powers.

A few years later Fay reviewed the English translation of the second edition. This time, while again expressing disagreement with Renouvin on a number of points, he went even further than before in praising the book. He declared that "one can not fail to admire the clarity, grasp, and judiciousness with which M. Renouvin has sifted the mass of documentary evidence, punctured and discarded untenable legends, and written what seems to the reviewer quite the best comprehensive treatment in any language which he has read on this difficult and thorny subject."[30] No finer tribute could have been paid to the quality of *Les origines immédiates de la guerre*.

During the three and a half decades that have elapsed since his debut as a diplomatic historian, Renouvin enhanced his reputation in a variety of ways. But more than anything else historical synthesis proved to be his forte. Here he performed impressively, so much so that he stood out even in a land where the art of synthesis boasts many consummate practitioners. Although he by no means stopped conducting original investigations, he threw himself increasingly into this broader type of endeavor.

28. *Ibid.*, p. 355.
29. *Ibid.*
30. *Ibid.*, XXXIII (1927–28), 878.

Renouvin's skill in fusing and elucidating the findings of recent research was demonstrated in the pages of his *La crise européenne et la grande guerre (1904–1918)*.[31] Published in 1934, it promptly won recognition as a major pioneering effort. Although more than one fourth of the book dealt with developments that antedated August 1914, its significance lay in the fact that it represented the first serious attempt to write a truly comprehensive history of the war years. Renouvin had become interested in the subject when he commenced his critical investigations into the sources on the July crisis. For him the origins of the struggle were quite inseparable from its entire course during the following four and a quarter years. Indeed, from 1922 to 1931, when he was awarded a professorship at the Sorbonne, the historiography of the war remained his single most consistent preoccupation.[32] The work which he finally published in 1934 thus meant something very special to him.

The best of the previously published general histories of the conflict stressed the military aspect. Renouvin's approach was far broader. To each of the disparate but interrelated facets of the struggle—military, naval, diplomatic, economic, social, and psychological—he gave a nicely proportioned share of his attention. Moreover, he treated not only Europe but the Far East, the United States, and Latin America. His discussion of conditions and happenings in these faraway regions betrayed an expertise that reflected the depth as well as the range of his scholarship.

Grappling with an immense amount of material, Renouvin performed prodigies of compression and condensation. Yet he retained enough detail to convey the authentic flavor, even the dramatic, exciting quality of the period. He brought his own recapitulatory conclusions into the narrative without appreciably impairing its smooth, natural flow. The problem of organization, always difficult in an undertaking of this type, he resolved by skilfully blending the topical and chronological approaches and by trusting to his own sense of proportion. A lucid style, a high

31. Paris, 1934. This volume appeared as part of the "Peuples et civilisations" series edited jointly by Louis Halphen and Philippe Sagnac.
32. Renouvin to author, August 2, 1960.

degree of factual accuracy, and an objective or at least reasoned treatment of controversial issues served to underscore the general excellence of the volume. As one reviewer remarked, what Renouvin had achieved was "synthesis in the finest French manner."[33]

In some respects such a judgment was even more applicable to *La question d'Extrême-Orient, 1840-1940,*[34] which appeared a dozen years later. In this work, which Renouvin chose to write because it fitted so perfectly into his expanding purview as a diplomatic historian, he again exhibited his flair for synthesis, but he did so with a narrative and analytical brilliance that signalized the full maturation of the talent first disclosed in *Les origines immédiates de la guerre. La question d'Extrême-Orient* traced with superb accuracy, clarity and compactness the successive phases of international relations in the Far East and the Pacific during a hundred years of spectacular and momentous change. Renouvin's description of the motives and moves of the great powers, which was grounded in the best available knowledge, represented one of the finest expositions of its kind in any language. To provide the necessary background for an understanding of this diplomatic story, Renouvin summarized the important developments that took place within China and Japan. He also recapitulated the relevant happenings in Indo-China, Siam, Burma, and the Pacific Islands. He was of course no Orientalist, and this he was careful to emphasize.[35] Yet, in depicting the peoples and institutions of the Far East, he displayed a comprehension of the subject that would have brought no discredit even on the most knowledgeable specialist in the history of the area.

The bibliographies appended to each of the chapters disclosed how far-flung had been Renouvin's quest for up-to-date and dependable information. But considerably more impressive was the craftsmanship with which he wove these data together. Trenchant in content and beautifully proportioned in form, the work was highly lauded even by those who did not find it flawless.

33. Charles Seymour in his discussion of the book in *American historical review,* XL (1934–35), 742.

34. Paris, 1946.

35. See *La question d'Extrême-Orient, 1840–1940,* p. 1 n.

Thus John K. Fairbank, after calling attention to some inadequacies in Renouvin's treatment of the Asiatic background, explained that he had raised "these minor points only because M. Renouvin's high standing in the field of diplomatic history makes it unnecessary to dilate upon his masterly grasp of the subject of this book and the great precision and finesse of his presentation of it."[36]

In the years directly following the publication of *Les origines immédiates de la guerre*, Renouvin had collaborated with several other distinguished scholars to produce, under the editorship of Henri Hauser, a diplomatic history of Europe from 1871 to 1914.[37] Shortly afterward he had published, with the European Center of the Carnegie Endowment for International Peace acting as sponsor, an incisive survey of European diplomacy from 1815 to 1914.[38] Then, just before the outbreak of World War II, he had co-authored a work entitled *La paix armée et la grande guerre (1871–1919)*.[39] These studies, together with *La crise européenne et la grande guerre* and *La question d'Extrême-Orient*, represented leisurely stages in Renouvin's progress toward the culminal four-volume history of international relations from 1815 to 1945 which he published in the 1950's. His teaching program at the Institut d'Études Politiques dovetailed nicely with the task of completing this ambitious undertaking. Displaying anew his talent for synthesis, the author assembled an enormous amount of material and welded it into a limpid, gracefully written, skilfully compressed and closely reasoned exposition. The bibliographies showed that Renouvin had overlooked relatively little in the way of important articles, monographs, and general works. Publications in several languages other than French— Russian, Polish, and Swedish as well as English, German, Italian, and Spanish—figured in this vast array of sources. Having kept

36. *American historical review*, LIII (1947–48), 340.
37. *Histoire diplomatique de l'Europe (1871–1914)* (2 vols.; Paris, 1929).
38. *Histoire diplomatique (1815–1914)* (Paris, 1930). This was a verbatim transcription of a course of lectures Renouvin had given in the academic year 1928–29 at the Institut des Hautes Études Internationales.
39. Paris, 1939. Renouvin's collaborators were Edmond Préclin and Georges Hardy.

abreast of recent research, Renouvin was able to maintain a high level of both up-to-dateness and accuracy throughout the many phases and ramifications of his narrative.

No one was more aware than he that despite the proliferation of documentary publications, there were still innumerable gaps or thinly covered spots in the evidence. Consequently, a host of significant questions could be answered not at all or only in the most tentative and guarded fashion. While duly noting these lacunae and indicating the methodological problems they raised, Renouvin squeezed what he could out of the data at his disposal and even ventured some shrewd hypotheses along the way. In the process he compiled an excellent summation of the best available knowledge.

The marvelous lucidity and compactness of his treatment, which evoked universal admiration, matched the almost Olympian detachment, the combination of steadfast judiciousness and cool objectivity, with which he viewed each of the episodes and individuals he discussed. His methods varied, but he relied mainly on an alternation of the topical and chronological, the analytical and narrative approaches. He displayed keen perspective in appraising the meaning of what transpired amidst the kaleidoscopic succession of events. Cutting through much of the underbrush, he made the large trees and the contour of the forest stand out in bold relief. Frequent summaries stressed saliences and interrelationships, thereby enhancing the cogency of the exposition. To be sure, the distribution of emphasis left something to be desired. Renouvin gave the periods 1815–1914 and 1914–45 an equal amount of space. But such a lopsided division hardly detracted from the achievement as a whole. As a general yet pithy and searching recapitulation of the principal happenings in the world's diplomatic arena during the vast era under review, it represented a veritable tour de force, surpassing all previous works of comparable scope. True, although some fresh details were introduced, the interpretations contained nothing really original or startlingly new. But several of them were extraordinarily suggestive. Every now and then flashes of insight illumined or clarified the reconstruction of events, the description of actors and their motives. The familiar thus acquired a richness of dimension which made it more meaningful than it had been before.

The four volumes formed the second half of a series which Renouvin himself had planned and edited and which covered the history of international relations since the Middle Ages.[40] At the very outset the reader's attention was drawn to the forces that shaped or influenced the course of international affairs. These forces Renouvin identified as political, socio-psychological, ideological, and economic in character. The first three overlapped a good deal and were at times quite indistinguishable. To be sure, all of them were constantly operative, but with varying degrees of intensity and effectiveness in different periods and circumstances. It was therefore impossible, Renouvin concluded, to establish any definite hierarchy among them; the fluctuating nature of their roles ruled out any rigid classification on the basis of relative importance. In any case, so far as he was concerned, the purpose of the study of international relations was neither to establish "historical laws" nor to provide lessons. Rather, it was to try to comprehend the complex interaction of those "causes" that had produced the world's "great transformations."[41]

Although Renouvin thus declined to accept any theoretical, hard-and-fast rating of the forces at work in the sphere of diplomacy, he tended in practice to ascribe a primary role to one or another of the noneconomic categories. This was quite evident, for example, in his treatment of the period from 1815 to 1871, his analysis of the origins of World War I, and his reconstruction of the troubled years that preceded the coming of the second holocaust. Exponents of the economic interpretation of history were bound to demur, but the evidence which Renouvin marshaled seemed to be against them. Although admittedly no economic or any other kind of determinist, he was in actuality far from blind to the importance of the role played by economic interests in the

40. Pierre Renouvin (ed.), *Histoires des relations internationales* (8 vols.; Paris, 1953–58). The volumes written by Renouvin are *Le XIXᵉ siècle. I. De 1815 à 1871: l'Europe des nationalités et l'éveil de nouveaux mondes* (Paris, 1954); *Le XIXᵉ siècle. II. De 1871 à 1914: l'apogée de l'Europe* (Paris, 1955); *Les crises du XXᵉ siècle. I. De 1914 à 1929* (Paris, 1957); *Les crises du XXᵉ siècle. II. De 1929 à 1945* (Paris, 1958).
41. *Le XIXᵉ siècle. I. De 1815 à 1871*, p. 404.

international domain as well as in the realm of domestic affairs. Indeed, he maintained that they figured so significantly as motives or pretexts that it was imperative for the diplomatic historian not to lose sight of them.[42] He himself never failed to bring them into his analysis, if only to show that although they were influential, they were not necessarily decisive. He conceded that at certain moments they did predominate, but he concluded quite correctly that at least in the succession of periods with which he was concerned, such moments were comparatively rare.

One of the instances in which they exerted a controlling influence was the subjection of the Far East to European penetration.[43] They played a significant although in the last analysis an essentially contributory role in the growth of the national movements that presented European diplomacy with some of its severest tests. The socio-psychological impact generated by the currents of national sentiment proved the decisive factor.[44] On the other hand, in the case of the revolts which felled Spanish and Portuguese rule in Latin America, economic interests were preponderant.[45] But this had few parallels elsewhere. Although commercial considerations exerted a powerful and palpable influence on the behavior of the European nations before 1914, the outbreak of World War I could hardly be explained in terms of trade rivalry.[46] To be sure, the Franco-German and Russo-German difficulties that cropped up during this period were related to a conflict of economic interests, but the latter apparently played only a secondary role in producing these complications.[47] Even in the oft-cited case of Anglo-German commercial rivalry after 1890, the available evidence did not support the thesis that British businessmen favored a resort to arms to eliminate German competition. In fact, they showed themselves hostile to the idea of military intervention of any kind in July 1914. As for the leaders of German industry, there was no proof that they wanted war.

42. *Les crises du XX$^e$ siècle. I. De 1914 à 1929*, p. 218.
43. *Le XIX$^e$ siècle. I. De 1815 à 1871*, pp. 400–401, 403.
44. *Ibid.*, pp. 401–2.
45. *Ibid.*, p. 402.
46. *Le XIX$^e$ siècle. II. De 1871 à 1914*, p. 382.
47. *Ibid.*

The pith of the matter was that although economic rivalry did affect the psychology of nations, it tended mainly to reinforce already existing suspicions and to strengthen the "desire for power." Thereby it increased the chances of a general war, but it was not the direct cause.[48]

Admittedly the state of international relations would have been decidedly different in 1914 if profound changes had not taken place in the economic sphere during the preceding half-century. But surely, Renouvin contended, it could not be argued that the conflict was the inevitable result of clashing material interests. Actually, the war did not break out until competing political designs came into violent collision. Thus, economic considerations figured in these designs. But it was not thoughts of material gain that determined the behavior of governments and peoples. The explanation for their conduct was to be found in the impact upon them of national feeling and passion.[49] Here Renouvin placed himself on apparently unassailable ground. Nothing in the voluminous data he had sifted conflicted with the thesis that the first great struggle of the twentieth century sprang from non-economic causes.

Turning to more recent developments, Renouvin continued his appraisal of the underlying forces in international relations. In this context he scrutinized the repercussions of the world-wide depression that started in 1929. He noted that the ferment it produced assumed divergent forms in the various countries and concluded from his examination of the evidence that the reason for this was political: the existence of long-standing attitudinal differences between the nations.[50] Adverting to the central fact of international affairs from 1933 onward, the bellicosity of Germany, Renouvin rejected as completely unproved the contention that economic pressures forced the Nazis to embark upon a policy of conquest.[51] Was such a policy really imposed by the need for economic expansion, as argued by certain writers, or was it at

48. *Ibid.*
49. *Ibid.*, p. 384.
50. See *Les crises du XXᵉ siècle. II. De 1929 à 1945*, p. 21.
51. *Ibid.*, pp. 195–96.

bottom the result of something else? Addressing himself to this question, Renouvin pointed out that economic necessities were never invoked at the conferences in which Hitler divulged to his subordinates the motives and goals of his foreign policy. Moreover, it was quite plain that Germany could have satisfied her need for economic expansion without resorting to arms. It was therefore possible to maintain that the foreign policy of the Nazis, far from having been determined by economic preoccupations, stemmed instead from an essentially different source: the craving for political and military preponderance.[52] Did economic considerations push the Western powers into the series of disastrous blunders they committed on the eve of World War II? Renouvin did not think so. He was inclined to ascribe the behavior of England and France mainly to "the currents of collective psychology,"[53] by which he meant the political attitudes then prevalent in those two countries, as distinguished from purely material concerns. Given the present state of our knowledge, the distinction thus made by Renouvin and the thesis he rested on it seemed plausible enough. While economic interests obviously helped to fashion the Anglo-French image of what was right, desirable, and necessary, they apparently failed to produce nearly as much effect as the imperatives of national security and prestige.

The last major topic treated by Renouvin was the world in 1945, immediately after the cessation of hostilities. In assessing the already emerging rivalry between the United States and the Soviet Union, he analyzed the American decision, reached toward the end of the year, to extend loans to the countries of Western Europe. Although he noted the economic considerations that undoubtedly helped to produce this decision, he correctly insisted that political preoccupations were uppermost in Washington: the stated aim of the American program, which foreshadowed the Marshall Plan, was to preserve "a civilization of free men and free institutions."[54] As for the Russians, although Renouvin did not say so, it was clear that the mainsprings of their behavior,

52. *Ibid.*, pp. 196–97.
53. *Ibid.*, p. 199.
54. *Ibid.*, p. 397.

their motives and aims, were likewise political in character.

In addition to the forces that determined or influenced the direction of international relations, there were of course the actors who occupied the center of the stage, the men who held positions of authority in the various countries, particularly those states in Europe and outside it that had long been or were in the process of becoming great powers. In this connection, it should be noted that the governments of such extra-European countries as the United States and Japan, to which Renouvin paid heed as soon as they began to loom on the international horizon, received increasing attention as the chronicle unfolded. When he had reached the end of World War I, Renouvin appropriately titled his next chapter "The decline of Europe."[55] He was obviously interested in the rulers, statesmen, and diplomats from all the lands that figured to a greater or lesser degree in successive alignments and alliances, in the tale of adventures, crises, and wars. Almost at the very beginning of his first volume, where he sketched some of the larger contours of the story he proposed to tell, he cautioned against slighting the personal factor. How, he queried, could one neglect the actor's temperament, his conception of the national destiny, his understanding or misapprehension of the underlying forces?[56] With the period of 1815-71 in mind, he went on to elaborate this point as follows:

[Any] explanation [of the course of international relations] would remain incomplete and deceptive if it failed to consider the behavior and initiatives of the statesmen. No one can doubt this in the case of Cavour, Bismarck, or Napoleon III. But how many other instances, at first glance less obvious, ought to come to mind! How, for example, can one fail to see the personal role of Canning in the dissolution of the Holy Alliance, or the influence of Palmerston's temperament in the prodromes of the revolutions of 1848? How can one forget that the France of 1830, under a sovereign other than Louis Philippe, could have become once again the agent of a great upheaval, or that the provisional government of 1848 was unwilling to give armed support to the Italian and German unitary movements? And when Russia, in

55. *Les crises du XX^e siècle. I. De 1914 à 1929*, chap. v, pp. 130–53.
56. *Le XIX^e siècle. I. De 1815 à 1871*, p. 28.

1853, by rekindling the Ottoman crisis, opened the way for transformations in Central Europe, did she not do so as a consequence of the personal wishes of the tsar? Analogous statements of fact are suggested by the Egypt of Mehemet Ali, the Japan of Okubo, the Spanish America of San Martín and Bolívar. To be sure, the initiatives of the statesmen were successful only insofar as the way had been prepared for them by the operation of the underlying forces; but when these forces did not find a man capable of directing them, they came to nought: this was true of the German unitary movement of 1848. Undoubtedly one can argue with some plausibility that Italian unity would ultimately have been achieved even without Cavour and Napoleon III, or German unity without Bismarck. But when? If they had been delayed for thirty years, would not the consequences for the life of Europe and the world have been entirely different?[57]

Proceeding with his analysis, Renouvin cited the years from 1871 to 1890 as an example of how important at times the role of the personal factor could be despite the constant and pervasive impact of the underlying forces. Throughout those years Bismarck, invested with the office of German chancellor, bestrode the international scene like a colossus. In this rather unusual situation, the man became indistinguishable from something called "Bismarckianism," which was a socio-psychological reality.[58] But very different, according to Renouvin, was the interval from Bismarck's fall to 1914. This period he characterized as one in which the statesmen played a comparatively insignificant role. Their actions appeared to be dominated by conditions which they themselves perhaps failed to see clearly but which in any case they felt powerless to master. There were a few exceptions, but they occurred outside Europe: in Japan and in the United States of Theodore Roosevelt.[59] After World War I, Europe too had its exceptions. One of these was Hitler. The personal element in his career could hardly be underestimated, even though he acted out a collective desire for power and domination.[60]

Renouvin not only recounted what the statesmen did; he also

57. *Ibid.*, pp. 403–4.
58. *Le XIXe siècle. II. De 1871 à 1914*, p. 378.
59. *Ibid.*, p. 379.
60. See *Les crises du XXe siècle. II. De 1929 à 1945*, p. 193.

sought to indicate what they were like. In so doing, he showed remarkable perceptiveness. The portrayal of Napoleon III stood out as perhaps the finest in the entire work. Penetrating too were the vignettes of Alexander I, Metternich, Palmerston, Frederick William IV, Cavour, Bismarck and Hitler. These sketches related character traits to aims and policies. They added so much in the way of depth and pattern that it was regrettable Renouvin did not compose more of them. He missed many excellent opportunities, especially for the period 1914–45. As a consequence, in this respect the last two volumes did not equal the first and second.

Despite his flair for depicting the occasionally decisive, frequently important, but never negligible role of the personal factor, Renouvin showed no inclination to pursue this aspect of diplomatic history when he completed his four-volume work in 1958. Instead, he pushed on in the opposite direction. Anxious to do something about the lacunae he considered most serious, he decided to amass as much new data as possible on the forces that shaped the course of international relations from 1848, the year of revolutions, to the end of World War II. According to Renouvin's own description of the project, it would embrace among other things "demographic, economic, and financial influences and the role of religious questions and national sentiment."[61] The value of this project is self-evident. So is Renouvin's unique fitness to undertake it. The results of his research will be eagerly awaited.

Needless to say, what Renouvin may yet accomplish will have to be taken into account before any final estimate can be made of his place in the historiography of the twentieth century. However, his writings are already considerable, and they bear the stamp of a true blend of science and art. To be sure, he is not primarily an innovator; he has done relatively little to push back the frontiers of knowledge. But he stands out as one of the most judicious and lucid historians of our generation. He is also eminently rewarding. Within his chosen domain, he has assembled virtually everything we know, tested, refined, and fused it, and made it more luminous.

61. Renouvin to author, May 2, 1960.

# XIII

## *Francesco Ruffini (1863–1934)*

S. WILLIAM HALPERIN

FRANCESCO RUFFINI was many things. He was a distinguished historian and canonist whose writings are held in the highest esteem by scholars the world over. He was an inspiring teacher and a fecund stimulator of scholarly interest in unexplored areas of investigation. He was an ardent patriot whose love of country balked at no sacrifice. He was a genuine liberal to whom all tyranny was anathema. He was a loyal friend. Above all, he was true to his innermost convictions, ready to do battle for them even in the most disheartening circumstances. Ruffini, the man, has received no finer tribute than these words of Benedetto Croce:

> That which really unites human beings is something deeper than . . . agreement in the matter of ideas: it is agreement in their attitude toward life. And here Francesco Ruffini was a teacher, and a prop and comfort to his friends. The latter admired in him the simplicity of resoluteness toward that which is duty: a resoluteness which almost excluded the moment of perplexity, which almost left no room for the very virtue of courage, because he did not even suspect that he could do otherwise than that which, in following the path of honor, he was doing.[1]

Ruffini was born in Lessolo, in the Piedmontese section of Italy, on April 10, 1863. His family had neither noble lineage nor wealth, but some of its members had distinguished themselves as scholars, as civil servants, and in the liberal professions. The pre-

---

1. Benedetto Croce, "Francesco Ruffini," *Critica*, XXXII (1934), 230.

mature death of the head of the household forced heavy responsibilities upon Ruffini's mother. She acquired a small farm and sought to make it pay for the education of her children. To see their sons secure a university training was a widespread ambition among even the most modest families of provincial Piedmont. It was at the *collegio civico* of Ivrea that Ruffini completed his classical studies. Armed with a scholarship, he entered the University of Turin in 1882. His proclivities were decidedly literary; but yielding, perhaps, to practical considerations and pressure from home, he matriculated in the school of jurisprudence.[2]

His favorite professors, those who most deeply and permanently influenced his intellectual development, were Giuseppe Carle and Cesare Nani. From Carle he gained an insight into the processes governing the evolution of those interlocking and interacting ideas which, in turn, fashioned the course of legal history. From Carle he also learned to appreciate the national traditions behind movements of thought and to perceive the ideological and spiritual roots as well as the imposing but superficial externals of political and juridical institutions. Nani's analytical mind, his rigorous adherence to the niceties of historical method, and his careful and exact researches left a lasting impression on Ruffini.[3]

Shortly after the completion of his work at the university he decided in favor of an academic career. He chose the field of ecclesiastical law. Because it was just beginning to be cultivated methodically and in a thoroughly secular spirit in Italy, it offered many unexplored areas. But since his own country lacked, as yet, a scientific tradition in this branch of study, Ruffini went to Germany in 1889 to secure more advanced training. He attended the courses of Professor Emil Friedberg at the University of Leipzig and came away an enthusiastic disciple of that celebrated scholar. Upon his return to Italy he taught ecclesiastical law at the universities at Pavia and Genoa and then, in 1899, was invited to occupy the chair of legal history at the University of Turin. Finally, in 1908, he was transferred, at his own request, to

2. Gioele Solari, "La vita e l'opera scientifica di Francesco Ruffini (1863–1934)," *Rivista internazionale di filosofia del diritto*, XV (1935), 191.
3. *Ibid.*, p. 192.

the chair of ecclesiastical law in the same institution.[4] This post he retained for twenty-three years.

In 1900 Ruffini married Ava Avondo, who belonged to a wealthy and aristocratic Piedmontese family. But this union ended tragically. The birth of a son, Edoardo, was for the mother the beginning of a long illness that proved incurable. Her death in 1910 was a stunning blow to Ruffini. However, his child, the self-effacing devotion of his sister-in-law, Giulia Avondo, and the historical researches which were claiming more and more of his attention afforded him some solace.[5]

Academic honors were showered upon him. For a number of years he was president of the Accademia delle Scienze di Torino and vice-president of the Deputazione di Storia Patria per le antiche Provincie. He presided over the faculty of the University of Turin from 1904 to 1907 and was rector of the institution from 1910 to 1913. But these time-consuming professional activities and the innumerable hours lavished upon his studies failed to keep him out of the political arena. Here, from the outset, he wielded all the influence he could muster to promote the liberal cause. He had the greatest respect for those who sincerely professed a given faith; but he was, and remained to the end of his life, an uncompromising foe of every species of intolerance and fanaticism.[6] He fervently believed that the preservation of religious and political liberty was vital to the highest interests of the nation and humanity. His creed was epitomized in the word "freedom."

His first major opportunity in the field of practical politics came in 1906, when he served as departmental chief under Boselli, who was then minister of public instruction. It was not, however, until the outbreak of the European war in the summer of 1914 that he came into his own as a public figure. He strongly supported the interventionist policy of Salandra, on whose recommendation he was named a senator of the kingdom on December 30, 1914.

4. *Ibid.*, pp. 192–93, 194, 195; Mario Falco, "Francesco Ruffini," *Rivista di diritto civile*, XXVI (1934), 390.
5. Solari, *loc. cit.*, pp. 195–96.
6. Mario Falco, "Francesco Ruffini," *Rivista di diritto privato*, IV (1934), 206.

Throughout the years of Italy's participation in the struggle against the Central Powers he gave unstintingly of himself to the national cause. He became, almost overnight, an impassioned propagandist whose every nerve was strained to awaken in others the kind of patriotism which was electrifying him. The scientific habit and outlook were momentarily abandoned. He now presented himself to his compatriots as an apostle preaching the gospel of self-sacrifice and faith in Italy's high destiny. To those who persisted in their opposition to the war he recalled the farsighted boldness of Cavour[7] and the high-minded teachings of Mazzini.[8] Following the disaster of Caporetto, he endeavored to remind his gloom-ridden countrymen of the deplorable situation in which Piedmont-Sardinia found herself after the battle of Novara and of the remarkable recovery she achieved thereafter under Victor Emmanuel II.[9] He extolled the martyrdom of Cesare Battisti, who sensed that Italy needed heroism and the spirit of self-sacrifice above all else and who foresaw that only struggle—not inglorious passivity or pusillanimous bargaining—could bring a fulfilment of her legitimate aspirations.[10]

Speeches and tracts were not all he contributed to the war effort. In 1915 he organized a committee in Turin to aid the national military effort. The work of this committee called for the expenditure of large sums, and when financial difficulties were encountered he sacrificed all his possessions to take care of the deficit.[11] When Boselli formed his national union cabinet in June, 1916, Ruffini was appointed minister of public instruction. His ministerial career proved short lived, however, ending with the fall of the Boselli government in October, 1917. His last important activity during this period was his participation in the work of the interparliamentary committee which sought to promote complete concord between the Allies.[12]

The immediate aftermath of the war found him preoccupied

7. *L'insegnamento di Cavour* (Milan, 1916).
8. *L'insegnamento di Mazzini* (Milan, 1917).
9. *Vittorio Emanuele II* (Milan, 1918).
10. *Cesare Battisti* (Milan, 1918).
11. Solari, *loc. cit.*, p. 197; Mario Falco, "Francesco Ruffini," *Rivista di diritto civile*, XXVI (1934), 391.
12. Solari, *loc. cit.*, p. 198.

with a number of things, among them the Wilsonian program and the projected League of Nations, of which he was a fervent champion,[13] the problems and prospects of political Zionism,[14] and the repercussions of the recently concluded hostilities on existing political and constitutional arrangements.[15] He continued active, during these first post-war years, in the ranks of the liberal party. Notable in this connection is the speech he delivered in the senate on December 8, 1919. With characteristic courage and vision, he summoned the liberal elements of the country to do what they could to prevent the nation from falling under the sway of the extremist parties. Imbued, as always, with optimism, tolerance, and humanitarianism, he believed the liberal state capable of absorbing and fructifying all the interests and energies of those who dwelt within its borders.[16]

After the advent of Fascism, Ruffini continued to be a staunch champion of personal and political liberty, and his refusal to take the oath demanded of all professors by Mussolini cost him his post at the University of Turin in 1931. His son, who had been teaching Italian legal history at the University of Perugia, was dismissed for the same reason. The closing years of his life witnessed a steady withdrawal from politics and public office, even from the Committee on Intellectual Cooperation, established by the League of Nations, to which he had given much of his time and energy from 1923 to 1927.[17] He surrendered himself entirely to his studies, and it was while he was busily at work on them that he was fatally stricken. He died on March 29, 1934, and was buried in his native province without official honors, without speeches, with the very same simplicity which throughout the long and fruitful life had been the hallmark of the man.

But simplicity was not his only engaging trait, as the author of this essay discovered when he met Ruffini in the summer of

13. *Il presidente Wilson* (Milan, 1919).
14. *Sionismo e società delle nazioni* (Bologna, 1919).
15. *Guerra e riforme costituzionali* (Turin, 1920).
16. Solari, *loc. cit.*, pp. 198, 199.
17. As a member of this committee, Ruffini had prepared a report on the protection of scientific works which was destined to serve as the point of departure for all subsequent legislation on this matter.

1932. He was a charming and gracious host, delightfully informal and affable. What stood out most of all, however, was his extreme gentleness. The ensuing conversation touched upon many things of common interest, and the present writer came away with the feeling that he had met not only a great scholar but a lovable man. What he saw and felt on this occasion has been affirmed and reaffirmed by all those who knew Ruffini well—friends, colleagues, and students.

The death of Francesco Ruffini robbed his country of one of its outstanding jurists.[18] It was he, together with Professor Francesco Scaduto, of the University of Rome,[19] who restored the study of canon law in Italy. The first scientific elaboration of Italian ecclesiastical law was due in large part to him. His translation of Friedberg's classic treatise[20] helped to diffuse among Italians a systematic knowledge of the constitutional and administrative law of the church.[21] His own writings in this field are legion. They deal with a wide assortment of topics and vary markedly in length and scope, but the scholarship which produced them is uniformly sound. The best known of all, perhaps, is his *Corso di diritto ecclesiastico*,[22] which quickly established itself as a standard treatment. His early essays deal, for the most part, with the role of canon law in the development of Italian private law. He subsequently devoted considerable attention to the study of ecclesiastical institutions viewed in their historical evolution and in the light of prevailing juridical norms. Not to be overlooked are his contributions to the expanding literature in the field of public law. He trained a number of Italy's leading canonists of today, including Mario Falco and Arturo Carlo Jemolo. Such was Ruffini the jurist.

18. Cf. the estimate of Ruffini as a jurist in Falco, "Francesco Ruffini," *Rivista di diritto privato*, IV (1934), 202–3; Arturo Carlo Jemolo, "Francesco Ruffini," *Archivio giuridico*, CXII (1934), 111–12.

19. Scaduto was the author of *Diritto ecclesiastico vigente in Italia* (2 vols.; Turin, 1892–94).

20. *Trattato del diritto ecclesiastico cattolico ed evangelico del Friedberg* (Turin, 1893).

21. On the importance of this translation see Solari, *loc. cit.*, p. 194.

22. Turin, 1924.

Ruffini's career as a historian, which extends over a period of more than forty years, began with the publication of his justly esteemed and famous *Lineamenti storici della relazioni fra lo stato e la chiesa in Italia*.[23] This succinct and pithy outline was a direct outgrowth of his interest in the development of Italian ecclesiastical law. By far the greater part of it deals with the situation in the various sections of the peninsula prior to unification. Despite its brevity, it is an indispensable manual. It filled a serious lacuna, for of general histories of the relations between church and state in Italy there was then a dearth. It performed still another important service: it pointed the way to further studies of a comparable type.

Ruffini's interest in problems of ecclesiastical policy and the relations of church and state soon crystallized into a sustained preoccupation with the vicissitudes of toleration in Italy and the rest of Europe. Out of this preoccupation was born the idea of surveying briefly the history of religious liberty. The task proved a much bigger one than he had anticipated, and it was not until 1900 that it was completed. The study was published shortly thereafter under the title: *La libertà religiosa: storia dell'idea*.[24] After a few introductory pages on the ancient and medieval periods it traces the slow and painful progress of the idea of religious liberty, considered both in its theoretical formulations and as the subject of legislative enactment, from the sixteenth century to the close of the eighteenth. The writings of philosophers, theologians, political theorists, jurists, essayists, dramatists, and statesmen who at one time or another concerned themselves with the problem of religious toleration are analyzed and appraised, as are also the texts of governmental pronouncements which constitute landmarks in the history of this great theme.

The historian of religious liberty was led, before long, to address himself to a closely related subject: the genesis of Cavour's very liberal views on ecclesiastical policy. The appearance, in 1908, of the celebrated "Le origini elvetiche della formula del

23. Turin, 1891.
24. Turin, 1901.

272

conte di Cavour: 'Libera chiesa in libero stato,' "[25] inaugurated a long series of studies on the great Piedmontese. The predominant and, indeed, decisive role played by Swiss liberal Protestantism in the development of Cavour's politico-religious thought is ably and convincingly set forth. During his youth the future statesman spent much time in Geneva, and it was there that he first came under the influence of ideas which were at complete variance with those which prevailed in his own country after 1815. What Cavour saw and learned in Switzerland enabled him to view with keener understanding the liberal Catholicism which raised its head in France during the period of the July Monarchy. His attitude toward this movement forms the subject of a suggestive essay which Ruffini published in the *Stampa* of Turin on August 9, 1910.[26]

In Switzerland, while he was investigating the origins of the famous Cavourian formula, Ruffini stumbled upon something which was to absorb his energies for years to come: a sheaf of unpublished and hitherto unknown documents that turned out to be letters written by Cavour between 1828 and 1845—from his eighteenth to his thirty-fifth year—to his Geneva cousin, Adèle de Sellon, and her husband, Baron Paul Emile Maurice. Before chancing upon this treasure of information, without which his two-volume *La giovinezza del conte di Cavour: saggi storici secondo lettere e documenti inediti*[27] could not have been written, Ruffini had not had the faintest intention of working on a life of Cavour. But previous inclinations and plans now counted for nought. "This," he himself tells us, "was the beginning of everything. The saying, 'Opportunity makes the thief,' may very well be applied to me with this variation: opportunity, or, better, the document, made the biographer."[28] The letters which Ruffini was thus privileged to see are invaluable for the light they shed

25. It is one of the essays in *Festschrift Emil Friedberg zum siebzigsten Geburtstage* (Leipzig, 1908).
26. This article is entitled "Il cattolicismo liberale (1844)."
27. Turin, 1912.
28. I, 18. This and subsequent references are to the second (1937–38) edition of this work.

on the personality and intimate life of the young Cavour. In them are mirrored his thoughts, his feelings, certain of his idiosyncrasies. Ruffini supplemented their contents with material drawn from letters in the Cavourian archives at Santena, from those parts of the count's diary which had escaped the attention of Berti, and from other unpublished documents in sundry private and public archives, including those of Vienna, to produce his great work on the youth of Cavour. The formative years of the statesman are here painstakingly and sympathetically reconstructed. The portraiture is full and rich, revealing its subject's warmth, his precocious intellectual development, the range and depth of his interests. The world in which he matured comes to life: his family; the people who in one way or another influenced his mental and emotional growth; the theories and doctrines which attracted his attention; the places he visited; the events, in Italy and abroad, which he pondered. The story possesses a remarkable unity. When Cavour was only sixteen Charles Albert wrote a letter containing the following passage about the lad, who was then serving as one of his pages: "Le petit Camille Cavour a fait le Jacobin et je l'ai mis à ma porte; pleurs, lamentations de toute la famille." The entire history of Cavour's youth, Ruffini remarks, is epitomized in the prince's words: "incoercible manifestations of political and religious liberalism; indignation and opposition on the part of his large family, especially those of its members who were blindly devoted to the old regime; suspicion and persecution on the part of the government."[29]

The intimate picture of the youthful Cavour which had emerged from the pages of *La giovinezza del conte di Cavour* was further enriched by Ruffini's *Camillo di Cavour e Mélanie Waldor (secondo lettere e documenti inediti).*[30] Written with admirable tact, and based in part on unpublished letters from the Cavourian archives in Santena, it recounts the brief liaison between the twenty-eight-year-old count and a French woman fourteen years his senior. She had been, for a time, the mistress of Alexander Dumas, *père,* and was herself a writer of some reputation. This

29. *Ibid.,* I, 48.
30. Turin, 1914.

erotic interlude ran a course that was not at all extraordinary, but its few vicissitudes, however commonplace, throw invaluable light upon certain aspects of the young man's psychology. The correspondence between the lovers reveals, among other things, the "invincibly realistic, positive, *raisonneur*" foundation of his character. He was, to be sure, an "idealist"; but he had, as Ruffini insists, a profound and sustained abhorrence for "sentimentality" of any kind.[31]

The war years halted Ruffini's researches, but the very morrow of the armistice found him directing his attention to a totally different chapter of the Cavourian saga: the great statesman's relations with two of his bitterest political adversaries—Angelo Brofferio, the Piedmontese writer and politician, and Francesco Domenico Guerrazzi, the famous Tuscan patriot. In 1920 he published three articles on various phases of this theme in successive issues of the *Nuova antologia*.[32] They are substantial and exceedingly valuable essays. Ruffini analyzes the reasons for the aversion which Brofferio and Guerrazzi felt for Cavour, an aversion that was personal as well as political. Especially telling are the unflattering sections devoted to Brofferio, whose dogged and deviously manifested hostility evoked reprisals in kind from his doughty opponent. For ten long years Brofferio and Cavour fought one another in parliament and in the press. The struggle went on without interruption and with increasing bitterness until the count's death. There can be little doubt that Brofferio was Cavour's "vero castigo di Dio." Guerrazzi was likewise a persistent and vigorous foe; but he, unlike Brofferio, enjoyed the admiration and respect of his distinguished adversary. The crescendo of the Cavour-Guerrazzi feud was reached in May, 1860, when the two men clashed in parliament over the question of ratifying the treaty with France.

Ever since 1915, when Italy entered the war, there had been an

31. P. 152.
32. "L'antipatia del Brofferio e del Guerrazzi per il conte di Cavour," CCXCII (1920), 193–208; "Il Brofferio ed il Guerrazzi all'opposizione contro il conte di Cavour," *ibid.*, pp. 302–20; "La rottura del Brofferio e del Guerrazzi con il conte di Cavour," CCXCIII (1920), 19–33.

upsurge of interest in the perennial Roman question. The already formidable literature on the subject had undergone tremendous accretions, and to many it seemed that a new phase of the thorny issue was in the offing. Ruffini, whose interest in the problem was of long standing, had followed closely its most recent vicissitudes. In an effort to elucidate some of these he wrote a series of articles which appeared in 1921 and once again in successive issues of the *Nuova antologia*.[33] These essays, which attracted considerable attention and lent further impetus to the already spirited nation-wide discussion of certain issues connected with the Italo-papal feud, are of capital importance for the student of the Roman question. They contain much valuable information, abound in trenchant analyses, and skilfully take the reader through the intricacies of their complex theme.

Shortly after the completion of these articles, Ruffini turned his attention to Alessandro Manzoni. Many things about the great Lombard writer had for long interested him—above all, the religious values from which much of his inspiration was derived. It was this intriguing aspect of the man that Ruffini now resolved to explore. The projected study was conceived on a vast scale. It was to deal with every phase of Manzoni's religious life. The ensuing investigations quickly converged on the writer's addiction to Jansenist ideas. His relations with Jansenism, to be sure, had attracted the attention of scholars long before Ruffini turned to them, but so far no exhaustive elucidation of the subject had appeared. Pushing far beyond the limits reached even by his most enterprising predecessors, Ruffini came to the conclusion that Manzoni had found in Jansenism the deep spiritual satisfaction that he craved and which he had vainly sought elsewhere. The first important fruit of his researches was an article calling attention to the period of Manzoni's life which centered around the year 1817.[34] This period, according to Ruffini, witnessed a serious

33. "Il potere temporale negli scopi di guerra degli ex-imperi centrali," CCXCV (1921), 289–301; "Progetti e propositi germanici per risolvere la questione romana," CCXCVI (1921), 24–40; "Sovranità temporale, congressi della pace e società delle nazioni," *ibid.*, pp. 118–130; "La questione romana e l'ora presente," *ibid.*, pp. 193–206.

34. "Il 'masso' del natale manzoniano e il giansenismo," *Rivista d'Italia*, XXVIII (1925), 143–62.

spiritual crisis, in the course of which Manzoni turned resolutely to Grégoire, the head of French Jansenism, and manifested a sharp aversion for Lamennais, who at the time was still one of ultramontanism's most applauded spokesmen. To a further elaboration and documentation of Manzonian Jansenism, Ruffini devoted several years of patient and minute research. In the course of his investigations he came upon unpublished sources which proved of crucial importance. Heralded by the publication of two suggestive articles,[35] the two-volume *La vita religiosa di Alessandro Manzoni*[36] finally made its appearance. It is a highly absorbing and trenchant study. Ruffini manages to penetrate into the innermost intimacy of Manzoni's religious convictions. He exhibits, in all their fulness, his powers of analysis, his resourcefulness in piecing together scattered bits of evidence, his insight and subtlety in assaying the nuances of feeling and belief. The usefulness of the work is appreciably enhanced by several learned digressions, such as those, for example, on the history of the Jansenist movement, Pascal, and the religious life of France during the Restoration.

A few years before the completion of *La vita religiosa di Alessandro Manzoni* Ruffini began work on a comparable study of Cavour's religious ideas and experiences. Here he was on familiar terrain and finally at grips with a subject which he had long before tentatively outlined but thereafter repeatedly put aside as other preoccupations bobbed up to monopolize his attention. Unfortunately, the task, so tardily undertaken, was never finished. Death intervened in the midst of his labors,[37] and only a few precious fragments of what was to have been a large and comprehensive work have been published.

There were impressive elements of similarity in the religious experiences of Manzoni and Cavour which could hardly have failed to make this newest project all the more meaningful and inviting. Both men went through an acute religious crisis in their youth, and both of them very early in their lives were exposed to

35. "Manzoni e Lamennais," *Cultura*, IX (1930), 255–67; "Il 'miracolo' nella fede, nella vita e nell'arte di Alessandro Manzoni," *ibid.*, pp. 665–78.
36. Bari, 1931.
37. Jemolo, *loc. cit.*, p. 110.

Jansenist ideas. In Manzoni these ideas took root, but not in Cavour. The Jansenist element in the latter's background became the first preoccupation of Ruffini. *I giansenisti piemontesi e la conversione della madre di Cavour*[38] constitutes a fundamental and, in many respects, original contribution. Piedmontese Jansenism was merely a reflection of its French parent, and as Ruffini points out, was kept alive by a small coterie which included Tardy, an ecclesiastic who was an intimate friend of the Cavour family. Tardy turned out to be for Cavour's mother what Degola, the well-known Jansenist leader, was for the wife of Manzoni. As a matter of fact, Tardy followed Degola's catechistic methods in bringing the good lady, who was a rigid Calvinist, into the Catholic fold. The conversion took place at Santena on October 21, 1811. Until his death in 1821 Tardy remained the spiritual adviser of the Cavour household, and it was he who served as the first confessor of young Camillo.

Of much greater moment in the evolution of Cavour's religious attitudes was the acute *crise de conscience* which began when he was little more than eighteen and which carried him from the orthodox and traditional Catholicism of his paternal ancestors to a militant rationalism and anticlericalism. First set forth briefly in an article dealing with Cavour's intellectual development,[39] it forms the subject of the trenchant second chapter of the posthumously published *Ultimi studi sul conte di Cavour.*[40] The significance, in this connection, of his sojourn in Geneva, where, for the first time, he breathed the pure air of reason, and of his careful perusal of the writings of Constant, Guizot, and Jouffroy is brilliantly elucidated and convincingly documented. A fitting introduction to this essay is provided in the first chapter, which is entitled "La devozione infantile del conte di Cavour." Based in part on unpublished documents from the archives at Santena, it underlines some of little Camillo's salient traits. That the youngster, when barely out of the infantile stage, showed an interest in

38. Turin, 1929. This study is one of a series published under the auspices of the Academy of Sciences of Turin.
39. "La cultura filosofica del conte di Cavour," *Cultura,* X (1931), 214–29.
40. Bari, 1936.

religious ceremonies is noteworthy; but even more so is the fact that a bit later, when he was in his early teens, he evidenced a certain amount of independence and an "incipient rationalism."[41] The remaining chapters of the volume are reprints of earlier articles.

The youthful Cavour for a time came under the sway of Socinian ideas. This fact, coupled with the long-standing desire to return to a subject originally encountered when he was working on his history of religious liberty, led Ruffini during the closing years of his life to direct some of his inexhaustible energies into still another channel of investigation. These researches embraced the history of Socinianism from its origins to the time when Cavour came into contact with it in Geneva. Death interrupted this project, too, but the results achieved were nevertheless imposing. They were incorporated in a series of erudite essays on the Italian Reformers and the checkered fortunes of the Socinian movement. Among the more important contributions are *Francesco Stancaro: contributo alla storia della riforma in Italia*[42] and *Metodisti e sociniani nella Ginevra della restaurazione*.[43] Also deserving of honorable mention are some of the articles published between 1928 and 1933.[44] One of the noteworthy by-products of Ruffini's preoccupation with the religious problems and experiences of certain sixteenth-century Italians is the essay on the ecclesiastical policy of Emmanuel Philibert.[45]

41. P. 11.
42. Rome, 1935. This monograph was originally published in Buonaiuti's *Ricerche religiose* in 1932–33.
43. Florence, 1936. The publication of this essay two years after Ruffini's death was supervised by Adolfo Omodeo, the noted Italian historian who also edited the *Ultimit studi sul conte di Cavour*.
44. E.g., "Il giureconsulto chierese Matteo Gribaldi Mofa e Calvino," *Rivista di storia del diritto italiano*, I (1928), 207–69, 417–32; "Matteo Gribaldi Mofa, Antonio Govea e lo studio generale di Mondovì," *Studi pubblicati dall regia università di Torino nel IV centenario della nascita di Emanuele Filiberto* (Turin, 1928), pp. 279–96; "La 'cabale italique' nella Ginevra del seicento," *Cultura*, X (1931), 786–808; "La Polonia del Cinquecento e le origini del socinianismo," *ibid.*, XI (1932), 248–59; "Voltaire e Rousseau contro i sociniani di Ginevra," *ibid.*, XII (1933), 83–116; "Carlo Alberto e il socinianismo ginevrino," *Atti dell'accademia delle scienze di Torino*, LXVIII (1933), 407–66.
45. "La politica ecclesiastica di Emanuele Filiberto," *Emanuele Filiberto*, ed. Costanzo Rinaudo (Turin, 1928), pp. 395–426.

More than those of any other historian, Ruffini's researches have given impetus in his own country to studies on the Italian Reformers and on the influence of specific Socinian and Jansenist doctrines.[46] From the very beginning of his academic career he deplored the dearth of scholarly interest in religious history. As his own work in this field progressed, he helped increasingly to focus attention on the contributions of Italians to the ferment of ideas which accompanied the great religious upheaval of the sixteenth century. As we have seen, Manzoni's relations with Jansenism had attracted the attention of scholars long before the appearance of Ruffini's study on the subject. But its publication caused this interest to bound forward powerfully. The conclusions advanced in *La vita religiosa di Alessandro Manzoni* evoked in academic circles a lively and sustained controversy which provided still another fillip to the progress of Manzonian studies.

The majority of Ruffini's historical writings bear the stamp of painstaking and exhaustive research. The documentation is uniformly careful and copious. There is a pronounced reliance on primary sources, both printed and manuscript. The latter variety made possible, as we have seen, the studies on Cavour and Manzoni, but a host of other writings are based entirely on published material. Not inconsiderable is Ruffini's indebtedness to the works of other scholars, and he is candid in acknowledging it. He tells us, in the preface to *La libertà religiosa,* that to do justice to a subject of this kind, a large modern library is essential. But Turin, where the study was completed, did not possess one. And so, because he was unable to procure some of the primary material he needed, he had to rely on references to it in the writings of other historians.[47] In the introduction to *La giovinezza del conte di Cavour* he pays his respects to the documentary publications of such predecessors as Chiala and Berti.[48] The opening pages of *La vita religiosa di Alessandro Manzoni* contain an appreciative allusion to the contributions of a small but indefatigable group of Manzonian scholars who for some time had been

46. Croce, *loc. cit.,* p. 229.
47. Pp. viii–ix.
48. I, 37–39.

investigating the emotional and religious experiences of the great Lombard.[49]

Ruffini maintains throughout a high standard of factual accuracy, thanks to his rigorously orthodox methods of establishing or verifying a given point. He was adept at handling critically historical evidence. His works bear witness to his skill in analyzing, collating, and appraising documentary material. They show, too, his deftness in establishing the settings in which individually important documents appear in their truest and fullest light. This penchant for panoramic backgrounds is one of the salient traits of the man as a historian. He knew how to extract the maximum from the data at his command. When the evidence was fragmentary he did not seek to bridge the hiatus by making rash deductions. When it was conflicting his acumen and analytical powers were generally equal to the situation. He was a resourceful investigator. He worked with tremendous enthusiasm, and when he was thrilled by a discovery he hid the fact from no one. He was patient and assiduously persistent even in the face of recurring and sometimes painful distractions. His early Cavourian researches were carried on at a time when his wife's illness was a source of constant preoccupation. The last and very productive decade of his life was spent among men who had turned their backs on his lifelong ideals. The studies on Manzoni, the religion of Cavour, and Socinianism had to compete for his attention with a political situation which finally brought dismissal from his professorial post.

Although Ruffini had little difficulty in mastering and organizing effectively the material he worked with, he was wont to minimize his own role in accounting for the finished product. Thus he relates that he intended originally to make the history of religious liberty the subject of a lecture. When the manuscript began to grow, he decided to make a sizable pamphlet out of it. But the pamphlet soon got out of hand and gave every indication of swelling into a robust tome. In the end, it appeared as a volume of 542 pages. And so, Ruffini concludes retrospectively, the

49. I, xii.

book emerged almost against his will; the process was like the downward course of a snowball that ended as an avalanche.[50] He fails to add, however, that he did an excellent job of controlling and directing this avalanche, thanks to a skilful combination of the chronological and topical approaches.

No less candid is his version of how he wrote *La giovinezza del conte di Cavour.* "The material dominated me, not I the material," he avers. "I proceeded like someone who discovers a vein of precious metal and who follows it in all its twists and turns, without giving thought to where it would end."[51] This statement must not be taken too seriously, for it springs from the author's excessive modesty. Actually, although important documents are reproduced in their entirety and the main thread of the story is thus continually encountered in the words of the protagonists themselves, the contents of these documents are carefully fitted into an elaborate pattern, the informing principle of which is the steady intellectual and emotional growth of Cavour. In each of the *saggi storici* announced in the subtitle, the data bearing on one particular period of Cavour's early life is skilfully integrated about a person, idea, or event that influenced the young man, with the result that each of these periods is invested with a distinctive character. An equally effective manipulation of material is evident in the essays that make up *Camillo di Cavour e Mélanie Waldor,* although here the principal problem confronting the author was that of making the most of rather exiguous data. The way in which this problem is handled affords the reader a typical illustration of Ruffini's technical competence.

His skill in organizing a vast amount of material is perhaps nowhere better demonstrated than in *La vita religiosa di Alessandro Manzoni,* although here, too, he is quite self-effacing in explaining how the work was written. The whole thing, he declares, sprang "automatically" from a theological dispute between the great writer and Alexis Billiet, a learned ecclesiastic who later became the Archbishop of Chambéry and a cardinal. The subject thus presented itself to him *sub specie controversiae;* and so this

50. *La libertà religiosa,* p. viii.
51. I, 21.

initial dispute had to remain the foundation of the study. The entire treatment does revolve, as a matter of fact, about it. Occupying the pivotal position is an unpublished letter in which allusion is made to the Manzoni-Billiet discussion: a letter of September 23, 1819, from Manzoni's mother to his spiritual adviser, Monsignor Luigi Tosi. The crucial passage of this document provides a principal clue to Manzoni's views on the basic question of grace. With this passage serving as the point of departure, the analysis is developed with the aid of material drawn from other letters, the testimony of unimpeachable witnesses, and Manzoni's writings. That a high degree of unity and thematic effectiveness is thus achieved is due to the author's resourcefulness in making the most of this particular technique.

Ruffini's works are more than readable; they possess a genuine literary quality—thanks to a style that combines fluency, verve, and elegance. It is a sensitive style, too, and yet not lacking in vigor. The author's flair for the well-turned phrase is evident, as is also his penchant for interpretation. His writings abound in considered observations of a general nature about specific periods, developments, and persons. That most of these generalizations will stand the test of time and new evidence is more than likely. The character and amount of the data and the acumen in analysis upon which they rest vouch, as much as anything can, for their soundness. The polemical note is not lacking, for much of Ruffini's work is definitely à thèse. In *La libertà religiosa* he was anxious to prove that modern toleration derived its "first and most fecund source" from the Socinian movement. A good part of his work on Cavour pulsates with the desire to explode certain traditional but grievously mistaken conceptions of the man which sprang from one-sided preoccupation with the period of his greatness and facile acceptance of judgments pronounced by certain of his contemporaries. *La vita religiosa di Alessandro Manzoni* was written to prove that the theological and moral doctrines of the French Jansenists and of their followers in Italy constitute the basis of the great Lombard's religious outlook and that he retained faith in those doctrines until the end of his life. Everything that could be adduced in favor of the central thesis is brought into the picture. And that this was by no means an easy task will be appreciated by those who know how energetically and stubbornly Manzoni at all times sought to keep secret his most intimate religious beliefs.

Ruffini tried always to combine comprehensiveness of treatment with depth of investigation, and he generally succeeded. But he found it necessary to sacrifice the former for the sake of the latter in one conspicuous instance: his history of religious liberty. Confronted with the task of covering a tremendous period and many countries, he saw fit to exclude several significant topics. These lacunae did not fail to evoke a certain amount of adverse criticism.

Religious values and problems in their manifold manifestations always intrigued Ruffini. The canonist constantly impinged upon the historian, and in this fact lies one of the keys to an understanding of what he was attempting. Indeed, we are told, on excellent authority, that *la religiosità*, "studied in its external and internal life, in its juridical and historical forms, analyzed in great individual consciences, constituted the keenest spiritual interest of his scientific activity."[52] This religiosity, according to Ruffini, was essentially liberty and conscience. As such, compulsion of any kind was repugnant to it. Moreover, it was the duty of the state, in dealing with ecclesiastical matters, to safeguard the manifestations of this religiosity within the limits imposed by its sovereign interests. This conception of religiosity and of ecclesiastical policy, affirmed by Ruffini from the first days of his career, affected profoundly the direction of his historical investigations.[53]

Ruffini reacted rather sharply against the excessive provincialism of Italian historiography. But his own cosmopolitanism of outlook never became a fetish and was not allowed to warp his perspective. Nevertheless, both *La giovinezza del conte di Cavour* and *La vita religiosa di Alessandro Manzoni* have been criticized in some quarters because, so it is alleged, too much attention is paid in them to non-Italian influences and not enough to what was transpiring in the peninsula. These critics freely admit the charge

52. Solari, *loc. cit.*, p. 206.
53. *Ibid.*, p. 207.

of provincialism, but they contend that Ruffini goes to the opposite extreme of "Europeanism."[54] To which there is only one rejoinder: Ruffini's "Europeanism," far from vitiating the soundness of his judgment, helped him to do justice to Cavour and Manzoni, who were so much under the influence of extra-Italian ideas.

To his researches Ruffini brought an unfailing sympathy for the men and women whose experiences he recounts. More than that, he tended to become identified with the protagonists of his principal works, Cavour and Manzoni, and particularly with the kind of political and religious liberalism which they personify—this, despite his rejection of Cavourian separatism[55] and his failure to concur in Manzoni's religious opinions.[56] Indeed, as one who knew him intimately puts it, "there was in the impassioned and persistent historical investigations of Ruffini a personal and almost autobiographical note, which consisted in affirming, through the minds of the two supreme exponents of the ideals which animated our Risorgimento, his own political and religious conscience."[57] His liberalism tinges, in varying degree, the products of his labors. To this his history of religious liberty, his analysis of Cavour's ideas, and his discussion of Manzoni's heterodox proclivities bear ample witness.

Though the bent of his mind was decidedly philosophical, Ruffini made no attempt to reduce historical phenomena and processes to a few laws or universally applicable principles. He did not seek to unearth the eternal or underlying truths of history. His treatment of the subjects that monopolized his attention reflects no particular view as to the dynamics of all major historical trends. And it would be rash, indeed, to make his unwavering interest in religiosity the springboard for deductions along this line. He did have, however, very positive ideas about the functions and duties of history and the historian. He believed that

54. See in this connection the review of *La vita religiosa di Alessandro Manzoni* by W. Maturi in the *Nuova rivista storica*, XV (1931), 328–29.

55. For a discussion of Ruffini's views on separatism see S. William Halperin, *The separation of church and state in Italian thought from Cavour to Mussolini* (Chicago, 1937), pp. 67–68.

56. *La vita religiosa di Alessandro Manzoni*, I, xv.

57. Solari, *loc. cit.*, p. 221.

historical research should not be content merely to enrich our knowledge of the past. It should seek, he felt, not only to inform but to educate. Its supreme purpose should be to aid in developing the public mind.[58]

The direction of Ruffini's investigations led him to take a particular interest in the educative value of biography. The lives and careers of great men, he averred, are replete with inspirational value; and the more one knew about them, the more could one love and be inspired by them. Indeed, one had to know their frailties as well as their strengths. What he has to say, in this connection, about his work on Cavour, is enlightening. When dealing with historical figures like the great Piedmontese, the biographer, Ruffini contends, must record every detail, however minute or unflattering. Nothing which pertains to such men can be considered "too petty or insignificant or superfluous; because genius . . . has the faculty of transmuting into historical gold everything . . . it has touched."[59] On another occasion, he remarks:

> There are some who took offense when I sought to clarify those . . . profound and decisive factors in the psychology of the count which were his youthful amours and errors; and they reproached me for having crossed the threshold of that intimate sacrarium to whose inviolability he and . . . the women who loved him had a right. . . . I must say, once and for all, that I have an absolutely different conception of the rights of history. I believe that only someone who has lived and died in obscurity can claim eternal obscurity. But with respect to those who still dominate, from beyond the grave, our present thought and life by virtue of the omnipotence of their genius, the least we can demand is to know what they were like.[60]

It might be said, he continues, that

> to attempt to bring these great makers of our history as close as possible to our common human denominator is almost to lessen . . . the educative efficacy of their example. As if . . . one could really love that artificial semidivinity which a very recent patriotic mythology would like to attribute to great historical figures and not, on the contrary, their eternal and common humanity.

58. *Ibid.*, p. 207.
59. *La giovinezza del conte di Cavour*, I, 43.
60. *Camillo di Cavour e Mélanie Waldor*, pp. 168–69.

And, Ruffini concludes, there is no better way to illustrate this "eternal and common humanity" of great men than to show "whom, how, and with what success they loved, and by whom, how, and with what success they were loved."[61] All of which did not prevent one obtuse reviewer of Ruffini's *Camillo di Cavour e Mélanie Waldor* from remarking: "Our modest opinion is this: when dealing with Cavour, it is well to study that which honors him and conceal his weaknesses."[62]

Ruffini's contributions to historical scholarship are many and highly significant. His *Lineamenti storici delle relazioni fra lo stato e la chiesa in Italia* has remained a fundamental work. *La libertà religiosa* placed him in the front rank of Italy's historians and won him considerable recognition in other countries as well. Despite some serious omissions, it is, in the words of J. B. Bury, an "illuminating contribution to the history of liberty."[63] It provides perhaps the fullest elucidation we possess of the significance of Socinus in the annals of toleration. Ruffini has given us a new and revealing picture of the youthful Cavour. His contributions in this field are of paramount importance. They have made indubitably clear the enormous significance of Cavour's early life for an understanding of the celebrated contriver of Italian unity. Ruffini himself remarks:

> By studying well the youth of Count Cavour, one manages to comprehend thoroughly his later heroic work. Indeed, this is perhaps the only way to do so. Because to him is applicable, and to no one more so, the beautiful dictum of Alfred de Vigny: "Qu'est ce qu'une grande vie? Une pensée da la jeunesse réalisée par l'âge mûr."[64]

Ruffini does not overstate the case, for the mentality and attitudes of the man who so suddenly skyrocketed to fame after 1848 were the result not of overnight improvisation but of many years of preparation and ripening—years when he was, to use his own melancholy words, "un obscur citoyen piémontais." Only in the

61. *Ibid.*, pp. 170, 171.
62. *Risorgimento italiano*, VII (1914), 474.
63. See Bury's preface to the English edition (London, 1912) of *La libertà religiosa*.
64. *La giovinezza del conte di Cavour*, I, 12.

light of this fact does the effulgent figure of the statesman become truly intelligible. Ruffini has effectively disposed of the charge, first made by Brofferio[65] and repeated by others since, that Cavour had no knowledge of literature and philosophy; and he has also made it clear that those who saw and admired in the great Piedmontese only the gifted politician or the resourceful diplomatist were seeing and admiring only one aspect of the man.[66] Indeed, he has relegated to a well-deserved limbo the long prevalent but grossly mistaken conception of Cavour as a man whose interests were exclusively political, economic, and diplomatic in character.[67] In its place he has given us a Cavour who from his earliest years manifested a keen and sustained interest in matters of the spirit and the intellect. Ruffini has done more than anyone else to explore and clarify the part played by Jansenism in the spiritual life of Manzoni. He has enriched our understanding of the significance of Jansenist ideas in the intellectual and religious history of Italy during the early decades of the nineteenth century. He has made fundamental contributions to our knowledge of the Italian Reformers and of the vicissitudes of the Socinian movement. It is therefore not surprising that at the time of his death he was universally recognized as a foremost Cavourian scholar, an outstanding authority on Manzoni, and an unsurpassed student of religious history. In a brief but pithy summary of his contributions to historical scholarship a number of his fellow-workers in this field called him "a historian of the highest importance."[68] Posterity is not likely to alter this judgment.

65. *Storia del parlamento subalpino* (Milan, 1866), I, 146.
66. See in this connection Ruffini's remarks in *Camillo di Cavour e Mélanie Waldor*, pp. 21–22.
67. See the illuminating observations on this point in *Ultimi studi sul conte di Cavour*, pp. 22–23.
68. See the appreciation of Ruffini by the editors of the *Nuova rivista storica*, XVIII (1934), 270.

# XIV

## Gustav von Schmoller (1838–1917)

PAULINE RELYEA ANDERSON

GUSTAV VON SCHMOLLER did not write history merely for the satisfaction of recreating the past. As a historian, he has made notable contributions in a field which he wished to make the basis for a realistic approach to the study of economics and politics. The founder of the younger historical school of economics, Schmoller used history as his method, not his goal. Since Schmoller early repudiated the classical economic theory of Adam Smith and Ricardo and despised the "abstract" rationalism of the Austrian school, as well as the neo-Hegelianism of Rodbertus and Marx, he turned to a method which would place man and values as the focus of economic study. Schmoller did not give up the aim of the economist of the nineteenth century—that of arriving, like the natural scientist, at laws of economic activity; he merely wished history to enlarge the field of observation from which theoretical economic assumptions could be tested and, as he argued, more validly stated than with a minimum of observation and a maximum of logic. It is clear that history written under the auspices of economics had many of its problems and materials set. Possibly without consciously weighing the need for and value of intensive study of internal history, Schmoller turned from the first to social, economic, administrative, and institutional life, making here the innovations which his predecessors in historical research had made in the study of foreign policy and political institutions.

Another powerful factor was at work in dictating Schmoller's

289

emphasis upon history and in determining the nature and materials of his research—his burning interest in politics. This interest led him to demand of himself and of his profession cooperation in a program of social reform.[1] Only a thorough history of each question, he thought, could lay the foundation for practicable suggestions of reform, could teach the country to understand its social problems, and could indicate the goals which should be pursued. No one may doubt that the importance in the Bismarckian Reich of the tariff question occasioned Schmoller's essay on mercantilism (1883) and, later, his extensive treatment of tariff history in the publications of the Verein für Sozialpolitik and in his *Grundriss der Volkswirtschaftslehre*. Similarly, the problems connected with *Gewerbeordnung* led to his investigation of the guild system, as did inner colonization to the essay "Die preussische Einwanderung und ländliche Kolonisation des 17. und 18. Jahrhunderts."[2] This interest of Schmoller in that which should be (*Seinsollen*) unifies his work and hence any essay about him. It led him to reject rationalism and idealism for realism and historism; to accept as subjects for research those set by the problems of his own age; and, finally, to organize his own and the knowledge of his contemporaries for use as a guide to the state in its measures of reform.

Schmoller was not alone in his interest in history, for the rush of new life lent to the age a desire to understand the course of its own development. It was the same with economics: new interest in material things aroused new interest in economic processes. Nor was Schmoller alone in his turn from intellectualism, idealism, and romanticism toward naturalism and realism. Every state in the western world was struggling to decide between individ-

1. See Erich Rothacker, "Historismus," *Schmollers Jahrbuch für Gesetzgebung, Verwaltung und Volkswirtschaft im Deutschen Reiche*, LXII (1938), No. 4–6, 4 ff. See also Joseph Schumpeter, "Gustav von Schmoller und die Probleme von Heute," *Schmollers Jahrbuch*, L (1926), No. 3, 1–52; also Schmoller's own preface to his *Zur Sozial- und Gewerbepolitik der Gegenwart* (Leipzig, 1890).

2. In *Umrisse und Untersuchungen zur Verfassungs-, Verwaltungs- und Wirtschaftsgeschichte* (Leipzig, 1898), pp. 562–627. This collection of essays gives an excellent idea of Schmoller's historical work.

ualism and stateism, democracy and autocracy; and reliance on state power increased as imperialism increased. The century, like Schmoller, worked many virgin fields of knowledge and, like him, sought to bring the fruits together in a new synthesis. Life in Germany exercised, in addition, its specific influence upon thought: here idealism was stronger than elsewhere, democracy weaker, techniques of historical research at a high level, and historical feeling rapidly developing. These vital influences molded Schmoller, who, in turn, left his mark upon his time.[3]

The southern German family and environment of Gustav Schmoller contributed to his interests.[4] Schmoller was born in Heilbronn in 1838. On the father's side his family had served the state of Württemberg since the seventeenth century; and the father (1791–1865), too, after being severely wounded in the Wars of Liberation, had settled in Heilbronn as a bureaucrat. The son mentions nothing else striking of his father except that he fascinated his children with stories of his youth in the campaigns against Napoleon. The mother's family, although originally in business, consisted of professional men, and the maternal grandfather and great-grandfather of Schmoller were famous botanists. Schmoller said of his grandfather's influence upon him, "In his greenhouses, among his collections, and in his library I first learned what science was";[5] and he spent many pleasant summer hours in the Gärtner household in Calw. Since Schmoller learned little at the *Gymnasium* in Heilbronn, where, he says, he had only

3. One should read in this connection the essay of Ernst Troeltsch, "Das neunzehnte Jahrhundert," *Aufsätze zur Geistesgeschichte und Religionssoziologie, gesammelte Schriften*, IV (Tübingen, 1925), 614 ff. Schmoller wrote of Bismarck: "In short, each person, even the greatest, has the shortcomings of his virtues, and each is a child of his age and of its ideas, a product of his course of life" (*Charakterbilder* [Munich and Leipzig, 1913], p. 45).

4. See *Reden und Ansprachen bei Gustav Schmollers 70. Geburtstag* (1908), *passim;* Carl Brinkmann, *Gustav Schmoller und die Volkswirtschaftslehre* (Stuttgart, 1937), pp. 11–16.

5. *Reden und Ansprachen*, p. 47. See Waldemar Mitscherlich, *Die Lehre von den beweglichen und starren Begriffen erläutert an der Wirtschaftswissenschaft* (Stuttgart, 1936), where the opinion is expressed that Schmoller's emphasis on process, development, and growth goes back to an early understanding of Darwinism.

one good teacher and where he conceived a lifelong distrust of philologists, his active mind remained all the more open to the stirring historical events of which his father told, to natural history, and to the scientific method which he was learning in Calw.

After 1847, the date of the marriage of Schmoller's sister Marie with Gustav Rümelin, Schmoller grew up in close contact with the man whom he admired above all others.[6] From this man, who rose from a secondary-school teacher to be minister of education of Württemberg in the fifties and later professor at Tübingen, who sat in the parliament of Frankfurt in 1848, and who was one of thirty chosen to offer the crown to Frederick William IV, Schmoller took his taste for politics, economics, psychology, statistics, and pedagogy. Through Rümelin he acquired, as early as 1848, his devotion to the Prussian state; he learned to prefer the *kleindeutsch* solution of the German problem; and with Rümelin he awaited the developments of 1870–71 as the beginning of a new era for Württemberg and Germany. When, in later years, Schmoller strengthened his admiration of Prussia, of the Hohenzollerns, and of Germany by a thorough knowledge of their history, he brought to fruition the impetus which Rümelin had given him.

Before entering upon his university career Schmoller joined his father's staff for a year and a half, every morning receiving instruction from his father in administrative law and in finance, before entering upon office work. "I learned to know my country and its people and carried on business with peasants and renters of the royal lands, with handicraftsmen and taxpayers. Before I even went to the university I understood the entire mechanism of administration, both in its executive and legal phases. I already had a clear idea of the relationship between all economic development and administration," said Schmoller later.[7] This experience matured Schmoller's judgment and taught him to raise pertinent questions touching economic and administrative problems. It taught him what to admire and what to disparage in estimating the effectiveness of a bureaucracy. It undoubtedly

6. *Charakterbilder,* pp. 141–89.
7. *Reden und Ansprachen,* p. 49.

gave him a permanent bias in favor of bureaucratic supremacy, with the result that history never showed him a better regime than that controlled by a well-trained bureaucracy. It likewise prescribed his university course; but it showed him, as well, that if he were to find solutions for the new problems of the social and economic life of a great state in the making, he could not be satisfied with a relearning of old formulas.

At Tübingen, Schmoller did not have much economics, and the greatest single influence among his professors remained the liberal Max Duncker, under whom he studied history and through whom he came in contact with the work of Ranke, Droysen, Nitzsch, and Gneist. These men deepened his love of history; but on his own initiative he must also have been studying the work of Roscher and Knies, who had employed history to develop an empirical method of study for economics. By 1860, in a prize essay-dissertation, "Darstellung der in Deutschland zur Zeit der Reformation herrschenden nationalökonomischen Ansichten," Schmoller indicated why he needed history and the historical point of view for his work:

> The subject of national economy is the life of man and the way in which this acts in the ever widening circle of the individual, the family, the community, the nation, finally of all humanity in its thousand fold relations and connections; it is not the whole life, it is only one aspect of it—the relation of man to production, possession, and consumption of worldly goods; but in this sphere it is the whole of man with his freedom and his necessity which acts and which, with his activities, forms the subject of science. If man were compelled only by necessity, we could rightfully call our science a mathematical one, and we should only need to seek for the natural laws involved; then we should have an eternally valid theory. But since this is not so, we must place economics among the social sciences, which cannot be separated from space, time, and nationality, and whose foundations we must seek, not alone, but primarily in history.[8]

In this essay Schmoller made a beginning of freeing economics from the dogma of the English and French philosophy of utilitar-

8. Quoted by Brinkmann, pp. 20–21. The essay appeared in *Zeitschrift für die gesamte Staatswissenschaft*, XVI (1860), 461–716.

ianism.[9] At twenty-two Schmoller saw what he wished to do and —in the large, at least—how he wished to do it.

Schmoller early made himself acquainted with the main currents of modern thought. It has been said that in the controversy over method with Carl Menger, the Austrian economist, he failed to triumph because he was inferior to Menger in ability to think logically;[10] and his proficiency in abstract thinking has been questioned. Yet Schmoller had read widely in philosophy and had thought through several systems, weighing their value to him as an economist and social reformer.[11] As the essays collected in the *Literaturgeschichte* show, he had read Fichte, Kant, and Hegel with care, had sought to understand each in relation to his period, and had appraised the applicability of the philosophy of each to the late nineteenth century. He rejected Kantian ethics as wrongly based in pure reason, maintaining that what ought to be (*Seinsollen*) could grow only out of what had been. Since man, he thought, could reflect upon his past, he had developed a conscience, which in turn set up standards and so influenced the course of history; but at all times such standards were in relation to the culture which produced them. Thus Schmoller threw aside the categorical imperative and rationalism for a realistic, historical-cultural understanding of ethical values.

Fichte had a deeper appeal for Schmoller as a philosopher who argued concretely, could see economic facts clearly, wished knowledge to be placed in the service of the age, and thought in terms of general welfare. He criticized severely Fichte's socialism, which, he thought, like the socialism of his own day, set up a machine in place of the historical, living organism; but he found it superior to English and French socialism because it was closer

9. *Handwörterbuch der Staatswissenschaften* (4th ed.), article on Schmoller by Meitzel.

10. Werner Sombart, *Die drei Nationalökonomien* (Munich and Leipzig, 1930), p. 154. Sombart holds that Schmoller was correct in his view but that he could not adequately demonstrate it.

11. Preface of the *Grundriss der Volkswirtschaftslehre* (Leipzig, 1908), I, v–vi, where Schmoller says that he was always interested in philosophy and psychology. Volume I of the *Grundriss* was reviewed by E. R. A. Seligman in *Political science quarterly*, XV (1900), 728–32.

to German character and culture. In short, he praised in Fichte the practical elements which constituted his divergence from pure idealism, while disagreeing with Fichte's separation of *Recht* and *Sitte*. For Schmoller the culture determined formal right and spiritual-moral values, and law based upon pure reason could never succeed.

> All life, even economic [he wrote], permeated by moral considerations, will grow more and more from the relationships, connections, and opposing tensions, organs, and institutions of free cultural life and will make, especially in economic life, more difficult and less seldom any divergence from that which is truly right and good.[12]

Hegel likewise found little favor with Schmoller, for his theory of history was to Schmoller a construct based on a priori reasoning. More exact than earlier theory, Schmoller thought it still not exact enough. Thus Schmoller, who had already repudiated the English classical economic theory, turned against German idealism as a fruitless method for approaching contemporary problems, both because it was unhistorical and because, as Schmoller wrote in an essay on Schiller, "the materialistic, egoistic ethics [*Sittenlehre*] of the French and the subjectivity and sensualism of the English became translated in German idealistic philosophy into the cult of individualism."[13]

Schmoller did not lack acquaintance with positivism and naturalism. It is often said that he owed most to Spencer and Comte, and he knew John Stuart Mill and Wundt, who is frequently called the "German Spencer." From Comte, Spencer, Mill, and Wundt, Schmoller gained the ability to use the empirical method, to think in terms of society, to analyze causality from many aspects, to compare cultures, to consider psychology and its influence upon cultural development, to make use of anthropology, prehistory and ethnography, and he strengthened his interest in naturalism and natural laws as applied to human culture.

---

12. *Literaturgeschichte der Staats- und Sozialwissenschaften* (Leipzig, 1888), p. 75. Reviewed by E. R. A. Seligman, *Political science quarterly*, IV (1889), 543–45.
13. *Ibid.*, p. 6.

Schmoller's *Grundriss* is written entirely in Spencer's spirit, although not every section is worked out in an identical way.[14] In this connection it should not be forgotten that positivism, with its aim of raising social disciplines to a science by means of "laws," appealed to Schmoller's love of science. Lastly, it may be pointed out that emphasis upon change belongs to a period of swift cultural transition, such as that in which Schmoller, as well as Comte, Spencer, and Mill, lived. Schmoller did not imitate them; at some points his experience touched theirs, as did that of Lorenz von Stein, Schäffle, Wagner, and others, for all of whom economic life had become something in flux, no longer explicable by reference to timeless laws.

Schmoller is commonly connected even more closely with Roscher, Knies, and Hildebrand, his predecessors in the use of the historical method in economics. Informed analyses seem thoroughly to justify not pressing these connections too far,[15] for Schmoller knew the philosophical and methodological shortcomings of these men as well as their contributions. The nineteenth century saw the development of separate disciplines and of experimental methodology; and Schmoller had a long line of useful predecessors and contemporaries—among them Hanssen and Hildebrand, who first began detailed investigations of individual institutions or periods; J. G. Hoffmann and Ernst Engel, who used statistics extensively; List, who used the comparative method of study and who first countered "international" with "national" economy; Knies, who introduced ethics into economics; and Mommsen, Niebuhr, Ranke, Savigny, and Dahlmann, whose historical work and method were necessary preliminaries. Schmoller made use of all, but he sought a synthesis different from any and laid out a way of his own. In his review of Roscher's *Geschichte der Nationalökonomik*, in 1875, Schmoller pointed out that the work was a transitional one between the school of Adam Smith

14. Ernst Troeltsch, *Der Historismus und seine Probleme, gesammelte Schriften* (Tübingen, 1922), III, 420 ff.

15. Max Weber, "Roscher und Knies und die logischen Probleme der historischen Nationalökonomie," *Schmollers Jahrbuch,* XXVII (1903), 1181 ff.; XXIX (1905), 1323 ff.; XXX (1906), 81 ff.; Thorstein Veblen, "Gustav Schmoller's economics," *Quarterly journal of economics,* XVI (1901–2), 69 ff.

and Schmoller's young historical group. His own plans went far ahead of this work.

After the success of his first essay Schmoller published further, in 1862, "Systematische Darstellung des Ergebnisses der zu Zoll-vereinszwecken im Jahre 1861 in Württemberg stattgehabten Ge-werbeaufnahme," and in the same year an anonymous work, *Der französische Handelsvertrag und seine Gegner: ein Wort der Verständigung von einem Süddeutschen.* Although the free-trade liberalism of the latter work made it impossible for Schmoller to hope for a career in protectionist Württemberg, both indicated his interest in, and knowledge of, contemporary conditions. In 1863 appeared "Die Lehre vom Einkommen in ihrem Zusam-menhang mit den Grundprinzipien der Steurlehre," wherein Schmoller tried to deal anew with the relationship between state and individual.[16]

His early publications helped to secure for Schmoller a post as professor extraordinarius of political science in Halle (1864). Here Schmoller spent the sixties, at last in close contact with the Prussian state and in a liberal group. He went frequently to Ber-lin, where he came in touch with Treitschke, Erdmannsdörffer, Droysen, Hermann Grimm, Dilthey, and others. During this pe-riod he developed in at least four important directions: he did his first extensive work in Prussian administrative, social, and eco-nomic history; he began to deal with the question of the worker and to consider the matter of socialism; he published the first of his historical-economic monographs, *Zur Geschichte der deutschen Kleingewerbe im 19. Jahrhundert;* and he was matur-ing the views which led to the plan for the Verein für Sozial-politik, founded in the autumn of 1872 to further co-operative research into contemporary economic and social problems.[17] The constitutional struggle of Bismarck in the sixties showed Schmol-

16. The first of the three essays appeared in *Württemberger Jahrbücher,* 1862, Heft 2; the second in brochure form, Frankfurt, 1862; the third in *Zeitschrift für die gesamte Staatswissenschaften,* Vol. XIX (1863).

17. Schmoller's part in the work of the Verein and the great scientific achievements of the organization are monuments to Schmoller and to the century. The monographs published by the Verein are too often overlooked. Cf. also Albion W. Small, *Origins of sociology* (Chicago, 1924), chaps. xv, xvi.

ler the importance of administrative forces, thus strengthening his interest in the history of the Prussian bureaucracy and sending him to the archives for new materials. At the same time, he realized that the extent of new social and economic problems in the Second Reich would call for vast knowledge, and he determined to place academic resources at the service of the government and the public.

In the early seventies Schmoller left Halle for the new German University of Strassburg. The years of his stay at Strassburg (1872–82) were among the most fruitful for Schmoller in purely historical research and writing. To this period belong the foundation of the Verein, the assumption of the editorship of the *Jahrbuch für Gesetzgebung, Verwaltungs- und Gewerberecht,* which has always been known as *Schmollers Jahrbuch,* the investigations into the history of Strassburg, and the famous controversy with Treitschke, in which conservatism and social liberalism stated their irreconcilable cases. The Verein für Sozialpolitik had its best days in the seventies, when Bismarck and even industrialists like Baron von Stumm looked favorably upon the "socialists of the chair" and heed was paid to the meetings and publications of the Verein.

In embarking on researches in the history of Strassburg, Schmoller performed an important service to historical effort. He opened local archives and placed his seminarists at work in them. He secured the co-operation of local officials and, in time, grants of city money for the work of publication of documents. He demonstrated how such detailed local history could be used as a test case for the study of wider economic changes. This latter aspect appears in the most important work, *Das strassburger Tücher- und Weberzunft: Urkunden und Darstellungen nebst Regesten und Glossar: ein Beitrag zur Geschichte der deutschen Weberei und des deutschen Gewerberechts vom 13. bis 17. Jahrhundert,*[18] in which Schmoller discussed almost all the problems of the economic-political town life of the middle ages on the basis of this concrete study. Delving into local history was in line with Schmol-

18. Strassburg, 1879.

ler's desire to understand the problems of his milieu by thorough acquaintance with their historical background. But the Strassburg researches served another end as well: they brought about gradually a change of emphasis in Schmoller's historical interest. He turned from Prussian history under Frederick William I to the general history of Prussian economic development. This purpose appears in the introduction to his essay, "Die russische Compagnie in Berlin," written at the end of 1882.[19] The change is significant for Schmoller's entire future work.

Since Schmoller had shifted his historical emphasis, his call in 1882 to succeed Adolf Held, secretary of the Verein, at the University of Berlin did not lead to the resumption, on the former scale, of the historical work begun at Halle and partly interrupted by the stay at Strassburg. In other ways as well, the Berlin post marked the beginning of a new life for Schmoller. Through Althoff, Prussian minister of education, Schmoller frequently gave advice in educational and cultural matters. In 1884, he became a member of the Prussian council of state; in 1887, of the Preussische Akademie der Wissenschaften; and subsequently, of a variety of German and foreign academies. He was made official historian of Brandenburg (1887) and associate editor of the re-organized *Forschungen zur brandenburgischen und preussischen Geschichte,* whose inspiration he soon became. In 1887 the Akadamie der Wissenschaften accepted his memorandum for the publication of the *Acta Borussica, Denkmäler der preussischen Staatsverwaltung im 18. Jahrhundert,* and in the next year work on these volumes began under Schmoller's direction. In 1899 Schmoller became a member of the upper house of the Prussian legislature (*Herrenhaus*) for the University of Berlin, and he held appointments to several commissions of investigation. Since he was already assisting with the publication of the monographs put out by the Verein, was writing for and editing *Schmollers Jahrbuch,* was connected with *Die staats- und sozialwissenschaftlichen Forschungen,* and was contributing articles and reviews to former publishers, Schmoller led an exhausting life. His daily

19. *Umrisse und Untersuchungen,* pp. 457 ff.

contact with privy councilors and statesmen enhanced his tendency to aloofness from all except a small circle of family and
friends. The eager student and scholar had become a man of
affairs.[20]

Schmoller continued in Berlin during the remainder of his life.
He gave up the last of his seminars in 1912 and died in 1917. As
was the case with earlier participation in administrative work, he
gained in stature for his scientific work by contact with public
figures and problems.[21] Few academic men have had his opportunities for participation in public life. He saw how he could be
useful to those who sought his advice, and hence what kind of
academic knowledge was needed and at what points. This made
him valuable as a teacher of future bureaucrats. He had occasion
to observe more precisely the importance of the administrative
unit and the necessity of attempting to keep it above party and
class interest. He gained new belief in the state and in society, as
against individual interest. To this public life in Prussia is due
some part of the wisdom and courage of the *Grundriss,* the general work in economics upon which Schmoller spent his scientific
effort during most of the Berlin years. To do this task he left his
Prussian history a torso, but he completed the expression of an
even deeper interest. He wrote in the preface to Volume II:

> However incomplete my *Grundriss* may remain, however little
> it may satisfy the theoretical economist or the individual historian,
> the effort at a general synthesis is not superfluous and not un-
> fruitful. It had to be undertaken by an economic historian, one
> who has always considered it a false charge against himself that
> he was striving for description, not for a general understanding of
> the laws of economic life. Only with such a representation created
> from the whole can one serve the greater purpose of all scientific
> understanding. I do not pride myself too much on my work when
> I say that I have written it in the service of the leading economic
> ideas and trends of our time and of the ideals which rule my life.
> Without coming too close to other fields, I believe I may say that
> it is clear that a *Grundriss* of economic theory has been written by
> a scholar who is as much an historian of constitutional, administra-

20. For further details on these matters see Brinkmann, pp. 115–16.
21. Cf. *Reden und Ansprachen, passim.*

tive, and economic life as an economist, who has followed the process of psychological and social development as well as economic and who, with the far greater means of present-day economic history, has attacked the work which Roscher began fifty years ago.[22]

Fundamental to an understanding of Gustav Schmoller is a knowledge of the philosophy of history and of the political and social values that he held. Although he had rejected German idealism and English laissez-faireism in favor of an empirical method of system-building, he had formulated, early in his career, his own views of history and of contemporary problems.

Schmoller's theory of change and progressive development had its roots in his own life and in the age in which he lived. All about Schmoller events had happened and were happening so quickly, and the change effected was so fundamental, that there could be no question of static systems, whether political, social, or economic. One of the basic appreciations of the historian—the feeling for process—was present in Schmoller from the start of his career. His first problem was to show the forces at work in conditioning the cultural process; and when once he had concluded that these were both spiritual and material, he sought to explain their connection. This led him to the natural-science concept of the integral causal relationship of all happening. It was the age, too, which showed him the complexity of causality. But the course of development proved more interesting to Schmoller than the why. Rejecting pure Darwinism, he held to the primacy of moral forces ("sittliche Kräfte"). Although he saw the struggle for existence and in the *Grundriss* dealt with the fall of empires, culture continued, he thought, to advance to new high points; struggle was natural and healthful, for weaker peoples fell and new forces took up the advance. Further, he assumed a general line of advance for all humanity, with moral forces slowly effecting a rise of economic, social, and political levels. That different peoples had had differing lengths of cultural existence he took as proof of the fact that they were not merely fulfilling a process of nature. "The time of flower of every people and state," he wrote in the *Grundriss*, "is

22. P. vi.

at once one of great internal spiritual-moral, technical, and organizational progress and then one of power-superiority or power-improvement in relation to foreign countries, whereby directly and indirectly wealth is increased." He recognized that the rhythm of economic life differed from the rhythms of other institutions, but he could not explain this.[23] Nor did he try to give an exhaustive picture of the connections between various forms of spiritual life and their relationship to institutions. He frankly left to the future the working-out of these things. In the meantime, in spite of the "cutthroat spirit of gain, social indifference, and the burdening of our social and political life with all manner of trials," he wrote in concluding the *Grundriss:*

> The time will come when all good and normally developed men will know how to reconcile a decent desire for gain and the search for individuality, self-assertion, egoism, with a sense of complete justice and of community of feeling. Let us hope that the way will not be so long as was that which led from the brutality of men of force to the culture of the men of today.[24]

Schmoller's belief that cultural change was leading to new and better cultural levels rested on his idea of justice (*Gerechtigkeit*).[25] The ideal of justice is native to man, Schmoller thought, and determines his action. It is the means by which he approaches the ideal, although he never reaches this goal. The setting-up of the ideal is complicated, and, again, it is dependent on the stage of the cultural development; yet it has never failed to break through the darkest ages and to resume the forming of the ideal "good." Thus the "ideal" became for Schmoller a part of history. Especially important to social and economic progress is what he called "verteilende Gerechtigkeit." This form of justice demands that

23. Cf. Paul Menzer, "Gustav von Schmollers Lehre von der Entwicklung," *Schmollers Jahrbuch,* LXII (1938), No. 4–6, 82 ff. The quotation from the *Grundriss* is given by Menzer, p. 87.

24. *Grundriss,* II, 678.

25. "Die Gerechtigkeit in der Volkswirtschaftslehre," *Zur Sozial- und Gewerbepolitik der Gegenwart* (Leipzig, 1890), pp. 204 ff. See also *Über einige Grundfragen des Rechts und der Volkswirtschaft: ein offenes Sendschreiben an Herrn Professor Dr. Heinrich von Treitschke* (Jena, 1875), *passim.*

men be given rights and goods in proportion to their ability and activity on behalf of the whole of society. Men are not equal, according to Schmoller, and do not, as of right, merit an equal share in society's goods and privileges. Society divides men into groups, classes, and ranks according to their activities and accords each group what seems just; the *Volksgefühl* has always granted more to those whose abilities and achievements have been beyond the average. Class struggles, with their bases in economic equality, have always resulted from this division of goods as new groups demanded recognition of their importance. Difficult as it is, however, to solve the problem of their demands, justice will give to each his due and will, even more importantly, give to the whole that which is due it—in time. Meanwhile, struggle must continue, but it will become milder as justice advances over the earth. "As no penal code and no judge is absolutely just," wrote Schmoller, "so no existing division of income and property is entirely just. But every succeeding epoch of human history has won a greater degree of justice in this field as well."[26]

Because Schmoller believed so thoroughly in the future, he could make plans for reform. Only in the measure that serious men gave their effort to further the "spiritual forces" could these be strengthened among the masses and progress furthered. Throughout his essay on justice, as well as in all his political writings, it is the commonweal which Schmoller considers. He is prepared to devote his own energies to this common good. Unlike some of his contemporaries, Schmoller does not see history working itself out as a natural process; man can assist in the progress of culture by raising the level and broadening the base of spiritual understanding. On this ground rested all Schmoller's work in the Verein and in his own and other journals, designed, as they were, to inform the citizen about his problems and to point the way to just solutions.

The specific content of Schmoller's justice and the nature of the injustices which he judged as problems are not far to seek. The highest cultural institution for Schmoller was the state, and

26. *Zur Sozial- und Gewerbepolitik*, p. 246.

303

its preservation was the prime necessity. The achievements of Prussia and Germany under Bismarck had given him great respect for political power, while the economic development of the Second Reich had seemed to prove that a strong state could guarantee progress in this field as well. The state easily appeared superior to the individual and as easily became for Schmoller the vehicle for reform. As he turned to the history of the modern state and found in Prussia of the seventeenth and eighteenth centuries a model, he grew more and more to believe in the value of a strong monarchy and a well-trained bureaucracy. He saw them as standing above party and class politics in the interest of the whole, reconciling opposing social forces, regulating economic conditions, and carrying out considered reforms. In his writings on Prussia he was able to show just how the eighteenth-century state had done these things, step by step gaining control over the towns, building the standing army, regulating the cloth manufacture and trade, developing a tax system. Although Schmoller realized the violence of the class struggle of his own day, saw the clash of interests in politics, and counted on the rise of a strong capitalistic group, he thought the state could cope with all these and restore harmony. He knew from history that the state of the past had often abused its power, and he realized the need for interstateism. Yet he believed that *Sitte* would restrain *Machtpolitik* and was even already bringing about internationalism at some points, notably in commerce. He supported all the new techniques for state power—protectionism, a navy, colonies, and foreign trade—as dictated by *raison d'état;* and he had no fear, apparently, that they would get out of hand. Even the outbreak of war in 1914 did not shake his faith that the state would survive and possibly begin a better life than before.[27]

It was Schmoller's belief in the supremacy of political power which dictated the nature of his periodization of history. Each period—that of the family group, of the village, mark, town, territorial state, modern state—appeared to him as differentiated from the preceding and subsequent periods by the nature of the political organization which obtained.

27. Franz Boese, "Aus Gustav von Schmollers letztem Lebensjahrzehnt," *Schmollers Jahrbuch,* LXII (1938), No. 4–6, 372.

Closely connected with his devotion to the state, especially to the characteristics of the old Prussian regime, was the love which Schmoller bore to the German people. Both led him to an almost exclusive interest in natural history, as did likewise his sensitiveness to the need for reform. To preserve the security of his people and to promote their good through the time-proved medium of the state constituted his goal, and hence set the materials with which he must work. It is interesting to note that even his essays on Bismarck dealt only with Bismarck's social and economic position and importance.[28] Schmoller's appreciation of the German people and their history contributed, no doubt, to an understanding of historical individuality. Although he was less precise in detail than the best of historians should be, this lack was due to his eagerness to generalize; he grasped the individuality of an institution or of an age as few before him. The love of German character also contributed to the bitterness with which Schmoller denounced socialism. He became convinced that there must be a German solution for the social ills of his country which would leave intact the German institutions he admired. The internationalism of the Marxists was anathema to him, just as Manchesterism was; neither seemed "just" in accordance with German ethics.

It is clear that, in spite of his views in 1848 and 1870, Schmoller had very little of the liberal in him. He cannot be labeled, because he avoided dogma in favor of the view which seemed to him historically sound. Hence, in approaching his social ideas, he may seem, at first and in comparison with Treitschke in his attack on Schmoller,[29] extremely progressive; but actually the pattern of his entire social philosophy was a variegated one. The key to this pattern lies in the following words:

> Our social ideal must not consist in democratic form but in the economic and moral uplift of our lower classes. To this end a certain measure of democracy is necessary; but it is not the main

28. "Vier Briefe über Bismarcks sozialpolitische und volkswirtschaftliche Stellung und Bedeutung," *Charakterbilder*, pp. 27–77.
29. Heinrich von Treitschke, "Der Sozialismus und seine Gönner," *Preussische Jahrbücher*, XXXIV (1874), 67 ff., 248 ff., and "Die gerechte Verteilung der Güter," *ibid.*, XXXV (1875), 409 ff.

thing, if Germany is to remain at her peak. More important is it—
or we should better say, so it seems to us—that monarchy and
bureaucracy retain the leadership as the strong backbone of the
state to lead us to victory in foreign affairs, to restore at home
peace between capital and labor, organized industry and organized unions, and to maintain what has been restored. One-
sided political control by organized labor would be a still greater
misfortune than that of the cartels. But both would mean class
victory with class hegemony.[30]

As Schmoller was not an individualist, so he was not a democrat.
He did not deny the historical value of democracy and still found
it desirable for certain peoples or places, but in Germany it was
not the solution dictated by tradition. Rather, the Prussian state
and the Prussian kings had always been friends and allies of the
lower classes and could not desert them; but, at the same time,
this monarchy had known how, through the army and bureaucracy, to win over the aristocracy which it had once had to conquer.[31] It would be a mistake to do away with this carefully
evolved machinery by means of which alone class struggle could
be reduced or abolished and the welfare of all made more secure.
Schmoller did not see man in the mass as having ever decided
epoch-making events, and eventually he opposed universal suf-
frage. He regarded parliamentary government as a form of class
rule, with now one class, now another, in control of the majority.
It was in line with his entire philosophy that he should oppose
Marxian socialism, but it was as much so that he should wish the
state to take every practicable step to make more just the income
of the proletariat and to raise the moral level. His goal was always the greater national unity, endangered, he knew, by socialism but capable of preservation through blood, language, common values, and institutions—bonds which he thought made in
the end for stronger nationalism than technical ones. Schmoller's realistic historism made him face the fact of class struggle,

30. Quoted by Wiese, "Aristokratie und Demokratie bei Gustav von
Schmoller," *Schmollers Jahrbuch*, LXII (1938), No. 329. Schmoller's constant fear was that one class would control instead of the neutral state.

31. *Grundriss*, II, 519 ff.; "Der deutsche Beamtenstaat," *Schmollers
Jahrbuch*, XVIII (1894), 712 ff.

just as his reading of history led him to believe in the possibility of spiritual growth. This very emphasis upon the ethical force in culture was the foundation stone of Schmoller's social-reform program. Both the men who made the program, as well as those for whom it was to be made, should have moral stature.

Schmoller avoided working out a theory of social justice to oppose to liberalism or socialism. He did not know how, in detail, he would carry out all that he proposed; but he thought it best to attack the nearest problem and proceed from there, keeping always in the foreground the need for practicable measures suited to the day and age. Schmoller was a social activist, and in the seventies at the time of the *Sendschreiben an Treitschke* the list of needs was large and Schmoller's lust for battle great. In later life there are signs that Schmoller felt the strong state created by Bismarck to be the best "carrier and executor of the social progress of mankind."[32] Schmoller may never have realized the ascendancy of the Bismarckian social policy; but it is certain that the Verein after the seventies lost in influence and that Schmoller's social-ethical goal was never reached.

In considering Schmoller's method of historical research and the application of this method to political economy, special attention will be given to the essay on mercantilism and its historical importance, as one of Schmoller's best and most famous studies in the history of Prussia in the eighteenth century, and to his use of this and similar material in the treatment of tariff policy in the *Grundriss*. Here Schmoller is using the historical approach to illuminate a matter of importance to the Second Reich.

In his essay on mercantilism Schmoller set out with the assumption that a phenomenon like mercantilism could only be grasped in its historical setting. It was his point of view that if a free-trader examined mercantilism in the light of his own theory of trade he would necessarily find disadvantages predominating, while a protectionist would find only advantages, and neither would be able to contribute to an understanding of the institution in its functional relationship to the culture of which it

32. *Charakterbilder*, p. 74. Cf., also, Friedrich Meinecke, "Drei Generationen deutscher Gelehrtenpolitik," *HZ*, CXXV (1921–22), 248–83.

formed a part. Schmoller, therefore, made it his task to provide this understanding, first, by examining the economic character of the seventeenth and eighteenth centuries when mercantilism obtained. In accordance with this theory of the primacy of political power, he asserted that "in all phases of economic development a leading and controlling role in the economic field falls to one or the other political organ of the group,"[33] and he expounded a theory of stages of culture based on stages of political development. For each stage Schmoller correlated the economic life of the group with the political life.[34] He drew upon published material for the prehistorical, ancient, and medieval stages (developed more in the *Grundriss* than in the essay on mercantilism); but, as he approached the period which he was emphasizing, he used primary sources. The group was handled as a whole, for Schmoller saw society operating as such, and the beginnings in one stage of phenomena characteristic of a subsequent stage were brought out to indicate the way of growth of an institution. Each successive stage stood forth as a cultural advance, and Schmoller assumed that spiritual forces had exercised a greater force in each notable forward step; but he did not make precise this point. He did not show what part *Sitte* played and what part economic necessity played in the effort, for example, to suppress the egoism of town organization for wider economic co-operation. Schmoller likewise correlated technical progress with the political and economic changes, pointing out, for the first time known to the writer, the part taken by geographical and technical discovery in forcing the building of the modern national state. As is to be expected, the modern state examined is Prussia; and her mercantilism, as developed by the margraves of Brandenburg and the kings of Prussia in the seventeenth and eighteenth centuries, was that described. The analysis of the building of a powerful political unit by means of an economic system, mercantilism, and of the perfecting of this economic system by the political power has been done with magnificent strokes. The picture of Prussia was

33. *Umrisse und Untersuchungen,* p. 2.
34. Such a *Stufenlehre* was new to economics and, as can readily be appreciated, helped to relate economics to the total culture.

set off against other states, illustrating Schmoller's use of the comparative method which is frequently found in his Prussian studies. Generalizations were made on the merits and demerits of the sytsem, and the points at which it broke down were indicated, for Schmoller did not deny that mercantilism, at least in its exaggerated form in international commerce, proved a deterrent to world-progress. This admission opened the way for Schmoller to show at a future date the historical place of liberalistic free trade, as he demonstrated the place of mercantilism in the eighteenth century.

In his analysis there was no new and clearer definition of mercantilism. The value of the essay lay in the method, whereby mercantilism was regarded as *Staatsbildung*, and, therefore, as taking its place in promoting culture. The liberating and creative forces in mercantilism were revealed in contradiction to the view that mercantilism was restrictive. The greatest lack in Schmoller's analysis was adequate consideration of the social classes and groups which profited by the system. Had he applied his criterion of justice, he might have made more complete the understanding of the nature of mercantilism and the need for change. This fault is one which too great emphasis on the state may easily produce. Yet the essay advanced the understanding of an important institution to a point which modern research has scarcely passed.[35]

Mercantilism is treated many times in several aspects in the *Grundriss*, but especially in the section dealing with the history of tariff policy. In this section tariff policy was traced back to the practice of prehistoric, ancient, and medieval times, with extensive reference to the mercantilistic town economy of the Hansa cities, to the territorial principalities of 1500–1700, and to the mercantilistic states of the seventeenth and eighteenth centuries. Considerable attention was paid to England's mercantilistic practices and their result in creating English imperial power. Against this picture Schmoller set that of Germany and Prussia,

35. Heckscher, the contemporary student of mercantilism, works from a different point of view but hardly from a different conception of mercantilism.

ending with Prussia's turn to power politics and economics. "Without the policy, the wars and mercantilism, Prussia would never have secured in Germany," Schmoller concluded this section, "a firm hold against East, South, West, and North. In the eighteenth or nineteenth century our fatherland would have been divided, like Poland, by the other great powers."[36] A treatment of free trade follows. As has been suggested, Schmoller has not failed to give this movement its historical setting, and he has recognized that it was made necessary by the abuses of mercantilistic practice; but he did not accept free trade, because he saw it as weakening the state. Hence he readily found sympathy for protectionism, the spread of which in less industrially developed states he considered healthy. He accepted the new *Machtpolitik*, however, and could not escape the implications of this for tariff policy, a dilemma which he does not squarely face; but he does understand—and this is one of the products of both his method and his wisdom—that other forces than the purely economic ones were and are at work in molding tariff policy.

Schmoller then drew his conclusions for present-day policy. His historical summary of tariff policy led him to the teaching that free trade and protection were not matters of principle.[37] They were only interchangeable means for promoting the welfare of the state. The tariff policy of a country should be based on a careful survey of domestic resources and an understanding of foreign competition. Everything, he argued, depended on a well-regulated system, and the means for achieving such a system were improving and would improve. He believed that the common interest was drawing special interests more and more under control, so that "the means of tariff policy are improving, being refined, humanized." Individual states, he warned, must strive toward internationalism; and he hoped that a public better informed by him would have a care for this, as well as for a tariff policy more clearly based on the economic welfare of the whole

36. *Grundriss*, II, 599.
37. *Ibid.*, pp. 647 ff. Cf. speech in the Verein in 1879, "Der Übergang Deutschlands zum Schutzzollsystem," *Zur Sozial- und Gewerbepolitik*, pp. 166 ff.

nation. Even so, he expected a long period of international struggle before the state system should have reached a level upon which peace would be possible. Man must endeavor to bring moderation and intelligence into play and so shorten the period of struggle.

Is the historical method as Schmoller handles it successful in laying the foundation for a theory of tariff policy? No one will deny that Schmoller has used sufficient historical material and has managed this material well. In so long a survey he has not been able to use primary sources extensively, but his bibliography was very large. He has not had time to sharpen his analysis in the essay on mercantilism, nor even to go so far in discussing the relation of the political power to economic systems other than the mercantilistic. But he has suggested the complicated nature of the fixing of tariffs. He has been able neither to let the material speak for itself nor to lead the reader logically into a statement of theory of tariff policy. At every turn Schmoller's philosophy, values, and assumptions are evident, while he ends largely with advice and expressions of faith. He does not ignore any clearly undesirable aspects of an institution—as judged by his own standards; but he believes that human understanding, *Sitte,* and *Recht* are improving and will correct these aspects. He has not advanced a new policy—for example, a new departure in tariff systems—but merely a more wisely administered combination of old systems. He has placed great confidence in improved techniques without indicating how these are to have their effect in counteracting established forces. Might they not be so revolutionary as to compel a complete change of political system, as he suggested was the case in the eighteenth and nineteenth centuries? Or might not the administrative personnel deteriorate rather than improve? What if the national state, whose interest is the determining factor for Schmoller, is as an institution itself destroyed? The whole theory would fall, and there would be no tariff policy, either as given by Schmoller or to be arrived at anew on the basis of his material. What if the modern state, by its very nature and contrary to Schmoller's faith, should remain torn by groups of interests and unable to devote itself to the common welfare? All these and many more questions arise. It cannot be said that the method is at fault, for another might have used the method otherwise. But it must be said that Schmoller has not succeeded in arriving at economic theory on the basis of historical material. He has succeeded at arriving at good advice, even practicable advice; but it is advice closely linked with the time in which it is given and specifically for Germany, as Schmoller intended it.[38] His historical analysis is still superior to his economic synthesis.

It is not fitting in this essay to sum up Schmoller's work as an economist and economic theorist. Students continued to carry on the historical method of economic study, but even in his lifetime many turned from Schmoller or went beyond him. The *Weltwirtschaftliches Archiv* was established (1913) as one means of promoting a counterinfluence to the historical approach to economics, and a former student of Schmoller has confirmed to the writer the opinion of the *Archiv*'s editor that the historical school did more to delay the development of sound economic theory in Germany than any other one force. Schmoller died in 1917 before he could witness the collapse of the political system on which he had staked his reform program. After his death little was said in praise of him until the late thirties, when the occasion of the centenary of his birth aroused new interest in his work.[39] The best of these studies, however, serve chiefly to indicate the tremendous methodological and philosophical problems with which Schmoller wrestled rather than the finality with which he settled them: "Schmoller is a milestone and not the goal." In giving up the theory of the ideal type of the older economic school, Schmoller gave up the clarity and precision of that theory without being able to set up against it a sharply etched "anschauliche" theory. A great wealth of material was presented, but the mate-

38. Arthur Spiethoff, "Die allgemeine Volkswirtschaftslehre als geschichtliche Theorie: die Wirtschaftsstile," *Schmollers Jahrbuch*, LVI (1932), No. 2, 51 ff.

39. Carl Brinkmann, published in 1937; and the double number of *Schmollers Jahrbuch* so often quoted above, *Gustav von Schmoller und die deutsche geschichtliche Volkswirtschaftslehre*, ed. Arthur Spiethoff (Berlin, 1938), *Schmollers Jahrbuch*, LXII (1938), No. 4–6.

rial served only to illustrate the older theory, for there was no new point of departure, no new line of thought in Schmoller's work on economic theory.[40]

Too severe a criticism of Schmoller as a theorist will cause one to overlook much which makes him valuable to the historian. In his effort to present reality in its complexity he took a necessary step toward greater objectivity. The effort to check accepted theory or belief against experience and to explain it thus constituted another needed step, and one which Schmoller carried further than Roscher or Knies. His effort to delineate the complexity of reality by making use of the findings and methods of other disciplines places him among the first of modern social scientists. His success in grasping the historical individuality of an institution or an age can only be the envy of the historian of any century. His understanding of the relation between the state and economic and social life had never before been equaled. Nor did appreciation of the total culture, as one sees it in the *Grundriss*, ever before find such brilliant expression. Only by spending some time with Schmoller's work can one fully realize how much he possessed and made use of the historical point of view.

It is this historical point of view which is best understood by the "historical method of economics." Schmoller was not a trained historian, although he understood the mechanics of historical research sufficiently. Even if he had been so trained, it is clear that he could not have used historical techniques alone to write the *Grundriss*.[41] What is more nearly his case is that (1) Schmoller proposed for himself and for his students and successors a long line of historical monographs on economic institutions which would furnish economists with more material than they could observe for themselves; (2) he then made—and hoped others would—use of such material, that is, of facts, to illustrate and

40. Cf. Spiethoff, "Gustav von Schmoller und die anschauliche Theorie der Volkswirtschaftslehre," *Schmollers Jahrbuch,* LXII (1938), No. 2, 16 ff.

41. Georg Weippert, "Gustav von Schmoller im Urteil Wilhelm Diltheys und Yorck von Wartenburgs," *ibid.*, pp. 64 ff. Dilthey makes this distinction between historical research and the historical point of view, which both he and Yorck recognized as quite different things. The historical point of view is Germany's contribution to history, not antiquarianism (*ibid.*, p. 69).

criticize existing institutions and theories, but in addition to this illustrative material he employed as tools what he had learned from his study of history—a sense of becoming, of change, a feeling for individuality, and the understanding of group activity, by which in the *Grundriss* he interpreted his facts and gave new emphases. Instead of the cross-sectional analysis of an institution, Schmoller preferred the long-time or vertical view, because his was primarily a historical point of view, with feeling for process uppermost, rather than a sociological one. Schmoller's "younger historical school" of economics was actually a school of realism in which the historical approach or historism was well developed. After a long period of rationalism, it placed again the emphasis upon empiricism. But Schmoller did not intend, certainly not after about 1895, to neglect synthesis. His own account of his method of teaching, whether history or economics, gives a clue to his true point of departure: (*a*) to make whatever he is describing live before the eyes of the students, and (*b*) to present the complexity of a phenomenon so that a student may appreciate as nearly as possible its true nature. This complexity might confuse some but was better than laying down a law which made things seem simple.[42]

Schmoller's contributions to Prussian history should not be omitted in a summary of his work. If colleagues and successors of his in economics have been critical, the reverse is true in the field of his historical work, where only admiration reigns.[43] This is due to the fact that, whatever his shortcomings, Schmoller innovated so much that the profession cannot but feel gratitude toward him. One needs only to recall that administrative history had hardly been touched upon before Schmoller; that in a decade of work he opened archival sources for this and produced some of the most stimulating pages ever yet written in the field—pages on

42. *Grundriss*, I, vi.
43. Cf. *Reden und Ansprachen, passim,* especially the testimony of Breysig and Koser. See also, Fritz Hartung, "Gustav von Schmoller und die preussische Geschichtsschreibung," *Schmollers Jahrbuch,* LXII (1938), No. 4–6, 277 ff.

army reform, on tax and tariff reforms, on absolutism in the eighteenth century. The organization of the *Acta Borussica* alone might stand as a sufficient monument to Schmoller, but in addition he was a member of the commission which published *Urkunden und Aktenstücke zur Geschichte des Grossen Kurfürst* and was responsible for an extension of this publication into internal and financial materials. The *Forschungen* and the Verein für Geschichte der Mark Brandenburg under his stimulus did their part likewise in contributing to sound internal history and documentary publication. It has been objected that Schmoller buried himself in the seventeenth and eighteenth centuries when he would not have dared explore his own age so thoroughly. Opposed to this criticism is the fact that Schmoller purposely attacked modern times instead of the ancient or medieval fields, seeking the roots of institutions of the nineteenth century and in time comparing conditions. One of the most valuable of his studies is that dealing with the towns under Frederick William I. Both the romanticists and the liberals had waxed sentimental in their support of town liberties; but Schmoller's researches soon showed another side to the town of the middle ages and of the sixteenth and seventeenth centuries. His reconstruction of the reforms for the towns was in itself a masterly piece of historical effort, for the procedure had been different in almost each case, and Schmoller was content only when he had examined the instructions and had followed through their execution. He felt repaid, however, in that he presented a brilliant example of the growth of state power over local autonomies, showing the care and patience needed by the central power for such work. He could make his research valuable because he knew what questions he wished to answer, why he was working. If he acquired the epithet of "Borusser" because he became so strong an admirer of Prussia, it is to his credit that he saw much at fault in his own age and took upon himself the responsibility of understanding why this was so and what were the more perfect prototypes of these faulty institutions. Nor can one forget that, although Schmoller never lost interest in and contact with Prussian history, he turned more and more to the wider field of western European culture. Yet, his greatest contribution to historical studies lies in the Prussian field.[44]

What of Schmoller's success in the third of his roles, that as a statesman and reformer? Certainly, Schmoller played it with the same energy and devotion as he did those of economist and historian, paralleling his time in the classroom and seminar with hours spent on public commissions and in conference. If there were any egoistic reasons for Schmoller's interest in reform, they did not outweigh his sincere concern for the general welfare. Knowing this, one wonders why he should not have become a policy-determining figure, even outside academic halls. Why should the administrators in whom he had such confidence not have adopted his goals and used his techniques for achieving them? Why should the Verein have lost, rather than gained, steadily in prestige? The answer seems to lie in part with an interesting circumstance—interesting for historians, at least. It was Schmoller's interest in the problems of his own age and in the future of his country which governed his interest in both history and economics. But these latter interests ultimately determined the views he held toward his age, robbing him, in ways almost too subtle to analyze, of sufficient force to inspire reform. It has been mentioned that he grew to accept the Bismarckian social solution rather than his own, possibly without realizing it. Thus he, like the bourgeois citizens whom he criticized, came to feel something of the complacency of the Second Reich. His historical study confirmed his faith in existing and traditional institutions, and he did not wish any radical change. The necessary adjustments were made in part through a turn to *Machtpolitik*. Schmoller concurred in this turn, while reiterating the need for internal reform. He, who had always appreciated the value of great men in the state, seems to have made little distinction between Bismarck and

44. It is interesting to know that William II declined to make Schmoller director of the Prussian state archives because of his interest in social history. This failure to attain one of the highest honors accorded to the historian of Prussian history must have hurt Schmoller, especially in view of his devotion to the Hohenzollerns and to their history.

his successors, trusting men like Bülow to carry out reform. He, who understood the social conflicts of his age, in the midst of his faith in man and history failed to understand the full force of the proletarian movement or the bitter meaning of the proletarization of the lower middle class. Schmoller became a shade too secure, a compromiser, not a leader of the new. His cardinal virtue, however, is that he exerted himself, that he kept abreast of contemporary problems, either examining them himself or stimulating members of the *Verein* to do so, that he knew himself a responsible member of the national and international community.

Schmoller does not create an impression of a passionate man who was moved to reform by love of humankind.[45] He seems rather to have looked always about with the practiced eye of a trained bureaucrat who takes the measure of his problem and sets confidently to work upon it. In this the difference between Schmoller and Friedrich Naumann, whose democratic teaching Schmoller scorned, is striking. History cannot choose the men who serve her, and those who write of these men must rest content if now and again they record valuable services where no sympathetic personality is to be found. Schmoller poured his sympathy, his love, his charm, his consideration for others, his religion, into his work, where all are transmuted into sincere workmanship, faith in human endeavor, patriotism, and a broad understanding of historical process. Werner Sombart said of Schmoller at his death (July 1, 1917):

> This was Gustav von Schmoller's faith, this did he make living in us [his students]: the conviction that knowledge which does not fulfill these conditions, which is not fundamental, which does not have its roots in the mother-earth of philosophy and history, is only a utilitarian knowledge [*Zweckwissen*], a technical knowledge [*Fachwissen*], a technology, but has no right to the honorable name of science.[46]

45. In his essay on Bismarck, Schmoller said that a man with work to do could not have a heart for everyone (*Charakterbilder,* p. 33).
46. Quoted in *Schmollers Jahrbuch,* LXII (1938), No. 2, 2.

# XV

# *Henri Sée (1864–1936)*

## HAROLD T. PARKER

THE movement of modern, scientific—shall we say, university?—
historical scholarship began later in France than in Germany.
When Ranke started his seminar in Berlin in 1833, French history
was still the province of nonprofessionals like Augustin Thierry
and Guizot. Only when in Germany members of the second generation of historical scholarship—pupils of Ranke, like Waitz
and Giesebrecht—were doing their mature work, did instructors
in France during the closing years of the 1860's begin to give
courses on historical method and to write monographs after the
German model. Among this group of instructors were many competent scholars and teachers—Monod, Luchaire, Lavisse, and
others—but the prophet of the movement was Fustel de Coulanges. In an age when Michelet was still living to resurrect a
somewhat imaginative past, and Guizot and Taine were still
imposing their systematizing minds upon the facts, Fustel naturally emphasized the careful study of the documents. "The best
historian is he who follows the sources most closely." Historical
reality, he furthermore observed, was complex, and it was the
duty of the historian to lay it bare and to explain it in all its complexity.

Among the later pupils of Fustel de Coulanges, and hence
among the members of the second generation of French historical
scholarship, was Henri Sée.[1] Like Fustel de Coulanges, Sée, until

1. In preparing this article I am indebted to Miss Katherine Hall, of the

he left to take his first position, was a Parisian, that is, a Parisian in everything except birth. He was born in the small town of Saint-Brice, a few miles north of Paris, on September 6, 1864.[2] But his childhood and youth—his growing years—were spent in Paris, and he attended the Lycée Henri-Quatre and then the Sorbonne. When it came time to select the subject for advanced work he considered choosing philosophy but, after some hesitation, decided for history. (As we know little of the early career of Sée, the reader in these first paragraphs must imagine for himself the hopes and fears and intellectual life which lie behind each sentence.) In history, at the Sorbonne, his teachers were Lavisse, Luchaire, Monod, and Fustel de Coulanges. As has already been suggested, the latter left the deepest and longest impression. From Fustel, Sée apparently gained insight into method, faith in the value of history and of scholarship, and a certain vision of how history should be written. From all his teachers he learned mastery of his tools. When, at the age of twenty-three, he was ready to start on his thesis he could read Medieval Latin and Old French, decipher the script of late medieval documents, and critically analyze and weigh a text.

For his thesis Sée had selected a topic in the late medieval field: Louis XI and his relations with the towns. At that time (in the 1880's), the history of the towns and of municipal organization in France during the middle ages had been fairly thoroughly surveyed down to the fourteenth century; but the story of the decline of communal liberties during the fourteenth and fifteenth centuries had been neglected and the relations of Louis XI to the

---

University of Chicago Libraries, for securing additional material that was neither in Chicago nor in Washington; to Mr. Harold Schultz, of Duke University, for locating a bibliography of the works of Sée; and to Mr. Richard Hooker, of the Central Y.M.C.A. College, Chicago, for copying a large number of references.

2. The biographical details of the following account of Sée's life are taken, unless stated otherwise, from A. Rébillon, "Nécrologie et bibliographie des travaux de Henri Sée," *Annales de Bretagne*, XLIII (1936), 2–11. A complete bibliography of Sée's writings is given in *ibid.*, 12–33. This paper is based on the items listed in that bibliography, except Nos. 22, 34, 41, 54, 66, 67, 70, 71, 99, 112, 114, 115, 116, 118, 119, 136, 138, 159, 174, 183, 190, 193, which were articles in magazines that could not be obtained.

towns studied only with respect to one municipality.[3] In preparation he explored documents at the Archives Nationales and Bibliothèque Nationale, visited the departmental archives of Hérault, Gironde, and Haute-Garonne, worked in the municipal archives of Dijon, Lyon, Perpignan, Toulouse, Angoulême, Poitiers, and Orléans, and gathered and then wrote up his material. The thesis was published in 1891, defended by Sée in his examination for the doctorate in March, 1892. The documentation was thorough; the treatment of the subject complete, or nearly so. Reviewing it in the *Revue historique*, Monod wrote: "The thesis of M. Henri Sée on *Louis XI et les villes* marks an important progress in our knowledge of the reign of Louis XI. . . . If his work remains incomplete, uncertain, and contradictory on certain points, it is, nevertheless, interesting, new, and written in a very attractive manner, which is not a slight merit in such a subject."[4] On the whole a favorable review, although, of course, no author is ever pleased.

In 1893, at the age of twenty-nine, Sée was appointed by the University of Rennes, in Brittany, as *chargé du cours* (in 1897 appointed professor) on modern and contemporary history. He took up his duties in October and immediately assumed the threefold task of teaching, research, and the direction of the research of his students. As a teacher, he gave courses first on political ideas in France in the seventeenth and eighteenth centuries and later on the history of French commerce and industry under the Old Regime and on the history of the agrarian regime in modern Europe. As a supervisor of research, he "initiated" his students, as he indicated, into "good critical method" and tried to "direct them toward the history of Brittany, and especially toward the economic and social history of the province, hitherto too neglected."[5] It is true that before the arrival of young Sée at Rennes, and before he had time to win influence, there had appeared each year in the provincial Breton revues a number of articles on local his-

3. *Louis XI et les villes* (Paris, 1892), pp. vii–ix.
4. XLIX (1892), 352, 354.
5. "Le travail d'histoire en province: la Bretagne (année 1902)," *Revue d'histoire moderne et contemporaine*, V (1903–4), 43.

tory. But these articles (although all dealing with Brittany) were scattered in subject matter according to the personal interests of amateur investigators and were often merely of antiquarian or genealogical interest.[6] Sée had his students work on topics like "Beggary and poor-relief in Brittany during the eighteenth century," "The *corvée* on the highways and the department of roads and bridges in Brittany during the eighteenth century," "The condition of the peasants in the district of Rennes according to the parish *cahiers*"[7]—that is, on topics whose results could be woven into a general history of Brittany or would help form the basis of a general social and economic history of France. So successful was Sée in organizing research that in 1906, after years of teaching at Rennes, he could write: "More and more numerous are those monographs which deal with the institutions and the economic and social history of Brittany. There has certainly been progress in the organization of historical research;"[8] and Camille Bloch could remark that "as professor, indeed, M. Henri Sée has created at the University of Rennes a real school of modern Breton history."[9] Furthermore, as Sée's reputation grew, the archivists and nonprofessional investigators in Brittany came to ask him for direction of their study. Aided by Sée's advice, these, too, produced articles and monographs on local history which were of value to the general historian. In this fashion, by Sée's quiet work and influence in a province, the history of France was enriched.

Sée himself, in his own investigations, was a tireless worker. During the first eight years of his stay at Rennes he pursued research along three separate lines: the political history of Britanny, with a monograph on *Les états de Bretagne au XVI*[e] *siècle;*[10] the intellectual history of the Old Regime, with three articles on the

6. *Ibid.,* pp. 42–43; "Le travail d'histoire en province: la Bretagne (année 1903)," *ibid.,* VI (1904–5), 184; "Le travail d'histoire moderne en province: la Bretagne (années 1904–1905)," *ibid.,* VIII (1906–7), 44.

7. "Le travail d'histoire en province: la Bretagne (année 1903)," *ibid.,* VI (1904–5), 185.

8. "Le travail d'histoire moderne en province: la Bretagne (années 1904–1905)," *ibid.,* VIII (1906–7), 44.

9. *La Révolution française,* LI (1906), 380.

10. Paris, 1895.

political ideas of Diderot, Fénelon, and Saint-Simon; finally, the broad subject of the rural classes and the manorial regime in medieval France, and here, as a preliminary to a larger book, he published two regional studies, *Études sur les classes serviles en Champagne du XIᵉ au XIVᵉ siècle*,[11] and *Études sur les classes rurales en Bretagne au moyen âge*.[12] In each of the studies of these eight years (except for the one on the servile classes of Champagne, where it was unnecessary), Sée displayed the ability and also the intelligence to utilize, to exploit, and to turn to account the documents which lay within his reach. This first period of research at Rennes was closed in 1901 by the publication of his large volume on *Les classes rurales et le régime domanial en France au moyen âge*.[13] Except by Molinier in the *Revue historique*, whose praise was reserved, the book was acclaimed by reviewers: "one of the most important that has been written on the agrarian regime of the middle ages, and one of the most conscientious"; "fills a gap . . . in an excellent manner"; "it was a very difficult task to which M. S. set himself some years ago; he has completed it admirably."[14]

During his second decade at Rennes, Sée, observing the need of regional studies on the condition of the rural classes under the Old Regime, devoted himself to the history of the Breton rural classes from the sixteenth century to the Revolution. So, while he continued to work on the political ideas of the Old Regime, he spent most of his own time—long hours, days, weeks, months, and years—in the archives of the departments of Brittany, poring over the manuscripts of the seigniories (manors), the ancient eighteenth-century tax rolls, the reports of the intendants, the *cahiers* of the parishes of 1789. The information thus acquired was used by Sée in a number of articles on the eighteenth-century agrarian regime in Brittany and France, in a long monograph on *Les*

11. Paris, 1895.
12. Paris, 1896.
13. Paris, 1901.
14. Reviewed by A. Molinier in *RH*, LXXVI (1901), 357–60; by "C. D." in *Revue d'économie politique*, XV (1901), 423; by Paul Darmstädter in *HZ*, LXXXVIII (1902), 314; by Ph. Sagnac in *Revue d'histoire moderne et contemporaine*, II (1900–1901), 670.

*classes rurales en Bretagne du XVᵉ siècle à la Révolution*,[15] and in
the preparation (in collaboration with André Lesort, archivist of
the department of Ille-et-Vilaine) of a thickly annotated edition
of the *Cahiers de doléances de la sénéchaussée de Rennes pour les
états-généraux de 1789*.[16] With the appearance of the monograph
and of the edition of the *cahiers*, the reviewers, on the whole,
were again favorable. The edition of *cahiers* was spoken of as
"valuable."[17] Of the monograph, the pro-royalist A. Roussel objected that Sée had painted too dark a picture of the condition of
the peasants under the Old Regime,[18] but no other reviewer expressed that opinion. By most, *Les classes rurales en Bretagne*
was praised highly: "a vast tableau of social history," "a capital
monograph," "not only an excellent work but a model," "this book
greatly honors him who wrote it."[19]

One reviewer turned from the book to the author and gave us
a glimpse of the personal qualities of Sée. Camille Bloch wrote
of Sée as "a modest scholar whose writings and conversation reveal solid erudition, rare breadth of view, a noble disinterested-
ness in pursuing long researches . . . a tireless worker."[20] And it
does seem that throughout his life Sée was moved to continuous
study by a disinterested desire to advance knowledge of the past
and was supported by an underlying faith in the value of history
and of scholarship. In his personal relations he was always cour-
teous and kind. One who knew him long wrote: "An unbearable
feeling to him was, I would not say to have wronged anyone, for
such a thing can scarcely be imagined, but to have been, even in

15. Paris, 1906.
16. 4 vols.; Paris, 1909–12.
17. Reviewed by Étienne Dejean in *La Révolution française*, LVIII
(1910), 272–79; by Marcel Marion in *Revue d'histoire moderne et contemporaine*, XIV (1910), 98.
18. *Revue des questions historiques*, LXXXI (1907), 685–87.
19. Reviewed by Henri Hauser in *RH*, XVC (1907), 365–66; by Ph.
Sagnac in *Revue d'histoire moderne et contemporaine*, VIII (1906–7), 362;
by Jean Lorédan in *Revue des études historiques*, LXXII (1906), 645. See
also reviews by Camille Bloch in *La Révolution française*, LI (1906), 367–
80; by Paul Darmstädter in *HZ*, XCIX (1907), 162–65; by "T. F. T." in
*EHR*, XXII (1907), 400–401.
20. *La Révolution française*, LI (1906), 380.

the smallest of things, a cause of inconvenience or annoyance."[21]

During the war of 1914—those days of grimness—Sée, except for a few book reviews, published nothing. Shortly after the war a severe illness left him not strong enough to continue teaching, and in 1920 he resigned as professor at the University of Rennes, accepting the title of "professeur honoraire." At the age of fifty-six, and with a fragile body, it might well seem that he had reached the end of his career. Nevertheless, the succeeding sixteen years, until his death in 1936, proved in scholarly publication to be the most productive of his life. During the 1890's he had published eight articles and two books; during the 1900's, ten articles and three books; and during the 1910's, six articles and the edition of the *cahiers*. During the 1920's he published one hundred and thirty-six articles and fourteen books; during the 1930's (to 1936), thirty-two articles, three books, and an annotated translation of the travels of Arthur Young. The articles after 1920 were, it is true, usually shorter than those which had appeared before then, and the books were also briefer and of a general, more synthetic character.[22] To them, however, must be added his "Bibliographical bulletin of economic and social history," which from 1925 to 1935 appeared in the *Revue historique* and in which each year he classified and carefully summarized from forty-five to sixty-seven books and from seventy-eight to ninety-one articles—not to speak of individual book reviews, perhaps ten to twenty annually. All this work was accomplished by living somewhat apart in his residence, Bois-Rondel, and by watching his health day after day, with his wife aiding him in protecting his time and in creating a serene atmosphere conducive to scholarly work.

In this maze of publication Sée again worked steadily along three main lines: the intellectual history of the Old Regime, with three books on French political ideas in the seventeenth and

21. Rébillon, *loc. cit.*, p. 9; see also, on his kindness, Léon Cahen's review of Sée's *Französische Wirtschaftsgeschichte* (Vol. II) in *Revue d'histoire moderne*, XIII (1938), 301–2.

22. These figures are based on the bibliography of Sée's writings in *Annales de Bretagne*, XLIII (1936), 12–33.

eighteenth centuries; the agrarian history of Europe, with the publication of an *Esquisse d'une histoire du régime agraire en Europe aux XVIII* *et XIX* *siècles*[23] and of occasional articles on the history of agriculture in France, as from time to time he discovered new material; and finally, more especially during this period, the history of French commerce and industry in the seventeenth and eighteenth centuries, on which he published numerous books and articles. His work on economic and social history culminated in the preparation of a general economic history of France from the fall of Rome to the war of 1914. As Sée could not find a French publisher, it was published in German, under the title *Französische Wirtchaftsgeschichte*.[24] Volume I appeared in 1930; Volume II, in 1936. In addition, in the 1920's he also became interested in the method and philosophy of history. There followed on the subject many articles and four books: *Matérialisme historique et interprétation économique de l'histoire*,[25] *Science et philosophie de l'histoire*,[26] *Évolution et révolution*,[27] and *Science et philosophie d'après la doctrine de M. Émile Meyerson*.[28] Finally, he published several articles on issues of current importance: the League of Nations, capitalism in the United States, Bernard Shaw and capitalism. With the appearance of these various books in the last fifteen years of his life Sée's reputation spread beyond the boundaries of France. In Germany, Belgium, Holland, England, and the United States, among professional modern European historians he became a well-known and a respected writer.

When viewing Sée's life as a whole, it is seen that he followed the career of a typical scholar. He attended a *lycée*, pursued advanced studies at a university, obtained a Doctor's degree, entered instruction, taught, pursued research, directed the research of others, and, after long years of teaching, retired—in Sée's case, somewhat earlier than is usual. In the changing character of his

23. Paris, 1921.
24. Jena, 1930 and 1936.
25. Paris, 1927.
26. Paris, 1928.
27. Paris, 1929.
28. Paris, 1932.

scholarly investigation he also passed through those stages which many a scholar has experienced. Starting out in one field, in this case the middle ages, he moved in his research to the field in which he was teaching—modern European history. Starting out with using the documents that could be found in the central archives, he turned to the local documents which lay within his reach and to subjects concerning the region in which he resided. Starting out with an almost exclusive devotion to specialized investigation, to the ignoring in publication (although not in teaching or in conversation) of general syntheses, philosophical questions, and current world-happenings, Sée in later life turned to the publication of general surveys of broad subjects—the syntheses of his own previous investigations, of years of meditation, and of wide reading of the monographs of others. Matured, furthermore, by observation of past and present experience and by reflection, he came to feel he had something of value to say on the state of the nation and the world; and, made more sure by age, he expressed his views in several articles. Finally, in his later years he turned to philosophize about the nature of history.

In one respect, perhaps, his life differed from that of many scholars: his career had been singularly complete. Not only had he engaged in every type of scholarly activity—the preparation and publication of editions of documents, of specialized monographs, general syntheses, and philosophical disquisitions—but he had also been able to round out nearly every task. During the 1890's he was working largely on the history of the rural classes and the manorial regime in the middle ages. That work was completed in 1901 with the publication of *Les classes rurales et le régime domanial en France au moyen âge*. During the 1900's the long years of investigation of the agrarian history of Brittany in early modern times had been brought to a successful conclusion, with the publication in 1906 of *Les classes rurales en Bretagne* and in 1909–12 of the *cahiers*. The twenty-seven years of teaching at Rennes on the political ideas in France during the seventeenth and eighteenth centuries, on the agrarian regime in modern Europe, and on the history of French commerce and industry in the seventeenth and eighteenth centuries had been summarized in a number of books published shortly after his retirement in 1920. The articles written in his later life on the philosophy of history had been used in the composition of four long essays on philosophical subjects. An entire life devoted to the economic and social history of France had been summarized in the *Französische Wirtschaftsgeschichte*, the last volume of which reached Sée a few weeks before his death. Doubtless, at the end there were still plans to be carried out, projects to complete, a French edition of his *Französische Wirtschaftsgeschichte* to prepare, for he died while working; but, on the whole, it had been granted to him that he should finish nearly everything he had begun.

In the course of his life Sée worked in five fields: medieval history, the agrarian history of Brittany, the intellectual history of the Old Regime, the economic history of France, and the philosophy of history. And as the nature and quality of his achievement were different in each field, it is necessary to consider briefly and objectively his accomplishment in each one. But it must, in addition, be realized that as we examine his achievement we are also (except in the first paragraph on the medieval field) discussing his abilities as an editor of documents, a writer of monographs, of syntheses, and finally of philosophical disquisitions.

In the field of medieval history Sée's contribution included monographs on the condition of the rural classes in the middle ages in Champagne and Brittany, and a longer work on the manorial regime and the rural classes in all of medieval France. The latter book was based on the few regional monographs then existing and on a wide sampling of medieval charters and chartularies. It traces the various transformations of the French manorial regime from the late Roman Empire to the fourteenth century and describes in great fulness its characteristics during the period of high feudalism. The book is marked by a calm mastery of the material. Although Sée himself in the preface referred to his work as a provisional synthesis, after forty years it still remains the standard account.

Of the other fields in which Sée worked, three were new: the agrarian history of Brittany, the intellectual history of the Old

Regime, and the economic history of France. From the standpoint of relative permanence, the danger of working in a new
field is that one's work will be only provisional, soon superseded
by later research. In Breton agrarian history, one source which
Sée used in his monographs and articles was the *cahiers* of grievances which each peasant parish drew up when in 1789 it participated in the election of the estates-general. As we have seen,
when Sée's work became known, the Commission de Recherche
et Publication des Documents relatifs à la vie économique de la
Révolution authorized Sée and André Lesort, archivist of the department of Ille-et-Vilaine, to publish the *cahiers* of the *sénéchaussée* of Rennes, which once embraced a large section of Brittany. The resulting four-volume publication was one of the larger
contributions of Sée to agrarian history and gives us the opportunity to examine his skill as an editor.

When Sée and Lesort undertook their task a number of editions
of *cahiers* from other regions of France had already been published, and previous editors and the commission mentioned above
had already partly worked out a method of publication. It had
already been decided that the complete *cahier* should be published; that it should be published from an authentic text, either
from the original *cahier* or from a copy certified by the president
of the assembly which had adopted it; and that each *cahier* should
be preceded by a short notice giving the location of the parish or
town, its population, taxation totals, and distribution for *capita-
tion, vingtièmes,* and *fouages,* a brief description of chief agricultural and industrial products, and finally a summary of the minutes of the meeting, including a list of those present. In all this
—publication of complete *cahier*, use of authentic text, notice
preceding each *cahier*—Sée and Lesort followed previous editors.

In addition, one editor, Camille Bloch, had discovered that in
the *bailliage* of Orléans *cahiers* emanating from assemblies having the same president were often similar and sometimes identical, and in publication he had grouped the *cahiers* by assemblies
having the same president.[29] Furthermore, certain other editors,

29. "Les cahiers de paroisses de 1789," *RH*, CIII (1910), 298; "L'œuvre
de la Commission des Documents relatifs à la vie économique de la Révo-

especially Émile Bridrey, had attempted, somewhat casually, to check by other documents the accuracy of the *cahiers*.[30] On these two points, Sée and Lesort perfected the method of their predecessors. Like Bloch, they grouped their *cahiers* by assemblies having the same president. But, where Bloch had not attempted the analysis of the interrelationships of dependence within each group, Sée and Lesort, by comparing the dates of the assemblies and the language of the cahiers, were able in a brief notice at the top of each group to point out not only which was the first *cahier* but also how the others were interrelated (or related to some general model *cahier*), and they sometimes arrived at relationships as complex as the following:

> The assemblies of all the parishes of this group consisting of the marquisate d'Épinay and of the barony of Nétumières had the same president, François-Gilles Guyot du Brossay, *procureur fiscal* of the marquisate d'Épinay and of the barony of Nétumières and of the jurisdiction of Bremanfany. The *cahier* of *Landavran* (March 29) is independent of the others; that of *Cornillé* (April 2) follows very closely that of *Saint-Jean-sur Vilaine* (March 31) and directly inspires those of *Marpiré* and of *Champeaux*, both of April 3 and whose text is identical; that of *La Chapelle d'Erbrée* (April 5) was profoundly influenced by those of Cornillé and of Marpiré, and it is the latter which inspired the only two articles which form the *cahier* of *Erbrée* (April 4). We have joined to this group the *cahier* of *Mondevert* (April 2) *tréve* d'Erbrée, which was adopted in an assembly presided over by J.-B. Hevin . . . ; this *cahier* has no analogy with the preceding ones.[31]

Furthermore, while Bloch was content to indicate in a remark or two where copying had occurred and where variants existed, Sée and Lesort followed the copying word for word and brought out by italics where a *cahier* followed a general model or another

---

lution française (1904–1910)," *ibid.*, CVI (1911), 321. See also Bloch's edition of the *Cahiers du bailliage d'Orléans.*

30. "Les cahiers de paroisses de 1789," *RH*, CIII (1910), 303. See also Émile Bridrey's edition of the *Cahiers du bailliage du Cotentin*, especially I, 70–71.

31. Sée and Lesort, *Cahiers de doléances de la sénéchaussée de Rennes* (Paris, 1909–12), I, 246. An even more complex interrelationship is found on p. 543 of the same volume.

*cahier* of the group, and by the absence of italics where it was independent or deviated, if only for a word or phrase. Finally, whereas previously only casual, general attempts had been made to check the accuracy of the *cahiers*, Sée and Lesort sought, as far as possible, to check the accuracy and truth of each item of each of their four hundred *cahiers*. For this purpose they ransacked a wide drift of material: the papers of the Breton clergy, the seignorial manuscripts, the archives of the intendance, estates, and parlement of Brittany, documents of the central government, brochures of 1788 and 1789, and a long list of books. The information thus secured was placed in the notes. When a *cahier* mentioned the *corvée* (work on the king's highway), the task of that parish is given; the tithe, the amount and distribution for that parish; certain seignorial dues, the amount and character of dues paid in that locality, and so on.

Preceding the four volumes of *cahiers* is an introduction, in which Sée and Lesort describe their method. To be read in conjunction with the introduction is an article by Sée,[32] which, penetrating, subtle, and acute, removes any doubt that Sée could analyze documents critically.[33] Taken as a whole, the four volumes of *cahiers* probably constitute one of the finest examples of editing in the modern field; and, as one studies it, one cannot help but be profoundly moved by the spirit—the ideal of careful workmanship and the faith in the value of scholarly endeavor—which the work embodies.

In the field of Breton agrarian history Sée's chief monograph—

32. "La rédaction et la valeur historique des cahiers de paroisses pour les états-généraux de 1789," *RH*, Vol CIII (1910). See also "Les cahiers de paroisses de la Bretagne en 1789," *La Révolution française*, XLVI (1904), 487–513.

33. The question, of course, arises: How much of the excellence of the work was due to Sée and how much to Lesort? Doubtless, both contributed. But, after reading Sée's two critical articles on the *cahiers* (see preceding note) and comparing them with the introduction to the *Cahiers*, it is my impression that much of the critical value of the edition was due to Sée. In any case, Sée's French edition of the *Voyages de Arthur Young* (Paris, 1931), with critical introduction and notes, proves that, even when working alone, Sée was a skilful editor, probably unsurpassed by any scholar of his generation.

indeed, the chief monograph of his life—was *Les classes rurales en Bretagne du XVIe siècle à la Révolution.* The book is a long one —five hundred and nineteen large pages—and depicts in detail the organization of property in Brittany, the characteristics of the seignorial regime (a chapter apiece—twelve in all—to each of the twelve obligations of the peasant to the seignior), the different types of farm lease, the burden of royal fiscality, the backward farming methods and attempts to improve them, and finally the material and moral condition of the peasantry. Sée paints a rather dark picture of the seignorial regime, and in the conclusions he rises to a quiet eloquence:

> It can be understood, therefore, why the discontent of the Breton peasants had been so keen when the Revolution opened, why their irritation had manifested itself with such sharpness in their parish *cahiers.* . . . They had suffered too much from the exploitation which, for so many centuries, had weighed upon them, to follow blindly the masters whose yoke they had just recently detested.[34]

The book is obviously the product of daily and prolonged contact with the manuscript sources. The description is always clear and full. Nevertheless, it has been objected that the documentation is insufficient and that Sée has painted a darker picture of the condition of the rural classes than the facts would warrant.[35] As this is Sée's chief monograph, it might be well to examine the charge and to scrutinize his methods of handling evidence.

Two defects may be noted at once. The controversial section of the book on the seignorial regime is based largely on the archives of various seigniories in Brittany. For the entire province Sée examined and used the archives of fifty-five seigniories, two baronies, one castellany, eight abbeys, and five commanderies.[36] Necessarily, this is a sampling of the material, for, as Sée himself notes, there was an "immense number" of seigniories in Brittany. But unnecessarily, of the seventy-one sets of documents exam-

34. *Les classes rurales en Bretagne,* p. 519.

35. In review of the book by A. Roussel in *Revue des questions historiques,* LXXXI (1907), 685–87.

36. *Les classes rurales en Bretagne,* pp. xii–xiv.

ined, fifty-two, or nearly three-fourths (73 per cent), come from a single department of Brittany, the department of Ille-et-Vilaine; the other fourth, from the other four departments.[37] Furthermore, in the book itself, of the illustrative examples used in the description of the seignorial regime in Brittany, 88 per cent are taken from the seigniories and abbeys of this department of Ille-et-Vilaine.[38] This concentration of evidence and of example from a single section of Brittany assumes that the seignorial regime of that section was typical—like that of the other sections.[39] The assumption may be correct. It has, of course, been checked by the examination of nineteen sets of documents from the other departments and in the chapter on the abuses of the regime by a use of the *cahiers* from these departments. But the failure to check it by, or to base the book on, an even wider sampling constitutes a weakness.

Strangely enough, furthermore, for a historian who was so thorough, Sée in the book itself does not cite all the evidence on which each general conclusion is based. His practice is to make a general statement concerning the regime, the sentence usually containing the word "often" or "frequently," and then to add in illustration an example, or two or three examples, of particular seigniories. *"Lods et ventes* [one-eighth of sale's price to the lord when property was sold] were very profitable for the seignior, as the accounts show very clearly. Consult, for example . . ."; then follow the figures for two seigniories.[40] "Often for each *péage* or

37. *Ibid.*
38. The seignorial regime is described on pp. 77–240. The examples which appear in those pages both in text and footnotes and which were taken from the manuscripts of the seigniories, baronies, castellannies, abbeys, and commanderies have been counted and distributed by departments. Of the 247 examples which appear, 217 were taken from the department of Ille-et-Vilaine, 13 from Loire-Inférieure, 11 from Côtes-du-Nord, 4 from Finistère, and 2 from Morbihan.
39. Or it may assume that the agricultural population of the department of Ille-et-Vilaine was three times the total for the other four departments. If that was the assumption, which I doubt, it was incorrect. See the census figures and deductions which may be drawn from them in the *Grande encyclopédie* under "Ille-et-Vilaine," "Côtes-du-Nord," "Finistère," "Loire-Inférieure," and "Morbihan."
40. *Les classes rurales en Bretagne,* p. 114.

## Harold T. Parker

*trépas,* there existed a tariff of dues which the different classes of merchandise had to pay. Here is, for example. . . ."[41] Each example is footnoted to the set of documents from which it is taken, but seldom are additional instances mentioned in the note. To write, as Sée does, that "often," "most often," "frequently," such and such a thing was true, and then to cite an example, does not always carry conviction, especially when the generalization concerns all Brittany and when the words "often" and "frequently" suggest a rather casual method of working.[42] To illustrate is not to prove, and Sée's method of arranging the evidence is really a method of description and not a method of proof.

This does not necessarily mean that the book is a bad book or that the conclusions are wrong. But the somewhat casual method of working, plus the fact that Sée was a liberal who approved of the society which developed out of the Revolution and condemned the society of the Old Regime, raises the question: Did Sée, in working with the documents and in arriving at general statements, see (that is, did his mind register) as typical only those instances which were in accord with his bias?[43] While it is impossible to answer this for most of his particular, detailed generalizations, nevertheless he arrived at five general conclusions concerning the seignorial regime in Brittany; and these may be tested, and one verified in detail.

41. *Ibid.,* pp. 137–38. See also pp. 78, nn. 1, 6; 81, n. 2; 84; 85; 87, n. 2; 88, n. 2; 90; 95; 105; 110; 115; 117, n. 1; 131 and n. 5; 133 and n. 1; 135–37; 138–39; 144–46; 151–52; 155–56; 163–67; 169; 172; 175; 188.

42. Probably the documents of all the seigniories are not sufficiently complete on all the points to render a statistical study possible. But, as Sée does give a large number of figures, it probably would have been better on important points, such as the increase in the rent of the mills or on the amount of the tithe, to have said, "Of the fifty-eight seigniories we have studied from all regions and of all types, we have figures on the rent of the mill over a period of years for nine; of these, all nine show a decided increase during the latter third of the eighteenth century"—and then to have cited the evidence for those nine.

43. There is also, of course, this problem: In his description did he yield to the literary temptation to select for illustration the clearest, most telling examples, which, however, in their cumulative effect would probably give a sharper and perhaps a darker picture than the mass of documents would warrant?

He concluded: (1) In Brittany, of those manorial charges which had been at the center of the system, the *taille personnelle* and the *corvée* (work on the lord's land) had in most cases disappeared, the seignorial dues in money were now usually insignificant, and only the dues in kind were still of some value to the lord.[44] (2) In addition, however, there existed a large number of miscellaneous dues and obligations: *lods et ventes, rachat* (a year's revenue when property was inherited), local tolls, the obligation of the peasant to use the lord's mill and pay the price set by his miller, and others.[45] (3) Furthermore, in the administration of the system abuses occurred: millers were fraudulent; frequent and expensive legal acknowledgment (*aveux*) of their obligations was required of the peasants; injustices prevailed in the collection of dues to the benefit of the seignior; extraordinary *corvées* were demanded; seignorial justice was employed to maintain seignorial usurpation; the seignior's agents were hard, pitiless, and unjust.[46] (4) Finally, during the second half of the eighteenth century the seigniors—anxious to increase their revenue—revived old rights which had fallen into disuse, reintroduced old measurements, and, in general, tightened up the seignorial regime at every point.[47] (5) The accumulation of dues and obligations weighed very heavily on the peasants, although perhaps not as heavily as one might suppose;[48] but it was the abuses and spirit of the administration which rendered the regime insupportable.[49] Together the dues and abuses constituted "une très dure exploitation."[50]

On points (1), (2), and (4), the evidence—always assuming a representative sample—is sufficient; besides, point (1) is against Sée's bias. Point (3), and hence the second half of point (5), that abuses in the administration of the regime existed, were common,

44. *Ibid.*, pp. 92, 96, 97, 102–3, 109, 508–9.
45. *Ibid.*, pp. 110, 112, 130, 137, 144, 149, 175, 509–10.
46. *Ibid.*, pp. 105–6, 112, 121–22, 125–26, 129, 181, 183–97, 205–6, 510–11.
47. *Ibid.*, pp. 204–7, 240, 511.
48. *Ibid.*, p. 181.
49. *Ibid.*, pp. 181, 196.
50. *Ibid.*, p. 505.

and weighed heavily, rest on those few rural *cahiers* of the departments of Morbihan, Loire-Inférieure, and Finistère, which Sée believed actually represented the views of the peasants.[51] The conclusion thus reached may be checked indirectly by an examination of Sée's edition of the *cahiers* of the *sénéchaussée* of Rennes, which comprised a large section of the other two Breton departments. An examination of that edition reveals that the *cahiers* were a reliable source in their statement of fact. Although Sée and Lesort had been able to check most of the individual items of the *cahiers,* a reading of their notes reveals that in every case where an item could be verified it turned out to be accurate or true.[52] On the basis of probability, therefore, if a *cahier* said that an abuse existed, it almost undoubtedly did. Furthermore, an inspection of the rural *cahiers* themselves reveals that, of the six abuses mentioned by Sée, five (all except the demand for extraordinary *corvées*) were mentioned rather frequently in the *cahiers,*[53] and hence he was justified in con-

51. *Ibid.,* pp. 179, 183–97.
52. See the notes to Sée and Lesort. There are one or two exceptions to accuracy.
53. Of the 336 rural *cahiers* in the *sénéchaussée* of Rennes, frauds of millers were mentioned by 31 per cent; abuses in the collection of dues, by 36 per cent; expensive *aveux,* by 24 per cent; harsh, unjust seignorial agents, by 33 per cent; complaint of seignorial justice, by 20 per cent; demand for extraordinary *corvées,* by 20 per cent. But many of these *cahiers* emanated from assemblies whose presiding officer was a seignorial official and who perhaps influenced the assembly to omit mention of abuses. To eliminate this factor of seignorial influence, it is necessary to compare the *cahiers* issuing from assemblies whose president was a seignorial official with those coming from assemblies without such a president. Of the 210 *cahiers* from assemblies with a seignorial official as president, frauds of millers were mentioned by 24 per cent; abuses in collection of dues, by 29 per cent; expensive *aveux,* by 17 per cent; harsh, unjust seignorial agents, by 27 per cent; complaint of seignorial justice, by 15 per cent; demand for extraordinary *corvées,* by 18 per cent. Of the 96 *cahiers* from assemblies without a seignorial official, frauds of millers were mentioned by 45 per cent; abuses in collection of dues, by 48 per cent; expensive *aveux,* by 34 per cent; harsh, unjust seignorial agents, by 43 per cent; complaint of seignorial justice, by 30 per cent; demand for extraordinary *corvées,* by 26 per cent. Presumably, if no seignorial officials had presided, the latter percentages would apply to all the rural *cahiers.*

These last percentages may still seem low; but it must be recalled

cluding that these abuses were common, widespread, and existed in the majority of the seigniories.

But that the demand for the extraordinary *corvée* was a widespread abuse cannot be demonstrated. And from the *cahiers* it is also difficult to prove any quantitative or qualitative statement concerning the severity of the seignorial regime. When, therefore, Sée in his general conclusion implied that the abuses weighed heavily on the country population (granted that they were exasperating, vexatious, and a burden) and that the entire regime constituted "une très dure exploitation," I take it that, overimpressed by the violence of certain *cahiers,* he was swept by his bias and perhaps by his eloquence beyond what the evidence would warrant, and it may be somewhat beyond reality. But even this remark grants the validity of most of his conclusions.

The qualities and characteristics of *Les classes rurales en Bretagne* are typical of Sée's other monographs and of the great mass of articles which he wrote on the medieval, agrarian, commercial, and industrial history of France. As a writer of monographs, Sée used the best possible sources, usually manuscript; he analyzed these sources critically; and in his description his mind

---

(1) that silence of a *cahier* does not necessarily mean that the abuse did not exist; (2) that nearly every *cahier* speaks of the abuse it mentions as common, existing not only in its own parish but also in the surrounding country; (3) that it sometimes happens that one parish of a given seigniory mentions an abuse while other parishes from the same seigniory will be silent—in that case, it could probably be assumed (except for the frauds of millers) that the abuse mentioned by one parish should probably have been mentioned by the other parishes; (4) finally, that in most cases we still cannot be sure we have eliminated entirely all seignorial or bourgeois influence which might have kept out the mention of abuses. In twelve parishes, however, we can tell either from the minutes of the meeting or from the *cahier* itself that there was a definite rejection of seignorial influence or that the *cahier* was read to the assembly and approved by it. In these twelve cases, where we can be fairly sure that the *cahier* approximated more closely the wishes of the assembly, undisturbed by outside influences, frauds of millers are mentioned by 58 per cent; abuses of collections, by 67 per cent; expensive *aveux,* by 58 per cent; harsh, unjust seignorial agents, by 83 per cent; complaint of seignorial justice, by 92 per cent; extraordinary *corvées,* by 33 per cent. Altogether the evidence would probably justify the conclusion I have drawn.

## Harold T. Parker

followed the documents on the whole without distortion, except when bias intervened, which was infrequently. His chief defect was to move a little too rapidly from the particular case to the general conclusion—from the documents of a single department to conclusions regarding all Brittany, from a few *cahiers* mentioning the extraordinary *corvée* to a general seignorial demand for extraordinary *corvées*, from the methods of a single business firm in Brittany to methods of all firms in western France. This slight haste may mean that an occasional, detailed generalization is erroneous and that a general conclusion was to be modified. But, on the whole, the excellence of his judgment is such that, although he uses fewer documents than a modern historian would consider requisite, his general conclusions are usually valid.

Turning, now, to Sée's works in other fields, the field of intellectual history of the Old Regime, when Sée entered it in the 1890's, was still new, and consequently he wrote at a time when it could still be considered scholarly to treat of men and topics which were important, before scholars in this worked field had to retreat to the obscure and minute. He wrote, therefore, a series of articles on the political ideas of Fénelon, Saint-Simon, Voltaire, Condorcet, and on related subjects. After the war these articles, with additional material, were brought together in two books: *Les idées politiques en France au XVIIᵉ siècle*[54] and *L'évolution de la pensée politique en France au XVIIIᵉ siècle*,[55] intended as an introduction to the field.[56] In the two books, through six large divisions, the history of political ideas is followed from the culmination of the absolutist doctrine (Bossuet) through the reaction against absolutism (Fénelon and Saint-Simon), the growth of liberal doctrine (Voltaire), and the growth of democratic doctrine (Rousseau), to the appearance of the reformers (Helvétius and Holbach) and the formation of the Revolutionary doctrine. Under each division the writers representing each doctrine or ten-

54. Paris, 1923.
55. Paris, 1925.
56. His *Les idées politiques en France au XVIIIᵉ siècle* (Paris, 1920) was largely a collection of extracts from the leading writers.

337

dency are discussed, a chapter to each writer; under the liberal doctrine, for example, a chapter each to Montesquieu, D'Argenson, and Voltaire.

The broad movement of political ideas during this period, the influence of events on this movement, and the relationship of each author to the general trend are traced with astonishing clarity. But the treatment of the individual writers is less satisfactory. Sée went to each author, read his major works, and then described the author's thought logically—described, for example, Voltaire's ideas on religion, on freedom of thought, on individual liberty, on the rights of man, on political liberty, a section to each major conception. The resulting chapters are neither penetrating, profound, nor subtle. There is, of course, the danger of being more subtle than the matter requires or than truth of description and explanation will stand; but in intellectual history Sée is never in that danger. In the chapters, furthermore, any chronological development of the author's thought is ignored; the influences which helped to shape his life and thinking and the influence which the author himself had on others are largely neglected. In extenuation it must be remembered that these books were intended as an introduction, but even as an introduction they must be supplemented.

In the field of economic and social history Sée's contribution included a mass of articles on the commercial and industrial history of Brittany in the seventeenth century—articles notable chiefly for the skill with which Sée selected topics of value to general French history and gave significance to local detail and for the exploitation of the papers of old commercial and business firms to describe the business techniques of the Old Regime and the commerce of Old-Regime France with Spain and Portugal to the south and with Holland and the Baltic states to the north. Sée's contribution also included five works of a general, more synthetic nature: *La France économique et sociale au XVIII<sup>e</sup> siècle*,[57] a static description of the society of the Old Regime; *L'évolution commerciale et industrielle de la France sous l'ancien*

57. Paris, 1925.

*régime*,[58] the development of French commerce and industry from 1600 to the Revolution; *La vie économique et sociale de la France sous la monarchie censitaire (1815–48)*;[59] *Les origines du capitalisme moderne*,[60] a brief history of European capitalism from the Renaissance; and finally the two-volume *Französische Wirtschaftsgeschichte*. In all these works of synthesis Sée displayed similar qualities: mastery of an almost unbelievable amount of secondary, monographic literature, including naturally the results of his own investigations; an ability to give the material a strong, intelligent organization, which yet weaves in all the factors and circumstances involved; a singular balance and objectivity of temper which gives each subject or factor its due; and a certain caution in presenting the results as tentative, a willingness to point out that here and there are possible problems on which further research is needed. The style, it is true, is seldom exciting, and there appears a slight liberal bias against the mercantilistic-corporative regime;[61] but otherwise it is difficult to find any flaws in these books. As a writer of syntheses, Sée was much more successful in economic, than in intellectual, history. Of the individual works, the *Französische Wirtschaftsgeschichte* impresses by the mass of its learning and by the strong clarity of its organization. But for deftness in weaving into a chronological account a variety of materials and factors, for skill in use of the comparative method—of the comparative history of capitalism in Italy, Holland, France, and England, and in the colonies— to demonstrate that everywhere increasing commerce has been the foundation factor behind the rise of capitalism and changes in its form, for quiet pointing of this central theme, yet for many-sided presentation of a complex development, *Les origines du capitalisme moderne* is a little masterpiece.

Through his writings on economic history there runs a philosophy, a certain view of historical reality which Sée developed more

58. Paris, 1925.
59. Paris, 1927.
60. Paris, 1926.
61. *La France économique et sociale*, pp. 106–8, 128–29; *L'évolution commerciale et industrielle de la France sous l'ancien régime* (Paris, 1925), pp. 78–80, 106, 108–9.

thoroughly in his four books on the philosophy of history.[62] As a scholar, Sée was primarily interested in understanding the past. In his view the reality with which the historian deals is infinitely complex: institutions, events, the action of individuals, economic phenomena, political phenomena, social phenomena, and intellectual phenomena, all intermingled, acting upon each other, and changing both individually and as a whole from year to year. So complex is this reality that it is impossible to establish, as in the physical sciences, mathematical relations among the facts—impossible, that is, to formulate scientific laws or to use the past to predict the future. In this respect, history is not, and cannot be, a science. It is also impossible in history to gain information through experiment or even through direct observation of reality. The historian can know the past "only by the trace which exists in monuments and especially in documents," and many of these traces have been lost and have dropped out altogether.

62. The key passages which contain Sée's general philosophy of history are the following: *Les origines du capitalisme moderne*, pp. 189, 196; *Matérialisme historique et interprétation économique de l'histoire*, 84, 124, 127; *Science et philosophie de l'histoire*, 79, 80–81, 84–85, 92, 96, 97, 101, 110, 116, 118, 122, 128–30, 135–36, 140, 141–42, 145 (n. 2), 150–51, 154, 173–74, 178, 223, 235, 254–55, 293, 350, 366, 394; *Science et philosophie d'après la doctrine de M. Émile Meyerson*, pp. 158, 161; *L'évolution commerciale et industrielle de la France sous l'ancien régime*, p. 373; "L'évolution commerciale et industrielle de la France sous l'ancien régime," *Revue de synthèse historique*, XXXV (1923), 89; "Remarques sur l'évolution du capitalisme et les origines de la grande industrie," *ibid.*, XXXVII (1924), 67; "La division de l'histoire en périodes à propos d'un ouvrage récent," *ibid.*, XLII (1926), 66, 67; "Remarques sur le concept de causalité en histoire," *ibid.*, XLVII (1929), 21; "La mémoire et l'étude de l'histoire," *La psychologie et la vie*, I (1927), 6–7; "De l'intuition en histoire," *ibid.*, III (1929), 115–16; "Interprétation d'une controverse sur les relations de l'histoire et de la sociologie," *Archiv für Sozialwissenschaft und Sozialpolitik*, LXV (1931), 90–92, 95; "Les idées de M. Paul Valéry sur l'histoire," *Mercure de France*, CCXXXIV (1932), 309–10; "Remarques sur la méthode en histoire économique et sociale," *RH*, CLXI (1929), 94, 96; "Taine, historien," *Grande revue*, CXXVI (1928), 640; "Les cadres d'une histoire économique de la France dans ses relations avec l'histoire générale et la science économique," *Revue d'économie politique*, XLIII (1929), 50; "L'activité commerciale de la Hollande à la fin du XVIIe siècle," *Revue d'histoire économique et sociale*, XIV (1926), 204; "Un type de document: le livre de raison d'un parlementaire breton au XVIIIe siècle," *Annales d'histoire économique et sociale*, III (1931), 237.

Nevertheless, a science (according to Sée, who is here following a philosopher of science whom he admired, E. Myerson) not only formulates laws but also seeks to explain reality in terms of causes and conditions, and it is Sée's hope that in this latter respect history may become a science. The task of the historian is then twofold. In monographs he is to examine the traces which have come down, by careful study to penetrate into every corner of reality, and to *describe* it in detail. In syntheses, he will try to *explain* the course of history. But explanation is difficult. There are so many possible causes of an event—some of them fundamental factors or tendencies, others casual, individual, even accidental. Change or evolution does not take place in a straight line or at an even rate; over a period of years, perhaps, in a given society, there are certain fundamental tendencies, but these are obscured by surface extremes and reactions. How to discern what are fundamental factors and fundamental tendencies and to be sure that one's discernment is correct?

Sée was convinced that the use of the comparative method was the solution. A comparison of different societies existing at the same time or in the same stages of development would bring out which causes were fundamental and which accidental or peculiar to a time and place.[63] Thus, comparison of the rise of capitalism in Italy, Germany, Holland, England, and France reveals that increasing commerce was the fundamental factor in the growth of capitalism and in changes in its form, with the presence of Jews, the Puritan spirit, and increase of land values operating only in certain cases.[64] A comparison of these societies of England and France in the eighteenth century reveals those fundamental differences—the extraordinary growth of capitalism and the absence of the seignorial regime in England, the contrary in France —which explain why their agrarian regimes diverged, in England toward large proprietorship, in France toward small peasant ownership.[65] Furthermore, a comparison of the same society at

63. *Science et philosophie de l'histoire,* pp. 142–43; "De l'intuition en histoire," *La psychologie et la vie,* III (1929), 115.
64. *Les origines du capitalisme moderne,* pp. 30, 34–35, 42.
65. *Ibid.,* pp. 173–74; *La France économique et sociale,* pp. 4–5, 13–14; "L'évolution du régime agraire en Angleterre depuis la fin du moyen âge," *Revue de synthèse historique,* XXXVIII (1924), 55, 79–82.

different times will reveal which tendencies of development in the society have been fundamental and relatively permanent and which surface and transient.[66] In this manner history might truly hope to become a science.[67]

In his philosophy Sée naturally gave a more specialized attention to the influence of economic phenomena. In his long essay on *Matérialisme historique et interprétation économique de l'histoire* he criticized Marx's doctrine that economic phenomena condition and determine all other historical facts and explain them. The doctrine, in Sée's opinion, is an abstraction—it will not fit all the facts; historical reality is too complex to be explained by a single, inflexible, unilateral hypothesis; finally, other phenomena react on economic phenomena, and there is interaction.[68] Nevertheless, as an economic historian, Sée, in his own works and to use his own words, granted to economic conditions "a preponderant influence."[69] They had affected in a dominant way the evolution of the seignorial regime,[70] the formulation of governmental economic policy,[71] the division of society into social classes, and the

66. *Science et philosophie de l'histoire*, pp. 142–43, 232–33; "Remarques sur la méthode en histoire économique et sociale," *RH*, CLXI (1929), 94; "Interprétation d'une controverse sur les relations de l'histoire et de la sociologie," *Archiv für Sozialwissenschaft und Sozialpolitik*, LXV (1931), 99–100. This comparison (of the same society at different times) will disclose, Sée was convinced after the study of four major revolutions, that in a revolution the only reforms which survive into the period of stabilization are those which continue the fundamental tendencies of evolution of the society in question. The reforms which have gone beyond that evolution constitute a surplus which is temporarily lost, although it may influence later generations and thus lead to further evolution. See *Évolution et révolution*, pp. 245–51; "Remarques sur le concept de causalité en histoire," *Revue de synthèse historique*, XLVII (1929), 22–23.

67. "La méthode comparative," *Revue de synthèse historique*, XXXVI (1923), 46.

68. *Matérialisme historique et interprétation économique de l'histoire*, pp. 77–86, 124; "Remarques sur la méthode en histoire économique et sociale," *RH*, CLXI (1929), 96–97. See also *La France économique et sociale*, pp. 6–7, 185–86; *Esquisse d'une histoire du régime agraire* (Paris, 1921), pp, 271–72; *La vie économique et les classes sociales* (Paris, 1924), pp. 1–2; *Les origines du capitalisme moderne*, p. 3.

69. *Science et philosophie de l'histoire*, p. 129.

70. *Les origines du capitalisme moderne*, pp. 12, 173–74; *Les classes rurales et le régime domanial en France au moyen âge*, pp. viii, 259, 615, 626.

71. *L'évolution commerciale et industrielle de la France sous l'ancien régime*, pp. 1–2.

strength and aspirations of each class.[72] Furthermore, economic phenomena themselves are less disturbed than other types by events and the action of powerful individuals.[73] By the mere effect of their mass they can balk or render vain any human efforts, whether of maintenance or reform, which run counter to the main economic trend. In the eighteenth century the force of steadily increasing commerce burst the bonds of the mercantilistic system of colonial regulation. In the face of that force the efforts of Spanish and English statesmen to maintain that system were fruitless.[74] The efforts of well-intentioned, capable French administrators under Louis XV and Louis XVI to improve French agriculture by promoting the partition of common lands were rendered sterile by the force of things—the backward methods of agriculture and the lack of capital in the hands of the peasants. After 1840, when these conditions were changed, the proposed reform went through smoothly, almost automatically.[75] The force of economic phenomena thus sweeps men down courses whose broad tendencies they do not see or, if vaguely aware, down which they sometimes have no desire to go. Although Sée acknowledges that the action of individuals and of legislatures often exercises an important and beneficent influence on economic phenomena (the abolition of the seignorial regime, for example),[76] his works convey a sense of fatalism which he probably did not intend.

Sée's philosophy was neither profound nor original. Most of its elements were borrowed: the complexity of historical reality

72. *Ibid.*, p. 3; *La vie économique et les classes sociales*, pp. 1–2, 123–24, 227–28; *La France économique et sociale*, pp. 6–7, 140, 182, 185; *Les origines du capitalisme moderne*, pp. 178–80, 183–87.

73. *Science et philosophie de l'histoire*, pp. 232–33; *Matérialisme historique et interprétation économique de l'histoire*, p. 120.

74. *L'évolution commerciale et industrielle de la France sous l'ancien régime*, pp. 1–2, 237–38; *Les origines du capitalisme moderne*, pp. 127–28; *La France économique et sociale*, pp. 121–22.

75. *La vie économique et les classes sociales*, pp. 1, 24, 119–21; *La France économique et sociale*, pp. 5–6; "Les forêts et la question du déboisement," *Annales de Bretagne*, XXXVI (1924–25), 23; "Notes sur les foires en France et particulièrement sur les foires de Caen au XVIIIe siècle," *Revue d'histoire économique et sociale*, XV (1927), 383.

76. *La vie économique et les classes sociales*, p. 121; *La France économique et sociale*, p. 6, 176–77.

from Fustel de Coulanges; the observation that history is based on traces left by the past, from Langlois and Seignobos; the division of causes into fundamental and casual, accidental, even irrational, from Cournot and Meyerson; the comparative method from Fustel, Seignobos, and perhaps Pirenne. But in borrowing, Sée more or less unconsciously chose those elements which were in accord with his spirit and experience, and he fused them into a logical whole. The result was a good, personal working philosophy, which, except for the praise of the comparative method, most scholars probably hold today and which, hence, seems commonplace. Sée's merit, first, was to think out for himself into a logical, coherent whole what remains with most scholars halfformed suppositions. Second, his merit was that he actually applied the comparative method fruitfully in three of his books.[77] His optimistic view that the comparative method will make history a science may be criticized; and his use of information gained from the fields of sociology and economics has been condemned. But certainly in history, where it is so easy to give the answers and to assume that they are correct, no tool should be overlooked which will render our judgment more precise and accurate, or any knowledge ignored, no matter from what field, that will enlarge our understanding of the past.

A few general considerations concerning Sée's style and biases remain to be noticed. Sée wrote at different levels of style, depending on the type of work he was doing. In his notices of books he was content with unremarkable comments ("very interesting," a "conscientious study," "documentation insufficient," or "the author could have been more impartial") and with a clear but unremarkable summary apparently written as the words fell off the pen. The articles are at a higher level: abrupt, vigorous, sometimes argumentative, but with the organization, although present, not always clear. In the monographs and books the thought has thickened out and become fuller; there is calm mastery of the material, quiet pointing of the theme; the organization is strong and clear. It is a style that can partly be

77. *Esquisse d'une histoire du régime agraire en Europe au XVIIIe et XIXe siècles; Les origines du capitalisme moderne; Évolution et révolution.*

defined by negatives. Sée did not have the type of mind that thinks in pictures, sees in details; he thought in terms of broad general ideas and institutions. The style, therefore, lacks vividness, the flash of illuminating brief quotation or detail, although the mass of description is often clear and full and not without cumulative effect. Brilliance and epigram are also wanting; there is scarcely a quotable phrase. Positively, its qualities are economy and flexibility (the prose fits the material like a glove, there is neither too much nor too little), a clarity which allows the subject to be seen completely but without vividness, and (at its best) a quiet vigor, rising at times to a quiet eloquence. It is a style well adapted to the impersonal, intellectual presentation of the subject, to Sée's scholarly code that in a work which is attemping to establish and present the truth the author's personality should be withdrawn, and the subject be allowed to stand by itself.[78]

Sée, however was not only a scholar, trying to be objective; he was also a Frenchman with certain political and economic views local to his time and place, and these influenced his work. Well known is Freeman's phrase: "History is past politics." Less familiar is the sardonic version of his dictum that "history is pres-

---

78. It is well to point out that Sée could write in other manners. In *La France économique et sociale*, which was written for popular consumption, the style is swifter and simpler, even epigrammatic. His biography of *Bertrand du Guesclin* (Paris, n.d.), for young people, is written with considerable charm in the "juvenile" style. In an article for the *Bulletin of the Business Historical Society* of Boston (translated as "Les armateurs de Saint-Malo au XVIIIᵉ siècle," *Revue d'histoire économique et sociale*, XVII [1929], 29) the opening paragraph contains a vivid and imaginative description of the port of Saint-Malo. He is capable of irony; but curiously enough—it is a trait revealing of his kindness—he exercises it only on the dead, on Bossuet, Victor Hugo, on the old École Normale Supérieure, and uses it only in familiar essays, never in scholarly works (see *Science et philosophie de l'histoire*, p. 14; "Le Cromwell de Victor Hugo et le Cromwell de l'histoire," *Mercure de France*, CC [1927], 6; "Fustel de Coulanges," *ibid.*, CCXVIII [1930], 514). Equally revealing is the fact that Sée, in reviewing works of scholarship, never praised or criticized a book for its style. The chief questions he asked were: Is it conscientious? Is it impartial? Is it true? For him the subject and truth were everything; and apparently he believed that in a scholarly work stylistic brilliance and intrusion of the author's personality were out of place; clarity and intelligence were enough.

ent politics," that as the present situation changes, the interests
and emphases of historians change, and new biases develop. Sée's
work represents this tendency in several ways. In a world which
seemed to be dominated by economic facts, it was natural for
historians, including Sée, to discover that economic facts had
been important in the past and to work out their history. Furthermore, in the struggle of opinion under the Third Republic
as to the desirability of a republican and democratic form of government, Sée, for a scholar, took a fairly active part. He was a
member of the Ligue des Droits de l'Homme (roughly corresponding to the American Civil Liberties Union), and he wrote
its history.[79] He ardently approved of the democratic society in
which he lived,[80] and that approval apparently affected, on certain points, his writing of history. Thus, whatever may be the
merit of the questions at issue, it was probably because he was
a liberal that he condemned the abuses of the Old Regime, held a
dark view of the condition of the eighteenth-century peasants, defended the *philosophes*,[81] rejected the (Cochin) conspiracy theory
of the Revolution,[82] and praised the Revolution itself as "the
greatest transformation which humanity has ever known."[83] Had

79. *Histoire de la Ligue des Droits de l'Homme (1898–1926)* (Paris,
1927).
80. *Ibid.*, pp. 12–13.
81. "Histoire des idées politiques, France, XVIIᵉ et XVIIIᵉ siècles,"
*Revue de synthèse historique*, VI (1903), 239–40; "Les idées politiques de
Diderot," *RH*, LXV (1897), 57, 60; "Condorcet, ses idées et son rôle
politique," *Revue de synthèse historique*, X (1905), 32.
82. *La vie économique et les classes sociales*, p. 172; *Science et philosophie de l'histoire*, pp. 99–100, 344–45.
83. *Les idées politiques en France au XVIIIᵉ siècle*, p. 254. Sée also had
the liberal's tolerance for revolutionary violence—when it had occurred in
the past. Thus, after describing from court records the Breton peasant up-
risings in 1790, the burning of seigniorial records, the looting of wine cellars
of the châteaux, the smashing of furniture, etc., Sée concludes: "The peasants
were working unconsciously at a great deed of human emancipation. The
witnesses' stories of pillage, drunkenness, thefts do seem to have a character rather common. But from these humble episodes dates a new era in
the history of humanity" ("Les troubles agraires en Haute Bretagne [1790–
1791]," *Bulletin d'histoire économique de la Révolution* [1920–21], p. 256;
see also *La France économique et sociale*, p. 154).

he been an aristocrat, he probably would have taken the other side.

Sée was not only a liberal, he was also a French patriot; and his national feeling occasionally colored (although it probably did not distort) his view of history. In his praise of France as a rural democracy;[84] in his treatment of nineteenth-century economic history to show that, while England and Germany expanded industry excessively at the expense of agriculture, France retained a well-balanced economy;[85] and in the concluding passage of *La France économique et sociale au XVIIIᵉ siècle*, written shortly after the war of 1914: "One can still, in a certain measure at least, apply to present-day France the words of Chaptal, in 1817: 'Of all the nations of Europe, it is still France which, reduced to its own resources, would experience the least privation' "[86]—in all these passages there shines through, restrained and strong, a love of France. In fairness to Sée it is well to note, however, that his biases are never extreme—they seem quite reasonable to a liberal mind—and they do not affect the great mass of his scholarly writing.[87]

Viewing Sée's achievement as a whole, it is seen that it is important more for its mass of description and explanation than for its suggestiveness. Save for his insistence that the nature of the medieval domain itself will explain all the characteristics of the

84. "La France, démocratie rurale: son influence et son rôle en Europe," *Scientia*, XXXIII (1923), 205, 213.

85. *La France économique et sociale*, p. 187.

86. *Ibid.*, p. 188.

87. Sée himself could not see that any of his work was affected by his sympathies, and hence, like most historians who are convinced of their impartiality, he sometimes seems naïve. Thus, in defending the *philosophes* against the charges of Taine that they were "creators of abstractions," Sée wrote: "It seems that a careful, truly scientific study of their doctrines would re-establish the reality of things and set forth the grandeur of the work accomplished by these thinkers, who, if they had been only creators of abstractions, would not have been able to contribute so powerfully to the founding of modern society." It is certainly reassuring to know in advance that a scientific study of the subject will confirm your prejudices. (Quotation taken from Sée, "Histoire des idées politiques, France, XVIIᵉ et XVIIIᵉ siècles," *Revue de synthèse historique*, VI [1903], 240.)

manorial regime, and his agrarian hypothesis that small peasant ownership in France may paradoxically be explained by the persistence of the seigniorial regime which protected the rights of the peasant over the land, while in England the weakening of the regime left the peasant unprotected—save for these, Sée has no brilliant theories to propose. Nevertheless, the mass of his work in medieval, agrarian, and economic history (excepting, that is, his excursions into intellectual history and into the philosophy of history) was marked by a high level of excellence. This was true whether he was working as an editor of documents, a writer of monographs, or an author of syntheses. Only as a philosopher of history was he unoriginal and somewhat commonplace.

The central fact about Sée—his work and his life—was not that he was a Frenchman or a liberal but that he was a scholar. The fundamental assumption of historical scholarship—that it is important to get the record straight—he accepted without question. "Accept" perhaps implies on the part of Sée a greater awareness of the assumption than was actually the case. With him it was less a formal intellectual tenet consciously held than an underlying understanding which was part of his growth and being. The second assumption of historical scholarship, that it is possible to get the record straight, he accepted less unconsciously and less naïvely. As a practical investigator, he was aware that the historian works by inference from traces of the past to a complex reality, and he quoted with approval Renan's phrase that history was "une petite science conjecturale."[88] Nevertheless, like his master Fustel, he believed that it was possible, even by conjecture, to get the record straight if one used scholarly methods—that is, if one would analyze the documents critically—and if in description and explanation one would allow one's mind to follow these documents without distortion. These

88. "De l'intuition en histoire," *La psychologie et la vie*, III (1929), 116; "Remarques sur le concept de causalité en histoire," *Revue de synthèse historique*, XLVII (1929), 25; *Science et philosophie d'après la doctrine de M. Émile Meyerson*, p. 155.

two assumptions—the importance and the possibility of getting close to historical reality by scholarly methods—were the foundations upon which he built his work.

So quiet and unobtrusive in his case was the excellence of the product that one is apt to miss Sée's other central quality. But the trait which distinguished Sée (I would not say from other scholars) as a worker in history was intelligence—a broad, general, objective intelligence. It was intelligence which led him in four separate cases—Louis XI and the towns, the agrarian history of Brittany, the intellectual history of the Old Regime, and the general economic history of France—to perceive that here were wide-open fields of investigation with a multitude of documents available. It was intelligence, once the study had begun, that enabled him—even in a new field, and even where others would have been smothered or confused by documentary and narrative detail—to discern what were the broad outlines of the subjects.[89] And the very defect of his monographs—his tendency to move a little too rapidly from the particular case to the general conclusion—was caused by an excess of intelligence (that is, not enough), by an ability to see rapidly the possible relation of each detail to the general plan or conception.

But even the most excellent and intelligent of scholarly work is only provisional and gradually disappears from view unless preserved from oblivion by the grace of style. Even during his lifetime Sée's conclusions were being slightly modified by investigations of others. In the medieval field he was compelled to acknowledge that his insistence that the nature of the medieval domain would explain all the characteristics of the manorial regime had been too exclusive: seignorial justice might have come from the dismemberment of the justice of the Carolingian state as well as from the nature of the domain, peasant use of common lands might have been derived in some regions from primitive, peasant communal ownership as well as from the custom of rent-

89. His intelligence, furthermore, enabled him, as witnessed in his bibliographical bulletins for the *Revue historique,* to see the whole field of world social and economic history and to notice where his work fitted in.

ing the use of the forest from the seignior.[90] As a large number of regional monographs and articles have appeared since Sée published his book on the manorial regime, it is perhaps already time for another general account. In French agrarian history his numerous articles on the attempted partition and enclosure of the common lands in the eighteenth century were superseded by the more thorough studies of Marc Bloch,[91] which, while confirming Sée's general conclusion, corrected statements of detail. In economic history his general syntheses were already being supplemented and whittled away.[92] In time, if interest in economic history continues, new syntheses will be needed. Perhaps of all of Sée's work his edition of the *Cahiers* and his chief monograph on *Les classes rurales en Bretagne* are most likely to possess relative permanence.

With his usual objectivity Sée apparently foresaw the fate that was to be his. Speaking of Renan, Sée wrote: "What does it matter, then, that the results of his work have since been supplemented, corrected, surpassed? It is the destiny of all scientific work."[93] But writing of Quicherat, a scholar who investigated the trial of Joan of Arc, Sée observed that, although his works have been forgotten and are no longer read except by specialists, the results have been incorporated in the fabric of science.[94] It

90. *Les classes rurales et le régime domanial en France au moyen âge*, pp. 120—23, 311–15, 434–35, 490–525; "Recent work in French economic history," *Economic history review*, I (1928–29), 141; *La vie économique et les classes sociales*, p. 54; *Les classes rurales en Bretagne*, p. 118.

91. "La lutte pour l'individualisme agraire dans la France du XVIIIᵉ siècle," *Annales d'histoire économique et sociale*, II (1930), 329–83, 511–56; Sée, "Bulletin bibliographique sur l'histoire économique et sociale," *RH*, CLXVIII (1931), 346–47.

92. See the bibliographical notes of Robert Schnerb at the end of each chapter of the posthumous French edition of Vol. I of Sée's *Französische Wirtschaftsgeschichte*. See also, for a minor point, P. Harsin, "De quand date le mot 'industrie?' " *Annales d'histoire économique et sociale*, II (1930), 235, 239; Sée, "Bulletin bibliographique sur l'histoire économique et sociale," *RH*, CLXV (1930), 137.

93. *Science et philosophie de l'histoire*, p. 380. See also *ibid.*, pp. 284–85; "Fustel de Coulanges," *Mercure de France*, CCXVIII (1930), 520.

94. *Science at philosophie de l'histoire*, p. 365. See also "La philosophie d'histoire d'Ernest Renan," *RH*, CLXX (1932), 48.

may be inferred that, in describing Renan and Quicherat, Sée was also thinking of his own work.

With his estimate of himself we would agree, although we would word it somewhat differently. In the field of history Sée was not a Marx, that is, an outsider who by his theories radically alters the interpretation of the past, or a Gibbon, who produces a literary masterpiece, or a Ranke or a Fustel de Coulanges, teachers who influence generations of scholars. In brief, Sée was one of those who are significant not for their personal achievement and influence but for their humble but important participation in a broader movement—in this case, the movement of modern scholarship. Insofar as modern scholarship has been of value and significance in modern civilization, the work of Henri Sée has its importance.

# XVI

## *Charles Seignobos (1854–1942)*

GORDON H. MCNEIL

PROFESSOR SEIGNOBOS enjoys today an international reputation which is perhaps unique among contemporary historians. His name is certainly well known to students of modern history. During a long career he has written more than his share of excellent historical works; he has made contributions to pedagogy, to the study of historical method, the social sciences, and the philosophy of history. Yet it must be admitted that his work, as a whole, has not been outstanding. He has founded no new school of history; his theories of method and historical philosophy lack the originality that characterizes the work of other disciples of Clio; and his reputation rests, in large part, on the pecuniarily satisfying but transitory fame of the writer of successful textbooks. There is a more enduring basis for his reputation to be found in the significance of his historical writings, in their qualities which are typical of his period in the history of France and Europe. In this his background was naturally an important factor.

Michel-Jean-Charles Seignobos was born September 10, 1854, at Lamastre, a small market village in the highlands of southern France near Lyon.[1] In religion his family was not Roman Catholic, as are the great majority of his countrymen, but had been Calvinist since the days of the Huguenots in the sixteenth century. Furthermore, it belonged to the liberal party in the French

1. The biographical material in this essay is taken from a five-page autobiographical sketch which Professor Seignobos very kindly sent to the author.

Protestant church. Thus his religious background was not a stern "fundamentalism" but a "modernist" creed, similar to that of the English Deists of the eighteenth century and the American Unitarians, rejecting both the Trinity and the divinity of Christ. That was the exceptional part of his background, which was not to be without influence when he came to write about the church in his various works. Otherwise his milieu was typical. His father was a *propriétaire,* a member of the independent landowning class that was and remains the backbone of the French nation, and Seignobos grew up in an agricultural community which economically and socially belonged to the end of the eighteenth, rather than to the nineteenth, century. His parents were prosperous enough to send him and his older brother in 1863 to nearby Tournon, where they lived with an old servant while attending the *lycée* in that town. This was during the Second Empire; French education had yet to be reformed, and his "very mediocre" teachers left him with a great deal of liberty, which he spent in reading what pleased him. After eight years he finished his studies at the *lycée* and passed the examinations.

That was in 1871. His father had been elected that same year to the National Assembly, which had been called to decide the future of a France decisively defeated by the armies of Germany. The son followed him to Paris, planning to continue his studies in one of the special faculties, there being, as yet, no regular course at the Sorbonne. He knew that he was not prepared for admission to the École Normale; so he began the study of law at the École de Droit. After one year, having found such studies "vain," he withdrew to enter the Lycée Louis-le-Grand and prepare for the École Normale competitive examinations, which he finally passed successfully in 1874. Here his professors included Fustel de Coulanges, one of the most famous medievalists of the day, and Ernest Lavisse, who helped him greatly in his career and with whom he later became very closely associated. During his three years as a *normalien* Seignobos also began to serve, as he says, an "apprenticeship" in the realities of political life through his father, who sat in the chamber of deputies with the moderately liberal Left Center during the first ten years of the Third

Republic, an apprenticeship which was of value later when he was to write the political history of the period.[2] During these years of widening experience he developed friendships with Mallarmé, Anatole France, and others of the Parnasse literary group.

He received the *agrégation* with the highest honors from the École Normale in 1877, and the way lay open for him to enter the French School of Athens. But having no particular interest in archeology, he accepted, instead, a governmental grant for a two-year study of German higher education, offered to him through the influence of Professor Lavisse. The France of the Third Republic believed that the German educational system had been an important factor in the victory of 1870–71, and the French authorities wished to study and copy it. Seignobos studied first at Göttingen. From there he went to the University of Berlin, where Ranke and Sybel were still teaching, and then to Leipzig and Munich, where he made the acquaintance of the world of the opera, returning to France by way of Heidelberg.

There had been no precedent for such grants for foreign study and observation, but Seignobos soon became used to pedagogical pioneering. On his return to France in 1879 he was appointed *maître de conférences* at the University of Dijon, a rank hitherto unknown in the French educational system. There were, as yet, few regularly enrolled students in the French universities, where public lectures were still the chief offering; and the young instructor spent his spare time in the archives of the medieval dukes of Burgundy at Dijon, doing research for his doctoral thesis, which earned him a *docteur ès lettres* in 1882. The following year he returned to Paris, to initiate at the Sorbonne still another academic rank, that of *Privatdozent*, supposedly copied from the German system. The position was, in fact, ambiguous; yet he held it for seven years—the first and last of that title. Then, after a period during which he served as professor of historical pedagogy, he

2. According to one writer, Seignobos in his youth had little respect for the republicans of this period, preferring the Orleanist faction of the monarchist party (Pierre Leguay, "M. Seignobos et l'histoire," *Mercure de France*, LXXXVIII [1910], 37).

became in succession *maître de conférences, professeur-adjoint,* and *professeur.*

Although now retired, Professor Seignobos continues to lecture at the Sorbonne on history and the social sciences and, at the beginning of each year, on historical method. The writer had the pleasure of hearing him during the year 1938–39 and can attest the quality and interest of his lectures—even on such a presumably dry and uninteresting topic as the methods and procedures of historical research. There he sat, a small and slight figure, with traditional beard, wing collar, and frock coat, striking the table with his hand for emphasis as he lectured with a verve and enthusiasm that was scarcely expected from a man of eighty-four.[3]

Successive generations of university students have come under the influence of Professor Seignobos during the six decades of his teaching career; and, although he has never taught at the secondary-school level, he has influenced an even larger number of younger students through his many textbooks. The first was a two-volume *Histoire de la civilisation,* published in 1885–86,[4] which was written for secondary girls' schools—for special textbooks had to be prepared for the weaker sex then. This was followed by three books which went through many editions, the *Histoire narrative et descriptive* of the ancient Orient, Greece, and Rome.[5] Even wider in scope was the subsequent series of textbooks covering the ancient, medieval, and modern fields for the sixth to the first classes. They were written for the revised system of secondary education which was introduced in 1902 and have

3. It is interesting to compare this description of Professor Seignobos with one published thirty years ago, which came to the author's attention after this paper was written. The similarity is striking (*ibid.,* p. 36).

4. *Histoire ancienne de l'Orient, des Grecs, histoire des Romains, le moyen âge jusqu'à Charlemagne* (Paris, 1885); *Le moyen âge depuis Charlemagne, la Renaissance et les temps modernes, période contemporaine* (Paris, 1886). There is a complete list of Professor Seignobos's publications, both books and articles, in J. Letaconnoux (ed.), *Études de politique et d'histoire* (Paris, 1934), which is a collection of selected articles by Professor Seignobos.

5. *Histoire narrative et descriptive des anciens peuples de l'Orient* (Paris, 1890); *Histoire narrative et descriptive de la Grèce ancienne* (Paris, 1891); *Histoire narrative et descriptive du peuple romain* (Paris, 1894).

been widely used in the French schools since that date.[6] Mention, too, should be made of his various Sorbonne lectures which have been published in the *Revue des cours et conférences* since 1893. Professor Seignobos has made other contributions to French education as well. There was the published report of his study of German universities, which turned out to be a rather harsh criticism of the teaching of history in the German schools. Prussianism and Hegelianism (one of his pet dislikes) had perverted German education, and he objected to much of the German theory and practice. But since 1871 there had been a return to the pure science; and France, he reported, had much to learn from Germany.[7] During the early years of the present century, while the French educational system was being reorganized, he was a frequent contributor to various journals, writing articles on methods and practices in historical pedagogy both at home and abroad.[8]

Yet it is on his work as a historian rather than as a pedagogue that the fame of Professor Seignobos is most solidly based. He received his education in an age when historical scholarship was concentrated on the ancient and medieval periods, and it was in this *Zeitgeist* that he wrote his doctoral thesis, *Le régime féodal en Bourgogne jusqu'en 1360.*[9] This study of medieval feudalism was confined to Burgundy because, as he said, it was a region small enough to be studied thoroughly, it was typical of the feudal regime as a whole, and there were abundant sources in the Dijon archives.[10] Unlike most theses, this was a broad institutional study, embracing the political, economic, and social aspects of the feudal regime over a period of centuries. The influence of his teacher at the École Normale, Fustel de Coulanges, can perhaps be seen in the emphasis he gave in discussing feudal institutions to the continuity from Roman times. Interesting, too, is the thesis that feudalism was an improvement over the Roman system

6. *Cours d'histoire Ch. Seignobos* (9 vols.; Paris, 1902–4).

7. "L'enseignement de l'histoire dans les universités allemandes," *Revue internationale de l'enseignement,* Vol. I (1881), reprinted in Letaconnoux, pp. 64–108.

8. Letaconnoux, pp. vii–viii and *passim.*

9. Paris, 1882. The supplementary thesis was entitled *De indole plebis romanae apud T. Livium.*

10. P. viii.

which it replaced; that what was harsh and brutal in medieval society was a remnant which had come down from imperial Rome.

That was a detailed study, based in large part on manuscript sources, and in the best traditions of historical research. Significantly, he was to do little more work of that type, and his reputation as a historian is founded, instead, on broader studies, which, although thoroughly scholarly, are still largely syntheses of the research done by others as well as by himself. In the early 1890's Ernest Lavisse and Alfred Rambaud began their co-operative *Histoire générale du IV^e siècle à nos jours;* and their young colleague Seignobos joined them as one of the founders of the series, becoming director of the project when Lavisse later entered the government. He himself contributed several sections. That on the feudal regime, drawn in part from his detailed work on Burgundy, has been widely used in the United States in translation.[11] It was a very good, factual summary of the subject, but this time there was no mention of the special thesis of the earlier work on the continuity of institutions from Roman times. In the same volume he wrote a chapter on the Crusades, in which the role of the church and religion was presented from the purely rational point of view;[12] and in a later volume he wrote on the revolution of 1848 and its aftermath in France, and on the Third Republic.[13]

The latter chapter reflected an interest in recent and contemporary history which was now to occupy all his attention, except for the general-survey textbooks already mentioned, and an interest which was to gain for him his chief fame as a historian. Actually, his position in the field had already been established with the publication of the *Histoire politique de l'Europe contemporaine* in 1897,[14] a work that was very well received by the reviewers and was honored by the Academy. He had lectured for

11. "Le régime féodal de ses débuts à la fin du XIII^e siècle," in E. Lavisse and A. Rambaud (eds.), *Histoire générale du IV^e siècle à nos jours* (Paris, 1893), II, 1–67.

12. "Les croisades," *ibid.,* pp. 294–351.

13. "La révolution de 1848 et la réaction en France," *ibid.,* XI (1899), 1–37; "La Troisième République," *ibid.,* XII (1901), 1–51.

14. *Histoire politique de l'Europe contemporaine, évolution des partis et des formes politiques, 1814–1896* (Paris, 1897).

a number of years on the period of European history since the Treaty of Vienna, and this volume was a natural product of those courses. The tangled web of nineteenth-century history, with its almost unmanageable mass of source material, was not easy to trace, particularly as he allowed himself practically no perspective of time, bringing the account up to almost the moment of writing. Although the work is factual to a fault, the organization is excellent. The internal development of each of the countries is traced separately in detail, with the international story, minus the unessential military and diplomatic events, left for independent treatment at the end. Such an arrangement has much to recommend it; yet the story it tells is fragmentary at best, and thirty years later, when Seignobos wrote again on European history, the system of organization was quite different from that used in this book. As the title reads, this is a political history, but those nonpolitical factors which have influenced political events are discussed at length. By and large, it is not the result of firsthand research, being based, for the most part, on many other detailed studies. No one man could have done the necessary research to write the whole story, and the imposing quantity of sources on nineteenth-century Europe had dissuaded French historians from writing anything but elementary textbooks on the subject. There are extensive bibliographies at the end of each chapter, but otherwise the mechanics of scholarly writing are lacking. Yet the facts are correct, the conclusions sound, and the whole work thoroughly historical.

Not the least of the book's merits are its objectivity and fairness. Although he wrote as a Frenchman and as a non-Catholic, it would be hard to take exception to his presentation of church affairs and the development of the German Empire. Particularly good is the analysis of the development of democracy in England during the century, for which he credited the "non-English," the Scotch, the Irish, the Welsh, and the political leaders from the northwest counties.[15] In one paragraph he gave a penetrating summary of the main thread of French political and institutional

15. *Ibid.*, p. 90.

development since the Revolution.[16] The German trend was not so clearly seen; yet one cannot blame a writer in 1897 for failing to perceive what many observers today cannot recognize—the inevitability of some form of German dominance of central Europe. The concluding chapter is a well-thought-out essay summarizing from the supranational, European point of view the main political trends of the nineteenth century. All in all, the book possesses merits which made it a classic, and it remains today probably the best study of the period.

The nineteenth century, and particularly the history of France, was now Seignobos's chosen field, and this one-volume survey was followed by detailed studies, chiefly on the revolution of 1848, published as articles in various reviews during the pre-war years.[17] The definitive result of this research, however, was again a survey, published after the war of 1914 in the co-operative *Histoire de France contemporaine*, edited by Lavisse. Seignobos contributed three volumes—*La révolution de 1848, le Second Empire (1848–1859), Le déclin de l'Empire et l'établissement de la Troisième République (1859–1875),* and *L'évolution de la Troisième République (1875–1914)*[18]—as well as a chapter in the final volume, "L'action de la guerre sur la vie française."[19] Again the subject is a broad one, the history of France from the revolution of 1848 to the war of 1914. It was a period through a large part of which he had lived himself, and more than once he drew on personal knowledge or observation for his material. But these volumes were based on extensive research, not only in the earlier chapters which covered the period on which he had already published articles, but in the later parts as well.

It would be difficult to summarize this work, for it presents the history of France for the period—political, military, diplomatic, economic, social, and intellectual—and there is no outstanding originality of interpretation. But it is a presentation that has yet to be equaled. The major part is political history; yet some of the

16. *Ibid.*, p. 96.
17. Letaconnoux, pp. xii–xiv.
18. Vols. VI–VIII (Paris, 1921).
19. IX (Paris, 1921), 485–504.

most successful sections concern the economic and social development of the nation, notably the chapter "La société française" in the first volume.[20] The geographical distribution of political parties is explained in detail,[21] and he shows a keen awareness of the importance of class distinctions in political life.[22] There are hints of a dislike of doctrinaire socialism[23] and of the Comte de Chambord, the royalist standard-bearer during the 1870's.[24] An obvious liking for the Third Republic and a dislike for its opponents, which included the church, can also be seen;[25] and there is a slight French prejudice in the discussion of the story of Alsace in 1870–71.[26] But such evidence of bias is hardly worth mentioning; and, as in the *Histoire politique,* the objectivity maintained throughout these volumes is noteworthy.

Contemporary political problems had also come to occupy Professor Seignobos's attention. Such an interest, presaged in his several works on political history, was to have been expected from the son of a delegate to the National Assembly and member of the chamber of deputies. Through his father he had observed at first hand the political life of the Republic—the personal interests, the ways of getting things done, and the very real difference between political theory and practice. Combining his observation with research, he wrote many articles, which were published in French, German, English, and American journals.[27] Some of these were semihistorical, such as one of the first on the separation of powers, in which the historical background of the doctrine and its practice were portrayed,[28] and another on the political evolution of Italy since 1860. The great majority dealt with France and French political problems, both of internal affairs and of international relations. Some of the best were concerned with con-

20. VI, 341–420.
21. VI, 158–85.
22. VII, 346 and *passim.*
23. E.g., VIII, 236–37.
24. VII, 376 and *passim.*
25. E.g., VIII, 33–34.
26. VII, 253.
27. Letaconnoux, pp. xii–xiv.
28. "La séparation des pouvoirs," *Revue de Paris,* I (1895), 709–32, reprinted in Letaconnoux, pp. 183–208.

temporary electoral questions, the geographical distribution of parties, and the significance of certain elections.

Before 1914 he had written on Franco-German relations and on the conflict between Austria and Serbia. With the outbreak of the war of 1914 his attention was turned to this subject almost exclusively; and, like his colleagues in the other warring countries, he devoted his talent to the writing of articles designed to bolster the national *esprit*. In 1915 a long essay, entitled "1815–1915," was published in the *Revue de Paris,* and later was issued separately in a series of war pamphlets.[29] The reader will find here a fairly good summary of the diplomatic history of this century between two great wars, with the interpretation to be expected under such circumstances (he speaks, for instance, of the "childish psychology" of the Germans), coupled with a rather idealistic view as to the final outcome and the eventual peace. This was followed by an analysis of some articles by the German historian Delbrück in the *Preussische Jahrbücher* during the prewar years.[30] In these articles, which were quoted extensively by Seignobos, this "intelligent Prussian" (the implication is that his intelligence was exceptional) expressed his dislike of the extreme nationalism and potentially dangerous foreign policy of the Empire and predicted a German defeat. Once that defeat had been accomplished, there came from Seignobos's pen articles on such subjects of current interest as the League of Nations, the past and future of Italy, the new Latvian state, Constantinople, the downfall of aristocracy in eastern Europe, Franco-German relations, and the possibility of converting Germany to the ways of peace.[31]

Closely allied to historical narrative and political science has been the interest of Professor Seignobos in the problems of methodology in history and the social sciences. This field of study has always interested him, he writes, and his investigation and study of comparative methodology has taken him into the realm of

29. Reprinted in Letaconnoux, pp. 209–40.
30. "Les inquiétudes d'un Prussien intelligent," *Revue de Paris,* II (1916), 752–76, reprinted in Letaconnoux, pp. 241–68.
31. Letaconnoux, pp. xiii–xv.

philosophy and the natural sciences. In 1887 he published an article on the psychological basis of historical knowledge in the *Revue philosophique*,[32] and a decade later the theories advanced there were stated again in the *Introduction aux études historiques*, which he wrote with Charles V. Langlois.[33] There had been other studies of historical method, notably Bernheim's *Lehrbuch;* but the *Introduction*, subsequently translated into English, has had a wide circulation and soon became one of the standard handbooks. Scientific method in research had advanced by leaps and bounds during the century, largely as a result of German scholarship. Yet it remained for two Frenchmen to publish the best summary and explanation of the method thus developed, in which the practical aspect is dominant and in which the successive steps in historical research and writing are explained in detail.

The book is not specifically concerned with philosophies of history; but Seignobos, in the sections written by him, discussed at length the psychological and philosophical problems of historical knowledge, as well as the question of causation. He insisted that history is subjective, inasmuch as it deals with written documents which, considering the obvious shortcomings of language as a means of communication, are by their nature subjective; and he distinguished it from the other sciences, which are concerned with the analysis of real objects. The problem is stated thus: "Facts which we did not see, described in language which does not permit us to represent them in our minds with exactness, form the data of history."[34] Time and again he pointed out to the reader the necessity of a healthy skepticism and the pitfalls that face the uncritical historian who accepts his sources at face value. Thus his approach to the problems of method is that of shrewd common sense, enlightened by experience and theory but rejecting all metaphysical formulas, Hegelian or otherwise.

32. "Les conditions psychologiques de la connaissance en histoire," *Revue philosophique*, XXIV (1887), 1–32, 168–97.
33. Paris, 1898.
34. *Introduction to the study of history*, trans. G. G. Berry (London, 1898), p. 221.

The interest of Seignobos in methodological problems was not limited to the field of history and pedagogy. He gave a series of lectures at the Collège Libre des Sciences Sociales, the first part of which was drawn from the *Introduction aux études historiques* but the second part of which was a discussion of historical method and its relation to the social sciences.[35] In this he pointed out the necessity of the historian's method for the various social sciences, which must gather facts from the past (and therefore use the various techniques of the historian), as well as from the present, by direct observation. He reviewed the methodological problems of social history and the related topic of collective action. This book was followed by a number of articles on specific problems. In the first of these, "Les conditions pratiques de la recherche des causes dans le travail historique,"[36] he stated clearly his theory—or rather lack of a theory—of causation, cautiously maintaining that historical knowledge was in too rudimentary a state to assimilate its methods with the natural sciences. Causation in history, he wrote, by the very nature of the material at hand, could not be treated as the philosopher or sociologist would have it, for history deals with sources which are incomplete at best and with facts which are unique, no two being alike. After still another essay, "L'inconnu et l'inconscient en histoire," he went even farther afield in the last article, "La méthode psychologique en sociologie," in which he criticized the Comtian school, which rejected psychological, subjective observation and insisted that *phénomènes de conscience* are an integral part of social phenomena and, as such, could not be neglected by the social scientist.[37]

Since his formal retirement Professor Seignobos has continued to give courses at the Sorbonne, and from time to time he has presented broad historical surveys. From the latter type of course have come in the last decade two small volumes on the history of France and the history of Europe. The first of these, a *Histoire*

35. *La méthode historique appliquée aux sciences sociales* (Paris, 1901).
36. *Bulletin de la société française de philosophie*, May 30, 1907, reprinted in Letaconnoux, pp. 26–59.
37. *Journal de psychologie*, IV (1907), Nos. 6–7, reprinted in Letaconnoux, pp. 3–25.

*sincère de la nation française*,[38] is the better of the two. His particular interest had always been the history of his own nation, and here he gave his personal, frank interpretation of the evolution of the French people, with a hint of patriotism that had been rigorously excluded from his other writings on his country's history. It is only a summary, an *esquisse*, of the complete story; and the style is deliberately simple. This book is an interesting illustration of the problems of emphasis in any history. He explained in the introduction that some political events have been decisive in French history, and these were discussed, while those without influence were ignored.[39] Similarly, the details of cultural history, he wrote, are foreign to the story of a people; and he consistently focused attention on the masses of the people and on the social history aspects of the narrative. Yet intellectual history was included as well—when it had influenced social history. He adhered to these principles of selection quite successfully, and the book is an organic unit of political, social, economic, and cultural history—an ideal often proclaimed but rarely achieved.

It was his intention, utilizing the mass of material that historians had accumulated, to explain for the lay reader the origins and historical development of contemporary France. His long life of study and teaching was turned to good account, and the entire book reveals the hand of one who knows the subject intimately. Beginning with the dawn of history in France (the sections on anthropology are particularly well done), the thread of continuity to the present was kept clearly in mind throughout the book—for example, in the discussion of the early and pagan survivals in contemporary Christianity,[40] or when he suggested that the Gallic tribal divisions have been perpetuated in the departmental boundaries of today.[41] In this book, as in his other writings, there is an emphasis on comparative etymology which adds

38. *Histoire sincère de la nation française, essai d'une histoire de l'évolution du peuple français* (Paris, 1933). The English translation appeared a year before the original edition (*The evolution of the French people*, trans. Catherine Alison Phillips [New York, 1932]).
39. *Histoire sincère de la nation française*, p. x.
40. *Ibid.*, pp. 63, 68–70.
41. *Ibid.*, p. 19.

both to the interest and to the understanding of the developments portrayed. Seignobos had returned from Germany with a belief that institutional history should be emphasized, only to reject it later. Yet here, as in some of his other volumes, there is a strong emphasis on the story of institutions, particularly in the sections on the medieval and early modern periods and in the story of the church. No American enthusiast of socioeconomic history could object to the space devoted to that phase of history in this book, particularly in the treatment of recent economic changes. By the beginning of the nineteenth century, Seignobos wrote, the evolution of France had been practically completed; yet he fully recognized the importance of recent and contemporary economic changes which have yet to exert their full effect.[42]

The success of this book led to a much more ambitious project, an *Essai d'une histoire comparée des peuples de l'Europe*,[43] a work in many respects similar to the *Histoire sincère de la nation française*. This, also, is a study dealing primarily with the larger developments and the masses, rather than with the unimportant, if picturesque, details about their rulers, and tracing the transformations that the peoples of Europe have undergone to arrive at the present. The style and presentation are simple and straightforward, enlivened only rarely with such observations as: "Literature has continued to be produced in the same form and spirit, divided between the necessity of pleasing the public and the desire to astonish it."[44] Writing in 1938, he saw an impending conflict between the opposing forces of totalitarianism and liberalism, which, aggravated by economic depression, boded no good for the future of Europe.[45]

This book was not so successful as the *Histoire sincère de la nation française*. Perhaps he was aware of this, for he had entitled it an *Essai d'une histoire*, and he admitted that it was even more rash a project than the preceding book. Actually, there were al-

42. *Ibid.*, pp. 488–89.
43. Paris, 1938. The English edition is entitled *The rise of European civilization,* trans. Catherine Alison Phillips (New York, 1938).
44. *Essai d'une histoire comparée des peuples de l'Europe,* p. 466.
45. *Ibid.*, p. 469.

most insurmountable difficulties. In fewer pages than the number used for the history of France alone, he attempted to narrate the history of a continent. True, he told the story of Europe, keeping the narrative consistently on the European plane, instead of discussing each of the various nations in turn, as he had in the *Histoire politique;* and, on the whole, the experiment was successful. A good balance between interpretation and detail was usually maintained; yet sometimes the details, particularly when drawn from minor countries, bog down the story and leave the narrative fragmentary. At times the generalizations are farfetched, as when he tried to show a unity in the period 1648–60 in European history which was nonexistent.[46] On the other hand, he sometimes failed to note common factors which did exist. In listing the oppressed nationalities in recent times, Ireland and certainly Alsace-Lorraine should have been included in the list.[47] Yet, when all is said, this most recent of his works remains the most original and interesting of them all.

Such a long and active career is perhaps ample justification for the reputation which Seignobos holds today among contemporary historians. Age alone would entitle him to his position, for he was born during the early years of the Second Empire, and his career as a historian and teacher has extended over six decades. Froude, in spite of grave faults in his work, lived to see his reputation as a historian bolstered by age and the mere quantity of his pen's output; while Seignobos has written only good history, and few historians have done good work in so many fields. Yet the significance of his work lies less in the intrinsic quality and value of his writings than in their representative character.

The best of recent historical tradition is represented in his work. He began to write when historical scholarship was breaking away from belles-lettres; and he was aware, perhaps to a fault, of the shortcomings of the historian who emphasized the artistic aspect of his work to the detriment of the purely scientific and historical.[48] Believing that there was an almost inevitable

46. *Ibid.,* pp. 275–77.
47. *Ibid.,* pp. 404–5.
48. "L'histoire," in L. Petit de Julleville (ed.), *Histoire de la langue et de la littérature française des origines à 1900,* VIII (1899), 305–10.

conflict between the two, he deliberately avoided any literary flavor in his own books, and they are noteworthy for their simple and clear style and vocabulary.

The period of his early years demanded scientific scholarship in the German tradition; and he was trained in that, contributing his share to the literature of research. Even in his works of synthesis he showed a fine respect for his sources, admitting it freely when there were lacunae and stating, whenever necessary, his inability to come to a conclusion on a disputed point. The tradition of his generation also set objectivity as an ideal, and his adherence to that ideal has been admirable. Wiser than some, he admitted the impossibility of maintaining complete objectivity, and he stated frankly in one of his earlier works his personal bias.

> Having adopted the tone of a scientific treatise, I have had no occasion for display of personal feelings toward any party or nation. I have, indeed, a preference for a liberal, unclerical, democratic, Western government; but I have a conscience too, and it has saved me, as I think, from the temptation to distort or ignore phenomena that are personally distasteful to me. If I am deceived in this, the reader is aware of the direction in which it is possible that I have had a leaning.[49]

One can see here and there in his writings a reflection of his preference for a liberal and lay society. His religious background had been Protestant and extremely liberal, and in his recent books he has written just a bit cynically about medieval Catholicism and the medieval fear of hell-fire which still exists.[50] As a liberal and democrat, his sympathies were naturally with the Third Republic in France and with democracy abroad,[51] and he has further declared his belief in the utility of history as a valid

---

49. *A political history of Europe since 1814,* trans. S. M. Macvane (New York, 1898), p. x.

50. See, e.g., *Essai d'une histoire comparée des peuples de l'Europe,* p. 466.

51. In 1922, when a friend, admitting that he had misjudged the potentialities of a militant Fascism, said to Professor Seignobos: "It was stupid of me to have quoted Napoleon in writing of Mussolini, 'One can do everything with bayonets except sit on them,'" he replied: "Yes, yes, but you can make others sit on them!"

instrument for political training in a lay democracy.[52] Otherwise, there is scant evidence in his writings of either this bias or of an excessive patriotism—no mean feat when one realizes that he wrote in a period when patriotism and the principle of a lay democracy were still a subject of violent discussion in France. His preference for liberalism and democracy has not taken him far from the accepted meaning of those terms during the early years of the Third Republic, and he has written critically of doctrinaire socialism in theory and in practice.

He rejected the economic interpretation of history as being fragmentary at best;[53] and he has likewise criticized other interpretations, such as the geographical and the institutional (to which he once adhered).[54] Yet he has continued to make use of these and other approaches to history on occasion. He might be listed as belonging to the political school of history. That has been his major interest, and in his last two books he has insisted on the fundamental importance of political events.[55] But, as we have seen, other interpretations have not been ignored, and throughout his work the approach has been eclectic rather than one-sided. Perhaps he can be assigned to a school of "accidental determinists." In the conclusion of the *Histoire politique de l'Europe contemporaine* he claimed that the political evolution of nineteenth-century Europe had been determined by the events of 1830, 1848, and 1870—events for which no general causes may be found.[56] Similarly, when he wrote on the problems of methodology and theory, again reflecting the interests of his generation, he avoided favoring any particular theory of causation; and when he wrote history he either gave the simplest and most immediate cause for

52. "L'enseignement de l'histoire comme instrument d'éducation politique," *Conférences du Musée Pédagogique, 1907, l'enseignement de l'histoire* (Paris, 1907), pp. 1–24, reprinted in Letaconnoux, pp, 109–32.
53. "Que reste-t-il de vivant dans le marxisme?" *Les enquêtes du Temps,* Aug. 27, 1933, reprinted in Letaconnoux, pp. 391–96; *Histoire de France contemporaine,* VIII, 236–37; *La méthode historique appliquée aux sciences sociales,* pp. 312–15.
54. See, e.g., *Essai d'une histoire comparée des peuples de l'Europe,* p. 3.
55. *Ibid.,* p. vi; *Histoire sincère de la nation française,* p. x.
56. P. 805. In spite of criticism, he maintained substantially the same thesis in the revised edition of 1926.

an event or, more often than not, left it unexplained. All of which is in the best tradition of recent historiography.

Practice, if not theory, among historians also requires an occasional glance beyond both the past and the present, and Seignobos has from time to time ventured to predict the future. Eight years before the Russian Revolution of 1905 he suggested that the Russian autocracy was approaching a change;[57] and, as we have seen, he had envisioned an impending conflict between liberalism and totalitarianism. But he also predicted on the eve of the war of 1914 that there would be no conflict between France and Germany, which cured him of making rash predictions.[58]

Students, however, step in where professors fear to tread. At the moment of writing, it is possible that the liberal, lay, democratic government and society that Seignobos has preferred and which he saw come into being in France during his lifetime will, as the result of the third conflict between France and Germany that he has witnessed, give way to a new regime which will bring forth a different ideal and interpretation of history. For we are told that history must be re-written by each new generation in terms of its own ideals. Yet, even if that were to take place, Seignobos's work would remain one of the best expressions in the field of historiography of the ideals and standards of the particular society for which he wrote—a society liberal but not radical, rational, and critical of outworn modes and ideas, yet hesitant to venture on untrodden paths. Therein lies the true significance of the work of Charles Seignobos.

57. *Histoire politique de l'Europe contemporaine*, p. 584.
58. "Que reste-t-il de vivant dans le marxisme?" *loc. cit.*, p. 396.

# Index

371

# Index

# Index

Military history, xi, xviii, xx–xxi, 46–47, 48, 62–66, 70
Mill, John Stuart, 77, 89, 295, 296
Mirabeau, Comte de, 83
*Mittwochgesellschaft*, 53
Molière, Jean Baptiste, 149
Moltke, Count Hemuth von, 60, 66
Mommsen, Theodor, 200, 203, 207, 296
Monod, Gabriel, xvii, 93, 153n, 318, 319, 320
Montague, F. C., 178
Montaiglon, Anatole de, 93
Montesquieu, Charles de Scondat, 338
Montgelas, Count Max, 53–54
Moroccan crises of 1905 and 1911, 249
Müller, Karl Alexander von, 218
Muret, Professor Pierre, 192–94
Mussolini, Benito, 270

Namier, L. B., 194n
Nani, Cesare, 267
Napoleon I, xxi, 38, 48, 62, 64, 143, 167, 174, 235, 291
Napoleon III, 75, 145, 263, 264, 265
National Socialists, 213–14, 261–62
Naturalism, 290, 295–96
Naudé, Wilhelm, 203
Naumann, Friedrich, 317
Nazism, 80, 118
Neo-Hegelianism, 289
Newcastle, Duke of, 193, 194n
Niebuhr, Barthold Georg, 296
Nissen, Heinrich, 200
Nitzsch, Karl Wilhelm, 123, 124, 293
Noorden, E. V., 45, 121
*Nuova antologia*, 275, 276

Objectivity, 367
Okubo, Toshimichi, 264
Old Regime, 320, 321, 322, 323, 324, 327–28, 333, 337, 338, 346, 349

Palmer, Robert, 162, 166n
Palmerston, Lord, 263, 265
Panama scandals, 102
Pan-Germans, 58, 59, 60
Pan-Hispanism, 15–16, 20–21
Papen, Franz von, 213

Paris, Gaston, 93
Paris Commune, 92, 103, 108
Paris Peace Conference, 157
Parnasse literary group, 354
Pascal, Blaise, 277
Pau, General, 156
Peel, Sir Robert, 190
Pérez Galdós, Benito, 5
Periodization, 304
Personal factor, role of, 263–65
Pertz, Georg Heinrich, 47
Pfister, Charles, 156
Philip II, xii, 219, 220
Philosophy of history, 327, 339–44, 352
Pietism, 217
Pirenne, Henri, 344
Poincaré, Raymond, xii, 54, 102, 111
Political historians of Germany, 212
Political history, xiv–xv, xvi, xviii, 71–72, 107–8, 124, 125, 127–28, 218
Political school of history, 368
Poole, R. Lane, 178
Positivism, xiii, 295–96
Préclin, Edmond, 257n
*Preussische Jahrbücher*, 50, 51, 54, 55, 72, 361
Prince Imperial (future Napoleon IV), 145
Prothero, Richard, 77, 178, 180, 181
Prussian school of historians, 81

Quicherat, Jules, 93, 350–51
Quinet, Edgar, 26

Rachfahl, Felix, 126n
Rambaud, Alfred, 153, 357
Ramsay, Sir James Henry, 190
Ranke, Leopold von, 43–44, 67, 68, 70, 80, 81–82, 120, 125, 128, 187, 200, 204, 206, 218, 293, 318, 351, 354
Ranke school, 67, 146, 187, 198–99
Rebelliau, Alfred, 154
Rébillon, A., 319n, 324n
Reformation, 67, 110, 200, 203, 293
Reforms in post-revolutionary periods, 342n
Religious history, xxi, 38, 229, 236–37, 272, 279–80, 284, 285, 287, 288
Renaissance, 67, 110, 188, 339